W9-CNA-402

MoneyBall Medicine discusses some of the remarkable innovations that are developing across the healthcare industry. Harry and Malorye provide readers with a front row seat to the most important emerging healthcare system challenges—and opportunities—of our time. We started Flatiron because we wanted to ensure that all cancer patients—not just those with the means and resources—have access to the same cutting-edge research. It is our hope that this book will stimulate discussions around the value of next-generation technology in healthcare so that the industry can continue to innovate.

Zach Weinberg
Cofounder, COO, and President
Flatiron Health

MoneyBall Medicine puts you at the center of healthcare's new frontier where medicine, technology, information, and business are converging and advancing with unprecedented speed and importance. The stakes could not be higher, and I recommend this book for anyone interested in learning more about this truly disruptive revolution in the ever-changing healthcare landscape.

Eric Schadt, PhD
Dean for Precision Medicine, Mount Sinai Health System
Professor, Genetics and Genomic Sciences at Mount Sinai

The political turbulence focused on what comes next for Medicaid, Medicare, and the Affordable Care Act (Obamacare) public exchange products simply reinforces the fundamentals of healthcare in the United States. Increased access, increased value, and better patient experience will be keys for all successful stakeholders.

In *MoneyBall Medicine*, Harry and Malorye describe the unique confluence of entrepreneurial innovation and the many entrenched and evolving healthcare components of the healthcare supply chain, and defines the parameters that predict who will win and who will lose.

Glenn D. Steele, Jr., MD, PhD
Chairman of xG Health Solutions
Vice-Chair of Health Transformation Alliance
Former CEO of Geisinger Health System

Data, data everywhere. Well, historically it's been everywhere but in healthcare, where our industry has been laggards in distributing, sharing, synthesizing, and analyzing data to make decisions for researchers, physicians, patients, and insurers. *MoneyBall Medicine* thoughtfully walks us through the change in healthcare, which has already commenced. Data will finally take center stage, especially in cancer care.

Mike Pellini, MD, MBA
Chairman and Former Chief Executive Officer
Foundation Medicine

The explosive force that's transforming healthcare is digital. Harry and Maloyre have aptly captured and described this tidal wave in a compelling compendium of examples and interviews. *MoneyBall Medicine* lays the foundation for understanding how new types of data will change the way we discover medicines, measure their impact, deploy, deliver, and even replace them.

Christine Lemke
Cofounder and President
Evidation Health, Inc.

We are all now living in a world of data-driven medicine. *MoneyBall Medicine* is a really important source for navigating in this new world.

Rory Riggs
Royalty Pharma—Cofounder and Chairman of the Investment Committee
Locus Analytics—CEO
Syntax—CEO

As a citizen scientist activist and the mom of children with a genetic condition, I welcome the effect on healthcare of meaningful data, carefully analyzed and appropriately utilized. *MoneyBall Medicine* artfully traverses the ever-evolving dynamic landscape and focuses in on the various levers and fulcrums that might make the difference, all the while keeping the consumer in the center.

Sharon Terry
President and Chief Executive Officer
Genetic Alliance

We face a perfect storm: a medical profession, reluctant to emerge from principles of apprenticeship and autonomous practice to evidence-based approaches, still largely rewarded by volume-based payments, and a healthcare industry, which has accumulated legacy structures never designed for efficiency and interoperability. The combination has resulted in an increasingly unaffordable U.S. healthcare delivery system, which covers only part of the populous and has outcomes at or below the level of other civilized countries. Expedient and systematic solutions are further impeded by privacy and safety concerns, which have resulted in well-intended, but impractical legislation and heavy regulatory burden. Glorikian and Branca's inspiring book highlights real (entrepreneurial) opportunity to use the power of multisource Big Data and emerging analytic approaches to get out of this misery and revolutionize the way healthcare is delivered to ever more data-conscious, engaged patients.

Christoph Wald, MD, PhD, MBA, FACR
Chairman, Department of Radiology and President of the Medical Staff
Lahey Hospital and Medical Center
Professor of Radiology, Tufts University Medical School

Data has become a significant strategic resource in healthcare. Just as sports, financial services, retail, and virtually all other industries have been shaped by data and analytics, so too will healthcare. Harry and Malorye have done an exceptional job of documenting and analyzing this remarkable transition in the largest and most complex sector in our economy—healthcare.

John Glaser, PhD
Vice President
Population Health and Global Strategy Cerner Corp.

The pace of scientific development is proceeding unlike any other time in the history of healthcare. Precision Medicine is becoming a reality. *MoneyBall Medicine* provides a compelling overview of how new technologies, diagnostic tests, and drugs are being introduced at record speed, and how these advancements and the resulting access to increasing amounts of patient-specific data are rapidly transforming the way healthcare can and will be delivered.

Jennifer Levin Carter MD, MPH
Founder and Chief Medical Officer
N-of-One, Inc.

The future of healthcare is inevitably data driven. As our ability to collect, sort, and analyze data improves, the predictability of what people need is enhanced. This will result in more precise medicine, with better customized and personalized treatment plans for our patients. This book is ahead of its time, bringing together concepts of new innovations aimed at improving healthcare delivery.

Kathryn Teng, MD, MBA
Physician Executive Leader and Division Chief
MetroHealth Medical Center

The convergence of Big Data and artificial intelligence is changing the paradigm for the entire healthcare sector—*MoneyBall Medicine* is a MUST-READ book for entrepreneurs hoping to make an impact in this complex ecosystem.

Dekel Gelbman, MBA
Chief Executive Officer
FDNA

If you want to understand the future of healthcare, you need to read *MoneyBall Medicine*. Paralleling the data-driven transformation of baseball, Harry Glorikian and Malorye Allison Branca delve into the data and analytic trends that are revolutionizing healthcare. As this book articulately describes, it's only through collecting, connecting, and understanding data that we will arrive at a patient-centered healthcare system. Grounded in firsthand accounts, rich in detail, and accessible to practitioners and experts alike, *MoneyBall Medicine* is a great read and worthwhile investment.

Robert Metcalf, MBA
Chief Executive Officer
Concert Genetics

Harry and Malorye's book provides a comprehensive look at how data is rapidly becoming the currency of modern medicine and how this is fueling a market comprised of a diverse set of technologies, approaches, and business opportunities.

Notably, of course, the goal must be to maximize the rate of exchange, from data to true clinical value. The book recognizes the diversity and lack of synchrony among the critical market factors that impact this exchange, that is, payers; providers; patients (needs, expectations, and hopes); physicians; and pharma.

By identifying and describing the concerns and priorities of this network, this book can serve as a solid base for advancing toward addressing an even bigger opportunity … that of the unstated and unmet clinical needs that we don't currently even consider.

Michael N. Liebman, PhD
Managing Director, IPQ Analytics, LLC
Adjunct Professor of Pharmacology and Physiology, Drexel College of Medicine

The U.S. healthcare system is undergoing sweeping change with profound implications for all Americans, and the change is not waiting for Congress or the White House to determine its fate. *MoneyBall Medicine* defines this pivotal time as we live it, showing how new expectations shape our healthcare, and how each of us as individuals will be changed by it too. I can't think of a more compelling and important book for future historians, who will no doubt wonder how our healthcare system was so dramatically transformed in the early twenty-first century.

Leah F. Binder, MA, MGA
President and CEO
The Leapfrog Group

"If the difference between evolution and revolution is the speed of change, then healthcare is now in the mode of revolutionary change," say authors Harry Glorikian and Malorye Allison Branca in *MoneyBall Medicine: Thriving in the New Data-Driven Healthcare Market*. Healthcare spending in the United States today is simply unsustainable. In this book, Glorikian and Branca reveal promising trends that will revolutionize healthcare. I believe their visions are spot on. If you want a glimpse into the future, read this book. It's fascinating and very well documented.

Tom Emerick
Former VP of Global Benefits at Walmart
Population Health Consultant
Cofounder of EdisonHealth
Coauthor of Cracking Health Costs *and* An Illustrated Guide to Personal Health

MoneyBall Medicine takes the reader on a deliberately pragmatic insider's journey of how raw, objective, hard data is already becoming the driver of better, more cost-effective medicinal decision-making in healthcare today.

This book offers something for everyone—from the backstories bringing observations to life to the references for deeper-diving, it delivers. In short, if you ever wondered why "It's the Economy, stupid" has become "It's the Data, stupid," read *MoneyBall Medicine*.

Susan Ward, PhD
Executive Director
Collaborative Trajectory Analysis Project (cTAP)

After painting a bleak portrait of our current healthcare landscape—an inefficient, often ineffective, and expensive system that's stuck in the twentieth century—Harry and Malorye offer readers a remarkably insightful look at how data-driven healthcare and drug development will offer patients customized, effective, and more cost-efficient solutions in the near future. In other words, this new data-driven model will empower patients to take a more active role in their healthcare decisions. *MoneyBall Medicine* is required reading for anyone interested in the evolution of medicine, healthcare practice, and data analytics.

Niven R. Narain
Cofounder, President, and CEO
Berg Health

MoneyBall Medicine

Thriving in the New Data-Driven Healthcare Market

MoneyBall Medicine

Thriving in the New Data-Driven Healthcare Market

Harry Glorikian
Malorye Allison Branca

CRC Press
Taylor & Francis Group
Boca Raton London New York

CRC Press is an imprint of the
Taylor & Francis Group, an **informa** business

A PRODUCTIVITY PRESS BOOK

CRC Press
Taylor & Francis Group
6000 Broken Sound Parkway NW, Suite 300
Boca Raton, FL 33487-2742

International Standard Book Number-13: 978-1-138-19804-3 (Hardback)
International Standard Book Number-13: 978-1-3152-7119-4 (eBook)

Library of Congress Cataloging-in-Publication Data

Names: Glorikian, Harry, author.
Title: Moneyball medicine : thriving in the new data-driven healthcare market / Harry Glorikian.
Description: Boca Raton : Taylor & Francis, 2018. | Includes bibliographical references and index.
Identifiers: LCCN 2017029976| ISBN 9781138198043 (hardback : alk. paper) |
ISBN 9781315271194 (ebook)
Subjects: LCSH: Health services administration--Data processing. | Medical technology--Management.
Classification: LCC RA971.6 .G65 2018 | DDC 362.10285--dc23
LC record available at https://lccn.loc.gov/2017029976

Visit the Taylor & Francis Web site at
http://www.taylorandfrancis.com

and the CRC Press Web site at
http://www.crcpress.com

Contents

Acknowledgments

MoneyBall Medicine would not have been possible without the information and insights provided by the experts who so kindly provided us with assistance. The support of the following individuals is greatly appreciated:

Leah Binder
President and Chief Executive Officer
The Leapfrog Group

Mark Boguski, MD, PhD
Chief Medical Officer–Precision Medicine
Inspirata, Inc.

Jennifer Carter, MD, MPH
Chief Medical Officer and Founder
N-of-One

Neil de Crescenzo, MBA
Chief Executive Officer, President, and
    Director
Change Healthcare

Keith Elliston, PhD
President and Chief Executive Officer
The tranSMART Foundation

Helmy Eltoukhy, PhD
Cofounder and Chief Executive Officer
Guardant Health

Tom Emerick, MBA
President
Emerick Consulting

Dekel Gelbman, MBA
Chief Executive Officer
FDNA

John Glaser, PhD
Senior Vice President, Population Health and
    Global Strategy
Cerner Corp.

Howard Grant, MD, JD
Lahey Clinic, President and Chief Executive
    Officer
Lahey Health

Ben Heywood, MBA
Cofounder, President
PatientsLikeMe

Jamie Heywood
Cofounder, Chairman
PatientsLikeMe

Leroy Hood, MD, PhD
President and Cofounder
Institute for Systems Biology

Anil Jain, MD, FACP
Cofounder, Senior VP, and Chief Medical
    Officer
Explorys, Inc.

Christine Lemke
Cofounder and President
Evidation Health

Michael Liebman, PhD
Managing Director and Cofounder
IPQ Analytics

Lisa Maki
Cofounder and Chief Executive Officer
PokitDok

Pete Meldrum
Former President and Chief Executive
    Officer
Myriad Genetics

Robert Metcalf, MBA
Chief Executive Officer
Concert Genetics

Niven Narain
Chief Executive Officer
Berg Health

Stan Norton
Vice President and Chief Technology
    Officer
Humedica

Mike Pellini, MD
Chairman and Former Chief Executive
    Officer
Foundation Medicine

Jeff Rice, MD, JD
Chief Executive Officer
Healthcare Bluebook

Barrett Rollins, MD, PhD
Chief Scientific Officer
Dana-Farber Cancer Institute

Eric Schadt, PhD
Chair, Genetics and Genomic Sciences
Mount Sinai Health System

Kenna Mills Shaw, PhD
Executive Director, Institute for Personalized
    Cancer Therapy
MD Anderson

Glenn Steele, MD, PhD
Chairman
xG Health Solutions

Jeroen Tas
Chief Innovation and Strategy Officer
Philips

Kathryn Teng, MD, MBA, FACP
Physician Executive Director, Adult Health &
    Wellness Service Line
MetroHealth Medical Center

Sharon Terry
President and Chief Executive Officer
Genetic Alliance

Eric Topol, MD
Professor of Genomics
The Scripps Research Institute

Vance Vanier, MD, MBA
Cofounder and Managing Director
Chicago Pacific Founders

Christoph Wald, MD, PhD, MBA
Chairman, Department of Radiology
Lahey Hospital and Medical Center

Susan Ward, PhD
Executive Director
Collaborative Trajectory Analysis Project
    (cTAP)

Zach Weinberg
Cofounder
Flatiron Health

Introduction: Welcome to the Age of *Moneyball Medicine*

Introduction

Why can't healthcare be more like financial services? Or retail? Or the automotive industry? Or... baseball? All of these fields use data and advanced analytics to help make better decisions and increase profits. In healthcare, decisions are often based on a single doctor's experiences or some other very limited dataset. Data sharing is restricted if not outright frowned upon, and there are probably more layers of regulation than in any other field.

But despite these hurdles, shouldn't healthcare, more than any other field, be data-driven—using as much data in the smartest way possible to get to the best solution? The U.S. healthcare market was worth $3.2 trillion in 2015, accounting for almost 18% of the nation's GDP (Centers for Medicare & Medicaid Services 2016e). That's a staggering $9,990 being spent per person, per year on health.

But if baseball team manager Billy Beane could use data and analytics to bring an underdog team to the front of the pack (Lewis 2004), couldn't the same tactics vastly improve a medical system that is the most expensive in the world, but by no means the highest quality or with the best safety record (James 2013; Davis 2014)?

As professionals who work in and track advances in the healthcare industry, we are regularly awed and inspired by the remarkable technological advances we witness: cochlear implants that allow the deaf to hear, new drugs that essentially cure deadly diseases such as malignant melanoma and hepatitis C, and machines that can decode the 3 billion base pairs in a human genome within days versus the years it used to take (Kolata 2013a).

At the same time, experts from other fields routinely express bafflement with the massive roadblocks to efficiency in healthcare. They ask questions such as:

- "Why can't my doctor just access my records from another hospital instantaneously? A credit card company can access my credit report within minutes if I authorize them to."
- "Shouldn't patients be able to get a price estimate before they go in for a visit or start a treatment? I can get that in any other market! And now, usually instantly online."
- "Shouldn't my doctor be able to double check his recommendations for me against those that many other doctors have made for similar patients in the past?"

The list goes on. Even when a solution is proposed (or launched) for some of these challenges, there is no guarantee the market will respond favorably or that consumers will find the solution palatable. The misfortunes of numerous health IT services, such as Revolution Health and Google Health, demonstrate just how hard it is even for industry titans to overcome these obstacles (Versel 2010; Chase 2011; McGee 2011). It may seem like a huge opportunity, but modernizing the U.S. healthcare system is fraught with difficulty and many mistakes will be made as it evolves.

The failure of novel healthcare enterprises is often attributed to some of the features that make healthcare unique. People in the industry like to say "healthcare is different," and there are some features that make healthcare unique:

The Regulatory Environment: When lives are at stake, that's an even bigger concern than money. As a result, healthcare is probably the most heavily regulated of all fields. For example, it's estimated that it takes about $2.8 billion and possibly 10–20 years to bring a drug from research and design through the U.S. federal regulatory system (DiMasi, Grabowski, and Hansen 2016; PhRMA 2016). Diagnostics and medical devices, likewise, undergo strict and time-consuming evaluations. Hospitals and providers operate under a range of legal requirements, including a mandate to treat all patients who come to the emergency room, regardless of their insurance status (American College of Emergency Physicians 2017), and antitrust laws. The Health Insurance Portability and Accountability Act (HIPAA), meanwhile, was enacted in the mid-1990s partly to ensure patient record privacy (Department of Health & Human Services 2015). However, misinterpretation of the rule has sometimes turned it into a hurdle to family members trying to access a loved one's record, or patients trying to share their records with their other providers (Westgate 2015).

Patient Resistance: In the United States, people are also particularly concerned about healthcare privacy. They don't want to share health data if it might someday be used to embarrass them, or deprive them of a job or insurance. For example, although the 2008 Genetic Information Nondiscrimination Act (GINA) protects patients against discrimination in employment or health insurance based on their DNA, it doesn't protect patients with respect to long-term care, disability or life insurances, leaving some patients to decide against testing—even when the results could impact their care (Peikoff 2014). That also makes it very difficult for researchers to share patient-related data.

Further, most patients aren't particularly interested in managing their own data until they are sick, at which point that becomes very difficult. This may help account for the failure of early online health records, such as Google Health. Also, it's one thing to shop for a car, but quite another to look around for a heart failure specialist. Further, most patients believe that the most expensive doctor is likely to be the best, even though there are no data to support this belief. As a result, few patients are truly managing their own care. More often, they stick to their doctors and do what they are told.

Physician and Hospital Resistance: It's costly and time-consuming for providers to share data between sites and they fear losing patients by making it easier for them to go somewhere else. As a result, over time we have developed a system where doctors and hospitals essentially own the patient data they collect. And comparison of providers or hospitals is virtually nonexistent, save for a few websites created by entrepreneurs and the federal government.

All of this and more have helped make healthcare "special" for a long time. But we believe that a combination of factors will push our industry into the data-driven age.

For one thing, as individuals and as a nation, we can no longer just keep paying more and more for healthcare. It is impinging on our ability to pay for other necessities, such as infrastructure and education. Budget deficit fights over entitlements and the rise of high-deductible health plans (HDHPs), which subject patients to more out-of-pocket costs, have made that clear. Neither the government nor individual patients have an unlimited amount of money to pay for healthcare. And this situation is not unique to the United States. The rest of the world is also facing a healthcare cost crunch, and they are looking at the United States' movement toward data-driven, outcomes-based medicine, as a model for how they can improve their own healthcare systems. This would be a dramatic turnaround, since currently, the U.S. is often cited as an example of how higher cost doesn't necessarily lead to better care.

Further, the tools to collect, analyze, and share even very complicated types of healthcare data are steadily maturing. Certainly, there is a lot of data out there that has been collected in very different formats, but big pools of standardized data, whether it is clinical or biologic, are becoming more common. Progress is also being made on improving our ability to share data.

The stage isn't just set; the change is happening. Advances in technology and pressures to control spiraling healthcare costs are forcing it. Since the United States accounts for the vast majority of healthcare technology innovation, we have the opportunity to be the global leader and create a framework for a higher-quality, more efficient, and more cost-effective healthcare system.

Healthcare reform, of course, is the loose cannon in this scenario. Congress has been fighting furiously over the question of whether health insurance should be a right or a choice for decades. With the passage of the Patient Protection and Affordable Care Act (ACA, also referred to as Obamacare) in 2010, it appeared that the nation was on the path toward national standards for health insurance, which reassured hospitals and providers who were glad to see more patients insured (Department of Health & Human Services 2017b).

The 2016 U.S. presidential election upended that and since then, the legislature has introduced a number of bills aimed at repealing and replacing the ACA. However, many of the experts we spoke to have said that certain trends are likely to continue no matter who is in the Oval Office. As budgets are constrained and competition increases, all the players in the healthcare system need to become more efficient and to be better able to demonstrate the value they provide. Data will be crucial in determining the winners from the losers.

This book aims to highlight exactly where data and advanced analytics are advancing healthcare and creating new and evolving business opportunities.

We hope this book will inspire others to be a part of this revolution and help ensure that the new system well serves the billions of people who will depend upon it. Within these pages, we aim to explain through examples why, how, and what the new data-driven healthcare system is most likely to look like. We'll discuss everything from digital healthcare to value-based purchasing, looking at the full range of ways that experts are using data to improve the healthcare system and what the next step in that evolution could be.

It's our goal that entrepreneurs, patients, healthcare professionals, and those who aspire to work in this field will use the information and ideas here to assist their planning and help them either cope with the changes, or thrive via their own innovations, in the era of *MoneyBall Medicine*.

After all, if we can create a healthcare system that rewards the highest possible quality care at a reasonable cost, it would be a home run for everyone.

Chapter 1

The $10 Trillion Healthcare Industry's *Moneyball* Moment

The leaps and bounds in information technology that have transformed all kinds of industries are now finally transforming healthcare.

Barrett J. Rollins
Chief Scientific Officer, Dana-Farber Cancer Institute and Linde
Family Professor of Medicine, Harvard Medical School, Boston

After watching a relative struggle to manage his child's leukemia treatment, tech entrepreneur Nat Turner decided it was time to change how that process works (Ong 2013). The cancer-stricken boy's father was frantically traveling across the country, hauling stacks of DVDs and medical files with him because his child's doctors had limited ability to share information with one another.

Turner and his business partner, Zach Weinberg, had both seen family try to navigate the cancer treatment process before. Although the two men had no healthcare experience, they had previously founded a data-driven advertising software firm, Invite Media, which was acquired by Google in 2010, reportedly for $81 million (Ong 2013). They wondered if they could use a similar, analytics-focused approach to improve the cancer treatment process. So together in 2012, Turner and Weinberg founded Flatiron Health (Shontell 2012; Ong 2013; Raths 2017).

Prior to founding their new company, Turner and Weinberg spent about a year and a half interviewing oncologists, practice administrators, nurses, researchers, and hospital executives, finding out what worked in the oncology clinical workflow and what didn't. Drawing on their own families' experiences and all that feedback from the market, they saw a system increasingly at odds with the vast amount of patient data being collected.

Eventually, they turned their sights on electronic health records (EHRs) (Shontell 2012; Raths 2017), which are sometimes also referred to as electronic medical records (EMRs). But Turner and Weinberg had lots of new ideas about how these should perform.

EHRs, they had found, were not working for doctors—the software was complicating, rather than simplifying, their workflow. At the same time, the number of EHRs was booming. "Only 15% of doctors' offices had EHRs in the late 2000s, and 90% do today," Weinberg explained to us (Weinberg 2017). That's because of the 2009 HITECH law, which spurred the "adoption and meaningful use of health information technology" by providing financial incentives for medical providers to adopt EHRs (Department of Health & Human Services 2014). Unfortunately, many of those systems were disappointing. By 2015, only about a third of doctors were satisfied with their EHR systems (Advisory Board 2015). Also, the law did little to ensure that the systems spoke to each other, meaning your own doctor might be "wired" but he or she was probably not connected to your other healthcare providers.

In short, despite the surge in EHRs, moving data around in oncology practices was still a very "clunky process," Weinberg says, mirroring what providers see across all specialties. Seeing a clear unmet need, Flatiron acquired EHR developer OncoEMR from Altos Solutions in 2014 (Business Wire 2014), and folded it into their own OncoCloud suite, which now includes analytics, billing, a patient portal, and clinical trial management.

One of Flatiron's goals is improving clinical trial participation. Only about 3% of cancer patients are enrolled in cutting-edge clinical trial research (IOM [Institute of Medicine] 2010). This slows medical progress, because the more patients are involved in trials, the more data would be available to share, thereby benefiting many more people.

The two men wanted to help oncologists determine whether or not a patient was a candidate for a clinical trial. Instead of patients trekking around the country from doctor to doctor, could an oncologist use just a few clicks of a mouse to identify the right trial for the patient sitting in front of him? "It's actually very complicated to find out if you're eligible [for a trial]," Turner has said. "It's like 120 variables and there's no way to know quickly. We hope to speed that up for physicians because clinical trials are huge for cancer" (Shontell 2012). Hence, they developed OncoTrials, an EHR-enabled software tool that lets clinical research teams identify and screen patients for clinical trials.

That relates to the big disconnect between what an individual doctor might see in their own practice and the published results from clinical trials and other research studies. Drugs sometimes perform differently in the real world, where the patient population is less homogeneous, than they do in clinical trials. Study results may also not be generalizable to all patients with a particular type of cancer, because the composition of the clinical trial is not representative of the population (Chen et al. 2014). So even if a particular doctor sees a lot of certain types of cancers, for example breast cancers, they are still only seeing a small fraction of all patients who ever get that disease, and the doctor may not be aware of all the results from relevant clinical trials, let alone from other practices.

The questions about "what works best in a specific cancer" have increased dramatically over the years, Weinberg says. "We have a growth in combination therapies, better understanding of the patient population due to next-generation sequencing (NGS) and other genomic tools, and people are now looking at immune-related factors." Much of those data are tucked away in proprietary databases, however, and too little of them reflect what goes on in the real world.

Since clinical trials can cost tens of millions of dollars (Sertkaya et al. 2016), and it can take more than a decade to fully vet a drug, it is important to find better ways to answer those questions. That recognition led Flatiron's founders to start gathering real-world evidence (RWE) from EHRs into a new type of database that could accelerate research.

Unlike clinical trial data, which are very carefully collected under specific parameters and measure only certain variables that are of interest to the study sponsor (e.g., a drug or device company), RWE is loosely defined as data that come from a variety of databases (such as insurance claims, digital devices, and EHRs) that may better capture the "real-world" use of a treatment. Importantly, "RWE is not just 'Big Data'—it's the *integration* of multiple sources of data" [emphasis ours] (Network for Excellence in Health Innovation 2015).

But how would they get those data in an industry that rarely shares patient information? Turner and Weinberg came up with an intriguing model: oncologists who buy their software give Flatiron access.

Today, Flatiron Health has a growing business providing specialized software to oncologists, pharmaceutical companies, and other researchers. At the heart of their business is an ability to gather complex health data. They work with more than 265 oncology clinics, three academic institutions, and 11 of the world's top pharmaceutical oncology firms. The company has been well financed along the way by some notable investors. Google Ventures led a 2014 round, putting $130 million into the company: that was Google's largest medical software financing to date (Hay 2014). In 2016, Roche led a $175 million round (Benner 2016). "The interesting thing is that Roche is both an investor and a client," explains Weinberg. "But they don't get any special client-privileges because of that."

What's more, in what may be the ultimate early vindication of their business model, Flatiron's database was used in 14 studies presented at the 2017 American Society of Clinical Oncology (ASCO) meeting, which is the world's most renowned showcase for new data on cancer drugs (Ramsey 2017).

It's *Moneyball Medicine* in action.

The challenges Turner and Weinberg ran into getting Flatiron up and running highlight some of the systemic inefficiencies and IT-related barriers that plague all aspects of healthcare (see the sidebar *Creating Internet Technology Solutions for the New Healthcare Environment*). As Weinberg points out, in some ways, IT and healthcare are like oil and water. Overcoming that disparity is going to be one of the major challenges in creating a data-driven healthcare system. But it is unquestionably a trend with momentum.

SIDEBAR: CREATING INTERNET TECHNOLOGY SOLUTIONS FOR THE NEW HEALTHCARE ENVIRONMENT

Zach Weinberg
Cofounder, Flatiron Health

After a year and half of field research, one of the first things Zach Weinberg and his partner Nat Turner realized about oncology was that "it was different from other fields in medicine," Weinberg says. Unlike when you have a headache, arthritis, or even knee surgery, "When you have cancer, your interaction with the medical system becomes pretty much continuous and intense. You also have lots of medical records, and one of your priorities is to get all those records together in one place and make sure your oncologist, more than anyone else, has access to them as soon as possible," he explains (Weinberg 2017).

Weinberg and Turner set out to make oncology practices data-driven: creating a set of tools that would make practices more efficient and press the field forward faster.

The chasm between the IT world and healthcare is massive, however, as they quickly learned. "There are people on both the health and IT sides who have a certain amount of hubris," he says. "They each think they know better." Checking your ego at the door, he advises, is the best approach if you really want to succeed. It's crucial to learn each other's language and to admit when you do not understand something. "There is a reason you are not a doctor, and there is a reason a doctor is not a software engineer," he says.

Founded in 2012, Flatiron today employs both those kinds of professionals. Weinberg is pleased that "a lot of our engineers spend time consulting our oncologists, and the doctors also feel comfortable going to the engineers and saying 'Hey, could we do this?'"

Building the company wasn't easy of course. Healthcare puts a priority on safety and privacy, and there have been few incentives to share clinical information or data. "Most of today's EHRs don't talk to each other," Weinberg explains. That, however, created an opportunity for companies such as Flatiron. "We addressed this problem by brute force," he says. "We built a hub with spokes that pull all the data together."

Today, Flatiron sells software to community oncology clinics. Those datasets produce the "real-world evidence" that is now so coveted for finding out what truly works in oncology.

To get that model off the ground, Flatiron's team had to get buy-in from oncologists and researchers, many of whom are naturally skeptical and may have had brutal experiences with software before. "A lot of times you could just see from their faces that they were not going to be convinced," Weinberg says. "But I remember one guy who really got it. Within 30 minutes he was so excited, he was totally on board." Those were the types of experiences that kept the team going.

Multiple tech companies have failed miserably in healthcare, including mammoths such as Microsoft and Google. "Many tech folks stumbled because they didn't appreciate the reality of healthcare. They simply said 'we can do better' and dove in," Weinberg says. "But today, we are seeing a merging of the disciplines in a way that is actually working."

With plenty of clients and more than $328 million in financing, Flatiron has the kind of momentum other start-ups in this field aspire to.

Cancer happens to be a particularly fertile field for this type of disruption. On top of the operational aspects that impede optimal cancer treatments, the science is changing at an unbelievably fast pace. New findings in this field are emerging at a rapid rate, compounding the information gap between traditional treatments and newer methods that might be significant improvements over standard therapies.

In recent decades, survival rates have risen for many cancers. This is due, in part, to biomedical research that has shown that cancer tumors of the same type (e.g., breast cancer) can vary substantially (i.e., be molecularly heterogeneous) from person to person. Even a single tumor can vary in response to its microenvironment or by the expansion of subpopulations of cells with particular genomic mutations (Fluegen et al. 2017; Konrad et al. 2017). In response to this recognition, there has been a big surge in the number of therapies directed to specific molecular targets (e.g., HER2, KRAS, and BRAF).

This new way of treating cancers from its molecular profile instead of its organ of origin isn't just a theory—the National Cancer Institute's Molecular Analysis for Therapy Choice (NCI-MATCH) Trial and other groups are already doing this (National Cancer Institute 2017c), and the FDA has approved the first drug that treats cancer with PD-1 mutations (Schattner 2017), regardless of tumor origin, as we'll describe in greater detail in Chapter 3.

But this trend of structuring clinical trials using molecular profiling is in early stages. So many doctors still have little experience outside of their specialty and are unlikely to have data available to them about treatments that were initially targeted to other cancer types. Therefore, it's possible that out of all the oncologists in the country, there are only a handful who have experience with a particular type of tumor and its mutations (Memorial Sloan Kettering Cancer Center 2011).

The fragmentation of data and hyperspecialization of doctors are what lead many patients to travel, sometimes great distances, to seek out an oncologist with particular expertise in their type of cancer. This growing emphasis on data is already changing cancer care and has the potential to influence a wide variety of noncancer disorders, such as chronic diseases like diabetes, as we will describe in Chapter 2.

In upcoming chapters, we will describe how physicians and hospitals are integrating this molecular and genomic information into patient care in a range of fields, how data have the potential to alter the research and care delivery workflows, and how the integration with technology is transforming healthcare.

Healthcare: Meet Digital

So why this trend, and why now? Analytics-intensive, evidence-based approaches have revolutionized dozens of other fields, including baseball (Lewis 2004), but things have been much slower in healthcare. Despite the tremendous amounts of data collected on patients (from routine physical exams to blood work performed before a surgery), concerns about privacy, heavy regulation, a longstanding culture of secrecy, and ultracompetitiveness have hamstrung the field.

Doctors and hospitals guarded patient records, price transparency was unheard of, and no one could agree on "fair" ways to measure quality. Additionally, researchers in public and private institutions also held on to most of their data, fearing that someone would use them to "scoop them." The list of hurdles goes on and on. Though some of these issues are valid and others have largely been addressed in the past few years, some are just ways to protect the status quo.

Security of healthcare data remains a challenge for companies and healthcare providers, especially when data sharing would be useful. But the reasons for this have evolved over time. Jeroen Tas, chief innovation and strategy officer at Philips Healthcare, compares the healthcare industry to Internet banking. "Twenty years ago Internet banking was thought of as unsafe; now everyone does online banking and security isn't such a big issue," he says. "There is large-scale infrastructure in play that can do [authentication, identification] with a high level of security."

Barrett Rollins, chief scientific officer of Dana-Farber, agrees: "[it's] passed the tipping point where this is an engineering problem, not a conceptual problem." Salient to the comparison is the ability to go to an ATM owned by any bank and retrieve money from your bank account. It's unlikely that a physician would be able to pull up a patient's medical record for procedures performed at a different hospital in the same way—but this should be a manageable problem.

Neil de Crescenzo, president and CEO of Change Healthcare, says things that are taken for granted in other sectors are not possible currently in healthcare (see the sidebar *Transforming Healthcare by Combining Data Streams*). Although sharing data between healthcare providers has improved in the past several years, limited interoperability between EHRs and continued privacy concerns remain as barriers that have largely been addressed in other industries, such as the mobile banking sector, as described above. And Tas notes, "[there's] no such thing as 100%." He continues, "[There will] always be those who don't want to share their data, but in an emergency situation they are likely to change their minds."

SIDEBAR: TRANSFORMING HEALTHCARE BY COMBINING DATA STREAMS

Neil de Crescenzo, MBA

Chief Executive Office, President, and Director, Change Healthcare
Former Senior Vice President and General Manager, Oracle Global Health Sciences

"The healthcare enterprise is going to become oriented around data management, analytics, and data liquidity," says Neil de Crescenzo, CEO and President of Change Healthcare (de Crescenzo 2017). "To move forward, we need to learn from how data has transformed other industries."

The first step, he says, is to translate as much data as possible into a digital format. "We're making good progress in that direction, especially through the steady growth in electronic medical records. And that's happening around the world," de Crescenzo says. This is a key change that will drive the evolution of healthcare.

There are also new types of data, such as those from sensors and personal tracking devices. Further, sophisticated algorithms and analytics that were once accessible only to highly specialized professionals can now be used by a much wider range of people. These analytics are also much faster. "People in genomic medicine, for example, are running queries in real time that once took 12 hours to run," he explains.

But the most important trends he sees are higher accuracy, utility, and liquidity of data. "We finally have the ability to take healthcare data from many sources, put it into a common form, and process it at multiple sites," he says. "That's going to be transformative."

By definition, Big Data are huge volumes of data that are difficult to analyze. We've already reached that point with whole genome sequence data. Now we have to reach that point with other data types, including clinical data. Ideally, there would be a standard clinical care document that would allow clinicians to pull specific data and share it between institutions.

"We have made some progress toward that but that's been much slower," says de Crescenzo. The CommonWell Alliance, which includes some of the biggest IT providers in the healthcare industry, has devoted itself to such data exchange, or interoperability. But achieving that across the industry is taking much longer than anticipated.

There are a lot of things that are taken for granted in other sectors that are still far behind in healthcare. For example, everyone who sends a package expects tracking information. But for most patients, it's impossible to determine which doctors they've seen in the last month, let alone in the last year. "That's an enormous logistical challenge and it's going to take a lot of work," de Crescenzo says.

The overall idea is to digitize more data, make it more liquid, and use analytics to make it easier to track and analyze. But that will be a big change in the healthcare sector, which until now has been all about privacy and secrecy. All that sensor data that are building up on patients' personal trackers, for example, needs to start making its way into doctors' offices. Meanwhile, more of the tools found mainly in medical settings, such as EKG monitors, need to get into patients' homes. Then, the data from those devices need to be piped to physicians.

Another big change is around reimbursement, which will have a huge impact on all the players, including pharmaceutical companies and hospitals. For example, no one—neither the doctor nor the drug company—is paid based on whether patients take the drugs they are prescribed or not. But compliance makes a big difference in whether people get better. "As we shift to value-based care, there will be bigger incentives to make sure certain patients are getting optimal care, and following their doctors' recommendations," de Crescenzo says.

Flatiron is just one of many start-ups, healthcare organizations, and other groups trying to use Big Data and sophisticated analytics to improve healthcare and take advantage of market opportunities (Kocher and Roberts 2014). New enterprises are developing products, such as Athena Health's Epocrates medical reference app, that streamline processes that have long been too cumbersome. Others, such as PokitDok and Castlight Health, are helping to shed light on the cost and quality data that have been mostly shielded from most people's view until recently (see Chapter 6). Still others, such as Health Catalyst, are developing software and other tools that can be shared across healthcare institutions and providers. Health Catalyst's healthcare.ai is an open source repository for predictive algorithms, tools, and documentation that healthcare professionals can use to build models for diverse healthcare challenges, such as readmission for chronic obstructive pulmonary disease or central line-associated bloodstream infections (Mason 2016).

The healthcare insurance industry is similarly finding itself being transformed by Big Data, trying to keep their businesses relevant and viable in a fast-changing market (Marr 2015). Aetna's CEO, Marc Bertolini, for example, has spoken openly about the company's need to reconfigure its business model. Aetna has been acquiring health IT companies and looking at ways to apply its experience in underwriting and other assets to the new landscape (Aetna 2014b; Markland 2014). "Aetna [now] views itself as a health IT company with an insurance component" one observer wrote (Chase 2012). Likewise, insurer Humana's CMO Roy Beveridge, recently said that because of the rise in value-based care, "Sometimes I think we're becoming more of a data analytics company than anything else" (Sweeney 2017a).

Even companies that haven't been traditionally associated with healthcare are expanding into the healthcare market. Many of these are technology companies that are finding healthcare to be an extension of their evolving business models. Apple, known primarily for computers and cell phones, jumped into the field with its HealthKit app in 2014 (Bonnington 2014) and further expanded their presence by integrating biometric sensors and third-party fitness-related apps for their Apple Watch (Apple 2016; Wakabayashi 2016). Tech giant IBM has been asserting itself in healthcare with its Watson Health artificial intelligence solution, particularly for oncology (IBM Watson 2017) and genomics (IBM Watson 2016). Xerox, synonymous with copiers, is working to digitize the data, making it easier to share and analyze (Xerox 2016). All of these are addressed in later chapters.

Each of these organizations have one thing in common: They want to be at the forefront of the new higher-quality, more efficient, and more cost-effective data-driven healthcare system.

Investors are interested too. Since 2010, venture capitalists (VCs) have invested billions in the health IT market, with the public market and debt financings bringing total corporate funding alone to $12.4 billion (Mercom Capital Group 2015). Investment in this sector has been growing. Both 2014 and 2015 were record years, with VCs funding worth a total of $8.8 billion (Mom and Adams 2016). A Rock Health mid-2016 analysis found that year on pace with the previous two, belying expectations that growth would be flat or even lower. Flatiron was one of the companies that have scored big in the past several years, netting $313 million in funding by the end of the first half of 2016. Other winners included Jawbone and Health Catalyst, which had amassed $948 million and $223 million, respectively, by that time (Mom and Adams 2016).

But you don't have to be a health IT start-up to benefit from this new emphasis on data. As we will try to describe, many sectors of the approximately $9.6 trillion global healthcare market are already being affected, and many more will be over time.

If the difference between evolution and revolution is the speed of change, then healthcare is now in the mode of revolutionary change. Medical information that was once kept on paper and rarely shared is now being stored electronically and can be widely dispersed. A broader range of data are being collected, including genomic and other biomarker data, prices for healthcare services, clinical trial results, failed experimental drugs, findings from microbiome research, and more.

Healthcare databases are also becoming interconnected and groups are beginning to combine and analyze data in more ways than ever before. For example, the Electronic Medical Records and Genomics (eMERGE) Network is a national organization of biorepositories linked to EHRs for large-scale genomic research (eMERGE Network 2017). This consortium is not only leveraging massive amounts of both genomic and clinical data to look at disease, but it's also using this information to investigate public health-related issues such as methicillin-resistant *Staphylococcus aureus* (MRSA) (Jackson et al. 2016) and how research subjects feel about consent and data sharing (Smith et al. 2016).

Collecting the data is just the beginning—it's the interpretation of the data and finding novel insights contained within that are changing the healthcare landscape. In our interview, Stan Norton, vice president and chief technology officer at UnitedHealth Group's data analytics arm Humedica, said, "I think Big Data is an overloaded term in some ways. Because it's not just that the volume of data is bigger. We also have new data and totally new uses for it" (Norton 2017). This has led to big steps forward in how data are analyzed and protected, making it easier to gain real knowledge from data and to share it.

More databases are also open to public viewing, and innovators are beginning to find new uses for it. When the government began releasing Medicare claims data, for example, entrepreneurs began looking for ways to use those to help patients compare prices for healthcare. And the *New England Journal of Medicine* recently held a competition (NEJM Sprint Data Analysis Challenge) for researchers to discover a novel finding using a dataset from one of their recent publications (*New England Journal of Medicine* 2017). Furthermore, we have seen an explosion in technologies to collect data, such as mobile phone apps and wearables (e.g., fitness trackers). The global mobile health market alone has been forecasted to reach more than $49 billion by 2020 (Grand View Research 2015), and there is considerable interest in leveraging the vast amount of data collected by mobile devices.

Not only are we seeing big advances in science and IT, but also there is growing pressure to ensure that we are paying for quality in healthcare, not just quantity—a topic we delve into in Chapter 7. Over the next few years, decisions about everything, from which insurance company to choose to which treatment to use, will increasingly be based on data and their analysis. This is leading to tremendous disruption of the existing healthcare marketplace, as well as opportunities for innovators who can think fast and move quickly by creating new jobs and companies.

But it isn't just about the disruption, as Othman Laraki, CEO of Color Genomics, cautions in a Recode Decode interview with Kara Swisher, "Those [companies] that focus on the disruption without getting the science right… will be destroyed" (Swisher 2017). Diagnostics company Theranos is a recent case in point. Once thought to be a major disruptor to the laboratory testing industry by claiming to be able to run dozens of tests on a fingertip's worth of blood, the company and its founder, Elizabeth Holmes, are now embroiled in legal battles and accusations of scientific fraud (Stockton 2016). Companies that get both the science and the business right will be the winners in the competitive healthcare technology landscape. In the end, if managed correctly, we'll have achieved the triple aim of healthcare: a more efficient, higher-quality system that provides better outcomes at a lower cost.

We are already beginning to witness a big change in how technology is used in healthcare. Healthcare costs have reached a level that many do not think is sustainable (see the section *Health Cost Crisis*). Going forward, we'll see a surge in the use of technology, such as remote monitoring and telemedicine (see the section *Quantified Self*), and greater efficiencies in existing technologies, such as genomic sequencing machines, to drive down costs and improve outcomes. For less than the price of some imaging tests, patients might be able to have their entire genome analyzed. Going well beyond the long-ballyhooed $1,000 genome, genetic sequencing giant Illumina recently announced a new sequencer that could usher in the $100 genome—putting this vast amount of data in the hands of more patients and doctors (Business Wire 2017). What does this mean for the average person and their healthcare provider? More information that can help determine how best to manage clinical care is being delivered to *both* the patient and their healthcare providers. But the implications of the technology-driven data deluge extend far beyond the walls of the exam room to areas such as the organization of health systems and drug development.

Health Cost Crisis

New pressure to cut costs is a major factor influencing healthcare today. Modern medicine has made astonishing progress. But unlike other industries, where new technology often lowers prices, healthcare prices and costs have continued to rise, and typically at rates higher than overall inflation. Expensive new treatments and imaging machines have helped propel the worldwide healthcare market to an estimated $9.59 trillion (Pricewaterhouse Cooper 2015). According to the World Bank's data from 2014, health costs account for more than 9.9% of gross domestic product (GDP) globally and are higher than 10% in 25 countries already (World Bank 2017). The United States spent a whopping 17.1% of GDP on healthcare (World Bank 2017). Although the rise of healthcare costs has slowed a little since 2014, overall global healthcare costs are expected to keep rising steadily (Organisation for Economic Co-operation and Development [OECD] 2017).

There are also substantial waste and inefficiencies in healthcare—factors that could be costing the United States $1 trillion (Sahni et al. 2015). This includes costs related to overtreatment and unnecessary treatments, bloated administrative infrastructures, fraud, and overspending that result from an inability to effectively shop for the best price (Sahni et al. 2015). And where other industries have embraced continuous improvement models, where processes are measured so that they can be made more efficient, healthcare has only recently begun to adopt that mindset.

If there is as much unnecessary and poor quality care in the system as has been reported, there's also considerable room for improvement (Redberg 2011; Institute of Medicine of the National Academies 2012; National Academies 2012). Leveraging claims data is one way to identify areas of overspending or inappropriate treatment, and several companies are working on that. But health benefits consultant and coauthor of *Cracking Health Costs* Tom Emerick told us that many companies aren't using these data wisely. Basing quality of care on claims data can be misleading, he says, since you can't tell if the diagnosis was accurate or if the treatment failed. A recent NEJM Catalyst survey of physicians and healthcare executives concurred, finding that respondents believe claims data will be less valuable in the next 5 years, whereas patient-generated and genomic data will become more important (Compton-Phillips and NEJM Catalyst 2017). But how insurers could integrate nonclaims data into their reimbursement processes is unclear.

Unsustainable healthcare costs are spurring many more governments, insurers, employers, and individuals worldwide to seek cost-effective alternatives—or simply skip obtaining care at all. A recent Gallup poll found that 31% of Americans surveyed had put off medical care because of costs (Dugan 2017). Many U.S. health plans now have limited networks (which exclude certain doctors and hospitals), and deductibles are in the thousands of dollars. As a result, many more patients are delaying or skipping recommended care, which can lead to sicker patients and more expensive care needed by the time patients actually seek out medical treatment (American College of Physicians 2016; The Commonwealth Fund 2016; Wharam et al. 2017).

Taxpayers, meanwhile, are footing a larger and larger bill. Medicaid and Medicare are straining state and federal budgets, and costs for healthcare for prisoners, who are not typically eligible for federal healthcare programs, are also ballooning in some states (Pew Charitable Trusts 2014; Andrews 2015; Centers for Medicare & Medicaid Services 2017c). These problems aren't relegated only to the United States. In the United Kingdom, for example, healthcare councils are removing some expensive drugs off of formularies in an attempt to reduce costs, leading some patients and doctors to complain about rationing (Cooper 2015).

If patients are skipping care or can't get coverage for a particular facility, that's lost revenue for those doctors and hospitals, and can lead to more expensive care when the patient eventually seeks medical help. As the number of patients with high-deductible health plans doubled from 2009 to 2012 (when the total was almost 20%), hospitals reported an increase in bad debt (Hancock 2013). But price-conscious patients who seek out price and quality information often find themselves stymied by a lack of data, as we'll describe in Chapter 6.

Cost consciousness has further encouraged a marked emphasis on quality and demonstrable improvement in patient outcomes. Hospitals are now increasingly graded (and penalized) by insurers based on their abilities to prevent a variety of problems, from hospital-acquired infections and surgical complications to readmissions within 30 days of hospital discharge, so they have a vested interest to create programs that will enable them to reach the right metrics. Physicians are being asked to take on more financial risk for their role in keeping patients healthier through quality payment programs that require them to submit performance outcomes for their patients (Department of Health & Human Services 2017a). But for metrics that aren't assessed or directly tied to payment, institutions and providers have little incentive to shift practices to performance-based models, particularly if the cost savings will be passed on to third-party payers. In Chapter 7, we'll describe how data are already transforming the move to value-based healthcare and what is next to come.

Quantified Self

Consumers have seen how technology and data have changed user relationships to other industries, like banking, and are starting to demand similar improvements in healthcare. In many ways, says Anil Jain, senior vice president and chief medical officer for Explorys, an IBM company, the patients are the ones driving the real change—an observation shared by several of the leaders we interviewed for this book. One new and rising trend: the increasing role of wearable devices.

Unlike what you might think, the wearable trend isn't driven solely by the younger generation. Evidation Health is a healthcare technology company that partners with companies to develop and analyze wearable devices and the digital biomarkers they generate (see Chapter 10). Christine Lemke, cofounder and president of Evidation, found, based on more than 1 million patients in their database, that the younger crowd adopts wearables more quickly, although they may lose interest and move on to the next thing; whereas the older crowd is slower to take up a wearable device, but will eventually stick with it. Each device can yield millions, billions, or even more data points on a single individual over time. Incorporating the massive amounts of data collected by these devices into EHRs will be challenging, and turning the data into something meaningful for patient care will require a variety of individuals, from engaged physicians to data scientists who can transform the raw data into actionable insights.

The partnership between medical device manufacturer Medtronic and fitness wearable company Fitbit exemplifies the opportunities wearable devices bring to healthcare. In the United States, there are nearly 30 million patients with type 2 diabetes. Medtronic's continuous blood glucose monitoring systems can give physicians important data about the control a patient has over their glucose levels, while Fitbits can automatically track a patient's physical activity. Bringing the two pieces together through a mobile phone app, the iPro2 myLog, "provides new tools and insights, so that physicians can optimize therapy and patients can better understand how to manage their diabetes," said Medtronic vice president Laura Stoltenberg in a press release (Medtronic 2016).

Physical activity information from a wearable that can be combined with other types of health data, like blood glucose monitoring, isn't the only area where data from a device will transform healthcare. Consider patients who take certain medications, such as warfarin, a blood thinner, and require periodic blood tests. A late 2016 report by Deloitte U.K. Centre for Health Solutions on the challenges facing primary care physicians in the National Health Service (United Kingdom) highlighted Health Call, a partnership between Inhealthcare Limited and County Durham and Darlington NHS Foundation Trust (DeloitteUK 2017). Through Health Call, patients self-monitor and submit test results through on online portal or via telephone; clinical nurse specialists determine the appropriate warfarin dosage and inform the patients if their dose needs to change and when another test is required. This type of remote monitoring has the potential to increase medication adherence and prevent complications if adverse events can be identified at an early stage or even before they occur.

Looking Forward

There is unquestionably going to be increasing demand for more standardization and optimization in healthcare. Doctors are typically very autonomous and usually base treatment decisions on their own experience. Some experts believe that's one of the key reasons we have so much variation in how medicine is practiced in this country. But price and quality vary for treatments and procedures, so it can be challenging for physicians to select the one with the best value. Standardization will benefit healthcare if the optimal practice (best outcomes for the highest quality and lowest cost) becomes the standard. Policy makers and others have long called for more standardization of healthcare, better measurement of outcomes, and an emphasis on *value*—not volume or price—to reduce health costs (Miller 2009; Institute of Medicine of the National Academies 2012). If the goal is more research into what treatments work best, more sharing of patient information to get solid answers, and better measurement of whether or not patients are getting the best outcomes, data analytics and sharing of data is the key to helping us get there.

As these changes are introduced, the healthcare landscape will change. Some healthcare professionals will see their autonomy eroded as clinical decision support mechanisms and data analytics transform how medicine is practiced. Others will see their responsibilities expanded, such as computer scientists and health data scientists. These are positions that, until recently, were relegated to academic institutions (or nonexistent), but are increasingly a part of many health systems. New job roles will be developed in the upcoming years to accommodate the integration of data with patient care. Physicians will find their patients are increasingly data-conscious and will have to have mechanisms to include this information in clinical care. Clinical support staff, such as advanced practice nurses, physician assistants, and health coaches, may find their responsibilities continue to grow, providing an opportunity for physicians to focus on more complex cases. Major sectors of healthcare, including hospitals, pharmaceutical companies, and insurers, will need to reshape their business models to thrive or risk being left behind.

As we will describe in the upcoming chapters, here are some key trends we are beginning to see transform healthcare:

- The growing use of databases, artificial intelligence, and new technologies to find genetic mutations underlying birth defects, cancers, and extremely rare conditions otherwise very difficult to diagnose.
- Patients becoming ever more active participants in healthcare, using social media to find others with similar disorders and spurring research into their own conditions using publicly available data and crowdsourcing sites.
- More hospital systems comparing their outcomes against those of their competitors, discerning which treatments work best, and identifying what the best practices are to prevent medical crises. Hospitals will increasingly evaluate the efficiency of all their employees, including physicians, as they adopt quality improvement strategies that have been used by other industries.
- Patients increasingly comparing prices and the quality of different doctors and medical facilities via online databases, leading to more competition by providers for these consumers.

- Growing use of artificial intelligence systems with specialized software to help diagnose conditions and recommend treatment options. These solutions will be able to sift through reams of data, such as images or lab results—they'll "know" far more than any doctor can.
- Pharmaceutical companies collaborating with hospitals to see how well their products are actually working in the "real world," where they are used on many more patients than in clinical trials. Pharma will also be using Big Data and digital health applications to select and evaluate new drug targets as well as influence patients.
- Technology advances, combined with data, allowing patients to access high-quality care at lower prices outside of the traditional medical establishments.

These are just some of the key ways in which the data revolution is reshaping healthcare. *MoneyBall Medicine* is already here. That's why so many entrepreneurs are flocking to healthcare now and founding companies that offer completely new ways of delivering care (such as retail clinics and remote monitoring), providing information about cost and quality, and giving guidance on how to purchase health insurance. The swiftest and smartest entrepreneurs will find the most powerful ways to use the data and help their organizations thrive in this new environment. And these innovators are not just coming from inside existing healthcare or information technology companies. Be prepared to see more commercial spinoffs from academia and a greater number of nontraditional companies seeking a place in the healthcare industry (see the section *Healthcare: Meet Digital* earlier in this chapter).

The volume and quality of data available and their accessibility is also going to keep improving. After the U.S. government pumped $19.5 billion into EHR adoption in 2009 with the Health Information Technology for Economic and Clinical Health (HITECH) Act, the health IT industry surged, and private and public investment followed. As noted earlier, hospital adoption of EHR systems has grown more than fivefold since 2008 (Charles, Gabriel, and Furukawa 2014). By 2014, 75.5% of hospitals had a basic EHR system that met the program's specifications (Charles, Gabriel, and Furukawa 2014).

These statistics can also be misleading without considering the wide variation from state to state. For example, although five states had more than 90% meeting the requirement, 25 states were below the average. Fewer than half (49.6%) of West Virginia's hospitals met even the basic EHR threshold (Charles, Gabriel, and Furukawa 2014). By 2013, about 78% of doctors' offices, meanwhile, had some type of EHR system, and just under 50% of those systems were considered basic (Centers for Disease Control and Prevention 2017a). Expect to see more states improve their hospital and provider utilization of EHRs to help minimize duplication of care, improve communication between different providers, and collect patient data that can be leveraged to improve care on a population level.

Although EHR utilization has increased substantially, most of those systems still can't—or just don't—share information. Part of this is due to a lack of a common standards. Think of the situation with EHRs like the relationship between cell phone service providers and cell phone manufacturers. With cell phones, no matter who you obtain service from, you can still make phone calls and communicate with people who have different carriers or devices. But there are differences in the technological platforms that can make transferring your data from one provider to another (i.e., buying a new type of phone or switching to a different service carrier) more difficult. Just like with cell phone technologies, no matter which EHR system a health system uses, it can collect basic health information and is required to have the ability to export some components of this information. But true sharing of data across these EHR systems doesn't often occur. This is a major problem for patients who move from one health system to another or who need to share records between doctors, like the cousin of Flatiron Health's Nat Turner, who was described at the beginning of this chapter.

In addition, much of healthcare is structured as silos, meaning patients typically don't have a "medical home" that serves as their point of contact for all healthcare interactions, from primary care providers to specialists and institutions (Patient-Centered Primary Care Collaborative 2017). Instead, the average patient might see an internist once a year for a physical and routine bloodwork, a cardiologist every 6 months for their previous heart attack, a dermatologist for a yearly check for skin cancer, and a gastroenterologist to manage their Crohn's disease. If these providers aren't all in the same hospital system or physician network, there's a good chance that what happens at one physician's office doesn't get fully communicated to the others, from treatment plans to medication decisions. Providers don't get any financial benefit by helping their patients take their data to another provider, and it's unclear how value-based payments for physicians will take improved patient outcomes that involve multiple specialists into consideration.

Some providers, third-party payers, and entrepreneurial software companies are starting to embrace what they call "interoperability" as the easy electronic sharing of health data (Aetna 2016). This means being able to have a patient's primary care records, hospital records, even prescription history shared between all healthcare providers who care for the patient. Health systems like Geisinger are leading the way. Geisinger and xG Health Solutions developed an app for rheumatologists that was able to transfer patient data between Geisinger's Epic EHR and the Cerner EHR framework using Health Level 7 standards (Monegain 2014). Eventually, being able to transfer health information seamlessly with other healthcare facilities is going to become a competitive advantage, and technology such as blockchain (see Chapter 10) will play a large role in making this happen.

Since much of the change will be driven by mergers and acquisitions, companies will need to have quality and cost data available, at least to investors, for deals to take place and to make it possible for new partners to share data. As we will present in later chapters, there's a misalignment between hospital/provider incentives and those of insurers. Right now, third-party payers reap almost 90% of the financial benefits of EHRs and process initiatives designed to improve patient outcomes while lowering costs—not the health systems that pay millions to implement them (Palabindala, Pamarthy, and Jonnalagadda 2016). The imbalance between who is paying and who is benefitting is sure to shift as hospitals' and providers' reimbursements are increasingly tied to patient outcomes. As a result, software and processes that help them reduce complications and preventable readmission rates, more efficiently manage patients with chronic diseases, and choose the most cost-effective treatments will be in demand. Health systems and providers that leverage their patient data will have a competitive advantage compared to facilities and physicians that don't. Learning how to gather those data and get the most out of analyzing them will prepare them for the new cost-and-quality transparent healthcare system.

In this landscape of big changes and rapid innovation, the United States has the opportunity to lead the world by encouraging the types of tools, services, and processes that all countries need.

Just as other industries have been transformed by data, software, and business process improvement methods including Six Sigma, Agile, and Lean, this is healthcare's moment to breakthrough and adopt truly modern operating practices. However, big obstacles still stand in the way. As noted, many providers are still wary of data sharing, and there are substantial technical difficulties to making that happen. Building big databases, getting good use out of them, and linking them is currently hard to do and usually expensive. We have made tremendous advances, and with the combination of more pressure to reduce costs and the new tools, a data-driven health system that drives toward better outcomes is well within our reach. The changes happening within the health system to move toward value-based care, reduce health costs, and improve health outcomes for patients are starting to take hold—but how far these initiatives will go and how fast it happens will depend on our willingness to collect the data, perform the analysis, and transform current processes based on those insights. Welcome to *Moneyball Medicine*.

Chapter 2

Precision Medicine, Data-Driven Diagnosis and Treatment

Precision medicine is about how to have care that is personalized for an individual and match the right patients to the right care, getting decisions correct and individually optimal.

Zeeshan Syed
Clinical Associate Professor at Stanford University School of Medicine (Siwicki 2017)

In 2014, after 5-year-old Korei Parker developed some unusual bruising and bleeding of her gums, her mother took her to nearby St. Jude Children's Research Hospital for tests and discovered Korei was suffering from severe acquired aplastic anemia—a noncancerous condition in which the body doesn't produce enough red blood cells and leaves patients prone to infections. Treatments for aplastic anemia include antibiotics, antivirals, and antifungal drugs to keep the patient infection-free. Korei was initially treated with the antifungal medication, voriconazole, but doctors found she metabolized the drug too quickly. "She took adult dosages, and it didn't seem to do anything for her," her mother said in an interview with *Scientific American* (Maron 2016).

But Korei was at St. Jude, where doctors have been performing genetic testing for variants that could impact how a patient metabolizes certain medications for all new patients since 2011. These tests look for variants that might predict whether a patient will respond to a drug or if they are at risk for an adverse event (negative side effect from the medication). Thanks to the genetic testing, doctors were able to prescribe an alternate medication that relied on a different biological mechanism to be metabolized, one not affected by the variants in Korei's genome, and the child remained infection-free (Maron 2016).

Dan Roden, senior vice president for Personalized Medicine at Vanderbilt University Medical Center, has said, "The era of precision medicine is upon us" (Maron 2016). As we will describe in this chapter and the next, implementing precision medicine in a clinical setting relies on both the analysis of enormous quantities of data *and* the ability to gain meaningful insights from those results. Those data can come from lab tests, gadgets, public databases, or electronic records; but the goal is to give a precise diagnosis, based on all the patient's individual characteristics. (Note: Precision medicine is also often referred to as personalized medicine.) For some patients, this can mean being prescribed a different medication dose or even a different drug from most people with the same condition, based on their genetic background. For others, it can mean the condition is diagnosed before the patient exhibits noticeable symptoms, and in time for preventive medication or other interventions to take effect. From pharmacogenomics to imaging, new discoveries are moving from the research lab to the patient's bedside, and all of it is being driven by *Moneyball Medicine*—reaching optimal performance at the most reasonable cost.

Precision medicine has been estimated to be a market worth about $40 billion currently, and is expected to exceed $87 billion by 2023, according to a recent forecast (Global Market Insights Inc. 2017). It encompasses treatment-guiding testing in a range of conditions, with oncology currently accounting for more than 30% of the market, and is steadily expanding into new indications. Will the established dominant companies, such as Roche, keep a tight rein on this burgeoning field? Or will upstarts disrupt the market with new innovations? That's the *Moneyball* question for precision medicine.

Precision Medicine: Welcome to the N-of-1

The term "precision medicine" is somewhat of a contradiction. At its core, precision medicine is about treating a patient based on their *individual* biological and environmental risk factors. And though most doctors will say they have always treated patients individually, patient management has generally started with what tends to work for most people with a certain condition. For example, patients who need a blood thinner will often be prescribed warfarin or clopidogrel. Taken at the precise dose the patient needs, these medications can prevent blood clots, which can be a complication of some cardiac surgeries. If the dose is too low, a clot can form and the patient can suffer a stroke. But if the dose is too high, the patient may have uncontrolled bleeding. Getting to a drug dosing algorithm, or risk prediction for a disease, requires a great many patients whose clinical data are analyzed, In short, precision medicine for the patient depends on the results from studies in large populations.

Historically, doctors have relied on readily available patient measurements, such as weight, sex, race, or ethnicity, and characteristics such as whether the patient smokes or has certain comorbidities, to set the dose for many drugs. The patient's initial dose would be based on these measurements, then tweaked or changed if they failed to respond to therapy or suffered an adverse event or complication. Depending on the drug and the patient, reaching the right dose could take some time, leaving the patient at risk of complications from too little or too much medication in the interim.

For the past several years, institutions such as St. Jude and Vanderbilt have integrated genomic information with clinical management for patients such as Korei, including those undergoing certain cardiac procedures, and patients with cancer, as we'll describe in the next chapter. Instead of relying solely on algorithms designed for the average patient, physicians are now attempting to personalize treatment based on patients' genomes, proteomes—even their microbiomes. You could say that treating a patient with precision medicine begins to approximate a clinical trial with a sample size $n=1$.

But getting to the point where physicians can successfully treat patients with precision medicine requires incredibly large datasets to make the connections between biological mechanisms, patient characteristics, and genomic variation. There also has to be the technical infrastructure to enable this type of treatment, from physicians' knowledge of the right genomic test to order, to ordering the test, through getting the results in an interpretable format back to the physician. These are not inconsequential challenges. Though there are numerous success stories such as Korei Parker's, there has also been substantial hype about the capabilities of precision medicine and genomic medicine. In particular, that they not only cure cancer but public health problems like cardiovascular disease, stroke, and diabetes (Husten 2015).

These datasets can be comprised of a great many individuals with a few data points each, or a smaller number of patients, each with many data points. This is because it's usually not sufficient to perform a study in a few dozen patients if the condition is common, the environmental exposure is widespread, or the genetic variant is extremely common in the population. You might need thousands of patients. For imaging studies, where MRI data are evaluated, there may be fewer subjects, but each may have thousands, or even millions, of individual data points. These complex datasets and the studies that are performed with them form the basis for precision medicine. From cancer, to drug response, to the best practices for patients with diabetes or obesity; Big Data and the rapidly evolving tools to mine and visualize the data make it possible.

As we mentioned in Chapter 1, most providers and medical systems have traditionally kept their patients' health data private. In our interview, Eric Topol, genomic medicine researcher at the Scripps Research Institute, explained, "A lot of data has been gathered by sequencing cancer genomes, but it is not properly aggregated yet. The holdup isn't necessarily the analytics, it's the willingness of different centers to work together and administrative hurdles such as Institutional Review Boards (IRBs), privacy, etc." (Topol 2017). And this problem isn't specific to cancer research.

Recognition that this fragmentation of data has hindered patient care, research, and precision medicine initiatives has been the impetus for many organizations to combine data through data-sharing agreements and groups. Increasingly, researchers are looking for ways to put clinical data to use without compromising patient privacy (see the sidebar *The Next Frontier—Marrying Clinical and Research Data*).

The eMERGE Network, described in Chapter 1 (see the section *Healthcare: Meet Digital*) is just one of many academic consortia that have been created to address this problem. By pooling their data, participating institutions are able to perform studies on significantly bigger patient populations. These large studies have been used for a number of genomic studies in the last several years, supporting precision medicine initiatives. And this type of collaboration across academic institutions extends beyond genomics, investigating public health and other epidemiologic concerns.

SIDEBAR: THE NEXT FRONTIER—MARRYING CLINICAL AND RESEARCH DATA

Keith Elliston, PhD
President and CEO, The tranSMART Foundation

Many experts now believe patient clinical data are the bonanza of the future. Combining that with the biological kind gathered by researchers can, they say, create synergies that will move medicine forward by leaps and bounds. That nexus of data are expected to fuel the next great wave of medical research.

"The most untapped resource in medical science today is the data from billions of patients interacting with the healthcare system," says Keith Elliston, president and CEO of The tranSMART Foundation, a nonprofit, research collaboration engine in our interview

(Elliston 2017). But high hurdles exist to accessing clinical data. For one thing, there are major privacy concerns and many regulations against sharing information about patients. Those who hold this type of data are also very protective of it. They are concerned someone else may lure their patients away or exploit for profit the data that has been so painstakingly collected.

Finally, interoperable software systems are needed to combine data from multiple sources, analyze, and then share it. Those are just some of the barriers faced by groups such as tranSMART—a unique foundation that provides members with access to fully developed, open-source, IT platforms and public data for translational research. Contributors submit tools to tranSMART and its community then tests and optimizes them. Some of the most recent features on the site are a SmartR plugin (from ITTM/University of Luxembourg/eTRIKS), genomics-based cohort selection (Janssen), GWAS enhancements (Pfizer), and XNAT image database integration (Imperial College London and Erasmus Medical Center). Some tools also connect users to other popular data sources. For example, one workflow links to the Qiagen Ingenuity Pathway Analysis.

As it grows, tranSMART hopes to advance data sharing and analytics to promote precision medicine. The group's 19 member organizations include academic groups, nonprofits, and commercial drug developers. They all have access to the site's tools and public data tranSMART has collected, but members can also use these tools to analyze their proprietary data as well.

"We have a lot of data at tranSMART to share already," explains Elliston. Many of the group's members are also handling large amounts of proprietary data. Pfizer alone, for example, has data from 140 clinical trials in their tranSMART system, he says. The National Cancer Institute (NCI) also has data from numerous studies, including a Cancer Genome Atlas project that included several thousand patients; those data are available to other researchers as long as they register on the site.

"The challenges to data-sharing are sociological, political, and economic," explains Elliston. But the benefits are so huge, it's imperative to keep working on this problem. He points to recent results from the National Health and Nutrition Examination Survey, which is a population survey led by the Centers for Disease Control and Prevention (CDC) (see Patel et al. 2016a). They have released over 255 files with data from four surveys, which involved almost 42,000 patients and more than 1,100 variables. Those variables included phenotype and environmental information, as well as demographic information and details from physical exams and lab results.

"Data resources like this," Elliston believes, "will show the true potential of precision medicine. One major challenge has been making it possible for those with clinical data to actually merge their information with others. Too many different software systems are usually involved. tranSMART is working closely with one particular platform, the i2b2 (Informatics for Integrating Biology and the Bedside) system. We think this can be the platform of the future for integrating clinical and research data," he says (Elliston 2017).

While academic collaborations have been tremendously successful, the federal government is also taking steps to mine its data for precision medicine purposes. There are nearly 9 million patients currently enrolled in the U.S. Department of Veterans Affairs (VA) healthcare system (National Center for Veterans Analysis and Statistics 2016). The VA database contains more than 30 petabytes (1 petabyte=1 million gigabytes) of data from more than 2 decades of patient care—longitudinal information that would be impossible to collect due to the large number of patients and cost associated with collecting data. It's one of the reasons the VA database is so incredibly valuable as a resource for clinical research and precision medicine.

The VA has demonstrated a commitment to leveraging its massive amount of patient data through a recent partnership with Flow Health, a technology company that works with companies to mine their data and perform complex analytics using a variety of techniques such as cognitive computing. The goal of the collaboration is to develop a knowledge map for patient management, using Flow Health's data analytics capabilities to enable the VA to use precision medicine (HIT Consultant 2016). Although the data will be de-identified for researchers, it is hoped that it will ultimately inform clinical practices in the future for patients, for diagnosis and treatment of disease (FlowHealth 2017).

While the VA-Flow Health partnership is still in early stages, a collaboration between AliveCor and the Mayo Clinic demonstrate how leveraging large datasets of health data can change patient management. AliveCor is a provider of an FDA-cleared mobile electrocardiogram (ECG) technology, delivered on a mobile platform (smartphone) (AliveCor 2017). Using the Mayo Clinic data with AliveCor's deep learning techniques, the goal of the partnership was to uncover additional clinical (non-heart-related) information in 10 million ECG readings (Attia et al. 2016).

Their study demonstrated how advanced analyses from massive amounts of electrocardiogram data can be used to track potassium levels in patients with cardiovascular and/or kidney disease who are undergoing hemodialysis. Maintaining normal potassium levels is difficult in this population, and potentially life-threatening changes can occur without warning.

Doctors were able to predict potassium levels with low error (~10% of measured blood potassium) using data from the noninvasive ECG, with or without a baseline blood test (Attia et al. 2016).

In addition to personalizing each patient's predicted potassium level, the combined data from the patients allowed the doctors to develop a model that could be used for all patients based on T wave characteristics from the ECG. The implications are that this method may allow doctors or nurse practitioners to remotely monitor potassium levels in patients undergoing dialysis, which has substantial clinical significance and may prevent negative outcomes from unexpected abnormal potassium levels (Attia et al. 2016).

Not only has the partnership between Mayo Clinic and AliveCor supported precision medicine for patients (i.e., prediction of potassium levels), the technology has the potential to reduce costs and improve patient care, since patients can be monitored remotely through the AliveCor device and smartphone software. The 10 million ECG readings and other large datasets will be the key to future precision medicine initiatives.

Assistant in the Exam Room

It's impossible for physicians today to stay current on all of the emerging research in a field. Although the Internet has made dissemination of research from across the world easier, there's simply too much data to assess, too many new articles, and clinical trials recruiting patients from far-flung locations. Furthermore, in resource-scarce areas, these challenges may be compounded by a lack of specialists to interpret the highly technical information. That's why there is substantial interest in the use of artificial intelligence (AI) and cognitive computing, data analytics, and integrated bioinformatics to help physicians make sense of it all.

This is certainly the case for clinical decision support systems (CDS). At their core, CDSs use analytics to provide information that a doctor can use to guide evidence-based patient management. (Note: Evidence-based medicine is defined as the incorporation of systematic research into the provider's clinical decision-making process [Sackett and Rosenberg 1995].) These systems can be the link between the mountains of scientific evidence that accrue yearly and the doctor, helping them stay up-to-date on relevant management guidelines and recommendations. While individual health systems can develop and implement their own CDS, there are commercial entities, such as the clinical decision support resource UpToDate, that can be used as well. For example, a physician in Alaska credited UpToDate with helping him determine the correct diagnosis for a patient with an unusual presentation of a rare disorder, and identify current management and treatment recommendations for the disease (Wolters Kluwer 2017).

A recent retrospective study evaluated the use of a CDS to identify patients with sepsis or systemic inflammatory response syndrome (SIRS) (Amland and Hahn-Cover 2016). Patients with sepsis or SIRS are at substantial risk of septic shock, multiorgan failure, and death, if they are not appropriately treated in a timely manner. But identifying these at-risk patients has traditionally relied on physicians' capacity to recognize a variety of symptoms that together suggest sepsis/SIRS, but independently may result from other disorders. Certain hospital departments (e.g., intensive care, emergency departments), where patients were known to be at risk, sometimes had sepsis screening tools that combined multiple factors into risk scores that enabled early diagnosis. However, patients outside of these departments could also be at risk, and in absence of an automatic screening tool, might be less likely to receive an early diagnosis and treatment.

In the study by Amland and colleagues, a sepsis CDS was implemented within an electronic health record (EHR) system at multiple hospitals. As patient characteristics (e.g., heart rate, temperature) and lab values (e.g., white blood cell count) were input in the EHR, the CDS would send an alert when a certain threshold of risk factors was met. Approximately 25% of the alerts were in patients identified by the CDS before the physician suspected or recognized sepsis/SIRS, leading to diagnostic testing and treatment. The study's authors admit the technical challenges of designing and implementing a CDS, but note the "powerful impact" of the CDS to identify sepsis/SIRS in patients (Amland and Hahn-Cover 2016).

CDS can take many forms and can be separate from or overlaid on an existing EHR system and some EHRs are building CDS into their platforms. For many conditions, particularly those with a genetic basis, advances in technology have led to a significant upswing in published data, making it difficult for providers to keep up with the latest research (Masic, Miokovic, and Muhamedagic 2008). This makes an automatic CDS, such as UpToDate (described above) or other software integrated with an EHR that aggregates and extracts key findings from medical studies so important for clinical care and the adherence to evidence-based medicine and guidelines.

For example, Avhana Health, a start-up, developed a CDS that informs the doctor which clinical guidelines apply to specific patients (Baum 2015). It does this by extracting the patient's medical record from the EHR through their proprietary interface, analyzing the record to determine which clinical guidelines are applicable, and returning that information to the physician. The Avhana CDS works in concert with the physician, who selects which guidelines they want to follow, and doesn't replace professional judgment (Baum 2015).

Community Medical Centers in Fresno, California, have used a CDS from ZynxHealth to provide nurses and doctors access to medical research, so they can make evidence-based decisions for patient care (McCarthy 2016). The ZynxHealth CDS works with Community Medical Centers' Epic EHR system and doctors can create customized, evidence-based care templates that the medical system can use across providers (McCarthy 2016). These templates can ensure that patients are treated consistently, no matter which doctor they see.

It's not difficult to imagine how a CDS can save money, reduce unnecessary procedures, and help doctors keep patients on track—in short, CDS can be an integral component of value-based care (see Chapter 7). Just imagine the average patient going to their doctor for an annual exam. Based on their recent bloodwork and prior history, the CDS might alert the physician to specific interventions they could recommend to the patient. For patients with chronic diseases, like diabetes or heart disease, the CDS might analyze the control the patient has over their disease or alert the physician if the patient has failed to have regular labs drawn. And as we'll describe in the next section, CDS can even prevent the patient from having a negative reaction to a medication, by warning the physician about other medications the patient takes or a genetic variant that influences how a drug works.

This is precisely what ActiveHealth Management, a subsidiary of Aetna, has done with its CareEngine CDS technology. In a retrospective study of more than 130,000 health plan members, emergency room visits and hospital admissions were reduced by 8% and there was a savings of $8.02 per covered member per month when CareEngine was used. Additionally, out of 13 measured quality benchmarks, more than half improved with use of the CareEngine CDS (Vemireddy 2014). Over all of its customers in the past decade, the CareEngine CDS has saved over $8 billion (ActiveHealth Management 2017).

Though precise definitions for AI (deep learning and cognitive computing) are still debated, a broad definition of AI, "the science of making computers do things that require intelligence when done by humans" that encompasses "learning, reasoning, problem-solving, perception, and language-understanding" will be used in this book (Copeland 2000) (see Chapter 10). This broad definition is applicable to both self-learning systems that require no human interaction and to technologies that use advanced computer science techniques like data-mining and pattern recognition that require input and training from humans. Some experts believe the healthcare sector for AI could be worth more than $6 billion by 2021, creating a lot of interest among entrepreneurs and existing biotech companies, who would like to grab some of that market share (Captain 2016).

Radiology and imaging are two areas where AI is beginning to make headway. A 2012 white paper by the Radiology Quality Institute described variable error rates based on the technology and condition ranging from less than 1% to more than 30% and disagreements between physicians was similarly variable (Radiology Quality Institute 2012). DeepMind, Alphabet's AI for healthcare, IBM's Watson, and other AI/cognitive learning systems are taking patient images and coming up with a likely diagnosis—sometimes beating the doctor's diagnosis for accuracy.

For example, DeepMind was trained to identify diabetic retinopathy and diabetic macular edema, both complications of diabetes (Gulshan et al. 2016). Diabetic retinopathy is a disease caused by blocked blood vessels in the eye, resulting in visual deterioration and, if untreated, blindness (Knight 2016). Patients may be in the early stages of the disease, when it is treatable, without any noticeable symptoms, making early diagnosis through retinal imaging so important. Using more than 128,000 retinal images, researchers trained DeepMind to recognize the disorders from healthy eyes, then tested its performance in nearly 5,000 patients who were evaluated by a panel of board-certified ophthalmologists (Gulshan et al. 2016). DeepMind performed as well as the panel at detecting diabetic retinopathy and diabetic macular edema, making it especially valuable in low-resource settings where a specialist may not be available (Knight 2016).

Philips' radiology solution, Illumeo, aims to reduce time for diagnosis through integration and analysis of patient data. Illumeo, described as "adaptive intelligence" is designed with evidence-based practices in mind: the system can alert physicians to pertinent, built-in guidelines and give context to imaging studies with patient-level data, such as problem lists or laboratory results (Philips 2017). These have the potential to standardize care across radiology departments and improve patient care (Jha and Topol 2016; Philips 2017).

A recent editorial published in the *Journal of the American Medical Association* makes the case for using AI in radiology for "cognitively simple tasks" like "screening for lung cancer on CT" or "to confirm that support lines are in proper position" (Jha and Topol 2016). Christoph Wald agrees that AI technology, such as IBM Watson Health, has huge potential. Wald is the chairman of the Department of Radiology at Lahey Hospital and Medical Center. "In radiology there are tasks that are repetitive or require certain challenging perceptive and information integration, these might be done better by a machine assisting the radiologist. But we're 5–10 years away from very robust and potentially FDA approved [AI systems]," he said in an interview with us. "Developing AI technology that produces meaningful results will require close collaboration of computer scientists with clinicians to help them define meaningful use cases and clinically useful output parameters" (Wald 2017).

Although Wald doesn't envision AI technology making a sizeable impact on clinical care for several years, there is emerging evidence to suggest the benefits will be seen sooner, rather than later. In January 2017, Arterys was granted FDA 510(k) clearance for its cloud-based AI platform (Marr 2017). The company's Cardio DL imaging solution provides doctors with an accurate representation of cardiac ventricular function in an average of 15 seconds, far faster than the 30 minutes to 1 hour that a human takes to do the same assessment (Marr 2017). Getting FDA clearance for AI-enabled technology may be easier for companies in the upcoming years: The FDA released guidance documents in 2016 pertaining to digital health and recently announced the formation of a new center at the FDA dedicated to the oversight and coordination of digital health devices (including AI-enabled software) (Graham 2016a; Molteni 2017).

As promising as these solutions are, the ultimate goal of using AI and advanced analytics doesn't appear to be replacing doctors, but rather to work *with* them to improve patient care. William Morris, associate chief information officer of the Cleveland Clinic has said that cognitive computing systems, such as Watson, are "there to augment the clinical thought process, not to replace it" (Kuhrt 2017a).

IBM Watson Health's general manager Deborah DiSanzo believes AI technology will improve radiologists' efficiency. She has said her company's offering can prioritize images for radiologists to view, identifying those with nothing to see and putting those with concerning features first. With the ability to analyze existing data that may be available in a patient's EHR, Watson can also provide meaningful context to the radiologist reading the images (Parmar 2017).

Clearly, CDS and AI/cognitive computing technology has the potential to pass on substantial savings to medical facilities and to improve outcomes for patients themselves—key components of value-based care. If a patient can be more accurately (or more quickly) diagnosed because the CDS can use pattern matching to fit the patient's symptoms to a disorder, or a physician can follow a customized algorithm to assign treatments to patients, unnecessary medical procedures can be minimized, lowering the risks and harm associated with overtreatment or the wrong treatment. And evidence-based clinical guidelines may be more likely to be followed, if doctors and patients are reminded of their applicability at the point of contact.

Pharmacogenetics: Avoiding the Risks, Maximizing the Benefits of Drugs

According to the CDC, nearly a quarter of Americans ages 45–64, and almost half of those 65 and older, take statins to reduce their cholesterol and lower their risk of heart attack (National Center for Health Statistics 2016). Lovastatin was the first commercially available statin, approved by the FDA in 1987 (Endo 2010). Initially, Lovastatin and the other statins that followed, seemed to be miracle drugs, reducing LDL levels and the frequency of heart attacks by more than 25% (Scandinavian Simvastatin Survival Study Group 1994; Shepherd et al. 1995).

But in the early 2000s, reports of severe adverse reactions and even deaths began to make news. An 82-year-old Kansas woman died following a chronic muscle disease caused by her statin (Brody 2002). In clinical trials, only about 1% of the patients developed elevated liver enzymes and about 0.1% developed severe muscle pain (Tuller 2004). But with millions of people taking statins, real-world evidence suggests these complications and others may be more common than initially thought (Fernandez et al. 2011), and there remains controversy over the use of statin therapy for patients in specific risk categories to prevent cardiovascular events (Ganda and Mitri 2016; Honore et al. 2017).

Growing awareness of statin-induced complications coincided with technological advances in genomic sequencing. Clinical researchers began to investigate whether individual variants in a patient's genome could be responsible for whether or not they developed complications from taking statins and other drugs, a new field of research called "pharmacogenetics" or "pharmacogenomics." Genomic variants involved in the absorption, digestion, excretion, or metabolism of various drugs can be tested in a single blood draw, and if a variant is found, doctors can choose to alter the dose of a drug or select another medication entirely. More than 100 drugs, from cancer therapies to statins to medications used for depression, whose actions are influenced by genomic factors are listed on the FDA's Table of Pharmacogenomic Biomarkers in Drug Labeling (Center for Drug Evaluation and Research and U.S. Food and Drug Administration 2017).

Patients at medical centers around the country, like Korei Parker, who was described at the beginning of this chapter, sometimes find that pharmacogenomic tests offer crucial information for their treatment. At Vanderbilt University Medical Center, for example, the PREDICT (Pharmacogenomic Resource for Enhanced Decisions in Care & Treatment) program tests patients who are considered at risk for needing certain drugs, such as statins (Vanderbilt University Medical Center 2017). Stanford Health Care's Center for Personalized Wellness offers pharmacogenomic analysis for some drug therapies (Stanford Health Care 2017). St. Jude Children's Research Hospital has been testing new patients for potential drug interactions for several years.

But the challenge of pharmacogenomics isn't simply identifying which variants affect a drug's performance—it's developing the patient management guideline and implementing it in the clinic. Mayo Clinic published a study recently describing their implementation of pharmacogenomics testing. CDS alerts were developed for the health system's EHR for 18 drug-gene interactions. Although the study's authors reported 100% adherence to the initiative, there were some lengthy delays and several points of concern, such as the need to develop educational resources for physicians, noted throughout the process (Caraballo et al. 2016; St. Sauver et al. 2016).

The Clinical Pharmacogenetics Implementation Consortium (CPIC) is trying to solve these problems. With dozens of members from healthcare organizations, industries, and outside observers, CPIC has developed more than 30 clinical guidelines to help physicians choose the right dose for a patient, based in part on the patient's genetic background.

With the drug simvastatin, for example, statin-induced myopathy (muscle pain) can occur at lower doses for patients who have a C variant at a particular location in the gene *SLCO1B1*, so doctors are recommended to start patients on a lower than typical dose or to switch to another drug completely if the lower dose isn't effective (Ramsey et al. 2014). And abacavir, an antiretroviral drug for patients who have HIV, isn't recommended if they have a particular variant in the gene *HLA-B* due to severe side effects (Martin et al. 2014).

Once a guideline has been developed, it still needs to make it into routine clinical practice. This means the treating doctor has to be aware of the guideline and how the recommendations impact drug selection or dose for each patient. Seamless CDS integration of the guidelines and dosing algorithms with providers' EHR systems can make this happen, but it also requires that the genomic testing be done ahead of time and the results of those tests be analyzed, stored securely, and structured in a way that makes the interpretation simple for the provider.

At each of these steps, there's tremendous opportunity for entrepreneurs and existing companies to create solutions for these problems. Although many drugs now have labeling guidelines encouraging or requiring genomic testing be performed prior to prescribing, doctors may not always have that information at hand when the patient is in their office. With electronic prescribing becoming the norm in medical centers and doctors' offices across the country, a CDS integrated into the EHR system could alert physicians at the point of contact, allowing them to order the corresponding genomic test or review the patient's results before selecting a medication or dose. Some EHR developers and software companies are beginning to meet these challenges.

YouScript, a software developed by technology company Genelex, uses complex analytics on patient data, including their genetic information and medications they may be taking, to assess the risk for adverse events (YouScript 2017). EHRs such as Epic and AllScripts have adopted YouScript to use over their EHR platforms (Pallardy 2016; YouScript 2017). There's evidence that this approach may not only prevent adverse events, but positively impact downstream outcomes as well. Several research studies have been performed testing the performance of YouScript in various patient populations. Overall, pharmacogenomic testing combined with the YouScript CDS, in patients 65 years old and older, led to reductions in emergency room visits, hospitalizations, and overall cost of care compared to patients who were untested (Brixner et al. 2016). A more recent prospective trial of patients ages 50 and older taking multiple medications found similar results (Elliott et al. 2017).

Where medical centers should store large quantities of genomic data generated from pharmacogenomic testing is unclear, since it needs to be readily accessible by clinicians at point-of-care to be useful, and there are multiple issues related to data access, patient privacy, and physician adoption that are still being investigated. Eric Topol, the genomic researcher we spoke with (see the section *Precision Medicine: Welcome to the N-of-1*), highlights the continuing challenge in collecting pharmacogenomics data and disseminating the information to clinicians. "How will new data, or greater quantities of it, impact more common conditions such as cardiovascular disease?" he asks. "We know, for example, that every single drug used for heart disease has some type of pharmacogenomic effect. But many such effects are still unknown. Can we build a data set that encompasses all the sequence variants that impact these drugs effects?" (Topol 2017).

With increasing emphasis on evidence- and value-based care, pharmacogenomic tests that can prevent adverse side effects (and improve medication compliance) are likely to gain greater acceptance in the future. The FDA approval of the cancer drug pembrolizumab (Keytruda) (described more fully in the next chapter) is a game changer for pharmacogenetics testing. By approving a drug based on a patient's genetic mutation, rather than for a specific indication, such as colorectal cancer, the FDA has opened the door on the potential for pharma to develop similar, targeted treatments for a variety of noncancer conditions.

CRISPR: A Breakthrough Technology

There is a notable method that has the potential to dramatically change the way we think about genetic diseases: CRISPR (short for Clustered Regularly Interspaced Short Palindromic Repeats).

CRISPR are a defense mechanism for bacteria against viruses. Much like how the human immune system can recognize previous viruses or bacteria after vaccination, bacteria use CRISPR to detect and destroy viruses. This finding was published in 2007 in *Science* (Barrangou et al. 2007). CRISPR is the natural next step in the precision medicine paradigm: moving from identifying genomic variants to fixing them.

Six years later, scientists developed a way to turn this bacterial defense mechanism into a gene editing machine in human and mouse cells (Cong et al. 2013). What is groundbreaking about the CRISPR method is its specificity—scientists can excise a genomic mutation with incredible accuracy and without undesirable off-target effects, something that wasn't really possible with earlier gene editing methods (Broad Institute 2017). Some genetic disorders, like sickle cell anemia that is caused by a single nucleotide base change, could become a thing of the past—if researchers can translate promising cell and animal studies into human trials.

The potential applications of CRISPR have not gone unnoticed by entrepreneurs who have launched numerous start-ups using this technology. Three of these start-ups have made the decision to go public. In February 2016, Massachusetts-based Editas Medicine raised $94.4 million in an initial public offering (IPO) of stock. Months later, another Massachusetts start-up, Intellia Therapeutics, topped $100 million with its IPO and in October 2016, Switzerland-based CRISPR Therapeutics raised $56 million with its IPO (Adams 2016).

These companies have attracted the attention and financial backing of several pharmaceutical companies for their programs. As we describe in Chapter 8, pharma is developing both traditional and nontraditional partnerships in order to move potential treatments through the development pipeline more quickly and to obtain licensing agreements when new treatments come to market. CRISPR Therapeutics has a joint venture with Bayer for its severe combined immunodeficiency and hemophilia programs and collaborations with Vertex for three additional programs (CRISPR Therapeutics 2017). Intellia is working with Regeneron and Novartis on three of its programs (Intellia Therapeutics 2017) while Juno Therapeutics has the commercial rights to Editas' gene editing of T cells for cancer treatment program (Editas Medicine 2017).

For these companies and others using CRISPR gene editing, the race is on to deliver a therapy in the clinic. Recently, Editas presented data at the American Society of Gene & Cell Therapy conference demonstrating the use of their CRISPR platform in a nonhuman primate model of inherited retinal disease (Boye et al. 2017) and for ß-Hemoglobinopathies (Gori 2017). Intellia Therapeutics is poised to start nonhuman primate studies for transthyretin amyloidosis and animal model studies for hepatitis B (Intellia Therapeutics 2017).

How does CRISPR play into *Moneyball Medicine*? First, the success of CRISPR for any disorder relies on the accurate identification and characterization of genetic variants. Here is where Big Data and accessible databases of variant information are essential. Second, if and when the programs move from clinical trials to market launch, studies will have to be done to assess the impact on patient outcomes and determine the value of these treatments. Clearly, a technology that has the potential to permanently cure diseases, such as sickle cell anemia or hemophilia, will be enormously valuable. As with any treatment, putting a dollar figure on potential cost savings will be challenging. In the meantime, opportunities are growing for those looking to use this technology.

Public Health in the Precision Medicine Era

As we described in the beginning of this chapter, precision medicine uses the information obtained through research studies on large populations and applies it to an individual patient. But it's not just single patients who can benefit from precision medicine—it also has the potential to change the direction of clinical research, health policy, and guidelines for patient management at the population level. This is one of the points made in April 2016 by Muin Khoury, Director of the Office of Public Health Genomics at the CDC, and we'll present several examples in this chapter and the next to show how it is starting to be implemented (Khoury 2016).

Cardiovascular disease is one area of focus where Big Data and advanced analytics are starting to change how doctors treat patients and identify those who may be at risk. Public health experts and epidemiologists are also using this information to create new health policies, geared toward the population as a whole. Because cardiovascular disease is so common, very large study populations are needed to identify genetic and environmental risk factors or to assess the benefits and risks of interventions. But developing a research program to evaluate tens of thousands, or even hundreds of thousands, of patients is not only extremely costly, but also time consuming and operationally challenging. Even after the research has been done, those discoveries still have to make it into the clinic where they can be assessed on a great many patients in yet more studies before being integrated into clinical management guidelines or healthcare policy.

This is where Big Data and techniques like machine learning and AI can make a difference. Guidelines rely on the interpretation of published scientific studies, proprietary information from pharma and other company databases, and the expert opinion of clinicians. Incorporating "grey literature," such as conference proceedings or government reports, and real-world evidence could further improve adherence to guidelines. But the current process of moving from research to clinical practice is lengthy, averaging 17 years (Morris, Wooding, and Grant 2011), presenting an opportunity for cognitive computing methods to comb through databases and analyze the data more quickly, in turn supporting value-based care through rapid assessment of treatments.

The American Heart Association (AHA) is partnering with pharmaceutical giant Astra Zeneca and multiple research institutions, including Intermountain Medical Center Heart Institute, the Duke Clinical Research Institute, and the Stanford Cardiovascular Institute, to create the AHA Precision Medicine Platform (Versel 2016; American Heart Association 2017). One unusual aspect about this venture is that the data repository will be hosted in the cloud by Amazon. This arrangement will ensure all participants have access to the data, which can be a challenge in large research studies where study sites may have different EHRs. (We've already discussed in Chapter 1 how interoperability between EHR systems is rudimentary at best.) Additionally, data storage limits are minimized by using cloud technology. Through analysis of the combined clinical data, researchers hope to hasten the research process to identify risk factors and potential treatments for cardiovascular disease (American Heart Association 2017).

Tech giant IBM and the Cleveland Clinic are developing a transition plan for health systems to transition to value-based care and population health in a new 5-year partnership (Landi 2016). As with the AHA Precision Medicine Platform, the IBM-Cleveland Clinic agreement will leverage clinical data in the EHR. In addition, claims data and information about patients' social determinants of health (e.g., income, education) will also be used to help researchers identify evidence-based population health strategies (Landi 2016).

With chronic diseases such as type 2 diabetes and cardiovascular disease becoming a more pressing issue, it's not surprising that some doctors and researchers are attempting to leverage powerful data analytic techniques to improve patient outcomes (see the sidebar *Data Analytics for Patient Management*). Patients with these and other chronic disorders often suffer from other comorbidities. But clinical management guidelines don't always take into account these other disorders or explicitly provide guidance for how a guideline might need to change in response to specific comorbidities or even medications the patient might be taking. This creates an opportunity for an AI-based clinical decision support system to analyze a patient's medical record and give the doctor management recommendations personalized for the patient.

SIDEBAR: DATA ANALYTICS FOR PATIENT MANAGEMENT

Michael Liebman, PhD

Managing Director and Cofounder, IPQ Analytics

"Technology generates a lot of data, and that can drive a lot of business development," said Michael Liebman when we spoke with him, but the key question is "What should I do if the patient has X disease?" (Liebman 2017)

Liebman is the Managing Director of IPQ Analytics, and his company is focused on answering that question using data and analytics. Their approach involves working "back from the clinical side" to get an optimal diagnosis, no matter how many conditions (i.e., comorbidities) the patient suffers from. In addition, patients all have a range of risk factors as well, and some may be more compliant with their medication regimens than others. All these factors can influence the patient's response to treatment.

That also means any one study is rife with confounding variables. Was it the average age of the patients, their comorbidities, their compliance, or something else that led to variation in outcomes? IPQ Analytics tries to answer such questions by "Building a unified model of disease processes and implementing it into an ontology that can be applied across multiple diseases," Liebman says. In short, it's a way to take all that into account, but still be able to analyze the data you have on hand.

For one study, the group analyzed data from the National Health Service (Italy) in collaboration with their National Research Council on patients with diabetes and high blood pressure to help to evaluate the level of patient complexity. Liebman's group found that the average patient had five or more comorbidities. That meant clinical presentation varied dramatically from patient to patient. What's more, the patients were taking a range of different drugs, which makes coming up with guidelines that much more difficult.

One striking finding was that physicians creating prescribing guidelines for diabetes and high blood pressure were not taking into account all those possible comorbidities. "Guidelines are typically developed around the 'ideal' patient, and not what is real," says Liebman. Further, most physicians don't even prescribe based on guidelines, they rely on their own experience. "If I'm treating you for cancer, that's my focus, not your other problems, although I try to consider them," he explains.

Liebman points out that there is a big emphasis on precision medicine now, but he sees proper diagnosis as a lynchpin for that approach. "You need the right diagnosis to prescribe the right medicine," he points out. And that requires understanding all of the conditions that may be impacting a patient's health at any one time. "Certainly, if you sequence some part of a tumor, you will find genes that are related to its growth and spread," Liebman says. "Unfortunately, at this point that doesn't generalize as well as we wish it did. There are still a lot of individual differences."

IPQ Analytics is currently working on heart failure, hematologic cancers, breast cancer, liver cancer, and human papillomavirus. "I think the core problem is how thorough was the diagnosis," Liebman says. Without knowing all the factors that can impact the patient's health, a primary diagnosis isn't enough.

Further, he wants to see this approach become standard in medical practice and in medical training. "We're not helping medical students if we just tell them how to diagnose disease X or Y," he says. "We need to expose them to the broader description and help them understand how different factors impact each other."

AI-enabled and cognitive computing solutions such as IBM's Watson and Alphabet's DeepMind are garnering a lot of publicity for their potential to diagnose patients with rare disorders and fly through vast amounts of imaging data faster than their human counterparts. But to relegate these and other cognitive computing systems to radiology or oncology (see Chapter 10), is to underestimate their potential uses for highly prevalent diseases, such as heart disease, diabetic retinopathy, or asthma. Arterys' Cardio DL AI-enabled platform to characterize cardiac ventricle performance, is a case in point. Although determining how best to incorporate these solutions into the clinical workflow is still being studied, the enormous potential of this technology and the growing number of successful studies suggest it will substantially transform the practice of medicine and public health in the future.

Quest for 10,000 Steps per Day

Over the past few years, one of the biggest healthcare trends has been wearable activity trackers and other biosensors. In the past, specialty manufacturers, such as Garmin and Polar, catered to serious athletes with their devices, many of which measured heart rate in addition to distance, pace, or other activity variables. Instead of elite athletes, Garmin, Polar, Fitbit, Leaf, and others are targeting the average consumer. Many more people are becoming interested in tracking their daily steps, weight, nutrition, vital signs, and other health-related characteristics. As a result, the market for wearable devices has exploded in the past years and is expected to reach $34 billion by 2020 (Lamkin 2017).

The data captured by wearable devices and their connected mobile apps and websites is substantial and is starting to produce evidence it's also clinically valuable.

For example, a 42-year-old New Jersey man with no previous history of heart problems landed in the emergency department after a seizure. Doctors found he had an irregular heartbeat and the patient was successfully medicated. Despite the drugs, the patient continued to suffer from atrial fibrillation, a condition where the upper and lower chambers of the heart beat out of sync from one another. To determine the course of treatment, doctors needed to determine when the atrial fibrillation began, a difficult task for a condition that can be asymptomatic (Rudner et al. 2016). If the condition was newly onset and caused by the seizure, doctors could use electrical cardioversion to treat it. If the condition was chronic, that treatment could cause a stroke, but failing to treat it could have devastating consequences (Palladino 2016).

Using data collected from the patient's Fitbit Charge HR activity tracker and its corresponding mobile app, doctors were able to identify the start of the atrial fibrillation. The patient underwent electrical cardioversion. Doctors then verified that the man's activity tracker captured the change in heart rhythm consistent with the treatment (Rudner et al. 2016).

Similar stories have been widely publicized. After a nap following football practice, 17-year-old high school athlete Paul Houle Jr.'s Apple Watch showed his heart rate remained more than double his normal average. Knowing his heart rate shouldn't have still been that high after resting,

Houle went to the hospital. He was found to have rhabdomyolysis, a condition that can lead to multiorgan failure and death, if left untreated (Glance 2015; WCVB 2015). His family credits his watch with saving his life.

An 18-year-old U.K. student was alarmed when her Fitbit Surge showed her heart rate at 210 beats per minute. Doctors later determined she had a previously undetected heart problem and could have died, had she not called for an ambulance when she did (Duffy and Mullin 2016). Australian journalist Garry Barker's Apple Watch captured his irregular heartbeat, a condition that landed him in the hospital for atrial fibrillation treatment and a stent for a blocked artery—conditions for which he had been previously asymptomatic (Barker 2015).

But smart watches and activity trackers aren't the only wearable biosensors with the potential to change clinical care. Scientist Mike Snyder, from Stanford University, might well be called the poster child for the "narciss-ome" (Dennis 2012). This tongue-in-cheek nickname was bestowed after Snyder had his genome sequenced and collected an assortment of other molecular data over a 14-month period. Although Snyder had no family history or other risk factors for type 2 diabetes, his genome indicated a predisposition.

What makes Snyder's story so fascinating is that he watched the disease develop in real time by analyzing the data as he collected it. Following two viral infections and escalation of his blood glucose levels, Snyder was officially diagnosed with the disease, leading to lifestyle and dietary changes to manage his blood sugar levels (Chen et al. 2012).

Since the 2012 study that brought a certain level of notoriety to Snyder, his lab has continued to research technologies using a variety of "-omics" such as proteomics (analysis of proteins). With more and more people wearing Fitbits and using connected devices, such as scales, there is considerable interest in exploiting the data these devices collect. One of his latest papers takes a look at wearable biosensors and the "physiome," the collective physiological data, from patients (Li et al. 2017). Snyder's lab analyzed billions of individual data points from a small number of patients using devices that measured heart rate, temperature, sleeping patterns, even oxygen saturation. In addition to quantifying daily physiological patterns for each participant, data from the wearable devices was able to differentiate health status between them (Li et al. 2017). This study demonstrates how wearable sensors also have the potential of accurately capturing a patient's physical activity level, information that may be useful for both research and patient management.

Despite these and other examples, the use of wearable devices for research and clinical purposes is far from established. Christine Lemke of Evidation Health says that there are several key barriers to making the data that comes from wearable devices useful in the medical setting. First and foremost is that doctors aren't yet seeing the value in these data. Lemke notes there is too much noise in the data and physicians have few or no incentives to integrate the data into their practice. Doctors also want to see that the data are high quality and scientifically accurate, although Lemke says that this last point shouldn't necessarily be an issue. Speaking with us she says, "you just need to capture the anomalies, you don't need such precision. Anomalies and trends show up really well in the data. But doctors want to see validation studies and there aren't any currently" (Lemke 2017).

Additionally, getting the "raw" data aren't particularly helpful for patients or doctors. A mechanism that can translate the data files into something comprehensible is needed. For example, a raw data feed from a Garmin running watch might include instant speed, average speed, GPS coordinates, and heart rate, but not in any easily understandable format. A connected scale can keep track of multiple users in a household who weigh themselves at different intervals. Food and general exercise information can be input by a user into a website or mobile app, for example,

MyFitnessPal. But a raw data export from connected devices and biosensors might look just like lines of computer code or random characters. In either case, you need some sort of mechanism to "translate" the data and present it in a meaningful way—like graphs that show trends over time. Across many different types of devices and websites, this presents an opportunity for manufacturers to "play nicely with others," and some manufacturers are doing just that.

Apple's Health app, which we described in Chapter 1, and the Apple Watch Activity app, are cases in point. In addition to data collected through the Apple device itself, both the Health app and the Activity app can share and import data to and from third parties. So, customers who are Nike+ runners will find that running a half-marathon or an intense weight-training session increases their target number of calories for the day in the nutrition tracking app, MyFitnessPal. Engaged and intrepid users of these devices and apps can also track sleep, body measurements, and lab values—over time creating a valuable health blueprint that could be useful for doctors to use in patient management.

From a technical standpoint, putting patient-derived information into an EHR isn't necessarily that difficult. Data from FDA-approved devices, such as blood glucose monitors and wireless blood pressure cuffs, are already being integrated into EHR systems. Making the jump from FDA-approved devices to consumer-oriented ones is proving more challenging, but some healthcare organizations are moving in this direction.

Boston-area Partners HealthCare is one example. In 2013, Partners launched a program for patients to upload certain types of medical data into their EHR from devices at home, so patients like Sandra Rice, a 61-year-old woman with chronic hypertension, could send daily blood pressure readings directly to her physician's office (Sathian 2013). For some patients, these at-home measurements may be more reflective of their actual health, due to anxiety when they visit the doctor's office. Joseph Kvedar, director of Partners' Center for Connected Health, has indicated expansion of the program could include activity trackers such as pedometers or other mobile apps (Sathian 2013).

Technology company Glooko, developer of the Joslin Hypomap, is a company incorporating patient-derived data into EHRs. The Joslin Hypomap is a management system for patients with type 1 and type 2 diabetes that feeds glucose measurements from patient devices into physicians' EHR systems (Glooko 2017). In late 2014, Glooko added another feature to the Joslin Hypomap: the ability for patients to put in fitness activity from its mobile app or from third parties, such as Fitbit (Comstock 2014). Combined with nutrition data from Glooko's database, the amalgamation of data can be useful to physicians and allow them to spot nutrition and/or exercise trends that influence blood glucose levels—helping them manage their patients more effectively.

The idea of physicians integrating patient-collected data (such as their activity levels) in clinical practice is something Jeroen Tas thinks could help keep people on track with their health goals throughout the year. His goal is to capture more data in real time and then provide continuous interpretation of those data. Instead of counseling a patient once a year based on results from their physical, doctors should be looking at data throughout the year, proactively reaching out to patients when they see concerning trends.

Continuous patient monitoring is already making its way into the inpatient setting (see the sidebar *On Patient Monitoring*). Philips recently received FDA clearance to use a single-use sensor with the IntelliVue Guardian to monitor heart rate and respiration. The IntelliVue Guardian can predict health crises, such as cardiac arrests, in high-acuity inpatients before they occur by identifying subtle changes to the patient's vital signs. A pilot study at the Augusta (Georgia) Medical Center found the system reduced "predictable" codes by 88% (Versel 2017).

SIDEBAR: ON PATIENT MONITORING

Jeroen Tas

Chief Innovation and Strategy Officer, Philips

"Healthcare is not yet using the full potential of IT, compared to other industries such as financial systems, travel and other fields," says Jeroen Tas in an interview with us (Tas 2017). "But there is tremendous need and opportunity for new health IT systems to change the way we manage our own health and we deliver healthcare to patients. IT that is designed for healthcare and strategically utilized can help us to move towards a more proactive and preventative approach."

One of the many areas Philips is working on is patient monitoring. "Monitoring is going to become a key instrument in future healthcare," Tas says. "We'll be looking at how to use monitoring to optimize patient outcomes both inside and outside the hospital." That will include using data, such as vital signs and other clinical information, and predictive analytics to support the care professional in deciding when is the right time to discharge a particular patient. "We need to prevent them from leaving and then being quickly re-hospitalized," he explains. "Most patients are currently discharged with a treatment plan, but there is no continuous contact with the patient after they leave the hospital."

Anyone with a chronic condition can benefit from such monitoring, and patients who have major events, such as heart surgery, will also have lifelong health issues.

"We are already market leaders in patient monitoring," Tas says. "Now we want to extend remote monitoring services to people with chronic health issues." The company's monitoring devices allow real-time analysis of patient data and streaming of those data to the care team.

"You need the right intervention at the right time," Tas says. A cardiologist, for example, will want to see different data than some other specialist. That might include images as well as laboratory results. Clinicians will all be interested in how stringently a patient is complying with treatment plans and other things impacting their health. Is a complication unexpected, or is it predictable because of something happening in the patient's life? Answers to that type of question can save lives, time, and money.

Case studies at Philips have already shown impressive results. Patient outcomes were improved, hospital visits reduced, and costs lowered in a group of patients with congestive heart failure in the Netherlands, for example. Intensive monitoring of some Arizona-based patients with multiple chronic diseases, meanwhile, helped cut back on events requiring hospitalization and helped improve patient self-management and quality of life.

"For me, the goal is a connected integrated healthcare system with the patient at its center," Tas says. One major hurdle that remains is the fact that most medical data are still unstructured. "You usually get back a written report, not something that is data-oriented and has specific goals, nudges and ideas for where the patient needs coaching, for example."

But the biggest thing holding up remote monitoring, according to Tas, is that it is very difficult to implement change, especially in well-established systems. "Ways of working in healthcare are rightly so based on the results from scientific studies and solutions are clinically validated. We need to build a strong evidence base where it comes to applying connected technologies and also validate new solutions. This doesn't happen overnight. And if you have been doing something one way your whole life, it takes a lot of effort to move in another direction," he says. "That's why this shift will take a lot more work and require cocreation where all stakeholders work together. We are constantly working with clinical partners to make it happen."

Extending this type of technology for patients with chronic conditions who need intensive ambulatory care can be a way to keep them on track. Tas thinks that patient monitoring will become a service as physicians look to optimize patient outcomes, from treatment to length of stay, so patients are discharged at just the right time and don't end up rehospitalized. He explains, right now, cardiac patients have a treatment plan for acute events, but no real mechanism for ongoing patient monitoring after they are discharged. This monitoring has the potential to impact not just the individual patient, but also how we look at disease. Eric Topol says, "For much of health, we still don't know what 'normal' really is. With blood pressure and blood glucose, for example, we've never before been able to do so much long-term, continuous monitoring. We'll be redefining normal for many of these conditions" (Topol 2017).

This is where medical grade devices, telehealth, and patient monitors wrapped in consumer-friendly packaging, will be the most useful. If someone has undergone heart surgery, has diabetes, or chronic obstructive pulmonary disease, Tas says, they will have issues for the rest of their life. But their physician can use patient-collected data to get a summary of their heart health and whether the patient is complying with the treatment plan outside of the hospital.

Beyond regular medical care, these devices also have the potential to change clinical trials. Patient-collected data can be inaccurate, particularly for things like medication compliance and fitness levels. In clinical trials, inaccurate information like this can compromise the study results (Breckenridge et al. 2017). But connected devices, such as Propeller Health's sensor, can track when a patient takes their medication and having this type of data available to clinical trial staff could help ensure the integrity of the study results. As Christine Lemke notes, wearable devices aren't yet collecting data for clinical trials. There's uncertainty about the accuracy of some of the devices and how best to ensure the data doesn't reduce study quality. Devices like Alphabet's Verily (formerly Google Life Sciences) dedicated clinical trials watch may soon prove to settle some of the debate (Mack 2017c), as we explain further in Chapter 10, *Digital Health*.

What's to Come

The quest for precision medicine isn't just relegated to the realm of oncology. As we've described in this chapter, data analytics is transforming the patient–provider relationship and the assistant in the exam room isn't a human—it's a computer. This will have far-reaching impacts on both patients and providers. There are a few medical centers on the cutting edge of bioinformatics and precision medicine that are already starting to embrace data analytics to personalize patient management.

As more medical centers implement EHRs and link them to biobanks with genomic information, increasing amounts of patient data will be available for large research and clinical projects and to develop algorithms that can be used to personalize medical care. But there remain significant challenges limiting greater expansion of precision medicine at hospitals nationwide. At the forefront are problems related to data: minimal data sharing, too little of the right data being collected, and the most appropriate analysis to perform. These issues are not insurmountable and numerous stakeholders, from academics to entrepreneurs, are already tackling them. The federal government has taken data sharing further by requiring data (anonymized or de-identified) generated using federal grant money to be deposited into publicly available databases, for example, ClinVar and ClinGen (Messner et al. 2016).

This data boom isn't going to be confined to information collected by a medical specialist, either. The role of wearable devices like fitness trackers and others used in telemedicine and other remote patient monitoring will continue to grow. It will be up to providers and their medical systems to figure out how best to reduce the "noise" in these data and how to integrate it with more traditional types of medical information, or risk being left behind. Here again, existing boundaries are being pushed as companies like Glooko work to show their devices add clinically useful information to patient management.

Probably the most disruptive technologies starting to make their way into healthcare are AI and cognitive computing platforms (see Chapter 10). For some specialists, such as radiologists, IBM Watson, Alphabet's DeepMind, and others are beginning to show they are as accurate—or better—at analyzing imaging results than the doctors are. Philips' Illumeo adaptive intelligence platform is helping radiologists reduce interobserver variability and add context to imaging studies (Philips 2017). In the case of Arterys' Cardio DL, it is as accurate as doctors, but substantially faster (Marr 2017). So, rather than eliminating radiology or pathology positions, this is an opportunity to reshape what those practices entail. Mundane tasks could be relegated to the AI system and could be used to prioritize results, helping doctors become more efficient and freeing up time for them to spend on difficult cases. As these systems are used at more medical centers, there will be more data available to train and refine the software, and their diagnostic abilities will improve.

Earlier in the chapter, we recounted how Alphabet's DeepMind AI was trained to recognize diabetic retinopathy and macular edema. We noted that this technology could be particularly useful in low resource settings, where telemedicine may be a patient's only option to see a specialist. But consider what could happen if doctors used images from the same patients, but taken 1, 5, or even 10 years before they received a diagnosis? With a large enough dataset, it's possible that the AI system could recognize healthy eyes compared to ones that were likely to develop retinopathy or edema in the subsequent years. When the disorder has an effective treatment or there is preventive care to minimize its damage, early diagnosis can be essential. If the AI system could be paired with an app and smartphone camera, patients might be able to do a self-checkup at home, and have the app let them know it's time to see a doctor, even before they may be noticing any symptoms.

CDS, either stand-alone options or integrated within EHRs, will play a significant role in helping doctors stay at the forefront of research. Over time, this will increase the amount of care that is evidence-based, driven by scientific research from millions of patients. In the next chapter, we'll describe how the field of oncology is already being dramatically transformed by precision medicine.

Chapter 3

Personally Tailored Cancer Treatment

We have passed the tipping point where using Big Data in oncology is no longer a conceptual problem, but just an engineering challenge.

Barrett J. Rollins
Chief Scientific Officer, Dana-Farber Cancer Institute and Linde
Family Professor of Medicine, Harvard Medical School, Boston

They were two cousins who spent "summers racing dirt bikes and Christmases at their grandmother's on the coast" (Harmon 2010). But when Thomas McLaughlin and Brandon Ryan each developed a deadly type of skin cancer at about the same time, the two young men had very different experiences. A *New York Times* article told how McLaughlin received an experimental new drug specifically tailored to a mutation (*BRAF*) found in both men's melanoma tumors. Ryan didn't.

These two young men's fates illustrated how dramatically cancer treatment is changing, bringing dozens of new treatments to patients and fueling a booming market.

The prognosis for a patient with metastatic melanoma in 2010 was grim, with a median survival of 8–18 months after diagnosis. The only FDA-approved chemotherapy at that time was dacarbazine, a treatment that elicited response rates of less than 15% and led to median overall survival of fewer than 8 months after the start of treatment (Chapman et al. 2011). In 2006, pharmaceutical companies Roche and Plexxicon teamed up to develop and commercialize PLX4032—an experimental melanoma treatment that targeted the *BRAF* V600E mutation (Roche 2006). Phase I and phase II clinical trials were promising, but a phase III trial was needed to determine whether the drug would actually improve survival compared to dacarbazine (Flaherty et al. 2010; Chapman et al. 2011).

This is where the paths of the two cousins tragically diverge. McLaughlin, with stage 4 cancer, was eligible first for the clinical trial, and able to take the experimental drug that targeted the specific *BRAF* mutation. Soon after he began treatment, he said his tumors began to "melt away." Ryan, diagnosed with stage 3 melanoma, wasn't initially eligible for the trial, which started by enrolling only the sickest patients. Months later, when his health had declined, he was randomized to the control arm and given the standard chemotherapy, but died soon after. McLaughlin, still taking what he called the "superpills," attended his less fortunate cousin's funeral (Harmon 2010). A year later, the FDA approved vemurafenib (Zelboraf) for patients with advanced inoperable or metastatic melanoma who have the *BRAF* V600E mutation, on the basis of the clinical trials that demonstrated a lower risk of death and longer median overall survival compared to patients receiving chemotherapy (Roche 2011).

Metastatic glioma, a type of brain cancer, was the diagnosis given to Allison Schablein, right before her fifth birthday. Surgery could remove only one of the tumors and the chemotherapy she was given couldn't prevent the remaining tumors from growing. But the Boston-area girl had a molecular profiling test done, a type of genomic testing, performed on the surgically removed tumor and the results helped doctors find a mutation (Hughes 2017).

The surprising part of their discovery? The mutation found in Allison's tumor had also been found in adult patients with melanoma, a skin cancer, and there was already a successful drug therapy, Tafinlar (dabrafenib), used with that population.

But Allison's doctors at Dana-Farber and Boston Children's Hospital were hesitant—no pediatric patients had ever taken that drug, and it was unclear if it would be successful in the young girl with brain cancer. However, the doctors offered her the treatment and Allison responded extremely well. After 8 weeks on the drug, her six remaining brain tumors had disappeared. Her experience ultimately paved the way for more than 100 other children to take the drug that was initially targeted for adults with melanoma (Hughes 2017).

Targeted cancer treatments like vemurafenib and dabrafenib have not only saved lives, they have fueled some of the biggest fields in medicine—oncology drug development and genomic testing. Today, this market encompasses dozens of fields, including targeted therapies, immuno-oncology, cancer vaccines, precision diagnostics, biomarker databases, liquid biopsies, and more. Several of these fields already command multibillion dollar markets, while others are emerging and still face challenges. But it's a combination of data and entrepreneurship that is fueling these markets and leading to newer ones to develop. It's an era of rapid re-engineering in oncology today, creating new opportunities and new challenges as well. This chapter will explore these fields and how they are evolving from both a scientific and a business perspective.

New Paradigm for Cancer Treatment

Stories like Thomas McLaughlin's and Allison's were virtually unheard of until almost a decade ago and only recently has precision medicine become a common phrase in medical care. Although precision medicine can apply to any condition, it has made the most progress in oncology. It's a welcomed change. Cancer is one of the fastest-rising diseases in the world. New diagnoses are expected to increase by 70% over the next 20 years, going from 14 million to 22 million, according to the World Health Organization (World Health Organization 2017).

That in turn, has fueled tremendous market growth. Oncology has become one of the top moneymaking fields in medicine, raking in more than $100 billion per year, with more than 500 companies in the field (IMS Health 2016). A whopping 800 cancer drugs and vaccines are in development (PhRMA 2015). The number of targeted drugs has surged, with more than 60 now approved along with 20 or so tests to guide choice of treatment (National Cancer Institute 2015; Abramson 2017). Because cancer is often deadly, many analysts believe treatments for the disease will continue to command high prices (Langreth and Koons 2015).

In the past, oncologists treated patients based on what type of cancer (e.g., papillary vs. follicular thyroid cancer) or its tissue of origin (e.g., breast, lung, bone) and how extensive it was. If a tumor could be surgically removed, it was, and then the patient might undergo radiation and/or medication (chemotherapy). Chemotherapy (chemo), however, is a blunt instrument designed to attack rapidly dividing cells. But it's not just cancer cells that rapidly divide; hair follicles and cells in the lining of the gut, for example, are also impacted by chemo. This sometimes results in hair loss and other common side effects, some of which can be debilitating. Furthermore, chemotherapy is not always effective for certain cancers, and just as bacteria become antibiotic-resistant, chemo may lose its effectiveness over time.

Researchers have long been searching for new ways to treat cancer. Genentech's Herceptin (trastuzumab), a drug that targets HER2 receptors in breast cancer, was the first precision medicine treatment, approved by the FDA in 1998 (Hall 2016). When scientists discovered that some particularly aggressive breast cancers have mutations causing them to overexpress the cellular receptor HER2 (human epidermal growth factor receptor 2, also called *ERBB2*), they developed Herceptin against that target. Today the drug is the mainstay of HER2+ and some metastatic breast cancer treatments, with annual worldwide sales of more than $6.5 billion (Pharmaceuticaltechnology.com 2016).

A little more than 10 years ago, researchers at Dana-Farber Cancer Institute in New York and Brigham and Women's Hospital in Boston, working with collaborators in Japan, found that patients with lung cancer tumors with genetic mutations in the *EGFR* gene responded to a drug that targeted the protein (Paez et al. 2004). Following publication of the study, these patients at the Dana-Farber and Brigham and Women's Cancer Center had their tumors tested for *EGFR* mutations and treatment was started based on the results of those tests (Dana-Farber Cancer Institute 2014).

These discoveries and others that followed were the start of today's precision medicine, a field that has resulted in substantial gains for cancer patients while also fueling a lucrative business environment with big opportunities for growth. According to a report by Concert Genetics, there are nearly 70,000 genetic tests on the market currently (Concert Genetics 2017a) and tests for cancer-related indications comprised 17% of all tests in the NIH's Genetic Test Registry in 2016, a growth of more than 150% over the previous year (Solomon 2016).

Improvements in genetic testing technology (e.g., next-generation sequencing) has made it possible for drug developers to create targeted therapies, such as the *BRAF*-targeting pill Thomas McLaughlin received. One big hitch, however, is that targeted drugs should only be prescribed to patients whose tumors carry the corresponding mutation. Otherwise, the drug is not likely to work.

Manufacturers were initially concerned that developing drugs for subsets of cancer patients would not be profitable; they preferred the traditional blockbuster approach of making a single pill that can be used in anyone with a particular disease, regardless of its underlying cause. That's why diseases such as asthma, cardiovascular disease, and diabetes are such popular targets. They offer huge populations of patients and better chances at blockbuster markets.

But despite the pushback, targeted therapies turned out to be profitable because drug makers can charge more for them. In 2015, the market for targeted therapies was approximately $27.8 billion and had a compound annual growth rate of 18% between 2011 and 2015 (Van Arnum 2016). The number of targeted drugs has surged, along with the tests to guide choice of treatment (Abramson 2017). With new cancer cases expected to rise to more than 20 million patients in the next 20 years (National Cancer Institute 2017a), the market potential for oncology is substantial.

Dawn of Precision Oncology

When doctors and scientists talk about precision medicine for oncology today, it typically refers to the use of genomic/molecular profiling of a patient's tumor to identify the particular type of cancer they have or to direct their treatment, including determining eligibility for specific clinical trials (see the sidebar *Dana-Farber's Profile System*). And just like precision medicine in other fields, such as cardiovascular disease or diabetes, getting to an answer for an individual patient requires prior data analysis of extremely large datasets, comprised of hundreds or thousands of patients that can be used to create tools like dosing algorithms or prognosis calculators (Druker 2017).

Often, when a patient is diagnosed with cancer, one of the first tests they may be offered is a genetic test. For patients with a cancer that might be hereditary, such as breast cancer caused by a *BRCA* mutation, a genetic test can be useful to identify the specific cancer syndrome responsible for the disease. Knowing whether or not the cancer is hereditary can help a patient understand if they are at risk for other types of cancer(s) and if any relatives are also at risk for developing the disease. For some cancers, knowing if it is hereditary can also provide important information about the likely progression of the disease and the patient's life expectancy.

Some cancers are inherited while others are caused by environmental exposures or acquired genetic mutations. Colorectal cancer, for example, may be the result of the inherited Lynch syndrome or may arise after repeated exposures to a carcinogen. Lynch syndrome is caused by a mutation in one of several genes, such as *MSH2*, which is a gene involved in DNA mismatch repair. If the gene has a mutation, it may not function correctly, and mistakes in DNA that occur during the cell division process might not be fixed (Strafford 2012).

In addition to heritable genetic mutations, tumors are being tested more routinely soon after diagnosis to understand the major "drivers" that help cancers grow and spread, so oncologists can then prescribe treatments that could inhibit the cancer. Such drivers have been discovered in many types of cancers and include *EGFR*, described earlier in the context of lung cancer, HER2 for breast cancer, *BCR-ABL* and *KRAS*. Such genes all occur in normal tissues too, but their mutated versions can be associated with cancer. This realization led to the birth of targeted therapies, as well as tremendous growth in the number of new anticancer drugs and the size of the cancer drug market.

SIDEBAR: DANA-FARBER'S PROFILE SYSTEM

Barrett J. Rollins, MD, PhD

Chief Scientific Officer, Dana-Farber Cancer Institute

Barrett J. Rollins heads a project called Profile, which collects all data from a patient's interactions with the healthcare system. Every patient at Dana-Farber Cancer Institute is offered genetic testing, and all of those results are stored in the database. "But the real data tsunami is the clinical data, where we have a huge amount of information generated—everything from routine physicals to preoperative blood work. When you make that information searchable, you have the ability to ask questions of a huge cohort," Rollins points out.

For example, Rollins can use the database to see how many stage 2 breast cancer patients who responded to a certain drug are still alive after 5 years. Then, the characteristics of those women can be compared to those who had the same type of cancer, received the drug, but died.

Because privacy is so important in healthcare, the key has been making sure that researchers and physicians using Profile can securely transfer data. For legal reasons, it was necessary to create a firewall between the clinical database and the research database. Hospitals aren't allowed to use clinical data for research without the patient's approval. "But once the Institutional Review Board approves a study, we can use the data from patients who have provided consent. We've also boiled down the consent form into a single page that contains everything required but takes less time to fill out."

The project is still in the early stages, but Rollins says they are already finding things such as previously unknown cancer-causing mutations. "We need to move to the next generation of analysis, using more patients and more data points," he says. "To achieve that, we would like to combine our data with that of other institutions."

Over the last 20 years, researchers have been increasingly successful at uncovering the genetic mechanisms underlying cancer, with more than two dozen markers now being used in available tests (National Cancer Institute 2015). They have also learned a lot about cancer in general.

For one thing, tumors in different parts of the body can have similar markers. That means for some cancers, it is becoming less important where the cancer is located (e.g., breast, lung, or skin). Instead, for these cancers, the specific mutation is the driver of what guides treatment. This is the same concept that led to Allison, described at the beginning of the chapter, being treated for her brain cancer with a drug that had previously been used for melanoma, and is behind the recent FDA approval of pembrolizumab (Keytruda) for patients with any advanced cancer with certain genetic mutations (Schattner 2017). As we'll explain later in the section *Improving Clinical Trials*, this is a fundamental shift from the current siloed approach to treating cancer and it's having a considerable impact on the design of clinical trials and could change how medical centers in the future will organize cancer treatment centers.

The mutations driving a tumor can also change over time; therefore, metastases may have a very different genetic makeup than the primary tumor, which is usually the first one discovered. That also means that repeated molecular testing may be needed when a patient suffers from a recurrence or when their primary treatment stops working. And these biomarkers work within complex biological pathways. Understanding those pathways is helping scientists determine which molecular signals are most important and how they influence each other.

Based on these realizations, more and more oncologists are recommending that patients get comprehensive molecular testing of their cancers. As John Glaser, Vice President, Population Health and Global Strategy at Cerner Corporation, describes, "at places like Geisinger Health System, Intermountain Health, and Kaiser Permanente, you see that they've been standardizing how they treat cancer. And for the top 20 to 30 types of cancer, genetic testing is now a routine part of treatment and is used to determine if you are at risk or to guide the treatment."

Role of Big Data in Oncology

As we stated previously, making precision medicine work for an individual patient with cancer relies on the analysis of dozens, hundreds, or even thousands of patients with the same cancer (or same genetic mutation). For many oncologists, however, even over a career spanning multiple decades, they may not see enough patients on their own to fill a database with the amount and type of information needed for precision medicine insights. Here is where Big Data and complex analytics come into play.

While building databases of variant information is essential, simply having the data isn't sufficient for precision medicine. This is even more important for tests that use multiple techniques (such as DNA sequencing *and* protein analysis) to determine a patient's genomic profile. Researchers have to be able to aggregate the data from a variety of databases, develop a computational model or algorithm that takes into account each of the components they are looking at (e.g., DNA mutations, protein expression, immune response), and then tie the result(s) to a clinical outcome, such as mortality or drug response. Data sharing and interoperability between systems become increasingly important as cancer treatment becomes more complex and based on molecular diagnostics (see the sidebar *The Value of Genomic Profiles*).

SIDEBAR: THE VALUE OF GENOMIC PROFILES

Mike Pellini, MD

Chairman and former Chief Executive Officer, Foundation Medicine

"Until now, we haven't been able to aggregate the data needed to tease out all of the important elements to truly guide clinical decision making for cancer diagnosis," Mike Pellini said in our interview (Pellini 2017). His company, Foundation Medicine, has invested in generating those data and then using it to give patients more options, including treatments and access to clinical trials.

"We work with researchers and clinicians to look at genomic profiles of patients with cancer coupled with their phenotypic data, including their response to specific drugs," he explains. The company's products include a next-generation sequencing test that checks for genomic alterations associated with solid tumors and another that does the same for blood-based, or hematological cancers. The company also offers a blood-based circulating DNA assay that can be used in cases where a biopsy is not possible. All three tests sequence dozens to hundreds of genes implicated in human cancer.

The strength of the type of database that Foundation Medicine is building should increase as the company collects more data. "What's striking, however, is that we started to see important findings after just the initial 100 to 1,000 patients," Pellini says. "We were able to look at some of the information from those patients and find correlations that had a direct impact not just on the treatment of individuals, but even on drug discovery programs." Those first hits were primarily in non-small cell lung cancer and in melanoma. "What that told us what that you don't necessarily need 100,000s of patients to find important things," he says. (Note that Foundation Medicine's HIPAA compliant database now contains information on more than 100,000 patient tumors.)

Pellini sees cancer treatment evolving rapidly now. "We've finally realized that the cancer doesn't necessarily know or care from which organ it originated," he says. As a result, the entire paradigm is shifting. It is the cancer's genomic profile that will largely guide treatment, not just its location in the body. But given the growing number of potentially clinically relevant genomic alterations, it's also becoming daunting for physicians to match each patient to the right treatments.

It's also important to find new druggable targets for drug discovery programs. These can be uncovered by determining which alterations are most often shared by patients. Foundation Medicine is one of several groups gathering these data and designing tests to accurately identify genomic alterations.

"Hospitals and other healthcare providers need to be collecting [these] data today. It's the right thing for patients, and in the long term, it will give us better drugs in oncology and elsewhere," Pellini says. Part of the challenge, he points out, is how to finance these types of programs, which can be very expensive. "We all know it's the best thing in the long-term, but how can they get value from [those] data today?" he asks. When aggregating genomic data, it is also crucial to have a sound privacy policy and program. "One must protect all of [those] data," Pellini says.

Foundation Medicine is collaborating with many cancer centers, hospitals, and organizations, such as Flatiron Health, to make sure this evolution of data aggregation and protection continues. "Due to the rising cost of healthcare, we need to find new ways to do things for patient care," he says. "Harnessing genomic and clinical data is one of the most important things we can do for humanity."

Other companies have created databases of patient information for similar purposes. But to truly treat patients using precision medicine, we need even more biomarkers to guide decisions about what treatment to use and when. Data from genomic studies, clinical trials, electronic health records, and more will be pivotal to finding those markers. Some of these markers will emerge from hospital or company databases, others will be big data projects involving tens of thousands of tumor samples and hundreds of potential markers. One of these company databases has a unique focus—hereditary cancers—that help predict a high risk of developing cancer (see the sidebar *Myriad Genetics' Mutation Database*).

SIDEBAR: MYRIAD GENETICS' MUTATION DATABASE

Pete Meldrum

Former President and CEO of Myriad Genetics

Myriad Genetics has one of the most extensive databases of heritable mutations known to increase a person's chances of developing cancer. In hereditary cancers, there can be thousands of potentially harmful mutations. Lots of mutations are also benign, causing no health problems at all. "So the more harmful mutations we track down, the more informative our tests become," says Pete Meldrum, a cofounder of Myriad and the company's former president and CEO, when he spoke with us (Meldrum 2017).

For more than 20 years, Myriad has been studying such mutations, including the ones in the *BRCA1* and *BRCA2* genes, which increase the risk of breast and ovarian cancer. (These are the same genes that prompted actress Angelina Jolie to have her highly publicized double mastectomy.) "Mutations in these genes can greatly elevate a person's chances of developing cancer. In some cases, the risk of getting the disease can be as high as 87%," Meldrum says.

Together, the *BRCA1* and *BRCA2* genes comprise about 15,700 base pairs, and Myriad has information on more than 16,000 mutations. "These are estimated to account for 98% of all possible mutations," Meldrum says. "As a result, our test provides a definitive diagnosis in 90% of cases. The best public database, meanwhile, can only provide a clear answer in about 70% of cases, meaning 30% of women using competitive tests based on public databases are being told they have a variant of unknown significance [VUS]," Meldrum says.

If women who use the Myriad test get a VUS result, the company will sequence all of their family members and look at their medical history to try and determine if the variant is harmful. That process works because there is a 50% chance that any one of a woman's siblings will carry the same mutations she has.

The company is also building databases of mutations in other cancers, including colon. They currently offer multiple tests for cancer risk, including the My Risk 25-gene panel that predicts risk of eight different kinds of cancer.

"It has taken many years and about $100 million for us to build our databases," Meldrum says. "We've also learned a lot from gathering and analyzing [these] data. Sure, a lot of it will become public over time. But the knowledge we've gathered will help us go forward and evolve as the playing field changes."

Most genomic databases today are located at individual institutions or companies, such as Dana-Farber or Myriad. Some, like Myriad, have invested millions of dollars into building their large database, while others, such as academic medical centers, may have versions that accumulated variant data from patients who were enrolled in clinical trials at the institution. Though their motivations may be different, many of these groups are not willing to share their data because they want their own researchers to have first crack at making discoveries from it, or because (in the case of Myriad) those data are the basis of their business model—that's how they derive their profits. But several organizations are trying to create large databases drawn from multiple sources that can be shared. These include the American Society of Clinical Oncology's CancerLinQ (with more than a million patient records already), Project Data Sphere (which focuses on phase III cancer trial data), the International Cancer Genome Consortium, and the National Institutes of Health's Cancer Genome Atlas and ClinVar.

It's the datafication of oncology, and it will profoundly change how cancer care is delivered. As noted, so many discoveries are being made that it is difficult for most oncologists to keep up with them. But that will become easier as the databases become populated and more people gain access to them. Open databases, which allow any qualified researcher access, will be particularly valuable. Another key will be powerful analytics. All these data will be useless without the ability to analyze it properly and the real value will come from its interpretation.

A growing number of companies, such as Foundation Medicine, Guardant Health, N-of-One, or institutions, such as the Dana-Farber Cancer Institute and MD Anderson Cancer Center, now offer specialized tumor testing services to help match cancer patients to optimal treatments, increasingly based on the molecular profile of the cancer, regardless of the tissue or organ where the cancer originated (see the section *Growth of Targeted Therapy*, below). And some test reports provide clinical trials information that a patient may qualify for based, in part, on that profile, helping doctors to narrow down potential options for their patient.

Eventually, instead of having to read up on the latest biomarkers or pour over clinical trials inclusion criteria, physicians will be able to see the recommended therapy as soon as they pull up their patient's test results. This has far-reaching implications, from the CDS systems that will facilitate the process (see Chapter 2 for an in-depth description of CDS), to identifying which clinical trials the patient is eligible for, to working with pharmaceutical companies to get the right drug(s) for the patient based on their molecular profile.

Growth of Targeted Therapy

The targeted approach to cancer treatment is often called personalized or precision medicine (see Chapter 2) because it aims to attack cancers based on molecular biology and guided by very specific tests. While it can apply to any condition, this approach has made the most progress in oncology.

As we mentioned earlier, Genentech's trastuzumab (Herceptin) was the first targeted cancer drug. When scientists discovered that some particularly aggressive breast cancers have mutations causing them to overexpress the cellular receptor HER2, they developed Herceptin against that target. First approved in 1998, today the drug is the mainstay of HER2-positive breast cancer treatment, with annual sales of more than $6 billion (Pharmaceutical-technology.com 2016). Like most targeted treatments, the drug is only meant to be used against tumors with this particular marker (HER2 overexpression).

Over the last 20 years, researchers have been increasingly successful at uncovering new such genetic mechanisms, with more than a dozen markers now being used in available tests (Bailey et al. 2014) (see Table 3.1).

They have also learned a lot about cancer in general. As mentioned before, tumors in different parts of the body can have similar markers. That means it is becoming less important where the cancer is located (e.g., breast, lung, or skin). Instead, the specific mutations in the cancer should help guide treatment. The mutations driving a tumor can also change over time: metastases may have a very different genetic makeup than the primary tumor, which is usually the first one discovered. That also means that repeated molecular testing may be needed.

Such mechanisms also work within complex biological pathways. More of one molecule can affect how much of another molecule is produced. Understanding those pathways is helping scientists determine which molecular signals are most important and how they influence each other.

Based on these realizations, more and more oncologists are recommending that patients get comprehensive molecular testing of their cancers. Britain recently broke new ground by announcing that every child diagnosed with cancer in that nation will have their malignancy's DNA sequenced to help match those children to the best treatments for their disease (Knapton 2017). This is possible due to a grant from the charity Children with Cancer U.K., which donated

Table 3.1   Selected Targeted Therapy Markers

Marker	Therapy	Cancer Type
ALK	Crizotinib	Non-Small-Cell Lung Cancer (NSCLC)
BCR-ABL	Imatinib	Chronic Myelogenous Leukemia (CML), Acute Myeloid Leukemia (AML)
BRAF	Vemurafenib, Trametinib, Dabrafenib	Colorectal Cancer, Thyroid Cancer, Melanoma
C-Kit	Imatinib	Gastrointestinal Stromal Tumor (GIST)
EGFR	Cetuximab, Panitumumab, Erlotinib, Gefitinib	Colorectal Cancer, Non-Small-Cell Lung Cancer (NSCLC)
HER2	Trastuzumab	Breast Cancer, Gastric Cancer
KRAS	Cetuximab, Panitumumab	Colorectal Cancer, Non-Small-Cell Lung Cancer (NSCLC), Pancreatic Cancer
PDGFRA	Imatinib	Gastrointestinal Stromal Tumor (GIST)

Source: Bailey, A. M. et al., *Discov Med* 17, 92: 101–14, 2014.

£1.5 million. As was reported in the *Telegraph*, Professor Louis Chesler of the Institute of Cancer research, was leading the initiative, and was quoted as saying "This funding will help us move towards a more comprehensive and structured approach to genetic testing to match children with cancer to specific targeted treatments, which could be an incredibly important step towards increasing survival and reducing the side effects of treatments" (Knapton 2017). Their aim is not only to match pediatric cancer patients to better drug options earlier, but help them avoid harmful side effects from drugs that would not help them anyway.

This approach is a much more complicated process, but hopefully more accurate too. As we discuss below, this will have significant implications for oncology and related fields.

Companies, hospitals, and research organizations are now building huge databases of molecular testing results from cancer patients to identify targets that are common, or shared, among them. Some of these mutations arise spontaneously, perhaps due to environmental conditions or just because of bad luck, for example, due to a random biological misstep during cell replication. Other mutations are heritable, and knowing about those makes it possible to detect cancer early, or even prevent it. That alone has become a big field in data-driven medicine.

Matching Cancers to Treatments

Finding an association between a genetic marker and the cancer is just one part of precision oncology. The goal is to amass huge amounts of marker data, and then link that to the clinical information now mostly locked away in patients' records. Tumors can then be precisely categorized, and patients offered treatments deemed most suitable for their particular malignancy.

It's important to note that some doctors may have little experience with certain types of cancer, especially those that are rare. Also, they may not have access to data about treatments that were initially targeted to other cancer types. Further, most of what we know about how to diagnose and treat any disease actually comes from research on a very small segment of the population—patients who have participated in a drug company-sponsored clinical trial. This limited patient population makes it even more critical that institutions capture outcomes data and link it to other patient data, such as lab results, imaging studies, or claims data that might be in a patient's electronic health record (EHR). Doing this would create a robust, longitudinal dataset that would be valuable to assess long-term outcomes of treatment. Though there have been a number of initiatives (e.g., Clinical Trials Awareness Week) to increase participation in clinical trials, overall patient engagement remains extremely low (<5%), particularly for some minority groups (Murthy, Krumholz, and Gross 2004; Aristizabal et al. 2015).

New findings in oncology are emerging at a rapid rate, compounding the information gap between traditional treatments and newer methods that might be significant improvements over standard therapies.

As noted earlier, tumors can also have a mix of acquired mutations, some of which may change in response to treatment, so picking the right drug is not always an easy task. Therefore, it's possible that out of all the oncologists in the country, there are only a handful who have experience with a particular type of tumor and its specific mutations (Memorial Sloan Kettering Cancer Center 2011). Focusing on the molecular underpinnings of cancer is a giant leap from when doctors treated cancer patients based entirely on which part of the body the disease originated in—which is all being driven by data.

In response to this new trend, a growing number of companies and institutions now offer specialized tumor testing services to help match cancer patients to optimal treatments. These include

The Clearity Foundation, Foundation Medicine, N-of-One (see the sidebar *Matching Patients to Optimal Treatments*), Perthera, and more. There will be intense competition among such tumor testing firms. Some are not just emphasizing the size of their databases and comprehensive annotation they do, they are also working to lower their prices and reduce their turnaround times.

SIDEBAR: MATCHING PATIENTS TO OPTIMAL TREATMENTS

Jennifer Carter, MD, MPH
Chief Medical Officer and Founder, N-of-One

One of the most anxious times in a cancer patient's life is when they are waiting to hear their prospects for treatment. Are there potent drugs available? Which treatments are best for that patient's specific disease?

Unfortunately, it can be complicated and time-consuming to get these answers because the field of cancer biomarkers is moving so quickly. It requires a lot of information to determine which markers matter most, and then to properly interpret test results. To address this challenge, N-of-One provides a service that analyzes a patient's molecular data, in the context of the company's extensive database of biomarker results, pulls together all the latest research and delivers answers sometimes as quickly as in minutes to a day.

N-of-One's team has analyzed clinical results on tens of thousands of patients. Their database and daily review of scientific literature, clinical trial results and other information sources allows them to advise physicians and clinical labs on the best treatment for any patient, including referring appropriate clinical trials.

The company interprets results from the entire range of cancer tests, including next generation sequencing (NGS), circulating tumor cells and DNA, copy number analysis and immunohistochemistry (IHC). "We've done the interpretation on tens of thousands of variants across hundreds of genes," says Jennifer Carter, Chief Medical Officer and Founder of the company, told us (Carter 2017). "We can also integrate data from multiple tests." The goal is to quickly match patients to the ideal treatment or trial options for their particular tumor.

"No two cancers are exactly alike," Carter explains. "Sorting out which mutations are driving a patient's disease, and what are the best treatment options is data- and information-intensive; we are focused on that."

Numerous variants have already been identified as drivers of tumor growth. The key question now is how do they interact and how many more are, as of yet, undetermined? Can some of these markers interfere or enhance the actions of others and thus the response to therapy? N-of-One is trying to help answer these questions.

The company doesn't do actual sample analysis. It interprets the results—but that is a lot of the work that goes into finding the best treatment. The company can use a lab's own bioinformatics platform to start, but it can also provide that analysis through partners, including Philips and Oracle. N-of-One has numerous other technology partners, and works with high-profile hospitals including Cedars-Sinai, Providence Health, Swedish Cancer Institute, Fox Chase Cancer Center, Intermountain Healthcare, and Mayo Clinic.

Carter sees future breakthroughs ahead. There's intense interest in finding biomarkers for immunotherapies right now, since this new class of drugs has proved so promising. "I think more and more what we are seeing is integration, combining copy number analysis, fusions, cytogenetics, NGS, and IHC," she says. "Although it's an older type of test, IHC now seems promising for predicting response for anti-PD1 immunotherapies." Another new opportunity lies in liquid biopsies, which are tests of blood samples that can replace invasive tissue testing.

In the end though, Carter sees the greatest promise in being able to understand how biological pathways interact. "What are all the factors that lead to resistance to treatment, and what are those that lead to a good response?" she asks. "Those are the questions we need to answer."

Harnessing the Immune System to Kill Cancer

As noted earlier, the surge of immuno-oncology is a recent development that holds tremendous potential to advance cancer care. This approach works by activating a patient's immune system against their cancer. It's an elegant idea that has been around for more than 100 years (Hoos and Britten 2012). But the field has limped along and began losing steam when there were no meaningful successes. Recently, however, a range of such treatments have delivered encouraging results and immuno-oncology is proving a disruptive innovation (Marabelle et al. 2016).

To understand how the various types of immune-oncology therapies work, a (very) basic primer on the immune system may be helpful:

The immune system can be divided into two types of responses: innate and adaptive. The innate immune system mounts a rapid, nonspecific defense against foreign pathogens through physical and chemical barriers (e.g., skin or mucous membranes), and certain types of cells (e.g., phagocytic leukocytes, dendritic cells, and natural killer cells) (Murphy, Travers, and Walport 2007).

The adaptive immune system is made of B cells and T cells. These mount antigen-specific responses. An adaptive immune response is significantly more complex than an innate response and takes longer. B cells, with the help of T cells, create antibodies that bind to molecules (antigens) on the surface of pathogens, such as viruses and bacteria, alerting the immune system to an invader. T cells play several roles. Some T cells, called cytotoxic T cells, have receptors that allow them to recognize cells that have specific antigens that designate them as invaders. These T cells secrete chemicals that break down the cell membranes of these invader cells, and cause the cells to self-destruct. Other T cells are "helper" cells; these T cells help to activate macrophages, cells that "eat" and "digest" pathogenic cells and other cellular debris (Murphy, Travers, and Walport 2007).

In immuno-oncology, scientists have found a way to harness the immune system and target cancer cells. Some cell therapies involve removing, re-engineering, and then replacing a patient's own T cells. And other methods include finding drugs that will help the T cell recognize a cancer cell—even when it's wearing a "mask" to appear healthy and normal. These drugs are called checkpoint inhibitors. Still other methods involve therapeutic vaccines that teach the immune system to recognize and attack cancer cells or bits of proteins (neoantigens) that are created by tumors, and oncolytic viral therapy, which uses genetically modified viruses to attack tumor cells (Farkona, Diamandis, and Blasutig 2016).

Neoantigens offer the potential for truly individualized therapies. Because they are unique to malignancies, it's believed that the immune system will be much less tolerant to them, as opposed to the antigens that are found in both tumor and normal tissues. That advantage, it is hoped, will make neoantigens much more effective at stimulating a strong immune response than the traditional shared, or conserved, antigens that have been the main focus of prior studies. Both categories of antigens are currently in development as the basis for cancer vaccines—treatments that would fire up a T-cell response, thereby allowing checkpoint inhibitors and other treatments to be even more effective.

Checkpoint inhibitors inhibit molecules that cancers use to evade the immune system; essentially, they remove the "mask" a cancer cell might be using to appear normal and evade destruction by the T cells. Ipilimumab (Yervoy) was the first checkpoint inhibitor approved. It's a monoclonal antibody that targets CTLA-4, a protein that normally acts as an "off switch" for the immune system. Other checkpoint inhibitors target PD1 (pembrolizumab [Keytruda], nivolumab [Opdivo]) or PD-L1 (atezolizumab [Tecentriq]), which also keep the immune system in check (American Cancer Society 2017).

In October 2015, Amgen announced that it received FDA approval for IMLYGIC (talimogene laherparepvec), its oncolytic viral therapy for recurrent, unresectable melanoma (Pol, Kroemer, and Galluzzi 2016). Results from a phase III clinical trial indicated a significantly higher number of stage III/IV melanoma patients received a durable response to IMLYGIC compared to patients in the control arm of the study (16% vs. 2%), a welcome result for a cancer notoriously difficult to treat (Galluzzi and Lugli 2013).

The tide has shifted so dramatically some analysts are predicting that more than 60% of all cancer treatment could involve immunotherapy within the next decade. It's estimated that the market for checkpoint inhibitors alone will reach more than $16.5 billion by 2020 and immunotherapies generally could reach a staggering market peak of $75 billion or more within the next decade (VisionGain 2015; Wood 2016; Beasley 2017).

What's most impressive about results from this new generation of immunotherapies is that their effects can be long lasting. Research data presented at the 2016 Annual Meeting of the American Association for Cancer Research showed that 34% of 107 advanced melanoma patients who received Opdivo (nivolumab), the anti-PD-1 checkpoint inhibitor, in a phase I clinical trial were still alive 5 years later (Goodman 2016). These results were similar to those in 2015 for Yervoy (ipilimumab), which targets CTLA-4, a different checkpoint inhibitor. That study, which included almost 5,000 patients, found 20% of patients getting Yervoy were still alive after 3 years (Schadendorf et al. 2015). Showing the striking graph of those data at a cancer meeting in 2013 (American Association for Cancer Research 2015), Bristol-Myers Squibb Oncology VP Renzo Canetta said, "Remember, these included patients with metastases in vital organs." That's advanced disease. Considering that advanced melanoma is typically fatal within months, these studies are highly encouraging.

Not all is rosy for immuno-oncology treatments, however. These treatments can also have serious side effects, as described in a recent *New York Times* article. Patients, such as Connecticut's Chuck Peal, are beginning to show up in emergency rooms with symptoms ranging from acute diabetic attacks to out-of-control immune system responses that mirror the flu and common cold (Richtel 2016). Some patients have even died from severe side effects of these new cancer therapies (Garde and Keshavan 2016) and doctors don't always make the connection between the cancer treatment and a side effect that can show up months later (Richtel 2016).

And a 20% response rate means relatively few patients are seeing the benefit of immuno-oncology, though individual trial results vary substantially. Results like the 2014 study published by Juno Therapeutics investigators that found 88% of patients with relapsed or refractory (nonresponsive to therapy) B cell acute lymphoblastic leukemia had complete response with their T cell-based therapy (Davila et al. 2014) are well publicized. But studies where the majority of patients do not respond to treatment or who experience recurrence of their cancer aren't as widely broadcasted and doctors would like to see many more patients achieve long-term cures (Zugazagoitia et al. 2016).

The key will be to determine what drug to use, when, and in combination with what other therapies. One recent report found that the number of combination trials involving immunotherapies has more than tripled over less than 2 years. As of April 2017, 765 such studies were ongoing (Evaluate 2017). Over time, cancer treatment will become more precise for individual patients. But to reach that point, researchers will need to find many more markers to guide treatment decisions and new drug development. These growing troves of data will help doctors match patients to drugs they have a higher chance of responding to.

New data and databases will play a key role in the success of immuno-oncology. The goal is to design a new treatment paradigm, where doctors will use drugs and/or vaccines that boost the immune response to attack the cancer, working in concert with older approaches, such as surgery and radiation.

Despite mixed study results and concern over serious side effects, scientific and clinical progress is being made and it's driving tremendous opportunity in the market. Drug trial results have led to a surge in investment in immuno-oncology by large and small drug makers alike. In December 2013, for example, start-up Juno Therapeutics, a start-up collaboration of the Fred Hutchinson Cancer Research Center, Memorial Sloan-Kettering Cancer Center, and Seattle Children's Research Institute, launched with $120 million in Series A funding—one of the largest biotech financings of its type in the sector's history (Fred Hutchinson Cancer Research Center 2013).

Neoantigen start-ups Gritstone Oncology and Neon Therapeutics both launched in October 2015, the former with over $100 million in start-up funding while the latter garnered $50 million (Carroll 2015). Academic spin-offs such as Palo Alto-based Forty Seven, which launched with $75 million in Series A funding and a program already in clinical trials, are also being launched (Lash 2016). Forty Seven was recently awarded $10.2 million by the California Institute for Regenerative Medicine to use their antibody that blocks a receptor (CD47) on the surface of cancer cells in patients with colorectal cancer (California Institute for Regenerative Medicine 2016). The CD47 receptor helps cancer cells evade the immune system (Weiskopf 2017). Forty-seven researchers will use their antibody in patients with the *KRAS* mutation, "turning the cancer into a target for both the immune system and an anticancer drug called cetuximab" (California Institute for Regenerative Medicine 2016).

Philanthropists are also putting significant resources toward immuno-oncology companies. Sean Parker, a former executive at both Facebook and Napster, pledged $250 million to a cancer institute and academic consortium that bears his name (Cha 2016). The institute recently joined forces with Bristol-Myers Squibb to accelerate immuno-oncology research (Parker Institute for Cancer Immunotherapy 2017).

These therapies will be highly individualized, as many immune responses are not shared, which means it may be necessary to tailor the treatments patient-by-patient, just as is done with cell therapies. To correctly identify which patients will respond successfully to immunotherapies will require large amounts of data and many patients. As a result, companies such as Gritstone and Neon have invested in informatics expertise and predictive models.

These points are not lost on researchers doing immuno-oncology research. To address lackluster participation in trials, researchers are beginning to develop smartphone apps that match patients with studies (Goldbaum 2016). Lab reports of some molecular profiling tests include a list of clinical trials the patient may be eligible for, while Foundation Medicine has partnered with EmergingMed to offer a "concierge service" to help clinicians and their patients identify potential clinical trials (Foundation Medicine 2014).

The vast amounts of data being collected in the course of treating patients will need to be combined with clinical data from EHRs and other sources in order to identify exactly what makes some patients respond spectacularly and others to continue to progress. That will require a new business process, which will be daunting to some companies.

Liquid Biopsies

Another exciting new area of research is liquid biopsies. Typically, doctors have to take actual tissue samples of solid tumors to do biomarker testing. These have numerous drawbacks, including the invasive nature of the procedure and sampling bias, where the results of the biopsy may not be representative of the entire tumor. The biopsy procedure could also potentially spread the tumor cells. But liquid biopsies filter tumor cells, DNA, and other molecules from a simple blood sample. This has the distinct advantage of being a noninvasive method to potentially diagnose and monitor a patient's cancer, compared to biopsies.

As they grow and spread, tumors release these biomarkers. Circulating tumor cells, cell-free circulating tumor DNA (ctDNA), exosomes (particles that transport molecules between cells and throughout the body), and biomarkers such as DNA and RNA can all be analyzed in a variety of ways, including the use of next-generation sequencing (NGS), PCR-based methods, and protein analysis.

Being able to use blood samples would help doctors to better follow up on cancer patients, switching them to more appropriate medications as their tumors evolve. The goal is to provide a more thorough picture of the patient's cancer and how it is evolving and spreading. Data from metastases can be compared to that of a primary tumor and the cancers genomic profile can be tracked over time. Because liquid biopsies are noninvasive, they could be repeated more often than typical solid tumor biopsies. Liquid biopsies might also lead to improved early detection (Karachaliou et al. 2015). In general, the earlier a cancer is detected, the easier it is to treat.

Several studies have recently been published that highlight the clinical validity and utility of liquid biopsies for a variety of cancer types, especially for lung cancer, which can be difficult to diagnose, and where repeated biopsies may not be possible. In one study, patients with non-small-cell lung cancer, ctDNA was assessed from urine, demonstrating how the liquid biopsy assay was able to capture *EGFR* mutations and that the results changed over time, correlating to treatment efficacy (Chen et al. 2017). Another research group used ctDNA isolated from broncholaveolar fluid to find *EGFR* mutations (Park et al. 2017). Liquid biopsy performed on blood samples linked increased expression of the PD-L1 protein to higher mortality for patients with lung cancer (Boffa et al. 2017).

Growing the databases of markers will again be critical. Illumina's liquid biopsy spin-off, Grail, is pushing to enroll more than 100,000 patients in its clinical trials to generate the massive data needed to find and interpret these biomarkers (Preston 2017). Grail's first clinical trial, the Circulating Cell-free Genome Atlas Study, is already underway with a goal of enrolling 10,000 patients to better understand the differences (heterogeneity) in liquid biopsy samples between patients with and without cancer (ClinicalTrials.gov 2017).

The market for liquid biopsy assays is still new, with many companies launching or developing liquid biopsy products. These companies include Biocept, Epic Sciences, Exosome Diagnostics, Foundation Medicine, Guardant Health (see the sidebar *Liquid Biopsies*), Grail, Inivata, Indi (Integrated Diagnostics), Personal Genome Diagnostics, Qiagen, Sequenom, Thermo Fisher Scientific, Trovagene, and others.

It's been estimated that this market could reach approximately $6 billion by 2020 and investors are betting big money on the technology (Grand View Research 2016c). In March 2017, Grail closed a $900 million Series B funding round and Freenome announced a $65 million Series A funding round (Preston 2017). That's nearly $1 billion for the sector in a single month. Competitors are trying to distinguish themselves based on the range of cancers they can detect, accuracy and costs among other factors, which can improve price and quality transparency for the tests.

SIDEBAR: LIQUID BIOPSIES

Helmy Eltoukhy, PhD

Cofounder and CEO of Guardant Health

The Holy Grail of cancer treatment is early detection. If doctors could identify malignancies soon enough, then they could prevent far more terminal cases of this disease. But finding tumors isn't always easy, and it usually involves taking tissue samples—an invasive process that also comes with risks.

That's why liquid biopsies have become one of the hottest fields in biotechnology. It's hoped that by using blood tests for cancer detection, the process can become lower risk and as it becomes more precise, perhaps more malignancies can be found early.

Guardant Health is one of the leaders in the burgeoning arena of liquid biopsies, and the company has their own unique approach. In our interview, Helmy Eltoukhy, Guardant Co-Founder and CEO, told us, "We wanted to proceed the same way Intel approached microprocessors and semiconductors via Moore's Law. We wanted to pick a platform that could similarly effectively scale, and then through a process I call compound innovation, make it improve in performance by 2–3× every year" (Eltoukhy 2017).

The company first focused on blood-based tests for advanced cancer patients, assuming valuable markers would be most abundant in these patients' blood. The goal is to help such patients avoid repeat biopsies while guiding them to the optimal next line treatments. That led to their first test. And as the testing platform has continued to improve, Guardant's team is now also looking at early stage cancer patients and those at high risk of developing the disease (i.e., those with germline mutations that are associated with cancers). Ultimately, the team wants to help these patients too, as well as people at average risk for the disease.

Their test platform identifies tumor DNA fragments in the blood, these are then tagged and millions of copies of them are made. Next, the fragments are sequenced, and errors in the reading of the code are cancelled out using the company's proprietary "digital inference engine." Results are available within 2 weeks and provide a complete genomic profile to guide treatment.

The Guardant 360 test became available in June 2014. "It is now one of the most successful cancer diagnostics ever launched," says Eltoukhy, who reports that more than 3,000 oncologists and most cancer centers are now using the product. "An important advantage is that it allows lung cancer patients to avoid biopsies," he adds. "That's a particularly invasive procedure. But now they can use a blood test and quickly start them on therapy."

Mutations that signal resistance to treatment are particularly difficult to pick up with traditional biopsies, Eltoukhy explains. "Heterogeneity of the tumor isn't as important in early stage cancer, but for deciding second line therapies, picking up acquired resistance mutations is usually critical."

One key mutation for lung cancer is T790M. Tyrosine kinase inhibitors (TKIs) targeting the epidermal growth factor receptor (*EGFR*) are commonly prescribed for patients with non-small-cell lung cancer (NSCLC). Unfortunately, the *EGFR* T790M is an acquired mutation that causes resistance to most approved *EGFR* TKIs. Now, however, we also have third-generation *EGFR* TKIs that work even in patients with that mutation. Guardant's test detects the mutation and helps guide prescribing for these patients. The test is also useful for other types of advanced cancers.

"We're working to shift cancer care from being reactive to proactive," Eltoukhy says. He sees such tests as not only crucial for patient care, but also for making clinical trials as productive as possible. "If you can do a test, and determine that the patient isn't going to respond to a certain drug anyway, why not avoid that altogether and give them another drug if it's available?" he asks.

Although liquid biopsies are promising, they are not without challenges. Recently, a study published in the *Journal of the American Medical Association* found no overlap in results for five of eight patients between a liquid biopsy assay, Guardant Health's *Guardant360*, and Foundation Medicine's *FoundationOne*, which uses a tissue sample (Kuderer et al. 2016). Clearly, liquid biopsy manufacturers will need robust data to get their tests approved and into clinical use.

Improving Clinical Trials

Currently, cancer clinical trials take many years, cost a lot of money, and fail often in the most expensive stage—phase III. To really cure cancer, it will be critical to pool data from as many patients as possible and then do trials that look at subtypes.

In the beginning of this chapter, we presented the story of Allison, the young girl with brain cancer who was successfully treated with a drug normally used for melanoma. She is just one of many patients who are being treated for their cancer based on the specific genomic mutation they have, instead of the cancer type. While that may seem like common sense, historically patients have been treated based where their cancer originated, and what "type" it was deemed. Breast cancer patients would be grouped together and treated differently than patients with lung cancer, and so on.

This new way of looking at cancers from the molecular standpoint, instead of the organ or tissue of origin, has also impacted how clinical trials are conducted. In 2012, a multicenter clinical trial began that turned traditional cancer care on its head by treating patients according to their mutations. This type of study was referred to as a "basket trial," since all of the patients with a specific mutation were put into a single basket for treatment. In 2015, the study was published, showing that some nonmelanoma cancers harboring a specific *BRAF* mutation responded well to traditional chemotherapy targeting the mutation (Hyman et al. 2015).

Today, the National Cancer Institute (NCI) is building on that clinical trial design with the NCI Molecular Analysis for Therapy Choice (NCI-MATCH) Trial, which opened in August 2015 with 10 treatment arms (National Cancer Institute 2017b). After preliminary analysis, the trial reopened in May 2016 with 24 treatment arms, and six others were added in March 2017 (Doroshow 2017). Each arm represents a targetable genomic mutation. Patients' tumors are tested for specific molecular variants and are grouped by the molecular signature of the cancer, not simply the type of cancer they have. The result is that all patients with a particular mutation will be treated with the same molecularly targeted therapy, regardless of their cancer type. Patients who fail to respond to one therapy may be eligible for another arm if their genomic profiling shows they harbor that mutation. Although NCI-MATCH is designed for adult patients only, a pediatric version is expected to begin recruiting in 2017 (National Cancer Institute 2017c).

The trend of structuring clinical trials in this way has started relatively recently, but there are numerous such trials already ongoing. A search of ClinicalTrials.gov suggests that more than 8,000 cancer trials using biomarkers are in the works. Long-term impacts of treating patients based on their molecular profile instead of their broad cancer type have not yet been determined and few medical centers are using this paradigm to treat patients currently (see the sidebar *Putting the Real Breakthrough into Precision Medicine*), so comparing outcomes of these patients to those of traditionally treated patients is yet to come. If the evidence supports this, it may lead to a dramatic shift in the way medical centers approach cancer care.

SIDEBAR: PUTTING THE REAL BREAKTHROUGH INTO PRECISION MEDICINE

Kenna Mills Shaw, PhD
Executive Director, Institute for Personalized Cancer Therapy, MD Anderson

Targeted therapy has been hailed as one of the major breakthroughs in oncology. This relatively new field entails designing drugs that hit at specific cancer-driving mutations. It makes great sense, and there have been several big wins, in terms of finding drugs that work in previously untreatable cancers. However, experts know that so far, we've still witnessed a very partial victory.

"The reality is that it is only a small number of patients that routinely receive precision medicine," said Kenna Shaw, Executive Director of the Institute for Personalized Cancer Therapy at MD Anderson, in our interview (Shaw 2017). In other words, relatively few cancers are actually undergoing the type of high-tech testing needed to match tumors to drugs. When the testing is done, "Overall, we see good responses in many patients who have known mutations, and where there is an FDA-approved drug that targets that mutation," she adds.

That's encouraging, but it's not the homerun people were hoping for. The growth in cancer mutation databases has certainly exploded. MD Anderson alone has data on mutations found in 20,000 plus patients. There are also multiple public databases adding cases daily, including the American Association for Cancer Research's Project GENIE (American Association for Cancer Research 2017).

So, why doesn't every cancer patient get tumor testing?

Part of the answer to that lies in the processes currently in place for diagnosing and prescribing for cancers. For one thing, it can cost patients several thousand dollars to do this type of analysis. And in the end, most patients may not have a mutation that matches an approved drug. That trend will change over time, as more actionable mutations are discovered, and more targeted therapies are approved. But even if a patient has a mutation that does match an approved targeted drug, the "standard of care" for their particular cancer may not include that treatment. As a result, off label treatment frequently will not be reimbursed. In those cases, "If the patient can pay, they can get the treatment, if not, they can't," Shaw explains.

That's because insurers don't usually let physicians bypass standards of care, even to prescribe newer treatments that make sense from a biological perspective. For prostate cancer, for example, there are a number of standard of care regimens that must be tried before any experimental or treatments of last resort. "Even if we find a potentially useful target, such as an anti-amplifying *EGFR* mutation, the patient's doctor could not prescribe an appropriate targeted therapy before trying all the standard of care regimens," Shaw says. As a result, for many types of cancer such testing is only done after the patient relapses despite standard therapy.

Certain rare tumor types, such as some sarcomas, do not have many standard of care regimens even available. "Those are the cases where we could see a real paradigm change," Shaw says. "For these patients, experimental therapy is clearly better and easily justifiable."

But understanding the importance of all the new genetic variants we are finding is still another huge barrier. "It is just not clear what many of these variants mean," she says. 95% of variants her team detects are of "unknown significance"—no clear drug match exists for them.

Furthermore, malignancies need to be reassessed after every round of treatment, because they evolve and develop new mutations over time. But it is often difficult to get those follow-up biopsies.

Shaw would like to see many more clinical trials. "We especially need to be doing trials on the less frequent mutations," she says. But the cost of sequencing and actually finding the right patients can be prohibitive.

What could help advance this field most? "In the ideal world, we would have every patient's cancer sequence data available centrally, with a unique identifier. We'd take just the data about the tumor type, sequencing results, allelic frequencies, etc. and put that in a centralized database. Experts would annotate [those] data with what else is known about these mutations," Shaw says. That last step is critical, because computers, she explains, are not that good at interpreting results from variants of unknown significance. Luckily, besides public efforts, a cadre of companies and academic groups are stepping up to the plate, curating such data, and offering services around it.

It's frustrating because the potential is there to make this information so much more widely used. "All the solutions exist to call mutations from tumors and report that back to physicians with actionable information," she says. "Now we just need to find a way to do that."

In addition to helping individuals get better treatment, data will also guide the discovery of new tests and medicines. It will advance public health by finding new information about what causes cancer or makes certain people more susceptible to it. All the advances taking place are driving the formation of more cancer start-ups, genomic services at hospitals, and cancer-related databases.

As noted, cancer drugs can command relatively high prices. It's not surprising for them to cost more than $10,000 per month (Beasley 2017), a cost that may not be tenable for many cancer patients, even when they have insurance (Bologna and Chakrabarti 2017). Each year, more than $100 billion is now spent on cancer treatments worldwide (IMS Health 2016). These high costs will also force changes in how cancer treatments are priced and reimbursed and a greater emphasis will be placed on the value they provide.

The drug Gleevec (imatinib), for example, has transformed chronic myelogenous leukemia from a lethal disease to one that is manageable as long as patients continue treatment. Gleevec costs a hefty $75,000 or so per year, and the drug's maker, Novartis, justifies the price based on how effective it is (Cowley 2013). But many cancer drugs have marginal benefits, providing only months or weeks of additional survival at extraordinary cost (Fojo, Mailankody, and Lo 2014). Furthermore, when physicians or medical centers decline to adopt use of a new drug, claims of "rationing" can be difficult to overcome (Bach, Saltz, and Wittes 2012).

Some countries are beginning to push back against such drugs. Germany, for example, did not approve either Bayer's colorectal cancer treatment Stivarga (regorafenib) or its prostate cancer drug Xofigo (radium Ra 223 dichloride) because they offered only slight benefits at much greater cost (Weintraub 2014). In the United States, meanwhile, pharmacy-benefits managers are starting to take aim at high-priced drugs, including those for cancer (Kelly and Berkrot 2015).

Cognitive Computing Comes to Oncology

As we described in the previous chapter, cognitive computing and advanced analytics, like those used by Alphabet's DeepMind and IBM's Watson, have the potential to radically change the way doctors approach diagnosis. This is especially evident in oncology, where patients with rare cancers can have a computer analyze their medical record, lab results, and imaging to come up with a probable diagnosis.

According to Anil Jain, CMO of Explorys, an IBM company, Watson is the culmination of many different models of decision support, from the very beginning of alerts in the clinical space (like potential drug interactions or the patient needing a medication). Historically, systems have been very Boolean logic-based with rigid rules—fine for noncontroversial, process-oriented decision support. But healthcare today needs to go beyond this, especially precision medicine.

As an example of the power Watson has to improve cancer treatments, Jain shares an experience with a University of North Carolina tumor board. For many patients, Watson came to the same answers as the group of doctors, but for roughly 30% of patients, the technology was able to find potential treatments that the physicians hadn't been able to find.

The University of Tokyo's experience with Watson is another case in point. Doctors there were stumped when a 60-year-old woman failed to respond to the standard treatment for her leukemia. After feeding information from the patient's medical record into Watson, the program compared her data to data from millions of research papers (Ng 2016).

The result?

Doctors had gotten the initial diagnosis wrong. Watson provided the correct diagnosis, a rare secondary form of leukemia, in a matter of minutes, leading the way for a new treatment that proved to be more effective (Rohaidi 2016). Although doctors were quick to point out that they would have gotten to the same answer over time, Watson's ability to parse through millions of research papers in a matter of minutes, instead of weeks, meant the patient could be started on the appropriate treatment more quickly.

Recently, IBM and sequencing giant, Illumina, announced a partnership that will see the cognitive computing tool be offered as a service to Illumina's customers alongside reagents and sequencing machines (Herper 2017a). Such a collaboration not only will benefit patients, but also the medical centers where they are seen. Instead of contracting out genomic analysis to a third party, hospitals that take advantage of the Illumina-IBM Watson partnership can keep the data analysis in-house, saving time and money (Herper 2017a).

As we described in Chapter 2 (see the section *Assistant in the Exam Room*), Watson and similar technologies aren't necessarily going to *replace* doctors, but will work alongside them, augmenting and enhancing the physicians' decision processes. This is particularly the case for radiology, where cognitive computing may be better than the doctors. The success for any cognitive solution to interpret imaging data relies on the quality and accuracy of the data used to train the system. The importance of high-quality imaging (and other types) of data can be seen in recent high-profile acquisitions. In 2015, IBM spent $1 billion to acquire Merge Healthcare, a software company that managed a massive amount of data for pharmaceutical firms and research institutes (Slabodkin 2015). Because having access to large databases of imaging is so essential for AI and cognitive computing software (regardless of the application) businesses that can offer those data will be in greater demand. It's analogous to genetic variant databases; developing proprietary imaging databases or partnering with institutions or businesses that have such databases already developed can be a significant business advantage in the AI/cognitive computing space. In the competitive oncology environment, that advantage can translate into real revenue.

Scientists train AI and cognitive computing software by feeding it tens of thousands of images, along with the relevant clinical information. Through pattern recognition and data mining, the software can read new images, based on the rules it "learned" from the training images. For example, Alphabet's DeepMind learned to tell the difference between benign (harmless) and malignant skin lesions, performing comparably to human doctors at identifying malignancies from images, and slightly better than human dermatologists for benign growths (Davis 2017).

Although there is substantial potential in joining cognitive computing solutions together with human expertise for oncology, doing so is relatively untested and there are considerable challenges. A widely publicized partnership between IBM Watson and MD Anderson Cancer Center was put on hold in early 2017, despite a successful pilot program that provided recommendations for patients with lung cancer, and agreed with experts approximately 90% of the time (Hernandez 2017). Setbacks included incompatibility between Watson and MD Anderson's EHR system (Herper 2017b). And to make cognitive computing a regular part of oncology care will require published studies demonstrating results similar to the University of Tokyo's case or the experience at the University of North Carolina's tumor board. Whether Watson, DeepMind, and others can deliver is still unclear, but early reports are positive.

But perhaps a bigger change will be how cancer is diagnosed and treatments are prescribed. As the data is collected and analyzed, it will become pivotal in making fast and accurate diagnoses. As noted, it is likely that some type of software-based, cognitive computing or decision support system will match the patient to a treatment, based on their unique characteristics.

IBM and Quest Diagnostics, for example, have partnered to create a service called Watson for Genomics. The service pairs IBM's famous Watson computer with detailed tumor analysis (Condon 2016). Dozens of companies are now vying for a piece of the cancer AI market (Dickson 2017). They include CureMetrix, Cyrcadia, Enlitic, Entopsis, Freenome, Globavir Biosciences, Insilico Medicine, Mendel Health, Notable Labs, Oncora Medical, Pathway Genomics, Proscia, SkinVision, WuXi, NextCODE, and others. Some of these groups are seeking to improve diagnostics or treatment, others are trying to spur drug discovery and development in oncology, and some are taking aim at workflow processes and more efficient staffing.

This new paradigm—or automated diagnosis—will have a ripple effect throughout the healthcare industry. Diagnostics, which are currently valued at far less than therapeutics, will become increasingly important. We could see the rise of value-based diagnostics, with much higher price tags than typical tests. Clearly, cancer centers with access to the most advanced tests and technology, as well as the largest datasets will have an advantage. However, it's also possible that, at some point, certain governments will insist that all tumor test results are shared, or some cancer centers themselves will decide to do so.

Future of Cancer Care

Cancer treatment is changing rapidly, and will continue to undergo further dramatic changes over the next 5 to 10 years. From changing clinical trial study designs to emerging technologies, the role of data can't be understated, since it will be what truly brings personalized precision medicine to patients. Already, experts in the field believe that testing tumors for multiple biomarkers should be standard practice. But there are still significant barriers to implementing precision medicine in most medical centers (see the sidebar *Putting the Real Breakthrough into Precision Medicine*).

For example, although some oncologists may believe there is substantial value in performing a multibiomarker test on a patient when they are first diagnosed with cancer, payers may not agree, leaving a physician to test one marker at a time until a mutation is identified. This may not be cost-effective compared to a multigene panel and inevitably delays finding appropriate clinical trials and targeted treatments. Even when an insurer is onboard, providers can find it difficult to navigate institutional systems to procure such a test for their patients. Thus, treatments that are mutation-specific and work across different tumor types, such as Keytruda, may find adoption difficult, because of current genomic testing protocols and a lack of payer reimbursement for the appropriate tests.

We foresee intense competition among tumor testing firms ahead. For example, companies are not just emphasizing the size of their variant databases and comprehensive annotation they do, they are also working to lower their prices and reduce their turnaround times. This information (i.e., turnaround time, prices, etc.), if kept in a publicly searchable database, could help physicians decide which is the best test to offer patients; so companies that share these data may find themselves at a competitive advantage against companies that keep that information private. As we will describe in later chapters, making these data public supports price and quality transparency, key factors in the move toward value-based care.

Databases of mutations and other markers will grow and proliferate, but their potential won't be maximized until the data sources can be connected in some way, enabling new insights to be made. A wider range of information, including data about a patient's characteristics and life history, will start being gathered and jointly analyzed. That will help establish a more comprehensive view of how cancer develops and how best to treat it. Each patient's treatment will be much more individualized and driven by data. That means it will have a higher probability of success compared to the usual trial and error approach.

Drug manufacturers, meanwhile, will have to change how they develop and market their drugs. They will no longer be able to sell a drug targeted to the organ involved; rather, their drugs will have to target specific molecules involved in cancer cell growth and survival. As mentioned earlier in this chapter, Keytruda is the first treatment approved by the FDA using this paradigm (Schattner 2017). Keytruda is an antibody targeting the PD-1 cellular pathway. It was first approved in 2014 for advanced melanoma and approvals for its use in non-small-cell lung cancer, head and neck squamous cell carcinoma, classical Hodgkin lymphoma, and urothelial carcinoma followed from 2015 to 2017 (Center for Drug Evaluation and Research and U.S. Food & Drug Administration 2017). In May 2017, the FDA approved the drug for patients with any solid, metastatic tumor with evidence of a defect in mismatch repair, the process of replacing incorrect nucleotides incorporated during DNA replication with the correct one (Schattner 2017).

The approval for Keytruda, while groundbreaking, is consistent with the federal government's recent expansive precision medicine initiatives. The National Cancer Institute's NCI-MATCH clinical trials (described in the section *Improving Clinical Trials*), for example, are testing and treating patients based on genetic mutations, not the cancer's organ or tissue of origin. One of the goals of the Precision Medicine Initiative is to use molecular (genomic) research to identify and develop new treatments for cancer (Collins and Varmus 2015).

The impact on drug development will likely be delayed for a few years, given the average timeline to develop a new drug is more than a decade (see Chapter 8). Companies that perform, or have access to, comprehensive molecular testing of patients who were enrolled in clinical trials will have an advantage getting approvals for drugs based on genomic mutations, as they can mine those data to find subsets of patients that may have responded positively to a drug, even if the overall study failed. Moving forward, it will be even more important for drug manufacturers to work with molecular diagnostics developers, to ensure they will have the right data to pursue approval based on a genomic mutation. Markets for these drugs may become much more fragmented, but costs can be spread out across a wider potential market. It won't be just a drug for patients with breast cancer, but for patients with ANY cancer with a particular mutation—a considerable market opportunity.

Hospitals and community-based oncologists will also have to make huge adjustments. There will clearly be a growing emphasis on data rather than the physician's own experience. Data specialists will be needed to help with gathering, analyzing and protecting all this patient data and there will be increased motivation to enroll more patients in clinical trials to collect the data. Oncology physicians may find themselves needing to stay on top of emerging therapies for other cancer types, because shared molecular mutations will direct treatment choice more than the tissue of origin. As a result, medical centers could find it advantageous to reorganize cancer treatment groups by biological pathway, rather than by the organ of origin (e.g., breast, lung, colon).

To be successful in the oncology landscape of the future will require more than just data specialists, however. Completely changing the way medical centers are designed to deliver cancer care based on biological pathway, similar in concept to the NCI-MATCH trial arms, would be truly revolutionary. Both organizational and management consultants would be needed to ensure the new structure streamlines medical center operations, maximizes provider efficiency, and improves the patient experience alongside outcomes. Providers who are experts in a particular cancer type (e.g., breast or lung cancer) will need additional training, optimally beginning in medical school, on genomics and precision medicine. Patients will expect once they have a cancer diagnosis that molecular testing will be performed, and their doctor will know how to interpret the results—opening up business opportunities for companies to develop software to help them do so.

As these technologies come together for cancer care, patients will begin to expect to get the right cancer treatment for the first time, based on the individual characteristics of their tumor. But health systems, providers, drug manufacturers, and others, such as companies that provide AI-enabled software for cancer diagnosis or treatment, will have to be cautious not to overstate the capabilities of precision medicine. However, if our predictions about the future of precision medicine for cancer come to fruition, we will see a more efficient system, less trial and error, and better outcomes for patients.

Chapter 4

Baby Testing Boom: Genomics-Based Prenatal Diagnostics

> I believe the uptake of these new noninvasive prenatal tests (NIPTs) has been the fastest in the history of molecular diagnostics.
>
> **Vance Vanier**
>
> *Principal at Chicago Pacific Founders and Former VP Global Commercial Operations for NIPT, Illumina, San Diego*

Stacie Chapman was almost 3 months pregnant in the spring of 2013 when her doctor called her at home. Chapman had recently undergone a noninvasive prenatal *screening* test (NIPT), the MaterniT21 PLUS, and the results were devastating. The child she was carrying tested positive for trisomy 18, caused by an extra copy of the 18th chromosome, and also known as Edwards syndrome (Daley 2014).

It's not surprising if you've never heard of Edwards syndrome. This trisomy is much less common than Down syndrome, which is caused by an extra copy of chromosome 21 and relatively well known. Edwards syndrome affects approximately 1 in every 5,000 infants. It would be more common, but is so severe that many Edwards pregnancies end in miscarriage. Only 5–10% of affected infants survive their first year. Severe intellectual disability and other medical issues are common (Genetics Home Reference 2017d).

For Stacie Chapman and her husband, this was tragic news. But she also couldn't understand how a test her doctor told her had a 99% detection rate could be wrong. Although the couple made plans for a termination to be done the following morning, her doctor persuaded her to wait and first have a more definitive *diagnostic* test, which is recommended to confirm the MaterniT21 PLUS results.

The outcome?

A year later, the Chapmans have a healthy toddler—who doesn't have Edwards syndrome—and the couple and their doctor are speaking out about popular misconceptions about these screening tests (Daley 2014).

Although the Chapman's story has a happy outcome, their experience is still a cautious tale about one of the fastest growing fields in medicine—noninvasive prenatal tests, or NIPTs.

Thanks to new genomics-based prenatal tests and a surge in the content of databases cataloguing genetic defects, it is possible to know much more about a baby's health prior to birth, or even before conception.

NIPTs are at the forefront of this new wave of prenatal testing technology and they have caught on fast. The first NIPT launched in the United States in October 2011, but the technology quickly attracted leading high profile entrants in Asia, including China's BGI. In its first year, the NIPT market was estimated to be $0.22 billion (Transparency Market Research 2014). The market grew to $1.19 billion in 2015 and is expected to reach more than $5 billion by 2025 (Grand View Research 2016d). Dozens of companies and laboratories are angling for a position in the NIPT market and there are many new opportunities as well, particularly for identifying a wider range of defects; earlier detection (including preconception); lowering prices; and related services, such as newborn screening.

The story of how prenatal testing evolved mirrors many of biotech's biggest successes, including the explosive growth of genetic tests after next-generation sequencing (NGS) technologies made the process less expensive and more efficient. People have an idea about a way to achieve a medical breakthrough, their original premise is good but not quite on the mark, they beat their heads against a wall for a decade or so, and then they realize they need to try a different way to achieve the same thing. The rest is history.

Evolution of Prenatal Testing

Until fairly recently, prenatal testing was limited and reserved to women deemed to be "high risk" due to advanced maternal age or a history of complications. Now, many women are confronted with multiple ultrasounds and a dizzying array of test options, almost the moment they find themselves to be pregnant, or even earlier in the case of assisted reproductive technologies.

Lab tests performed in the first trimester or beginning of the second trimester are used to screen women who may need more invasive testing. The most commonly used screens for genetic defects in unborn babies have been a set of protein markers found in blood, used in conjunction with ultrasound. For example, the quad screen test is a blood test that measures alpha-fetoprotein, human chorionic gonadotropin, estriol, and inhibin-A. It's usually performed between weeks 15 and 20, right after the start of the second trimester. Abnormal levels (either too low or too high) can indicate a potential problem with the developing fetus, such as neural tube defects like spina bifida, or chromosomal mutations like Down syndrome and Edwards syndrome (Office on Women's Health and U.S. Department of Health and Human Services 2017).

If the quad or other screening tests are abnormal, or earlier in the pregnancy if the mother is considered to be at higher risk for certain disorders, a diagnostic test such as chorionic villus sampling (CVS) or amniocentesis (see the sidebar *Amniocentesis and Chorionic Villus Sampling*) is recommended.

As noted earlier, this is an important distinction: lab tests that are performed early in a pregnancy are typically *screening* tests and not *diagnostic* tests. It may not seem like there's much of a difference between the two, but to pregnant women like Stacie Chapman, concerned about the health of their unborn child, there's a world of difference and there are very real impacts from conflating the two.

Many women apparently don't understand—or aren't adequately advised—that a positive screening test requires an invasive follow-up. As a result, they may simply make their decisions about the pregnancy or preparation for the child based on the screening result alone (Warsof, Larion, and Abuhamad 2015).

Why is it so important that a positive screening test be followed by a more invasive, diagnostic one? Understanding why has a lot to do with how common disorders are in the population being tested and correctly interpreting the performance of the test, like false-positive or detection rates. For example, let's take a hypothetical population of 100,000 people and a genetic disorder that occurs in 20 out of every 10,000 people who are tested. So in the hypothetical population, we'd expect to find 200 people with the disorder.

Let's assume the test has a 99% detection (sensitivity) and 95% specificity. This means that 99% of the time, the test will be positive when the disease is present—a true positive, and that 95% of the time, the test will be negative when the disease isn't present—a true negative. In our example, this means that the test will accurately identify 198/200 people who have the disease and 94,810/99,800 who don't have the disease. But it also means that 4,990/99,800 people will have a false positive result. So, the probability that the disease is actually present when someone has a positive test result (or, the positive predictive value of the test) is less than 4%.

Traditional methods, such as the first semester nuchal translucency screen and the second semester quad screen, have a 0.5%–7% false-positive rate (i.e., babies identified as having a defect, but who are healthy) (Park et al. 2016). That may seem like a relatively low rate, but it leads to unnecessary stress for expectant mothers and many more follow-up tests (i.e., amniocentesis or CVS) than are truly needed. Further, these traditional screening tests are only useful for detecting a small number of genetic defects, namely, aneuploidies, which involve either missing or duplicated whole chromosomes, or neural tube defects like spina bifida.

SIDEBAR: AMNIOCENTESIS AND CHORIONIC VILLUS SAMPLING (CVS)

Amniocentesis and CVS are actual *diagnostic* tests that can be performed during the first and second trimesters of pregnancy. That means their results are highly accurate. In CVS, a sample of cells is removed from the placenta to be tested, whereas in an amniocentesis, amniotic fluid and cells from the fetal sac that surrounds the fetus are removed for testing (Office on Women's Health and U.S. Department of Health and Human Services 2017). Both CVS and amniocentesis are invasive tests and come with increased risk for complications, including miscarriage (Tara, Lotfalizadeh, and Moeindarbari 2016; Wah et al. 2016).

The samples collected from CVS and amniocentesis procedures can be analyzed using a variety of methods. Karyotyping has long been a mainstay for evaluating large chromosomal anomalies. In fact, most people's first thoughts when they think about what a chromosome looks like probably comes from a karyotype image where the chromosomes are lined up in pairs. In karyotyping, the sample is stained and the chromosomes are visually examined under a microscope. It's easy to see, though, that although a karyotype can determine if there are extra or missing chromosomes, the resolution it provides is not sufficient to identify much more than gross abnormalities.

The use of fluorescent markers that bind to specific regions of chromosomes has improved utility of karyotyping in the past decade. These fluorescent markers can be used to literally "paint" each chromosome with color. Doctors and researchers can use these markers to highlight specific genetic regions and identify duplications, deletions of important genes, or places where parts of chromosomes were moved to other chromosomes and joined together. Although this has improved the utility of karyotyping, how well the method works depends on both the marker binding to the right place on a chromosome, the technical specifications of the microscope used to view them, and the expertise of the technician who interprets the findings (O'Connor 2008).

Shifting View of Genetic Risk

In the mid-2000s, microarray technology began rapidly advancing and finding new uses. DNA chips have been used for years to detect certain mutations, such as those in tumors, or to study portions of the human genome. Chromosomal microarrays (CMAs) are chips that contain the entire genome laid out on their surface in small fragments. Using samples from amniocentesis or CVS, the DNA is isolated from the fetal cells and cut into smaller pieces. A fluorescent marker is often attached to these fragments for subsequent visualization. The DNA fragments are then hybridized, or bound, to specific sequences on the microarray and later visualized.

This technique also gives genetic analysis using CMAs its name: array comparative genetic hybridization (aCGH). The technology is much more accurate than the traditional method of karyotyping, and high-resolution arrays have been developed that can identify very small (~200 base pairs) genetic variants (Urban et al. 2006). Several papers, including a meta-analysis of eight studies (Hillman et al. 2011) suggest that aCGH can detect some types of genetic problems, such as relatively small duplications and deletions or rearrangements, better than karyotyping (Sun et al. 2015; Choy et al. 2014; Wapner et al. 2012).

But there are also limitations to the aCGH method. Certain types of rearrangements, such as balanced translocations, aren't picked up by the technology, since they do not change the copy number of the gene present, just the location where it resides (Wapner et al. 2012). And some reports assessing aCGHs had surprise findings—the researchers detected a much higher level of genetic variations than expected. A small percent of those variations were deemed "variants of unknown significance" (VUSs) whose impact on health is still not clear (Manning and Hudgins 2010; Evangelidou et al. 2013).

Such cases will become less and less common, as data from aCGH and other genomic studies accumulate and the clinical consequences of specific genetic variants are determined. In the meantime, however, some parents will still be left in limbo after such tests—knowing that their fetus has an unusual genetic variation, but not knowing what the implications of that are.

Transformative Technology

Although substantial improvements have been made to karyotyping and aCGH technologies, they still require a starting sample taken during CVS or amniocentesis. Despite low numbers of complications associated with those procedures, the chance for miscarriage makes them unappealing to many women. To improve prenatal testing, scientists have been trying to find ways to capture whole fetal cells from maternal blood instead.

But harvesting such cells proved much more difficult than people anticipated, despite many years of work. Finally, in the late 1990s, researchers found evidence of fetal DNA fragments in maternal blood samples (Lo et al. 1997). These fragments, called cell-free fetal DNA (cffDNA), are released into the mother's circulation when placental cells break down. It turns out that cffDNA escapes into the bloodstream much more easily than whole fetal cells, which make up just 10 of every 200,000 billion cells in the mother's bloodstream. In contrast, cffDNA fragments make up approximately 10% of the genetic material found in a maternal blood sample, although this amount can be highly variable (Wang et al. 2013).

Researchers determined that, using standard laboratory tools, cffDNA can be detected as early as 7 weeks into the pregnancy (Hyett et al. 2005). Because these tests are noninvasive, there is significant appeal for pregnant women to use them, compared to the more invasive (with potential complications) CVS or amniocentesis.

In 2008, two rival labs published high-profile papers showing that cffDNA could be sequenced to detect whole-chromosome defects highly accurately (Chiu et al. 2008; Fan et al. 2008). They used a technique called massively parallel shotgun sequencing to analyze sections of DNA across the entire 3 billion base pair-long fetal genome. Specifically, they sequenced 5–10 million sections of sequence that were 25–36 base pairs long. Then, they mapped these to the reference human genome and started counting how much genetic material came from which parts of the fetal genome.

This advance boiled prenatal testing down to a counting problem, at least when an entire chromosome is duplicated or missing. In such cases, there's a fairly big difference between how much of that genetic material is present in a healthy individual and how much is found in someone with a defect. By sequencing specific fragments of cffDNA, researchers can stack those fragments up and see if there is too much or too little of a certain chromosome present.

That sparked a race to develop new prenatal tests that would be faster, more accurate, and able to be done earlier in pregnancy. Results from several large-scale NIPT clinical trials were first published in 2011 (Ehrich et al. 2011; Palomaki et al. 2011; Sehnert et al. 2011). These results were so positive that multiple medical societies published committee opinions, stating that women at high risk for a fetus with certain types of defects should be offered these tests (Gregg et al. 2013).

By October 2011, genomics pioneer Sequenom publicly launched the first of these products, MaterniT21, in the United States. Over the next few months, the company analyzed 100,000 of the tests (Sequenom 2013). Similar products quickly debuted by numerous start-ups, including Verinata Health, Ariosa Diagnostics, and Natera. Globally, the market further expanded into South and Southeast Asia, the Middle East, and Australia. Today's prenatal testing companies are competing based on accuracy, price, number of defects they detect, and also trying to find new applications for their services.

The adoption of NIPTs is one of the fastest technological transformations in modern medical history (see the sidebar *Explosive Field of Noninvasive Prenatal Testing*). These new tests have also dramatically changed the landscape of prenatal care, cutting rates of invasive procedures that were once mainstays of obstetric practices. The rise of these test is also bringing attention to the need for better genetic counseling.

As Martha Dudek, genetic counselor in Obstetrics and Gynecology at Vanderbilt University Medical Center has said, "Initially targeted for the high-risk pregnancy population, the screening is now more widely available to all women in pregnancy" (Pasley 2017). This point has an impact on the predictive value of the results that we'll come back to later in this chapter.

SIDEBAR: EXPLOSIVE FIELD OF NONINVASIVE PRENATAL TESTING

Vance Vanier, MD, MBA

Cofounder and Managing Director, Chicago Pacific Founders

Over the last few years, noninvasive prenatal testing has evolved at a particularly explosive rate.

For the prior two decades, doctors relied on several relatively ambiguous blood tests, usually done in combination with ultrasound, to estimate whether a fetus was likely to have one of several common defects. The best known of these blood tests measures alpha-fetoprotein.

Unfortunately, these older tests are not very accurate. "Five to 10 percent of times when doctors told a woman her fetus was at risk [of a defect], it turned out they were wrong," explains Vance Vanier, former president of prenatal testing company Verinata (acquired by Illumina in 2013 for $450 million), in our interview (Vanier 2017). Vanier is now a Managing Director of the investment firm Chicago Pacific Founders.

The science of prenatal diagnostics, however, took a dramatic leap forward when noninvasive testing became exponentially more accurate. Instead of testing proteins, labs are now analyzing cffDNA, which [come from] cells that are sloughed off from the fetus. These newer tests are ten times more accurate than the older tests that just looked at proteins.

Not only are the cffDNA-based tests more accurate, they also have the potential to look at a much broader set of conditions than those that are just protein-based. That means fewer women who want this information have to take the risk of miscarriage or infection associated with invasive procedures such as amniocentesis or chorionic villus sampling, which previously were necessary to get a more accurate view of the fetus's genetic health. What's more, it's now clear that this type of test is just as useful in "low risk" pregnancies as it is in those deemed at high risk of having a fetus with a birth defect (Bianchi et al. 2014).

"I believe the uptake of this test in the U.S. has been the fastest in the history of molecular diagnostics," says Vanier. "It has been slower in other parts of the world, since in many places governments end up paying for the test and have lengthy evaluation processes. But it is already getting momentum overseas, and has been particularly widely adopted in China."

Initially, this was just a substitution of one cffDNA test for the older protein-based tests. The older blood tests were used exclusively for the most common chromosomal defects—trisomies of chromosomes 13, 18, and 21. But cffDNA and adjunct technologies, such as subchromosomal analysis and whole genome screening, can detect a much broader set of chromosomal defects.

The upside of this is that patients who are very "risk averse" can get a lot more information about their fetus. The downside is that the newer tests can detect genetic variants of unknown relevance. The variant is so rare it's not known whether it will cause a problem or not. That can cause a lot of anxiety for some parents.

Regardless of these issues, this type of testing is increasing. "I think this has already fueled the growth in the overall field of genomic medicine," Vanier says. "More parents will get genomic data about their babies, and there will be greater interest in understanding what all that means. Someday, we'll know what these rare variations mean, and we'll be able to take more and more steps to treat genetic diseases, or at least to mitigate them."

While NIPTs are a huge advance, they are still only screening tests. They don't provide a definitive diagnosis, but indicate if a fetus is at higher risk of a defect and can sometimes pick up a potential cancer in the mother (see the sidebar *Maternal Cancer Detection*). A positive result (i.e., high risk of a defect) from a NIPT leads to referrals for a diagnostic test, such as CVS or amniocentesis. However, pre-implantation genetic diagnosis (PGD), which is available to patients undergoing *in vitro* fertilization (IVF), can provide doctors a method of assessing the genetic profile of the embryo before implantation.

A study from the CDC found assisted reproductive technology in the United States in 2014, which includes IVF, resulted in a live birth only 33% of the time (Sunderam et al. 2017) and many of the embryos created during the IVF process have chromosomal abnormalities (Kort et al. 2016; Shahine et al. 2016; Ubaldi et al. 2017). But PGD can improve the odds, by allowing doctors to select embryos that are most likely to be viable and avoid implanting those with certain genomic anomalies.

During PGD, generally one or two cells are removed from the developing embryo when eight cells have developed, around day 3 postfertilization (Kim et al. 2012). These cells are typically analyzed using polymerase chain reaction and/or fluorescent *in situ* hybridization. Single cell genome sequencing is also being investigated (Van der Aa et al. 2013; Xu et al. 2015; Patel et al. 2016b). In addition to aneuploidies (absence of a chromosome or presence of an additional chromosome), PGD can identify chromosome translocations, where sections from different chromosomes are switched, and even hereditary disorders (CombiMatrix 2016).

In May 2013, Marybeth Scheidts and David Levy's son Connor became the first child born following the PGD procedure (Geddes 2013). Thirteen embryos were created during the couple's IVF cycle, seven of which appeared normal. Of those seven seemingly normal embryos, only three had the correct number of chromosomes. One of those was implanted and 9 months later, Connor was born (Geddes 2013).

A couple with a family history of pantothenate kinase-associated neurodegeneration (PKAN) also turned to PGD to help them avoid having an affected child (Trachoo et al. 2017). During childhood, patients with PKAN begin to exhibit neurological and movement abnormalities, which become progressively worse due to increased iron in the brain (Genetics Home Reference 2017a). During the couple's IVF cycle, seven embryos were created: two were likely affected by the disease, three were likely carriers for PKAN, one was likely an unaffected noncarrier, and one embryo failed the genetic testing (i.e., initial DNA amplification was not successful). Amniocentesis was performed on the single unaffected embryo that was implanted and the results were consistent with the PGD results. Two years later, the child has normal growth and exhibits no neurological symptoms (Trachoo et al. 2017).

SIDEBAR: MATERNAL CANCER DETECTION: AN UNINTENDED CONSEQUENCE OF NIPT AND PGD

Expectant parents undergoing NIPT or PGD are counseled that these tests might find a serious genetic disorder is likely to affect their child. But it's altogether another thing to find the fetal test indicates the *mother* may have cancer.

When Eunice Lee was 10 weeks pregnant, the 40-year-old anesthesiologist had the Sequenom MaterniT21 PLUS NIPT to find out if her baby was at risk for a genetic disease. Two weeks after the test, Lee walked into her doctor's office to shocking news: the test had picked up some unusual genetic signatures and her doctor suggested she undergo a workup for cancer. A full-body MRI found a 7-cm tumor in her colon, which she had removed that evening (Hughes 2015).

NIPTs, which use circulating (cell-free) DNA to pick up fetal abnormalities, can also pick up circulating tumor DNA from the mother. In a study of more than 125,000 NIPT results, approximately 3,700 of the samples were positive for chromosomal aberrations.

In the aneuploid (abnormal chromosome) subset of samples, 10 maternal cancer cases were identified, eight of which were later confirmed (the remaining two patients were deemed too ill to contact) (Bianchi et al. 2015).

Lee's particular form of colon cancer is usually cured with surgery alone, so she decided to forgo chemotherapy. Several months later, Lee did the MaterniT21 test again, to see if the test would identify any circulating tumor DNA. "It was purely on my own initiative," Lee told a reporter for *BuzzFeed News*, "It was for my peace of mind" (Hughes 2015).

Lee's experience brings to attention a possibility that many who undergo NIPTs ignore or are simply unaware of. Diana Bianchi of Tufts Medical Center has said, "We need to do a better job up front to communicate with patients that we might find out something about their own health as well" (Nowogrodzki 2015). The possibility of a maternal cancer being identified through a NIPT isn't typically addressed in a pretest genetic counseling appointment, and although a survey of genetic counselors found roughly three-quarters would share the results with the patient, more than half said "they would feel uncomfortable or very uncomfortable counseling a patient with these results" (Giles et al. 2017).

NIPT companies have been quick to point out that while their tests can sometimes pick up on maternal cancers, they aren't designed or optimized to do so. Nevertheless, some of the companies have expressed interest in expanding their product lines to include cancer tests (Nowogrodzki 2015). A study performed in nonpregnant women found that NIPT identified 40.6% of early- and late-stage high-grade serous ovarian cancers (Cohen et al. 2016).

How to handle a woman whose NIPT suggests they might have cancer is still being debated, particularly because without other symptoms that could be used to hone in on a particular organ for additional testing, doctors have few options other than full-body scans or watchful waiting. But in this increasingly competitive NIPT market, accurate identification of maternal cancer could be a substantial advantage.

PGD has given parents undergoing IVF the ability to screen embryos prior to implantation, avoiding the consequences of carrying a child with devastating genetic diseases. However, as with NIPT, there is significant debate surrounding the use of this technology (see the section *Ethical and Social Consequences of NIPT and NBS*).

How *Moneyball Medicine* Is Transforming Prenatal and Neonatal Testing

There have been thousands of genetic defects described to date, the vast majority of which don't involve the addition or subtraction of an entire chromosome. But identifying trisomies (or the lack of a chromosome) with cffDNA testing is essentially all that is available today. That alone has had a huge impact on medical practices that offer prenatal testing, shifting their revenue flows. In particular, it has raised the rate of prenatal testing overall, but reduced the number of invasive procedures carried out, because the NIPTs are so much more accurate than the earlier noninvasive tests. It has also fueled the booming $1 billion plus NIPT testing market we described earlier.

Researchers and entrepreneurs think there are even more opportunities to improve this field and create new businesses.

Two of the biggest remaining challenges are (1) linking genetic variants with their clinical outcomes and (2) improving the analytical methods that allow researchers to accurately scan the 3 billion base pairs in a genome—not just for whole chromosome duplications or deletions, but even for a single base.

What's more, a major study published in 2012 suggested that the actual number of fetuses with genetic defects is much greater than previously thought, although many of these defects will not become apparent until later in childhood (Wapner et al. 2012). This creates bigger demand for more data, and comprehensive databases, but also opens up a Pandora's box of unintended consequences that ethicists are still working through (see the section *Ethical and Social Consequences of NIPT and NBS*).

Researchers continue to refine NIPTs and develop novel tools to provide a more accurate and detailed view of the fetal genome. At least two labs have already sequenced the entire genome of an unborn baby from the mother's blood sample (Fan et al. 2012; Kitzman et al. 2012). And unlike most current NIPTs, which only determine risk of Down syndrome, Edwards syndrome, and Patau syndrome, future iterations are likely to be able to screen for a growing number of disorders. Indeed, this has already been demonstrated by scientists using "direct haplotyping technology" with cffDNA samples from pregnancies at risk for certain inherited genetic disorders (Hui et al. 2017).

While current NIPTs are screening tests whose results have to be confirmed with another, more invasive test, there is significant interest in creating a NIPT that is *diagnostic* (Arcedi Biotech 2016). Using whole fetal cells instead of cffDNA could play a role in this. A recent study found approximately 13 whole fetal cells could be isolated from 30 mL of maternal blood and these cells could be subjected to both aCGH and sequencing technologies (Kolvraa et al. 2016).

Pre-implantation and prenatal screening are not the only areas that the confluence of big data, complex analytics, and cognitive computing are impacting. Newborn screening (NBS) is also becoming a lot more complicated.

NBS involves collecting a blood sample from babies shortly after birth and testing for a variety of (predominately) metabolic syndromes. By identifying newborns that potentially have a metabolic disorder so quickly, there is the potential to intervene, preventing or at least minimizing the damage.

Phenylketonuria (PKU) is one such disorder. PKU is caused by mutations in the gene that codes for the phenylalanine hydroxylase enzyme. These mutations prevent the gene from breaking down the amino acid phenylalanine, which builds up in the blood, affecting the brain. Untreated, PKU leads to permanent, severe intellectual disability and other problems like seizures and behavioral issues. But if the disease is diagnosed within the first month or two of life, dietary changes can be made, preventing the devastating neurological outcomes that used to be common with this disorder (Genetics Home Reference 2017b).

The exact composition of NBS varies from state to state, so a newborn with a serious disorder might escape notice until symptoms develop depending on where they are born. For example, although all states test babies for hemoglobinopathies, as of November 2014, fewer than half require and have fully implemented testing for severe combined immune deficiency (National Newborn Screening & Global Resource Center 2017). Differences between what states test for is one reason why whole exome sequencing (WES) and whole genome sequencing (WGS) are so intriguing as a supplement to, or replacement for, traditional NBS. They offer the potential to identify an at-risk infant who would not otherwise have been identified through the traditional NBS program.

But genomic tests and new treatments are complicating the historic premise of NBS to include *only* those disorders where an intervention is possible (Centerwall, Chinnock, and Pusavat 1960; Kwan and Puck 2015). As we present in Chapters 5 and 8, new technologies are making it possible to identify previously undiagnosable conditions and pharma is developing treatments for these "orphan" diseases. Consequently, as the technology continues to decrease in price and state labs update their technological capabilities, new disorders are likely to be included on states' NBS panels and the current patchwork of diseases tested for on a state-by-state basis could be eliminated, until all fifty states test for the same disorders.

Both WES and WGS are made possible by NGS technologies and are actively being assessed in clinical trials at medical centers across the United States to determine their utility, identify limitations, and assess operational challenges (Reinstein 2015; National Institutes of Health 2017). Some early studies have demonstrated generally positive results, showing a reduction in the number of false positives when compared to standard NBS methods, or the ability to diagnose rare disorders in sick infants (Saunders et al. 2012; Bodian et al. 2016).

The Newborn Sequencing in Genomic Medicine and Public Health Network is a collaboration of four academic medical centers and the NIH (Berg et al. 2017). These centers are investigating how WES and WGS could augment or replace traditional NBS methods and learn what disorders not currently tested for may be assessed using WES/WGS. At the University of California, San Francisco, doctors are using WES to identify variants associated with immunological and pharmacological outcomes from NBS samples.

You'll recall from Chapter 2 that pharmacogenomics variants are changes in the genome that affect the absorption, digestion, metabolism, or excretion of a medication. Knowing how a patient might metabolize a particular drug based on their genetic variants could help doctors choose an alternate dosing algorithm or a different medication entirely. And since the information would have been collected during NBS, the data would already be available to doctors at the time of prescribing (assuming the data has been analyzed, stored, and could be provided to the doctor in an easily interpretable format).

Thus, incorporating WGS/WES into existing NBS programs has the *potential* to provide parents with the opportunity to identify metabolic or endocrine disorders at a time when an intervention would be beneficial. In addition, there is also an opportunity to determine the risk for adult-onset disorders (e.g., *BRCA* mutations and risk for developing breast cancer) or characteristics that may influence medication choices. Minimally, incorporation of WGS/WES into NBS programs could follow the American College of Medical Genetics and Genomics (ACMG) guidelines for reporting incidental findings. First published in 2013, the ACMG developed and periodically updates a list of genes, currently numbering 59, associated with highly penetrant genetic disorders where an early intervention could improve patient outcomes (Kalia et al. 2017).

Although there is significant interest in the use of these techniques to improve upon NBS, there is no data to suggest that labs today would be able to perform WGS/WES at the same scale as traditional NBS testing. In addition, while the cost of these assays has dropped significantly in the past few years, they are still far beyond the cost of existing NBS testing, making it financially impractical for states to implement currently (Saunders 2017). This presents a business opportunity for private labs to offer sequencing and interpretation services for parents, but ethical (see below) and potential legal issues would have to be addressed to retain autonomy and to prevent discrimination in situations not covered by the Genetic Information Nondiscrimination Act of 2008.

NIPT is already changing how expectant parents think about prenatal testing and how much information they can learn about their baby, before it is born. Similarly, NBS in the future may be an opportunity to learn not only about any treatable metabolic disorders, highly penetrant hereditary diseases, or pharmacogenomic information that could prevent adverse drug events, but also about diseases that may not develop until adulthood—if at all. Currently, NIPTs and NBS are relatively limited in the information they provide. NIPTs still rely on invasive diagnostic testing to confirm a positive result, and there is little that can be done once a prenatal diagnosis is made. But the developments we describe here are beginning to make their way into the clinic, and as we'll show at the end of this chapter, a new option to fix genetic defects before a baby is born or shortly thereafter may soon be possible.

Ethical and Social Consequences of NIPT and NBS

Unlike genomic testing of adults, there are special considerations for testing of children. When the children have yet to be born, still another layer of complexity arises.

With the technical ability to accurately determine the sex of a fetus weeks into a pregnancy comes the concern widespread adoption of NIPT will lead to sex-selective termination (de Jong et al. 2010; Vanstone et al. 2014). Eight states have already passed legislation prohibiting the practice. Two states of those have gone further, prohibiting abortion based on a fetal abnormality (Green 2016). Disability rights activists are concerned that over time, fewer children will be born with these disorders—making NIPT a kind of "modern-day eugenics" (Green 2016).

As NIPT and NBS capabilities advance and a larger number of disorders can be accurately screened for, whether or not to test for say, the *BRCA* genes, becomes a difficult decision. If the test finds the fetus carries a mutation, it can influence the parent's reproductive decision-making for subsequent pregnancies and also indicate one of the parents (who may be asymptomatic at the time) also carries the mutation. But *BRCA*-related cancers arise in adulthood and interventions to reduce cancer risk are not performed until after the individual reaches adulthood—a time when they can decide for themselves whether or not they would want to have testing done. Prenatal and newborn testing for disorders like this remove an individual's ability to make those decisions for themselves (de Jong et al. 2010).

Right now, the tests are largely screening methods and diagnostic tests have to be performed to confirm a diagnosis. Patients sometimes don't realize the difference and are making decisions, such as declining more invasive tests, based solely on results from the screening test, causing further concern (Warsof, Larion, and Abuhamad 2015).

In February 2014, a large-scale study was published confirming that NIPTs were also much more accurate than the traditional tests among low-risk women, potentially expanding the market even further (Bianchi et al. 2014). As the technology continues to improve and doctors gain the ability to mitigate the effects of a genetic condition, or even fix it during the prenatal or neonatal period, debates over the ethical and social issues are sure to continue.

Future of Prenatal Testing

We have made a gigantic technological leap forward in the past decade from a prenatal screening process that was much more uncertain, sometimes more invasive, and directed only at high-risk pregnancies. Today, NIPTs are reframing prenatal testing choices and more women, even those with normal-risk pregnancies, are taking advantage of the opportunity to learn more from the testing available. Test developers may need new strategies to reach these women: doctors don't usually recommend testing in younger (i.e., low-risk) women, or those with no history of genetic disease in their family, and the predictive value of these tests in low-risk women is substantially lower than in high-risk women.

The widespread adoption of these tests is supporting the public's growing understanding of genetics. That, in turn, could fuel demand for a wider range of gene sequencing-related products, more accurate test options, and services, such as prenatal genetic counseling.

As we described, the key advances in this field have been the development of cffDNA testing, NGS, and CMAs. The amount of data collected through these new technologies has been substantial. These new technologies, combined with information from ever-growing genomic databases, can provide an unparalleled view of the prenatal and neonatal genomes.

But just as with oncology and other aspects of precision medicine, this information is incredibly complex and data sharing between companies is not common. In fact, the NIPT market has been under significant turmoil for several years, the result of ongoing lawsuits in the United States and overseas regarding patient infringement between labs performing the tests (Winnick 2012; Agarwal et al. 2013; Heger 2016). But competition between the companies can lead to improved tests for patients and allow them to choose based on the diagnostic performance of the test.

To continue to improve the predictive value of these tests, collaboration between companies or medical centers with large patient databases will be necessary to link genomic variation to clinical outcomes. As mentioned earlier, much of the variation that has been already linked to disease is either clearly problematic or clearly benign, but there remains a substantial proportion that are of unknown significance. For prenatal testing, addressing this uncertainty will be a key area of research as well as a business opportunity—the company that offers the most reliable results, will have a big advantage.

As a result, many groups, including clinical centers and some academic researchers, are busy building up their databases of genetic defects. As these grow, the number of VUSs will shrink. To maximize the value of these databases, researchers (and businesses) will need to collaborate and share the data. Right now, the *data* are considered valuable, but we are moving toward a future where the *interpretation* of the data is where the real opportunities are (see Chapter 10).

Someday, new start-ups will be able to access publicly available variant databases and create new software that interpret everything from risk of developing cancer later in life to whether the baby will have an allergic reaction to Tylenol, and expectant parents may even be able to view it on their mobile devices. For parents with more questions than could be answered within the mobile app, they could connect to genetic counselors via telemedicine and video conferencing. This isn't a sci-fi fantasy, it's taking technology that already exists and pushing it further. That's why clinical genomics is among the fastest-growing, big data fields.

What's more, new advances are also coming for treatment of genetic defects. Until recently, once a mutation was found there was little an expectant parent could do. The mother could decide to terminate the pregnancy or instead prepare for the birth of a child with whatever disability was identified. Technology like CRISPR (described in Chapter 2) and advanced gene and stem cell therapies are making a third option possible: fixing the problem while the fetus is still developing.

Several high-profile examples have emerged demonstrating the utility of these methods to cure patients from some disorders. A test of CRISPR using nonviable human embryos demonstrated the ability for scientists to alter a gene responsible for a blood disorder (Cyranoski and Reardon 2015) and a second team in 2016 was able to make the embryos resistant to HIV (Callaway 2016). More recently, the technique has been expanded to viable embryos, where attempts to fix ß-thalassemia and a G6PD deficiency were more successful than the earlier studies with nonviable embryos, although still variable (Tang et al. 2017). And a recent *New England Journal of Medicine* article that documented the use of gene therapy to cure sickle cell anemia in a boy (Ribeil et al. 2017) is encouraging hopes that the technique might one day be extended to the prenatal period.

We've moved past the days of identifying only high-risk patients for additional testing. Expectant parents are asking for more information about their fetus and what to expect as the baby grows older—and they're getting it. New treatments are being developed constantly that are changing the patient trajectories of rare diseases, so parents can now plan in advance for medical care and educational opportunities for babies with disabilities. Gene editing methods like CRISPR might give parents another option: fix the genetic mutation before the baby is born. Getting to the future of prenatal testing, where NIPTs are diagnostic, not just meant for screening, is likely to come in the near future, as techniques used for NIPTs are refined and the industry matures.

To manage the vast amounts of data generated by these tests, companies are increasingly turning toward cloud computing (see Chapter 10). This is democratizing not only the NIPT market, but precision medicine more generally, allowing start-ups to purchase only the data storage and software solutions they need at the time, with the ability to scale up (or down) seamlessly as their company's needs evolve. This means some financial and/or technical barriers for entrepreneurs looking to enter or expand into the NIPT market are lowered, and current NIPT providers might find it easier to expand into cancer tests, as described above.

The real benefit of expanding NIPT, so that nearly all expectant mothers undergo the test, would be in having clinically useful information about the baby available to physicians and other healthcare providers as the child ages. Where to store this type of data and how to ensure that it remains secure are not trivial concerns. Cloud computing and blockchain are two potential solutions.

Leveraging the potential of cloud computing, managing large variant databases, creating useful and easy-to-understand user (expectant parent) interfaces for websites or even mobile apps, and sifting through vast quantities of scientific literature to characterize individual variants require employees with experience in computer science and bioinformatics. In addition to clinicians and genetic counselors, these data-driven scientists will find numerous career opportunities in the NIPT market.

Despite the technical limitations and ethical considerations of NIPT, no one can refute that it has turned prenatal testing upside down. As the technology continues to improve, the results of these tests will have greater predictive value. As databases supporting the clinical interpretation of genomic variants continue to grow, expectant parents will be able to learn even more about a fetus's health prospects. These advances will lead to new business opportunities, increased medical services, and evolving options for prospective parents.

Chapter 5

New Hope for People with Rare Diseases

Ultimately, to get to our own big data moment, we'll need a federation of a lot of data-bases. Connecting to partners supports a whole new approach to medical research in which communities drive research.

Sharon Terry
President and Chief Executive Officer
Genetic Alliance, Washington, DC

In the age of Big Data, we're attempting to solve big population health problems—such as what are the most important factors driving heart disease or diabetes—by analyzing huge swaths of data points (see the section in Chapter 2, *Precision Medicine: Welcome to the N-of-1*). But researchers are also finding that advanced analytics, laboratory tools, and cognitive computing software can be used to help a different patient population: patients with rare diseases, or conditions that affect 200,000 patients or fewer, according to U.S. standards. More than 7,000 rare diseases have been documented worldwide affecting over 350 million people (National Center for Advancing Translational Sciences 2016; Global Genes 2017). Until recently, those patients have been relegated to observing the race for new drugs from the sidelines. But that has been changing.

The rare disease market is burgeoning for pharma and biotech as well—providing both opportunities and financial benefits. Data-driven advances and the Orphan Drug Act are making it more efficient and (sometimes) less costly to develop drugs for rare diseases, helping to drive substantial profits for pharma. Smaller pharma, biotech companies, and even academic researchers with one or two candidate drugs for rare diseases find themselves worthy of acquisition by the big companies or with licensing agreements as a way to reduce development costs, shorten the timeframe to bring a drug to market, and expand into new patient populations. The most expensive therapies on the market today are for rare diseases, with price tags exceeding $500,000 for the top seven drugs (Speights 2017).

This market essentially surged due to a confluence of factors. Although rare diseases affect smaller populations more than the typical "blockbuster" markets of common diseases, the price of treatment for rare diseases is inversely related to the patient population size. Insurers will generally pay for these lifesaving drugs, even at incredibly high prices (Jarvis 2013). That realization has led to interest from a broader group of drug developers. (For more, see the section *Drug Developers Rally around a Business Opportunity*, later in this chapter.) There are also hundreds of nonprofits focused on specific rare diseases, and more of them are taking a bigger role in investing and guiding research, besides providing support to patients. New technologies, meanwhile, are making it much more efficient to develop drugs, even for rare diseases, which are particularly hard to address, since the small patient populations generate less data.

In short, innovative drug developers, revved up nonprofits, and new data-fueled tools have led to big changes in this field over the last decade or so. Most patients still struggle to get help, and some start-ups in rare diseases may not achieve their goals. But, it is a more hopeful time in this arena than ever before. As we'll describe in this chapter, heavy use of data and analytics, a combination of emerging and maturing technologies, the engagement of citizen-scientists, the novel use of social media, and new business models are bringing new hope to these patients and new opportunities for entrepreneurs, data scientists, and healthcare and life sciences professionals.

Rare Disease Patient Odyssey

For any family searching for a rare disease diagnosis, the process can be harrowing. Leslie Gordon and Scott Berns, both of whom are doctors, knew something was wrong with their baby when his growth rate dramatically dropped off around 9 months (Henig 2005). Sam stopped growing properly and his baby teeth didn't come in on time. He also seemed stiff. "I'm his mother. I know there's something wrong here," Leslie said (Saey 2014). Gordon and Berns had Sam tested for various disorders that might explain his small stature without luck, until a colleague of Berns mentioned an extremely rare genetic condition not usually seen outside of textbooks: Hutchinson–Gilford progeria syndrome, typically referred to simply as progeria (Henig 2005). In 1998, before his second birthday, Sam was officially diagnosed with progeria.

As physicians, Sam's parents knew the prognosis was dire. Children with progeria suffer all the symptoms of old age, with symptoms emerging in the first 2 years of life. Their eyesight deteriorates, their skin thins, they lose their hair and body fat, and their joints and arteries stiffen. Heart attacks and strokes caused by cardiovascular disease are the leading causes of death in patients with progeria, occurring at an average 14.7 years (Gordon, Brown, and Collins 1993; Sarkar and Shinton 2001). Around the time Sam was diagnosed, there were only about 60 children in North America known to be living with the disorder (Henig 2005). Not only was Sam's health rapidly declining, but there was little hope for a cure on the horizon.

For one thing, it's very difficult to determine the underlying causes of such rare genetic diseases. It's like hunting for a needle in a haystack. In this case, the haystack is comprised of the 3 billion DNA base pairs in a human genome. Most of the human genome is identical from person to person, with about 10 million single nucleotide polymorphisms (SNPs) (changes in the DNA sequence) that make each of us unique (Genetics Home Reference 2017e). But most of those variants do not cause health problems. Figuring out if a variant causes a disease usually requires samples from hundreds or even thousands of patients to sort out the noise (benign variations) from the truly pathogenic ones.

Finding the gene for this particular disease, his family worried, might be especially hard.

Because of her scientific training, Gordon knew that basic research would be necessary to uncover the cause of progeria. Berns, who also had a public health degree from Harvard, knew that obtaining funding through the NIH was their best chance to receive support from science programs. Gordon and her husband quickly launched the Progeria Research Foundation (PRF).

Gordon served as the medical director and Berns worked on its board, with her sister Audrey Gordon, a lawyer, later becoming the PRF's executive director (Rothman 2014).

Sam's parents had the good fortune of connecting with Francis Collins early on. Collins is currently head of NIH, but in the early 2000s was head of the NIH's National Human Genome Research Institute. He led the public branch of the race to sequence the human genome and led the team that discovered the gene (*CFTR*) for cystic fibrosis in 1989 (Iannuzzi et al. 1989). Collins had once treated a patient with progeria, so he was familiar with the disease (Henig 2005).

They also got advice from Sharon and Patrick Terry, a couple who had essentially created a blueprint for accelerating research into rare diseases after their two children were diagnosed with PXE (pseudoxanthoma elasticum), an inherited condition that causes certain tissues in the body to become mineralized (Genetics Home Reference 2017c) (see the sidebar *Genetic Alliance's Efforts in Rare Disease Research*). With guidance from the Terrys and others, Sam's family set out to do everything they could to help children with progeria. The odds were stacked against them, as this disease is so extremely rare. But they ended up making good progress in an especially short period of time.

SIDEBAR: GENETIC ALLIANCE'S EFFORTS IN RARE DISEASE RESEARCH

Sharon Terry

President and CEO, Genetic Alliance

It happened out of the blue. Sharon Terry was taking her young children to a specialist to look at an odd skin rash they had each developed. She ended up learning they both had a rare, incurable genetic disease, with potentially serious effects. Not one to back away from a challenge, Terry and her husband dove straight into the business of finding new treatments for their kids. In the process, she became the longtime leader of a unique organization, Genetic Alliance, which provides resources and guidance to hundreds of advocacy groups and others seeking cures for rare diseases.

Over the 20-plus years she's been doing this work, she says some important steps have been taken. "One crucial thing we've realized is every disease can be stratified into subcategories," says Terry in our interview (Terry 2017). Even common diseases, such as diabetes or breast cancer, actually have lots of subtypes, many of which are rare. "As a result, the whole concept of rare disease is changing. It's no longer just about genetic syndromes, but includes a growing list of common disease subtypes as well," she explains.

Also, diseases don't exist as silos. There are bridges—or common biological pathways—from disease to disease. You might, for example, find a biological disruption in a type of diabetes that is also found in a rare genetic disease that presents in a very different way. "There are a limited number of phenotypes the body expresses. As a result, data about a phenotype in one condition may actually be relevant to another," says Terry.

These realizations have inspired some to take a new approach to medical research in general. One of the big challenges has always been getting a suitable cohort of patients for trials: to get statistically relevant results, researchers want all the patients in a trial to be similar, and they want lots of them. "For rare diseases, this has always been a particular problem," Terry explains. "We used to say that creating these cohorts was like 'finding a needle in a haystack.' But now, it seems more accurate to say that the entire haystack is made out of needles."

When Terry and her husband helped found the advocacy group PXE International they wanted to advance and spur research on a specific rare disease. They ended up developing a blueprint for rare disease research that included building tools for all advocacy groups to collect their own clinical information and biological samples, as well as helping them design research programs and clinical trials.

The vision at Genetic Alliance was to allow many other disease groups to follow this path. The group created a set of enabling tools, including a biorepository (http://www .biobank.org/) and registry (Genetic Alliance 2017a). The idea was that each group would use these tools to work on their own diseases. "But it turns out it is technically difficult for disease advocacy groups to capture information, even if they have the right tools. A few groups have copied the PXE model, but we have not yet achieved anything close to a critical mass and significant change in the pace of rare disease research," says Terry, underscoring the challenges of medical research in general, let alone in rare diseases.

Genetic Alliance has now shifted its focus to a new platform called Platform for Engaging Everyone Responsibly (www.peerplatform.org) (Genetic Alliance 2017b). This novel registry collects data from patients with any disease, while helping them learn about their condition. They can also share their own health data with researchers and advocacy groups if they choose. "We're hoping this will spur a generation of entirely new hypotheses and research that is not constrained by the old ways of defining cohorts," explains Terry.

The platform populates three levels of data. The first asks general questions and provides feedback about how one patient compares to others. The next level collects common data elements (http://www.nlm.nih.gov/cde/) established by the National Institutes of Health. These allow researchers to measure and report on the same things, in a similar fashion, across multiple diseases. Finally, at the third level, the questions get in depth and very specific to particular conditions. If patients choose to, they can also share their data securely with carefully screened researchers and other third parties.

"Ultimately, to get to our own Big Data moment, we'll need a federation of a lot of databases," says Terry. "Connecting to partners supports a whole new approach to medical research in which communities drive research" (Terry 2017).

Rapid Progress against Progeria

The PRF began by setting up a biological repository and started tracking down children with the disease, eventually finding a total of over 100 through an innovative public awareness campaign and a webpage on the PRF website: http://www.progeriaresearch.org/find-the-other-150/, which contains information about progeria in approximately 20 languages (Progeria Research Foundation 2016). With so few children affected, each new child who is identified adds tremendously to the data that can be generated about progeria.

In November 2001, there were a few hints where to look for the causative gene for progeria. W. Ted Brown, a leading expert on progeria and the doctor who confirmed Sam's diagnosis, was already targeting a region on chromosome 1 based on molecular analysis from a set of identical twins with the disorder that he had treated (Sarkar and Shinton 2001). By the following year, researchers at the University of Michigan were expanding on the data from Brown's lab, looking to see if the mutation on chromosome 1 affected nearby genes as well. Not long after, Francis Collins' post-doctoral researcher found two patients with a section of DNA that was inherited from only one parent—not from both parents as normal—and hypothesized the progeria gene must be in that region (Eriksson et al. 2003).

With the coincident timing of the Human Genome Project, Collins' researcher was able to see what genes were present in the region she had identified. After some additional sleuthing and molecular analysis of more patient samples from the PRF, the search for the gene that causes progeria was over (Rothman 2014).

Remarkably, just 5 years after Sam's diagnosis, they had determined that progeria is caused by mutations in the *LMNA* gene (Eriksson et al. 2003; Rothman 2014). This gene has about 25,000 base pairs, and the most common cause of progeria is a SNP—the 1824C>T (G608G) mutation—that results in a shortened protein. More than 20 other mutations have now been identified that cause the disorder (Eriksson et al. 2003; Taimen et al. 2009). Once the researchers identified the causative gene, Gordon's and Berg's attention then turned toward a cure.

Again, the researchers had a little luck. It turned out that *lamin A*, one of the variant proteins encoded by *LMNA*, was very well studied as a target for cancer research. There were already several drugs in development that act on the gene's product (Kelland et al. 2001). PRF sponsored some animal and other laboratory studies to see if any of these drugs seemed to block the damage caused by the *lamin A* mutation. They found a promising treatment (lonafarnib). Next, they enlisted Mark Kieran, a pediatric brain cancer specialist at Boston Children's Hospital and the Dana-Farber Cancer Institute, and one of the few specialists on this class of drugs, to help them design a study.

In 2007, a clinical trial was launched to study lonafarnib (a farnesyltransferase inhibitor) in children with classic progeria (Gordon et al. 2012). This remarkable study enrolled children from 16 countries. It was also unusual because there was no placebo (sugar pill), which is standard protocol for such trials. Instead of comparing the effects of the drug to a placebo, researchers used data about how the disease typically progresses to determine whether or not the drug was helping the children. Of 25 children who completed the study, all showed improvement in one of several ways: weight gain, hearing, bone structure, and/or flexibility of their blood vessels (Gordon et al. 2012).

That last finding was a "home run," according to Leslie Gordon, because changes in blood vessels are linked to the heart attacks and strokes that are the major causes of death among kids with progeria (Hamilton 2012). A second trial in 37 children, which combined lonafarnib with pravastatin and zoledronic acid, found only bone density was improved over using lonafarnib alone (Gordon et al. 2016). Finding a new drug typically takes about 20 years. But in less than a decade, PRF had identified the gene underlying progeria, found a potential treatment, and completed a clinical trial, with the results from a second clinical trial coming just 4 years later.

Sam Berns participated in the first trial, which he described as "rigorous." He went on to say, "I remind myself I'm helping researchers develop treatments for myself and other kids with progeria, and that drives me along" (Progeria Research Foundation 2012). Tragically, Sam died not long after the drug trial was over. But he was described by his mom as an otherwise typical kid who had friends and a "fantastic" life (Hamilton 2012). His family's fight against progeria is also the subject of a film called *Life According to Sam*, which was shown at the 2013 Sundance Film Festival (Fine 2013).

Progeria research has also contributed to research into common diseases of aging, as well as aging itself. "It has told us something pretty profound, namely that all of us are making little bits of this same toxic protein," Collins said. "Kids with progeria are making a lot. We're making a little bit. And as our cells get older and older, they start making more" (Hamilton 2012). Lab studies suggest that progerin production may be triggered by damage to telomeres, which are the ends of chromosomes and are already implicated in aging research (Cao et al. 2011). In addition, progeria, along with several other rare diseases, has provided substantial insight into the molecular mechanisms underlying skin cancer (Capell, Tlougan, and Orlow 2009).

Today, Sam's parents continue their work with the PRF. The organization has an ongoing campaign to find all children with progeria and an active fundraising arm. Importantly, PRF continues to work with scientists to identify new treatments for progeria. An ongoing clinical trial is evaluating the maximum tolerated dose for everolimus, an MTOR inhibitor, taken with lonafarnib. The PRF will finance and coordinate a phase II trial for the effectiveness of the drug combination (Progeria Research Foundation 2017b). The PRF maintains a cell and tissue bank that researchers can access for patient samples. These samples are an important component of ongoing basic research and early preclinical trials of medications (Progeria Research Foundation 2017a).

Rise of the Citizen-Scientist

For families of patients with rare diseases, it can seem like science moves at a snail's pace. Without a large population of affected individuals, it can be next to impossible for researchers to uncover the molecular basis for a rare disorder or gather enough patients for a clinical trial. Indeed, single arm clinical trials (performed without a control group or placebo) are common for very rare diseases because there are so few patients affected. Some ultrarare diseases may only affect one or two people worldwide. And obtaining research funding for these disorders can be difficult, which limits the progress scientists can make. But a growing number of patients and their families are taking steps to become more active participants in their medical research and are spearheading fundraising efforts designed to speed up the hunt for a cure.

The Terrys had mobilized as soon as they learned about their children's diagnosis with PXE in 1994 (see the sidebar *Genetic Alliance's Efforts in Rare Disease Research*). Patrick Terry was managing large construction projects at the time, and Sharon was a former nun and college chaplain. Though not scientists or doctors, like Gordon and Berns, together the Terrys read every article they could find about PXE and analyzed how medical research works. Patients with PXE often have unusual skin lesions, changes in their eyes, and even partial vision loss, as well as cardiovascular and digestive system symptoms. The disease is also rare, affecting only 1 in every 25,000 Americans (Genetics Home Reference 2017c).

They quickly realized that finding new drugs is a long and complex process. Although things have changed, rare disease research was practically nonexistent at that time. Drug companies were most interested in diseases that affect many people (such as heart disease, diabetes, or arthritis) and therefore have "blockbuster" potential.

The Terrys were also dismayed to learn that academic scientists tend not to collaborate very well, because the system doesn't reward them for doing so. Instead, they are very competitive, typically keeping their data secret until they have been first to publish about it. With a rare disease like PXE, the Terrys reasoned, coordination and collaboration would be key to making progress. Otherwise, how could they amass enough data points to make useful discoveries? And even more discouraging, scientists often didn't share their results with the very patients they were collecting samples from (Marcus 2011).

So, the Terrys mapped a strategy for rapidly accelerating the research process and managing much of it themselves. They launched a global advocacy group called PXE International, started raising money, established a blood and tissue bank and a patient registry, discovered the gene themselves working at night on a borrowed lab bench, patented the gene, created a diagnostic test, and began gathering data about how the disease progressed in different patients. They eventually also established several labs dedicated to research on drugs for PXE.

Those are all crucial ingredients for an effective research program. Blood and tissue samples are studied to understand the basic biology of the disease—what causes it, how it manifests, and how to follow its progress. It is also important to understand the disease's natural history, i.e., how it usually progresses. Most diseases progress differently among patients. Understanding how that process varies helps scientists to better design clinical trials and know the entire range of signs and symptoms of whether or not a treatment is working.

One key goal of such families now is to find drugs that may already be partially, or even wholly, developed that seem promising for "their" disease, as in the example described above of lonafarnib for progeria. Many drugs fail to reach market either because they don't work quite well enough in a particular condition, or because they just won't make enough money to warrant commercialization. Sometimes researchers can find new uses for such drugs, saving a lot of time in the development process. The key is understanding the basic biology of a condition: what molecules are affected by the genetic mutation? Then, researchers can sort through drugs that may have already been developed against the same molecular target.

In the process of setting this up for PXE, Sharon became the first nonscientist and member of an advocacy group listed on a gene patent, when she got her name on the patent for the PXE gene (PXE International 2004). The gene was discovered by Sharon and Pat at that borrowed lab bench space at Harvard with a collaboration with the University of Hawaii. As a discoverer of the gene, Sharon had the right to be named on the patent, and thought it was crucial for her name to be on that patent, because the Terrys didn't want anyone else to "own" the PXE gene and block research on it. Rather, they wanted as many people as possible doing research on PXE.

"We are stewards of this gene, and we are responsible for using it to develop diagnostics and therapeutics that are accessible and affordable," Sharon stated in PXE International's August 2004 press release announcing the patent (PXE International 2004). (Note: The Supreme Court has since made a ruling that invalidates the gene patents, including the PXE patent, but that ruling supports the Terrys' goal, which is to make it easier for researchers to work on rare disease genes [Denniston 2013].)

Patrick Terry is now a biotech entrepreneur and helped found the breakthrough personalized medicine company, Genomic Health. Sharon is president and CEO of the Genetic Alliance, an organization that provided the Terrys with tremendous support and lots of information during their odyssey (see the sidebar *Genetic Alliance's Efforts in Rare Disease Research*). She has written a detailed account of her family's journey for the journal *Health Affairs* (Terry 2003). Over the years, she has also counseled hundreds of families, including Sam Berns', on how to follow the same steps she and Patrick took when they learned their children had a rare genetic disease.

Leslie Gordon and Scott Berns' "mom and pop" story of rare disease drug research is exceptional, but it's not unique. More and more family members are getting involved in rare disease research for their loved ones. Brothers Ben and Jamie Heywood founded PatientsLikeMe, a website based platform that brings people with disorders together to share their experiences and their health data, after their brother Stephen was diagnosed with ALS at age 29 (PatientsLikeMe 2017). Amylynne Volker, mother of Nicholas Volker (see the section *Advancing Technologies: Precision Medicine for Rare Diseases*), started the One in a Billion Foundation, which focuses on the use of whole genome sequencing (Nicholas Volker, One in a Billion Foundation 2017). Patient and family engagement can take a variety of forms, from simply donating money to existing organizations or directly to hospitals and labs, to helping scientists determine what research studies should be performed and directing spending.

The Cystic Fibrosis Foundation, is another example. Cystic fibrosis (CF) is an inherited disease caused by mutations in the *CFTR* gene that prevents proper chloride ion movement in and out of cells and results in a severe buildup of mucus in the lungs and other organs (Tsui and Dorfman 2013; Cutting 2015). The frequency of the disorder varies by ethnic background, affecting approximately 1:2,500–3,500 Caucasian newborns, but is much less common in African Americans and Asian Americans (Genetics Home Reference 2012).

Because cystic fibrosis is relatively rare in the overall population, drug companies at the time had little interest in finding a treatment. Together with the Cystic Fibrosis Foundation, prominent Boston businessman Joe O'Donnell raised $175 million for research on a treatment for the disease (see the section in Chapter 8, *High-Throughput Screening*) (McGrory 2012). O'Donnell's son Joey had died at age 12 from CF. That's an extraordinary amount of money for one person to raise, and the story demonstrates how pivotal financing is in a high-cost arena such as drug development. The partnership between O'Donnell and the Foundation is one of the most productive to date in the realm of rare diseases. As a result of that collaboration, the drug ivacaftor (Kalydeco) was launched in 2012 by Vertex Pharmaceuticals, marking a major milestone in rare disease drug discovery and development.

Another inspiring story surrounds the Crowley family, whose children both have Pompe disease, a genetic lysosomal disorder that causes a deadly accumulation of glycogen in the body. The infantile early-onset form of the disease is particularly debilitating and usually lethal, killing patients in early childhood, while the later-onset type (which includes infantile onset without cardiomyopathy) is somewhat milder (Genetics Home Reference 2016; Leslie and Bailey 2017). The family received the first devastating diagnosis, for their daughter Megan, in 1998, when she was less than 2 years old. Further testing showed her younger brother Patrick was also affected (Moran 2016).

A couple years later, the children's father, John Crowley, heard wheelchair-bound Christopher Reeve give an inspiring talk (Davies 2010). With no cure in sight for his children, Crowley decided to take action himself and founded biotech firm Novazyme, which eventually grew into an 80-person company before its acquisition by pharmaceutical rare disease specialist, Genzyme, which eventually launched a drug that Crowley's children are now taking (Davies 2010). Since then, Crowley has gone on to found two other biotech companies, Orexigen Therapeutics in 2003 and Amicus Therapeutics in 2005, where he currently serves as Chairman and CEO, working on a broad range of rare diseases (Davies 2010; Amicus Therapeutics 2011).

In another example of how to speed rare disease research, patient advocacy groups are sharing their samples and clinical data to support their cause. The Collaborative Trajectory Analysis Project (cTAP) is a novel collaboration between advocacy groups, pharmaceutical companies, experts in statistical analysis, and leading researchers. It is just one example of diverse stakeholders working together to accelerate cures for rare disease (in cTAP's case, for Duchenne muscular dystrophy) through better use of limited patient data and advanced analytics. By bringing together these stakeholders, the group recently published two peer-reviewed studies that identified variation seen in Duchenne patients' abilities to perform a 6-minute walk test, an important measurement that is used in clinical trials (Goemans et al. 2016; Mercuri et al. 2016). Future clinical trials in this patient population can take into account this variation during study enrollment. This is analogous to better discrimination of patients with different cancer subtypes through genomic testing, in order to enroll patients that are as similar as possible. As we will describe in Chapter 10, wearable devices or other digital methods can capture differences in gait (Tupa et al. 2015), providing real-world evidence that might lead to better identification of patients who are likely to improve on a drug.

SIDEBAR: USING DATA TO IMPROVE CLINICAL TRIALS IN DUCHENNE

Susan J. Ward, PhD

Executive Director, Collaborative Trajectory Analysis Project (cTAP)

The frustration of some Duchenne patients' mothers, after a heartbreaking string of failed clinical trials, was one of the things that fueled creation of the Collaborative Trajectory Analysis Project (cTAP). It's a coalition of patient advocacy groups, major pharmaceutical and biotech companies, leading academic research groups, and experts in complex data analysis. At its core is a registry of data about the health of more than 1,300 patients, representing more than 10,000 clinic visits. The goal is to fix the problems hobbling Duchenne trials.

Duchenne is caused by a genetic mutation that mainly affects boys and prevents production of dystrophin—a protein key for proper muscle function. The disease is deadly and very difficult to treat. Despite a dozen or more trials, only two drugs have been approved. And in some cases, parents felt their children were doing well on a drug that was never approved. Some experts called for bigger trials. Because Duchenne is relatively rare, it's hard to get a lot of patients in a single trial.

But cTAP has a different view. They think novel statistical methods and better trial design can accelerate Duchenne drug development without needing big cohorts. Using innovative tools from James Signorovitch and the Analysis Group, they are analyzing the natural progression of the disease from a new perspective. Their goal is to create better processes and tools for trial design.

For example, it is widely stated that Duchenne patients become wheelchair bound around the age of 10–12. But several years ago, Susan Ward, now cTAP's Executive Director, had a passionate discussion with some Duchenne patient advocates about what constitutes "sufficient evidence" to declare that a drug "works." One mother was emphatic that if a patient was still walking at age 16, then the drug he was taking must be working: 16 year olds with Duchenne can't walk, she argued. She challenged Ward to go online and find evidence of patients that age still walking. "I did, and I found one, and then I found another, and another," Ward says (Ward 2017).

Ward then dug into the clinical trial data and was surprised by what she found. "It wasn't clear at that time how much variation there was in disease progression between individual patients," she says. The first publications demonstrating the variation in walking ability over time did not appear until 2013. "Until then, people had also not fully appreciated that the decline in mobility is not linear," she explains. Rather, a patient's ability to walk reaches a peak, levels off, then declines slowly until there is a sudden steep decline. The patient then becomes fully wheelchair-bound.

But there is tremendous variation in how long that "leveling off" period lasts. "You have some kids who can no longer walk by the age of 7, and others are still walking at age 16, 17 or older," Ward says.

A walking test has long been one of the major clinical endpoints in a Duchenne trial. But with so much variation between patients, it's often very difficult to spot trends in the data from such studies. cTAP's founders wondered if that could explain the trial failures.

So, with the encouragement and support of patient advocates, Ward and her collaborators launched cTAP in early 2015 to reinvent Duchenne trial design. She's heartened by the progress they've made so far, which has led to two publications already

(*Business Wire* 2016a). "We're gratified we've been able to bring lots of key players to the table," Ward says. That includes the leading academic groups and almost every company with drugs for Duchenne in clinical development.

"It is not always easy to get collaboration in research," Ward explains. People have worked for years collecting patient data, which is a precious resource. "Creating a structure that lets everyone in a community to learn as much as possible from patient data, equitably, without depriving the academic experts of the publications and grants they need to justify those years of hard work, is always a challenge," Ward says.

Today, there are numerous organizations, like the Heywood brothers' PatientsLikeMe, Genetic Alliance, PRF, the Cystic Fibrosis Foundation, and cTAP that are bringing together patients and families with rare diseases with doctors and scientists around the world. Many rare disease patient advocacy groups have created international registries, sometimes with biorepositories of patient samples, and are using that information, and their financial backing, to have a say in what kind of research is performed and who can use the samples (Mascalzoni, Paradiso, and Hansson 2014).

Advancing Technologies: Precision Medicine for Rare Diseases

Historically, rare disease research has been slow, partially due to the techniques available for research. Prior to the completion of the Human Genome Project, finding the causative gene for disease was laborious and extremely expensive. For example, in 1989, identifying *CFTR* as the gene responsible for cystic fibrosis took 8 years and required numerous molecular techniques such as positional cloning and animal models to confirm which variants conferred the disease (Tsui and Dorfman 2013). In addition to the time involved in locating the genes, there was substantial cost for each discovery. Rare disease research was even slower, with fewer patients to draw samples from.

With a completed map of the human genome, molecular techniques like sequencing took off and with it rare disease research. Today, massively parallel, high-throughput sequencing has enabled whole genome sequencing (WGS) and whole exome sequencing (WES). Patients with rare diseases can have their DNA sequenced, and in some cases, the cause of the disorder can be identified by comparing the sequences of patients to those of healthy individuals, like their parents, or others with presumably the same diagnosis.

Thanks to such advances, doctors are even able to diagnose conditions that have never been described before.

The poster child for the success in WES and WGS technology is Nicholas Volker. Dubbed *The First Child Saved by DNA Sequencing* by Matthew Herper of *Forbes*, Nicholas seemed to be on death's doorstep by the time he was 6 years old. Chronic inflammation had led to the removal of most of his colon and doctors were puzzled over what could have caused his illness (Herper 2011).

After more than a hundred surgeries, as a last resort Nicholas' doctors tried something novel: sequencing his DNA. Miraculously, not only did they find the genetic mutation that caused his extremely early-onset inflammatory bowel disease, but the diagnosis (an *XIAP* mutation) pointed doctors in the direction for a potential treatment: a core blood transplant (Zimmerman 2014). Years later, Nicholas is able to eat regular food and there are no signs of recurrence of his bowel disease (Herper 2011; Zimmerman 2014).

Matt Might, a computer scientist, and his wife Cristina found themselves in a similar situation with their son, Bertrand. Soon after his birth in December 2007, the Mights began to worry there was something wrong with their son. They described Bertrand as "jiggly" and often inconsolable (Might 2012; Mnookin 2014). It wasn't until their son's 6-month checkup that Bertrand's pediatrician agreed with the parents. Two months later, an appointment with a developmental specialist confirmed: their son had brain damage (Mnookin 2014).

This was the start of months of testing. An MRI found his brain was completely normal—the initial diagnosis by the developmental specialist had been wrong. Other diagnoses for rare disorders came and were ruled out one at a time: ataxia–telangiectasia, metabolic disorders, Allgrove syndrome, Rett syndrome, Schinzel-Giedion (Might 2012). At a loss for answers in their home of Salt Lake City, the Mights traveled across the country to Duke University where they met with a geneticist and other specialists (Might 2012; Mnookin 2014).

That meeting with geneticist Vandana Shashi proved to be a turning point for the Mights. A few months after their visit to Duke, Shashi contacted the couple to see if they would be interested in a new study using DNA sequencing for undiagnosed disorders. By comparing the DNA from both Matt and Cristina to Bertrand's, scientists hoped to find a red herring—the gene responsible for Bertrand's symptoms (Might 2012; Mnookin 2014).

Using WES, researchers at Duke narrowed down the possible results to roughly a dozen genes and honed in on one: *NGLY1*. The enzyme produced by *NGLY1* is involved in glycosylation, a process where sugar molecules are attached to fats and proteins (National Organization for Rare Disorders 2015). But this particular glycosylation disorder had not been seen before: Bertrand would be the first.

In May 2012, the Mights met with the Duke team once again. WES had likely found the genetic cause of Bertrand's illness and the couple was astonished to learn that each of them also had a different *NGYL1* variant and produced half the amount of N-glycanase 1 (the enzyme made by *NGLY1*) of people without the variants. Bertrand had inherited both variants, leaving him with no enzyme (Might 2012). Their daughter (who did not have the disorder) and any subsequent children had a 25% chance of having the same disease as Bertrand (Mnookin 2014). Though the doctors were careful to admit that without other patients with the same genetic mutation and symptoms, their finding wasn't definitive; but finding another child with the same disorder would be a challenge, if not impossible.

Soon after Bertrand's diagnosis, Matt wrote a blog post, "Hunting Down My Son's Killer," and posted the link on Twitter (Might 2012). In the following days, the post was shared across social media platforms, reaching untold millions of readers (see the section *Leveraging Social Media for Science* below). The end result: 15 more cases of *NGLY1* deficiency were found (Might 2012). In 2014, Might and another father wrote a commentary for *Genetics in Medicine* detailing how WES and communication between families and doctors is changing rare disease research (Might and Wilsey 2014).

Other rare disorders are benefitting from WES/WGS and other advanced molecular diagnostics. A patient was diagnosed with Bartter syndrome, a disorder that affects the kidneys, using WES (Choi et al. 2009), while in a pilot study of 12 patients with undiagnosed disorders, WES of the patient and their unaffected parents yielded a likely diagnosis in half (Need et al. 2012). Proteomics and metabolomics are two other approaches that have been used, along with genomics, to investigate Castleman disease (Newman et al. 2015).

But WGS and WES don't always find the "smoking gun" for patients with suspected genetic disorders. That's been the experience for Eric and Tricia Edwards, whose son Beckett has undergone both WES and WGS. Beckett's muscles were "floppy" after birth, and by the time he was 2 1/2 years old, he had begun to lose his emerging vocabulary (Mullin 2017). After WES revealed no likely genetic culprit for his disorder, the Edwards family underwent WGS. Including both parents can make it easier for doctors to find variants that might be the cause of the child's disorder, since genetic variants that the (unaffected) parents also have are presumed benign. But in Beckett's case, even scanning the entire genome yielded no obvious clues.

Liz Worthey, a geneticist at the HudsonAlpha Institute of Biotechnology, where Beckett's WGS was performed, has noted, "Often times in the genome we're finding the variant, but that gene or that region is just not associated with disease as far as we know, so we're not going to be able to say anything for sure" (Mullin 2017). This is a point also made by Isaac Kohane, a bioinformatician at Harvard Medical School. "Our ability to distinguish what actually might cause disease is still quite crude, so we have an unknown false-negative rate," he has said (Mullin 2017). This makes finding other patients with the same symptoms so important, since unrelated patients with the same genetic variants can point doctors to a new disease-causing mutation, like Matt Might found with *NGLY1*.

Molecular diagnostics are not the only technologies that are aiding rare disease research. For decades, clinical geneticists have relied on microarrays, genetic sequencing, metabolic tests, and many more technologies to make a diagnosis. Now, they have a new tool in their arsenal: a camera (see the sidebar *Applying Facial Recognition to Rare Disease Diagnosis*). Facial recognition software has been developed that can identify DiGeorge syndrome (22q11.2 deletion syndrome) (Kruszka et al. 2017) and this technology is being applied to other rare diseases.

SIDEBAR: APPLYING FACIAL RECOGNITION TO RARE DISEASE DIAGNOSIS

Dekel Gelbman, MBA

Chief Executive Officer, FDNA

Looking at children's faces to determine if they have a rare disease is an art practiced by geneticists for more than 50 years. Through experience, these specialists learned how the length of the ears, the spread of the eyes, the shape of the space between the lips and nose, and, most importantly, the pattern created by these traits (also called "gestalt"), pointed to particular genetic disorders. It's crucial to get the diagnosis right, because only once the genetic cause is correctly determined can patients get the most appropriate care and hopefully achieve better health.

With the dawn of genomics, this task was both made easier and more difficult, explains Dekel Gelbman, CEO of FDNA, which uses facial analysis software (Face2Gene) to help healthcare professionals to identify phenotypic signs of rare genetic conditions. "On the one hand, you could much more easily diagnose common conditions," he told us (Gelbman 2017). "But doctors also started getting many more cases with 'variants of unknown significance', which complicated things." Such variations are unusual and have not yet been clearly linked to any particular syndromes.

Enter FDNA.

The company was formed after its founders had done pioneering work in facial analysis and were looking for new applications, particularly in medicine, for their expertise. FDNA cofounder Moti Shniberg founded facial recognition firm Face.com, which was acquired by Facebook for approximately $55 million in 2012 (Tsotsis 2012). FDNA's other cofounder is Lior Wolf, a professor at Tel Aviv University and pioneer in the computer vision field.

After evaluating multiple opportunities, the team decided to focus on rare diseases both because of the good fit with their expertise and the tremendous unmet need. The company estimates that about 1 in 10 people, or 30 million total, in the United States have a rare disease. Globally, 350 million people have one of the over 7,000 known rare diseases. One thing that distinguishes the patient experience in this area, is that they must often go through a medical odyssey to get a firm diagnosis. Shortening that process could extend lives and save money.

FDNA develops artificial intelligence-based algorithms that can scan faces and highlight actionable genetic insights, starting from a simple facial photo and going deeper into a comprehensive patient phenotyping process. "The outcome is a comprehensive list of phenotypes our algorithms have detected," says Gelbman. Importantly, their tools can also predict other traits, for example, mental defects, that may not be visible, but are associated with the morphologic features detected. Gelbman notes that while the company started by manually guiding the computers to think like geneticists, they evolved to relying almost exclusively on deep learning—letting the computer systems teach themselves. "The interesting thing is," he says, "That once we made that switch users noticed and they said 'something seems better' with how the results were being delivered" (Gelbman 2017).

The company's business model is also innovative. They provide their app for free to physicians. In exchange they get to use the de-identified data the doctors generate. "We comply with all privacy requirement around the world," Gelbman says. "We have structured our IT system such that the patient health information is stored in separate 'vaults' from the de-identified information about lab data and phenotypes, which allows us to link information about genetics to phenotypic data, such as facial features."

Besides setting up the infrastructure to make this practical, the key challenge for FDNA has been getting enough data on each specific syndrome. New syndromes, after all, are being discovered every day, and some of them are extremely rare, with only a few patients reported even the whole world over. "We now have more than 2,000 syndromes where we have images data represented in our classifiers," says Gelbman. (The classifiers are sets of mathematical formulas that describe specific disorders.)

"It was a challenge to grow those first datasets," Gelbman admits. But now, he and his team are confident that their business will evolve along with medical science. "I believe that in 5 years, every child will be sequenced and phenotyping will be even more important than it is today, as this will tie back to the raw genomic data of a person and help 'unlock their code' to explain all disease states," he says. Already, genomics companies and other groups are interested in using the technology for research beyond rare diseases, including autism. "Who knows what other discoveries our data will lead to?" Gelbman says.

Advanced pattern/facial recognition methods, like the kind used by FDNA, are just one aspect of AI that is already being used for healthcare (see Chapter 10 for more on AI). As we described earlier (see Chapter 3), IBM Watson was able to correctly diagnose a patient in Tokyo with a rare form of cancer that doctors had misdiagnosed because it was able to scan through massive amounts of scientific research, matching the correct diagnosis to the data from the patient's medical record. University Hospital Marburg in Germany is using the system to help doctors there with undiagnosed patients. The cognitive computing system will be used to sift through the immense amount of published medical literature in hopes of finding a diagnosis for these patients (Medium 2016). Boston Children's Hospital is using the system to shorten the time to diagnosis for steroid resistant nephrotic syndrome, a rare kidney disease, and other undiagnosed disorders (Monegain 2015).

Mining the medical literature isn't confined to medical professionals with access to cognitive computing solutions like IBM Watson or DeepMind, however. Websites, such as FindZebra Findzebra.com and even the Google search engine, have the potential to find the proverbial "needle in a haystack" (Svenstrup, Jørgensen, and Winther 2015). Each rare disease that's identified and thoroughly described in the medical literature can make it easier to diagnose future patients with the disorder and to find variation within that patient population, as cTAP learned for Duchenne muscular dystrophy. For patients like Beckett Edwards that are still left without a diagnosis, stories like Bertrand Might's give hope that these technologies and finding others with a similar disorder will ultimately yield an answer.

Leveraging Social Media for Science

Although genetic sequencing was responsible for finding the cause of Bertrand Might's disorder, it is the power of social media that was responsible for the family finding others affected by the same glycosylation disorder (Mnookin 2014). Patients with rare diseases are using social media to find others with the same disorder and build a support network. The Progeria Research Foundation, Genetic Alliance, PatientsLikeMe, and other organizations provide information about their disease for patients who are newly diagnosed and connect them to other families who can offer advice about clinical trials, medications, and doctors who might be helpful. In fact, according to a 2011 report from the Pew Research Center, more than half of patients with rare diseases turned to peers for information and support (Fox 2011).

For Deb McGarry, a patient outside of Chicago, finding other patients with her rare disease online gave her information and encouragement about her outlook—something she didn't feel the doctors who diagnosed her provided (Meyer 2012). McGarry, who had a spontaneous coronary artery dissection (SCAD), said in an interview with the *Chicago Tribune*, "With rare diseases, you can't walk into your doctor's office and find the support and information you need. I think it's absolutely amazing to be able to get on your computer and find people who are experiencing the same thing as you" (Meyer 2012).

And patient advocacy groups are doing more than developing a support network for patients, some are also actively engaged in scientific discovery, like the PRF. McGarry and other patients from the online SCAD group are now working with the Mayo Clinic on a large-scale study of the disorder (Mayo Clinic 2017a). This is an important advance, since much of the medical literature for SCAD consists of case reports. Since working with the online community, Mayo Researchers have developed a patient registry and are working on several projects related to the treatment of SCAD. Sharonne Hayes, one of the doctors at Mayo, has said of patient-initiated research, "Still in its infancy, this may prove to be the new 'gold standard' for the study of uncommon medical conditions" (Loew 2011).

Future for Patients with Rare Diseases

As the amount of big data grows and expands, diagnosing and treating patients with rare diseases will get easier. Identifying the causative mutation has already progressed due to WES and WGS. As variant classification continues to improve, doctors will be able to say with greater certainty whether a variant is pathogenic or not. While that will improve genomic medicine overall, for patients with rare diseases it will be of even greater importance. Already, patient advocacy groups are creating their own patient databases and biorepositories for research and demanding a seat at the table with researchers.

Instead of the years that it took Bertrand Might to be diagnosed correctly, future patients might find it takes a matter of months, or even less time, as the technical aspects of genomic analysis improve. Matt Might, a computer scientist, used his skills to develop a precision medicine algorithm that puts the diagnostic odyssey into a step-by-step plan that parents, families, and clinicians can follow (Fliesler 2016). As Might stated at a White House summit on the Precision Medicine Initiative, "Patients are required to navigate the Byzantine academic-industrial complex on their own, with little to no resources for figuring out either what to do or how to do it. We can and must do better" (Fliesler 2016).

As search engines get better at handling queries and social media's influence continues to grow, it will be easier for patients with rare diseases to find each other (CG Life 2017). Many more types of data will start to be gathered and combined, leading to wholly unexpected discoveries. Though in their infancy for rare disorders, artificial intelligence and cognitive computing systems used by IBM Watson, Alphabet's DeepMind, and start-ups like FDNA are expected to aid doctors in diagnosing patients faster and more accurately by combing through medical literature and other data. Someday, rare diseases will increasingly be solved by algorithms—researchers will analyze data and pluck out pivotal discoveries.

In the meantime, it's essential to push for more collaboration and coordination to make these projects work as quickly as they possibly can. That progress is already taking place. Besides the advocacy groups (such as PXE, PRF, and others) groups such as cTAP are increasingly bringing together multiple stakeholders in an attempt to improve study quality and reduce the time involved in drug discovery and treatments for rare disease research (see the sidebar *Using Data to Improve Clinical Trials in Duchenne*, and see the section in Chapter 8, *High-Throughput Screening*). cTAP's members already include most of the leading companies doing research in this field, including BioMarin, Bristol-Myers Squibb, Pfizer, and Sarepta, and they are already making notable progress with multiple publications. Their model could be another blueprint for forwarding rare disease research.

Social media outreach is becoming increasingly important in the rare disease community to connect patients and families with one another and to serve as a liaison to the medical and scientific community (Stone 2015). Groups like this can be incredibly useful for pharmaceutical companies to find the necessary number of patients for clinical trials. And where rare disease drug research has historically fallen to a few companies or government labs only, there is renewed interest in rare diseases as pharmaceutical companies are seeing potential profits.

Drug Developers Rally around a Business Opportunity

Pharmaceutical companies typically prefer drug candidates that address diseases that affect millions, or at least hundreds of thousands of people, so they can reach the "blockbuster" sales level of $1 billion annually. But a combination of regulations and business models has spurred research in rarer diseases, even some that are considered "ultrarare." With new data and technologies, this surge could continue or grow.

Part of the credit for the new interest in rare diseases goes to the 1983 Orphan Drug Act, which provided key incentives, to encourage the development of drugs for rare, or orphan, diseases. The Act offered an exclusive license for 7 years (giving companies a virtual monopoly), a 50% tax break on R&D costs, waiving of the user fees associated with getting a drug reviewed, grants for early stage research, and more. The results were dramatic. Prior to 1983, only 10 orphan or rare disease, drugs were approved in 10 years (Branca 2017). By 2014, nearly half the drugs approved by the FDA were for rare diseases, the most approvals since the Act passed. The orphan drug market is anticipated to grow at a rate of more than 11% per year and is expected to reach $214 million by 2022, well surpassing the 4% annual growth rate for drugs that treat common conditions (Guzowski 2015; PharmaVoice 2017).

Another key factor is the realization that rare diseases require a different business model to succeed. As we'll describe in Chapter 8, finding promising drug targets and moving through clinical trials is a time-consuming and expensive process. The costs involved for rare diseases aren't lower simply because the affected patient population is small. Consequently, the prices of these drugs tend to be higher than their common-disease counterparts, whose development costs can be spread out over a larger patient population. While most of the industry has focused on blockbuster drugs for common diseases, pioneers such as Genzyme have built a business model around rare diseases and proven they can deliver a healthy profit if developed relatively quickly and priced to deliver returns.

As noted at the start of this chapter, the costliest drugs in the world are for rare diseases. Though only available in Europe, Glybera, a gene therapy treatment for familial lipoprotein lipase deficiency, launched as the most expensive drug in the world at a cost of more than $1 million per year. That price seems to have shown where the tipping point is though, as the drug will be withdrawn in fall 2017 due to lack of commercial viability. But six other drugs (Ravicti, Spinraza, Lumizyme, Carbaglu, Actimmune, and Solaris) have annual costs of more than $500,000, while another five are more than $400,000 per year (Speights 2017). The key is that despite these astronomical prices, there are so few patients taking these drugs that any single payer (i.e., an insurance company or government health program) is not paying that much for them overall, compared to what they spend on other medications.

This realization helped the larger pharma industry develop a much greater appreciation for rare disease drugs, fueling some high-profile acquisitions. Genzyme was acquired by traditional pharma company Sanofi in 2011 for more than $20 billion and Sanofi has indicated they are open to further acquisitions in the rare disease pharma market (Ward 2016). In 2011, Alexion Pharmaceuticals paid $610 million in cash, with up to $470 million in milestone payments, for Enobia, which was developing lead product candidate ENB-0040 (asfotase alfa)—a human recombinant targeted alkaline phosphatase enzyme-replacement therapy for patients suffering with hypophosphatasia (HPP). HPP is an ultrarare, life-threatening, genetic metabolic disorder (Stynes 2011).

Other more recent acquisitions have included Lexington, and Massachusetts-based Shire buying Dyax for $5.9 billion for the smaller company's treatments for the rare hereditary angioedema, which affects about 1 in every 50,000 people. Sanofi's Genzyme division paid $300 million for global rights to Caprelsa, a treatment for the rare cancer, medullary thyroid carcinoma. One of the biggest recent deals, however, was Alexion's $8.4 billion purchase of Synageva BioPharma, which was in late-stage development of a treatment for lysosomal acid lipase deficiency, a condition that affects about 3,000 people (Guzowski 2015).

A key feature of all these acquisitions is that they mostly involve relatively late-stage drug candidates for diseases with no other known treatment. Acquisitions and partnerships like these can be the key to shortening the costly development timeframe and can minimize some of the risks inherent with early-stage drug candidates.

From 1998 to 2002, Genzyme worked on four different potential treatments for Pompe, the rare disease that afflicts John Crowley's children (see the section *Rise of the Citizen-Scientist*). In addition to a candidate drug developed internally with Duke University and Erasmus Medical Center

(The Netherlands) scientists, Genzyme collaborated with two other companies on alternatives. Genzyme also acquired Crowley's company Novazyme, which was working on its own treatment for Pompe. The four candidate drugs' study results were analyzed in 2002 and clinical trials began in 2003 with the internally developed drug (Genzyme 2009). Just 3 years later in 2006, Genzyme launched Myozyme (alglucosidase alfa), an enzyme replacement therapy for Pompe, and large-scale production of the treatment led to FDA approval of Lumizyme in 2010 (Davies 2010; Guo, Kelton, and Guo 2012). All this happened at record speed—less than a decade, compared to typical drug development. Sales of Lumizyme/Myozyme in 2016 were €725 million (more than $800 million), growing at a rate of 13.5% over 2015 (Sanofi-Aventis Groupe 2017).

Will the surge in rare disease drugs continue? With healthy interest from pharma, new technologies, greater involvement of patient advocacy groups, and novel tools from groups such as Genetic Alliance and cTAP, further exciting developments could take place. One positive sign was that rare disease developer BioMarin netted $1 billion in sales for four of its drugs combined. While it took four drugs to get there, that's the traditional blockbuster milestone, sending a good signal (Orelli 2017).

Looking Forward

With WES/WGS and advanced technologies like cognitive computing and facial recognition software, bioinformaticians, data scientists, and computer scientists will find themselves in greater demand. Increasingly, they will be a part of the patient's care team, alongside the clinical geneticist, genetic counselor, and other specialists. In the past, WES/WGS was performed under research studies, as costs for these services were quite high, and not typically covered by a patient's health insurance. But as costs have come down and studies are beginning to find the clinical utility of WES/WGS for some conditions, many payers have taken the approach to reimburse for WES on a case-by-case basis. Cigna was the first major insurer to announce a formal coverage policy that included WES in late 2015, though it considered WGS experimental and unproven (Stewart 2016). Geisinger Health Plan developed a coverage policy for WES for children with certain conditions including autism spectrum disorder, complex epilepsy, and some congenital anomalies (Geisinger Health Plan 2014).

Currently, few insurers have taken steps, besides Cigna and Geisinger, to formalize a coverage policy for WES. How to more widely incorporate these tests, when it is unlikely payers will reimburse for the test or analysis of the results, has yet to be determined. This is an area that will be greatly transformed by an overall move toward value-based care (see Chapter 7). If it can be shown that performing WES or WGS is more cost-effective *and* can improve patient outcomes, over time more health centers will offer the tests to their patients and more payers will adopt reimbursement policies for them.

As mentioned in Chapter 2, CRISPR offers the potential to fix genetic mutations with incredible precision—down to a single base pair. There is substantial interest in applying CRISPR technology to rare diseases for cures or long-term treatments, and researchers are beginning to test the technique in cell lines and animal models. For example, chronic granulomatous disease (CGD) is a rare immunodeficiency disorder caused by mutations in the NOX2 protein. Patients with CGD suffer from frequent infections and are often treated with long-term antibiotics. Using stem cells from CGD patients, researchers were able to repair the NOX2 mutation with CRISPR. These cells were later implanted into mice, where the effects of the gene editing were long lasting (De Ravin et al. 2017).

Several start-ups have been founded in the last several years looking to capitalize on CRISPR. These include CRISPR Therapeutics which is collaborating with Bayer for severe combined immuno-deficiency and hemophilia programs (CRISPR Therapeutics 2017), and Editas, which is working on rare blood diseases (Gori 2017). As the technology improves, experts believe it's not a matter of *if* CRISPR will be rolled out to patients, but *when* (Ossola 2017).

Researchers are also finding rare disease research may impact research on treatment options for common disorders, which could appeal even more to pharmaceutical companies. A mutation in the gene SMS, found in a teenager with bone and neurological abnormalities in the NIH's Undiagnosed Diseases Program, is a candidate for osteoporosis treatments. New understanding of the biology behind progeria is helping researchers with studies on several aging-related conditions (Madhusoodanan 2017).

Social media is helping patients who are "one in a million" find others like them across the country and across the globe. Patient advocacy groups are finding new power in growing numbers, their fundraising capabilities, and their unique patient perspective to shape rare disease research. Innovative companies like Transparency Life Sciences are working with patients, providers and researchers, and others to change how clinical trials are performed, such as using "site-less" models, greater reliance on real world evidence, digital biomarkers from wearable devices, and outcomes that matter to patients. Given the added financial incentives, powerful new tools, and the new ways to share data even among small and dispersed groups of people, the progress we've seen already could greatly expand.

Having a rare disease can be one of the loneliest feelings in the world. Cathy Tralau-Stewart, interim director of the University of California San Francisco's Catalyst program, said, "It's an interesting time for rare diseases. It's been an area that no one would touch for a long time, because there's no money in it due to the small patient populations" (Fost 2017). But thanks to new technologies, massive amounts of data, and the groundbreaking work of people such as Sam Berns' family, the Crowleys, the Terrys, the O'Donnells, and others like them, new doors are finally opening for patients with rare diseases. That's also creating new opportunities for entrepreneurs, data scientists, and others who can help these patients achieve cures or at least live longer and better lives.

Chapter 6

Price and Quality Transparency: The Dawn of Medical Shopping

> When you have such huge variations in the quality and price of care, patients need to know their options based on solid data. [The] data [is] there and now we're trying to get it into consumers' hands.

Leah Binder
President and CEO, The Leapfrog Group

Michael Shopenn, an architectural photographer, needed a hip replacement. Journalist T.R. Reid needed a shoulder arthroplasty. Dave deBronkart, a patient advocate, needed a procedure to remove basal cell carcinoma from his face. Former art gallery manager Renee Martin was pregnant and in need of prenatal and delivery care. The young son of Jeff Rice needed foot surgery. What does this diverse group have in common? Each tried to shop for healthcare and discovered a system that obscures the costs of treatments and varies widely in price and quality, with few opportunities for the average patient to get straight answers. The difficulties encountered by these individuals mirror those that millions of patients face on a regular basis—problems that data, when formatted and presented the right way, has the potential to fix.

When Michael Shopenn started shopping around for a hip replacement in the mid-2000s, he had an eye-opening experience, as related in a 2013 *New York Times* article (Rosenthal 2013e). Shopenn's insurance company had already refused to pay for his hip replacement, which was due to a preexisting condition, leading him to try to figure out how to get a new hip at a price he could afford.

This process turned out to be very complex. In addition to figuring out how much the artificial hip (a medical device) would cost, Shopenn needed to know the surgeon's fee to implant it, how much the hospital would charge for the operating room and support staff, and so on. His research returned some surprising facts: Price of the procedure in the United States? That would be about $80,000—without the surgeon's fee. Price for exactly the same operation in Belgium?

Just $13,660, including all doctors' and hospital fees, the artificial hip itself, a week of rehab, medicine, crutches, and a round trip ticket from the United States (Rosenthal 2013e).

Michael Shopenn's experience with medical tourism, the term for obtaining medical treatment or procedures in another country to save costs while still receiving quality care, is far from unusual. The 2009 book *The Healing of America: A Global Quest for Better, Cheaper, and Fairer Healthcare* by T.R. Reid describes his experience traveling around the world visiting physicians and hospitals for his shoulder injury. Beginning in the United States, Reid found an orthopedic surgeon suggesting a total arthroplasty at a cost of tens of thousands of dollars (exact price unknown). Hesitant to go through with the surgery, Reid embarked on a journey that took him around the world to a variety of healthcare providers, even acupuncturists, for his shoulder, so he could compare the healthcare systems and costs of services in each country.

Reid found tremendous variation in both prices and in transparency. In France, for example, he reported that patients know exactly how much office visits and procedures will cost and how much insurance will reimburse them ahead of time (Reid 2009).

Renee Martin and her husband had health insurance, but maternity care was excluded. As she explained in a *New York Times* article, the couple negotiated charges for routine care, like an ultrasound, but were stymied when they contacted their local hospital to inquire about the total cost for maternity care: they just couldn't get a straight answer about how much it would cost.

Eventually, Martin was given a range from $4,000 to $45,000. Blood glucose testing, a fetal scan, and emergency room visits brought additional charges (Rosenthal 2013a). *New York Times* reporter Elisabeth Rosenthal described similar situations faced by other couples without maternity coverage. Some couples were able to take advantage of fixed-price plans that were developed by hospitals for such patients. But others were faced with restrictions, exclusions, and unplanned procedures, or specialist visits that could lead to substantial cost burdens (Rosenthal 2013a). Prenatal complications, a surgical delivery, or neonatal intensive care can easily accrue tens of thousands of dollars—and more.

Entrepreneur Jeff Rice turned his family's experience attempting to "shop" for healthcare into a business and a website to help others (see the sidebar *Bluebook for Helping Patients Save on Healthcare Costs*). Rice's Healthcare Bluebook and similar sites are attempting to innovate the confusing system Shopenn, Reid, and Martin all found, where the costs and quality associated with healthcare are largely hidden from patients.

SIDEBAR: BLUEBOOK FOR HELPING PATIENTS SAVE ON HEALTHCARE COSTS

Jeff Rice, MD, JD

CEO, Healthcare Bluebook

The idea for Healthcare Bluebook arose from Jeff Rice's personal experience. His young son needed foot surgery, and when he inquired beforehand, Rice learned it was going to cost $15,000 for the hospital's facility fee alone. In talking with his son's surgeon, however, Rice discovered the surgeon also performed procedures at another facility, where the cost would be just $1,500. That facility had the same quality, but was charging 1/10 the cost. So he decided to found a site, called Healthcare Bluebook, that could provide "fair" prices for procedures by collecting and analyzing price and quality data.

"This is of ever increasing importance, because more and more folks are on high deductible plans," Rice told us in an interview (Rice 2017). The leading cause of bankruptcy in this country is large healthcare bills, and prices vary widely within the same geographic region. Some providers charge as much as 10 times what their competitors bill. It's also important to remember that the third leading cause of death in this country is medical injuries from hospital care. Meanwhile, the United States spends four to five times on healthcare what other developed nations spend, but ranks much lower on many quality measures.

Where patients go for care is clearly very important. "People are thinking about their healthcare differently now," he says. "They are asking, what is the quality and cost? They are becoming consumers."

Rice has evolved his company's business model over the years, but the focus is still on giving people the information they need to make good decisions about where to get care. (For more, see the section *Providing the Data for Employers and Patients* later in this chapter.)

Healthcare pricing has long been highly secretive about everything from convenience, to quality and pricing. But the pressure is on to make the industry more transparent, and is driven primarily by government initiatives. Without federal or state requirements for institutions to divulge the data, prices, and quality metrics related to healthcare, they will likely remain hidden from consumers.

In the United States, the Obama administration led the way with Project Open Data, a government-wide effort to reframe data as an asset and make it publicly available (Burwell et al. 2012). In 2013, the government posted data on what different hospitals charge for particular procedures to the Hospital Compare website. That first data release included prices from approximately 3,300 hospitals for 100 of the most common inpatient services, 30 common outpatient services, and all physician and other supplier procedures and services performed on 11 or more Medicare beneficiaries (Bird 2013). In April 2014, another wave of pricing data, this time for doctors in independent practices, was released (Centers for Medicare & Medicaid Services 2014).

Those pricing data releases were crucial, because the Medicare payment rate is a key benchmark for healthcare pricing. Medicare is the single largest purchaser of healthcare services in the United States. Altogether, government-sponsored healthcare was estimated at $1.5 trillion in 2016 and accounted for 46% of health spending in 2015 (Centers for Medicare & Medicaid Services 2017d).

Reporters and others immediately began analyzing the data and describing the massive disparities between prices for identical services in the same region. For example, the *New York Times* reported that a hospital in Livingstone, NJ listed an average price of $70,000 to implant a pacemaker, while a hospital in Rahway, NJ—less than 25 miles away—charged more than $100,000 (Meier, McGinty, and Creswell 2013). Likewise, the *Washington Post* reported that Las Colinas Medical Center in Texas was listing an average charge of $160,832 for lower joint replacements, while "five miles away and on the same street," Baylor Medical Center listed an average charge of $42,632 for the identical service (Kliff and Keating 2013). The data, the *Post* reporters wrote, "reveal a healthcare system with tremendous, seemingly random variation in the costs of services."

This brought tremendous attention to a longstanding issue—price variation in healthcare, and spurred interest in using this type of data to help consumers finally shop based on price. But this data release hasn't been entirely successful in bringing price transparency or minimizing variation in pricing. Shopping around for healthcare continues to be as challenging as a competitive sport. As the *New York Times* eight-article series *Paying Till It Hurts* found, from colonoscopies to vaccines, getting a straight answer to the question, "How much does it cost?" is nearly impossible (Rosenthal 2013a,b,c,e,f, 2014a,b,c).

These examples highlight several problems with the current healthcare pricing situation. First, it can be difficult, if not impossible, to get a price for any one procedure. Second, assuming you can get a price, you'll find that costs can differ substantially from place to place—even in the same city.

These challenges have been exacerbated by the rise of High Deductible Health Plans (HDHPs), which are often combined with health spending accounts (HSAs)—a special type of savings account that let consumers put money aside for future health costs, like medications or office visit copays, tax-free. Such trends mean the cost of healthcare is being increasingly shifted from employers to employees. While this is currently regarded as a growing burden on consumers, it is meant to set the stage for savvy patients to start "shopping" more wisely for their care.

The patient as a consumer is an enticing concept, and one that has attracted considerable interest. There are, however, several obstacles to achieving this, including the lack of data available to healthcare shoppers. But as Leah Binder, CEO of The Leapfrog Group noted in our interview, the data to help consumers make better healthcare decisions exists. And Jeff Rice concurs, "It is convenient for providers to tell patients that they can't provide an estimate before the procedure, but if you were going to have Lasik surgery, they will tell you exactly what it will cost in advance. When the health system says 'we can't tell you' it means 'we won't.'" Consequently, organizations like Leah Binder's and entrepreneurs such as Jeff Rice and others are finding opportunities to provide the price and quality data a growing number of patients are looking for (see the section *Providing the Data to Employers and Patients* below).

Rise of High-Deductible Health Plans

As noted above, many experts anticipate more patients will be shopping for healthcare now because of the rise in HDHPs. Such plans offer lower monthly premiums for employees at the expense of requiring higher deductibles before reimbursement kicks in. This has the effect of requiring patients to pay more money out of their own pockets, through copays and deductibles (Collins et al. 2014). This type of plan has become increasingly popular as health costs have risen and employers have looked for new ways to control their own costs. In a 2015 survey, America's Health Insurance Plans (AHIP) found that HDHPs, coupled with HSAs, had increased their enrollment by 22% over a *single year*, rising to 19.7 million enrollees (AHIP Center for Policy and Research 2015). Many of the plans available to the uninsured on state or federal exchanges are also HDHPs (Herman 2014). Because of this trend, even patients with insurance are now spending an average of more than $5,100 on healthcare yearly, out of their own pockets (Health Care Cost Institute 2016).

Historically, most people with insurance have paid only a small portion of their overall premiums, and sometimes a copay for specialist visits or procedures. Their employers paid the bulk of the premium cost and employees largely had no understanding of the actual costs of their healthcare. This employer insurance-dominated system arose due to some unusual circumstances, including wage controls that were enacted following World War II (see the sidebar *How the U.S. Health Insurance System Evolved*), and the main goal was to ensure that doctors and hospitals were paid—creating a system that emphasized insurance plans with generous coverage.

The U.S. system is unique among other developed countries due to its emphasis on private insurance and lack of price controls—regulations that limit the costs for certain healthcare expenses or how much prices can increase over time. A 2009 OECD survey of 29 countries, excluding the United States, found that nearly all respondents' countries used various regulations to provide basic health coverage to their populations (Paris 2010). Health insurance in the Netherlands and Switzerland, paid for through private insurance funds, are tightly regulated to prevent market failures and ensure universal access to health insurance. In the 10 countries with multiple insurers, the OECD found several that allowed insurers to alter benefits, level of coverage, and/or premiums. But in many of those countries, benefits can only be expanded or increased and a basic level of services is required (Paris 2010).

These systems are in stark contrast to how healthcare works in the United States, where private, employer-based healthcare covers the majority of those with health insurance. Although there were some major changes in requiring basic levels of coverage through the Affordable Care Act (ACA), there is substantial variability between private and public insurers and it is not clear if the ACA's provisions for basic coverage will continue.

Now we are seeing a dramatic shift, as patients are responsible for more of their own bills. Some analysts argue that this trend is good. They believe that just as Shopenn and the other patients described at the beginning of this chapter did, more patients will ferret out bargains and/ or refuse unnecessary care when they are required to contribute more to their healthcare costs.

Others say that most patients can't effectively shop for care. Few can get access to information about prices or quality, and even information they get may be misleading or incomplete. For example, it may be possible to obtain a price for a surgeon and the hospital facility fees, but not the cost for the anesthesiologist. Or consumers might get the hospital's *average* price for a procedure, but not the price their insurance company will pay and how much their copay will be.

Professional medical associations in the United States. have also pushed back against publicizing cost and quality data, arguing patients aren't capable of interpreting it and that the information should remain private because it is essential for provider competition. Calculating which insurance plan provides the best coverage, reconciling hospital bills, and understanding what to ask for when shopping for healthcare can be difficult in the best of circumstances—and nearly impossible for many patients.

Even when patients are diligent about *shopping* for the best price for a procedure or medical care, some situations can prevent them from being able to *select* the best price. For example, their insurance companies may have contracts with particular providers that limit full reimbursement to services performed only with those providers—regardless of the actual cost of services. A doctor might suggest getting an MRI for migraine headaches that have increased in intensity. The patient might find an MRI provider that will perform the scan for $300, where the provider in their insurance network might charge $450. The out-of-network scan may only be reimbursed at 50%, leaving the patient to pay $150, but the in-network MRI may be reimbursed at 75%, 90%, or even 100%, so the patient could pay less out of pocket, while the insurance company covers the rest. Even when patients haven't yet met their deductible, some healthcare services are still covered, leaving patients to determine whether they are liable for all of the cost of a procedure or not.

Some experts believe programs that let patients shop around for the best price are inherently flawed, at least for insured patients, because they are only seeing the retail price, not the allowable charges the insurer has negotiated, making it impossible for patients to determine if they are paying the highest price for the lowest quality. With patients pressured by their healthcare plans to select providers that are "in network" in order to minimize their out-of-pocket costs, there is little incentive to shop around (Feyman 2017).

Also, acute situations may prevent patients from being able to make sure the care they receive is from the provider with the lowest cost. Imagine a woman in labor who isn't covered by a maternity policy—a situation like Renee Martin's, described earlier. That woman has spent the past 9 months shopping around for the best price for a typical vaginal delivery and selected her doctors and hospital around that. But during her labor, her doctor determines that she will need a cesarean delivery and pages the on-call anesthesiologist. All of a sudden, she's no longer in control of who that doctor might be or able to negotiate the rate for those services—those services or providers aren't "shoppable" (Feyman 2017). Patients who experience a traumatic event, like a car accident, and are taken to the nearest hospital face similar difficulties. Although having health insurance may minimize some of the costs, patients with high deductible health plans can still face substantial financial burdens when they lack real power to shop around for the best price for healthcare.

Whether patients are up to the task of shopping for healthcare or not, price is going to become increasingly important to them, health insurers, employers, and federal programs like Medicare and Medicaid. Rising healthcare costs are a huge and growing burden on everyone. Demand for pricing data is going to surge, and innovators like Jeff Rice and Leah Binder will be packaging it in ways to help patients and employers reduce their healthcare costs, giving the most cost-effective providers with the best quality a competitive edge. Hospitals and healthcare providers that aren't able to meet their patients' demands for price transparency will find themselves increasingly at a disadvantage.

SIDEBAR: HOW THE U.S. HEALTH INSURANCE SYSTEM EVOLVED

It may surprise you to learn that the U.S. health insurance system came about accidentally in response to events, rather than as a result of methodical planning. By the 1920s, numerous European nations had national health insurance systems. The United States, meanwhile, had started down a very different path. At that time, healthcare wasn't very expensive and doctors couldn't do very much. When private health insurance first became available in the late 1920s, it wasn't very popular. People preferred to save their money in case of medical emergencies.

The original insurance policies were designed with doctors and hospitals in mind— not patients. In 1929, Baylor Hospital in Waco, Texas, developed a hospitalization coverage plan to ensure the hospital would be reimbursed for patient care (Baylor Scott & White Hospital 2017; Austin 2009); that plan was easily extended to doctors' services and then replicated by other hospitals around the country (Austin 2009). These plans were the predecessors of the Blue Cross (hospitals) and Blue Shield (physicians) plans (Lichtenstein 2017). As incomes rose and technology advanced, health insurance became more popular. Regard for physicians and hospitals also improved over time, and people started to view health insurance as having greater value.

U.S. tax policies and the demand for labor also played into the rapid expansion of private health insurance during the 1940s. Wage controls enacted during World War II made it harder for employers to compete for workers based simply on wages. Employer-paid group health insurance premiums were determined to be a necessary business expense and exempted company health benefits from taxes (Austin 2009; Lichtenstein 2017). Now, employers could use health benefits to sweeten their offers to prospective employees.

The earliest health insurance policies charged everyone the same premiums, but companies soon started evaluating each individual's relative risk and charging them accordingly (Noah 2007). Large businesses were best able to mitigate this penalty on the sick, since they could spread the cost across their many employees. Meanwhile, small businesses or self-employed individuals who were sick would face the highest prices.

But that shift set the stage for a system where employers played an increasing role in providing health benefits, leaving most employees to pay only a fraction of what their health benefits actually cost.

Thus, the system evolved with no price visibility. Today, insurance companies negotiate prices with individual providers and healthcare networks, and both groups fight to keep the costs secret from their competitors. Patients rarely see the total price tag for their insurance, let alone the prices for their care. "For more than 80% of the public, their health costs are obscured," explained Leah Binder, president and CEO of employer coalition The Leapfrog Group, told us. "Those patients don't know what anything costs; they just feel helpless and confused when their premiums go up" (Binder 2017). Price transparency was one of the goals of some provisions of the ACA and a few states (e.g., Massachusetts and California) worked on similar legislation of their own (Viebeck 2014).

Paying for Quality, Not Just Quantity

Along with price, patients are beginning to demand quality information for their doctors and hospitals. But what does this mean, exactly? How can doctors and hospitals be rated in such a way as to make apples-to-apples comparisons? How can patients know that they are getting the best healthcare they can? There are no easy answers for these questions, but alongside reform and innovation for price transparency have come similar initiatives for healthcare quality. Some of these have been pushed by federal and state regulators while others have a more entrepreneurial basis.

In the United Kingdom, for example, information from how long a patient spends in the waiting room to the convenience of getting an appointment to clinical measurements were released by the National Health Service in 2012 to "give everyone a clear idea of which general practice surgeries, wards, accidents & emergencies, and hospitals are providing the best care—which will encourage others to make improvements" (Department of Health [U.K.] and Howe 2012).

Some controversy has dogged news magazine *U.S. News & World Report* for their methodology, which has been ranking hospitals in 16 specialties since 1990. The magazine was criticized for relying on physicians' ranking of their own colleagues to set its ratings. Ranking methods vary by specialty, but are now driven by data in 12 of the 16 specialties, including cancer, geriatrics, cardiology, and heart surgery (*U.S. News & World Report* 2016). However, surveys based on the opinions of fellow physicians are still used to rank hospitals in four other specialties, and there is some evidence that hospital reputation influenced ranking decisions, calling into question how accurate the rankings are (Sehgal 2010).

Importantly, evaluating hospitals by specialty highlights that hospitals rarely excel in all specialties. As Jeff Rice told us, "A hospital that is top tier in heart disease, for example, might not be as good in orthopedics."

Journalists aren't the only ones combing through the vast amounts of data to rank hospitals. The Centers for Medicare & Medicaid Services (CMS) recently combined existing quality data for seven categories into an overall star rating for hospitals (Centers for Medicare & Medicaid Services 2016b). Hospitals submit data for outcomes to CMS; some measurements are taken using only the Medicare population, while others include all patients in the hospital system (Centers for Medicare & Medicaid Services 2016b). CMS's analysis of 3,662 eligible hospitals showed overall ratings generally followed a bell curve, with most hospitals earning 3 stars, 102 hospitals earning the top rating (5 stars), and 133 hospitals with the lowest (1 star) (Advisory Board 2016b).

Another ranking system was developed by the American College of Surgeons. The National Surgical Quality Improvement Program (NSQIP) gives hospitals a way of measuring where they stand and to identify areas of focus where they lag in quality of surgical care compared to their peers (American College of Surgeons 2017). Unlike rankings from CMS, the data collected through the NSQIP program isn't designed for consumers—it's designed to enable hospitals to improve their facilities, through reductions in preventable complications like surgical site infections, and adoption of best practices (American College of Surgeons 2017).

Growing Cost and Quality Consciousness

The question of medical costs has gained substantial attention in the past several years with the publication of several exposés. A 2013 *New York Times* article by Nina Bernstein reported on New York's release of cost and charge data from more than 1,400 conditions and procedures from hospitals in the state. Comparing costs and charges based on diagnosis codes and levels of severity, Bernstein found dramatically variable costs and charge markups from hospital to hospital. Hospital trade groups opposed the release of the data, believing it would "confuse consumers, who rarely pay the sticker price for hospital care, especially if they have insurance" (Bernstein 2013).

In 2015, *Newsweek* ran a similar article on the markup of hospital care using 2012 data from CMS. Reporters found charges that were inflated more than 1,000% over what Medicare pays for care in the 50 hospitals that marked up the most. The average markup for the remaining 4,433 hospitals in the CMS database was just 340% (Potter 2015).

With negotiated rates between hospitals and insurance carriers a "black box," it's easy to see how shopping for healthcare is challenging and there is generally no way for the patient to know if they are receiving care at the most expensive price—charges that are passed on to the insurer, the uninsured, and underinsured.

Some experts have argued that this is just another reason to make sure that everyone has health insurance. However, in an era where patients are spending more on copays and deductibles, it's no longer just the uninsured that are becoming sensitive to prices for healthcare. Many more employers are offering only HDHPs, and the lowest-cost plans on the ACA-mandated health insurance exchanges, are HDHPs. As a result, a growing number of American workers are incurring big financial costs and starting to demand clear and up-front billing (TransUnion 2013). But as we've already described, getting those prices ahead of time is nearly impossible.

For patient advocate Dave deBronkart, trying to get the pricing for procedures related to a basal cell cancer meant going in circles between his insurance company and the hospital (Rosenberg 2016). As described in a *New York Times* blog post, deBronkart was speaking at a medical conference when a doctor noticed a spot on his face that looked suspicious. deBronkart, who had a $10,000 deductible for his health insurance, decided to take an unusual approach to getting the care he needed at a price he could afford. Initially, he solicited bids from doctors on his blog, e-PatientDave. Not surprisingly, he received no response, and calling around to hospitals proved equally fruitless. deBronkart said in the *New York Times* interview, "The actual information I needed in order to be an effective, responsible shopper was by policy blocked from me" (Rosenberg 2016).

This lack of transparency won't remain a competitive advantage for much longer, and price and quality clarity will change the healthcare system dramatically. We are already seeing such change.

In the past, insurers tried to offer their customers the most doctors and hospitals possible, in order to be competitive. They are now emphasizing approaches that limit choice for patients through restrictive networks (which cut out the most expensive providers) and centers of excellence, in which certain hospitals guarantee a set price for a procedure. Employers are also trying to provide incentives to encourage patients to use high-quality, lower-priced doctors and hospitals, reducing their healthcare costs. Providers and hospitals are pushing back, citing the need for patient choice, but when the patient can't afford to choose, it's hard to argue for it. With patients increasingly feeling the financial pain of healthcare consumption, they are demanding the data that will allow them to make informed decisions.

In addition to New York, other states, including Maine and Massachusetts, are beginning to follow the federal government's lead and provide the public pricing information based on insurance claims. However, when the nonprofit Catalyst for Payment Reform (CPR) and Health Care Incentives Improvement Institute (HCI[3]) released their joint 2016 Transparency Report Card, only three states received the top grade (A): Colorado, Maine, and New Hampshire. Oregon was the only state to receive a B grade, both Vermont and Virginia received Cs, and Arkansas received a D. *The entire rest of the United States received Fs* (deBrantes and Delbanco 2016).

The top-performing states were lauded for their consumer-focused websites, and collection and publication of data. Recommendations from the joint effort to raise transparency grades in the other states ranged from creation of transparency laws (numerous states lack commitment to price transparency legislation), a requirement for data sharing of the information that is collected by the state with consumers on publicly accessible websites; and shifting the voluntary collection of data by providers to an automatic/involuntary process. Eleven states were noted to have pending or recently passed legislation that once enacted, would address the deficiencies identified by the report (deBrantes and Delbanco 2016). Given that this report card has been published for the past 3 years with little improvement demonstrated by many states, without the federal government's requirement or individual state legislation to do so, healthcare pricing will remain in the shadows.

But simply putting the data at the consumer's fingertips is not going to be sufficient to turn patients into savvy healthcare shoppers, as noted in the CPR-HCI[3] report. The fact is that most Americans aren't able to shop for healthcare. Healthcare literacy is astoundingly low and uses both language and numerical comprehension skills. The Program for International Assessment of Adult Competencies placed more than half of American respondents at the three lowest levels for literacy and nearly two thirds at the lowest three levels for numeracy (Centers for Disease Control and Prevention 2016d). Deciding which insurance plan to choose, reconciling hospital bills, and understanding what to ask for when price shopping for healthcare can be difficult at best—for patients with low healthcare literacy, it may be close to impossible.

Judith Hibbard, from the University of Oregon, studies how patients interact with healthcare information. In a special section "Best Practices to Maximize Consumer Use" of the CPR-HCI[3] report, she writes, "The benefits of transparency are only realized, however, if consumers attend to and use the information in making choices… the way in which information is displayed and presented can make a difference in whether it is understood and used" (deBrantes and Delbanco 2016).

Hibbard identifies several methods that can be used to compensate for a lack of mathematical proficiency and burden of processing complex information: limiting the amount of information presented, minimizing choice, and reducing the use of technical terms. Interpreting the data for the user is another strategy to improve consumer utilization; "the best solution is to always pair price information with quality information." But as Hibbard cautions, consumers presented with only cost information may conflate price with quality (deBrantes and Delbanco 2016).

This is a point made in our conversations with Tom Emerick, president of Emerick Consulting and benefits management expert, and with Leah Binder, CEO of The Leapfrog Group. "Many consumers think 'more expensive equals better,' so they want more expensive procedures. But study after study has shown there is no correlation between price and quality. You simply can't predict quality based on price," says Binder. But quality metrics are also flawed, as Emerick explains (see the sidebar *How Employers Can Most Effectively Cut Costs*).

SIDEBAR: HOW EMPLOYERS CAN MOST EFFECTIVELY CUT COSTS

Tom Emerick, MBA

President, Emerick Consulting

For decades, employers have been paying a hefty portion of health costs, but not taking many steps to control them. There was a push to managed care in the 1980s–1990s, but that had a backlash effect when patients started to complain when they believed they were being denied necessary care, just to save costs. Now, the biggest trend is pushing more costs onto employees, in the form of higher premiums, copays and deductibles.

Tom Emerick, who has worked in benefits management for more than 30 years, thinks a completely different approach is what is needed. Based on his work, he says most networks have too many doctors practicing low quality care. "To cut costs companies need to make sure their employees are getting the best quality care," he told us in an interview (Emerick 2017). "Half of employees are currently receiving lower-than average quality care. But by redirecting those employees, companies can save a lot on misdiagnoses, medical errors, and unnecessary care."

Emerick sees a big problem with many of the new services now popping up that claim to sort high from low quality performing doctors. "The issue is that they tend to rate doctors on how many procedures they do. That seems logical at first, after all, you'd want a more experienced doctor," he says. "But would you rather see a doctor who does less procedures, or one who does many more, but also has bad outcomes for many of those?" Studies have shown that there is a great deal of variation in how often doctors do certain procedures, but there sometimes doesn't seem to be a good medical reason for that. And the outcomes for different doctors also vary a lot.

To really save big, he says companies "want to direct employees only to doctors who do clearly medically necessary and advisable surgeries. If they are doing too many unnecessary procedures, patients will suffer more side effects and poor outcomes." Key factors are: How often was the diagnosis right? How often did the procedure fail? Just looking at how many procedures physicians do is misleading.

Emerick also thinks employers are also asking for the wrong information from insurance companies. For example, many want to know "What is the cost for the average diabetic?" But those aren't usually the most expensive patients. Just a small fraction of patients, maybe 6%, are costing 80% of the dollars spent. It is by identifying those small numbers of very high cost patients, and making sure they get the best quality and most appropriate care that employers can best cut their costs.

One example of this approach is Lowe's Centers of Excellence program, which covers knee and hip surgery at selected facilities, at essentially no cost to the employee (Health Design Plus 2017). Centers of Excellence (COE) are hospitals or other medical centers that have highly skilled employees, typically with a focus on research and innovation. COEs often have requirements (e.g., volume of specific procedures, multidisciplinary teams) that are designed to standardize procedures and improve patient outcomes (Sugerman 2013). In the Lowe's program, the company even pays for travel if necessary

(Health Design Plus 2017). A key feature of such programs is that the employer negotiates a single fee for all the care related to the procedure, which makes it much easier to estimate and manage costs.

Beyond Hospitals and Doctors

Consumers don't just need price and quality transparency for healthcare services, but for diagnostics, drugs, and medical devices as well. With more than 65,000 genetic tests on the market today, the genetic testing industry is ripe for price and quality transparency. Concert Genetics, a Nashville-based healthcare technology company, is attempting to do exactly this (see the sidebar *Transparency in Genetic Testing*). Their GeneSource database contains information about tens of thousands of genetic tests, from price to lab turnaround times (Concert Genetics 2017b). Healthcare providers and hospitals can use this information to evaluate genetic tests from different labs—allowing them to make apples-to-apples comparisons and know up-front just how much these tests cost. Even more importantly, this information is available in an easy-to-understand format and can be used to order tests at the point of service. As a result, patients with high deductible health plans, whose doctors are aware of that, can make better decisions about where to get such tests.

SIDEBAR: TRANSPARENCY IN GENETIC TESTING

Robert Metcalf, MBA

CEO, Concert Genetics

With more than 65,000 genetic tests on the market today, picking the right one for a patient can be like finding a needle in a haystack. Concert Genetics aims to make that process a lot easier and more transparent. Metcalf, CEO of Concert Genetics, says the company has made sense out of a competitive and messy market by developing a new taxonomy based on vast amounts of data.

"Through a data collection and curation process we know every test that's on the market for genetic testing, single gene and multigene test," he explains. "We know the genes it tests for, the technology it uses, we know the clinical usage of those tests. And we use all that to go back and say 'These two tests are equivalent.'"

That type of comparison is essential for providers and hospitals trying to get a handle on the growing financial burden of genetic testing. The company's website offers a freely available Genetic Test Search to providers (and others) as a way to identify which genetic tests include the gene they're looking for, which labs offer those tests, list price and other data like turnaround time. Metcalf compared the situation to a drug formulary: "There's a lot of copying of tests, so can you get a similar test at a lower cost from another vendor?" (Metcalf 2017).

But limited access to proprietary databases of patient information make comparing two tests difficult. As he explains, "We're saying they are equivalent in context, but interpretation is still the Wild West." An example is Myriad Genetics, who held the patent on the *BRCA1* and *BRCA2* genes until 2013, after a Supreme Court ruling. That ruling resulted in a flood of competitors offering genetic tests for breast cancer. These new tests don't come with the vast amount of interpretive data for genetic variants that Myriad's test does, but public and shared databases have been developed that reduce Myriad's advantage.

Furthermore, Metcalf says that integrating the data with the clinical pathway is essential, especially as patients take on greater financial responsibility for their healthcare. For example, if doctors can tell their patients what their cost will be for equivalent tests, $400 vs. $4,000, how many doctors (or their patients) would still want the more expensive test? He explains, "We have the ability as a company to push more of that information to the point of decision."

But true price transparency can be difficult to come by. Negotiated rates for tests can depend on the insurance carrier or the lab's test volume. Taking the information from genetic test claims, Concert Genetics knows what's billed vs. what's allowed vs. what's actually paid, resolved down to a precise test ID. These data give them "a ton of information around price transparency that no one else has in the marketplace," shares Metcalf.

Metcalf sees genetic testing data changing the broad practice of medicine for patients and doctors: "[It] comes back to how do you know, in a data-driven way, when and what test to give? What is the diagnostic that fits with the situation and how do you get there in a world of personalized medicine?" he says. "We think about that as a data problem, with value-based decisions to be made." He expects that eventually, the data will be connected to downstream patient outcomes, helping doctors make evidence-based clinical decisions. "Over time, you'd want to be able to look at every time a particular test has been ordered with certain clinical criteria and assess the longitudinal impact."

Shopping for drugs is another area of growing importance, since prices for many are rising, and often at a dramatic rate. In 2014, Gilead Sciences made headlines when they introduced a breakthrough hepatitis C pill (Sovaldi) at a cost of $84,000 per year. Considering the costs associated with treating a patient with hepatitis C could exceed $100,000 (Razavi et al. 2013) and costs for a liver transplant are more than $500,000 (Transplant Living-UNOS 2017), Sovaldi and the competing drugs that followed shortly thereafter offered the promise of a cure at a fraction of the costs of treating someone over a lifetime for hepatitis C.

At first, insurance companies covered the cost and paid for the most eligible patients to get the pill. The drug was such an improvement over previous therapies that it seemed grossly unethical to deny it to qualified patients. But with more than 3 million Americans suffering from the disease, the cost of treating everyone who needed the drug would be staggering (Berkrot and Beasley 2014).

According to a *Wall Street Journal* analysis, state Medicaid plans alone spent $1.33 billion on hepatitis therapies during the year after the drug's launch. That was "nearly as much as the states spent in the previous three years combined" (Walker 2015). Some states have rationed the medication and restricted its use for patients on Medicaid (Barua et al. 2015), due to the high cost of the drug(s) and number of patients with hepatitis C. And though approximately one in three prisoners are infected or seropositive, most are not treated for the disease due to cost and institutional barriers such as length of time in the system (Centers for Disease Control and Prevention 2015). In fact, inmates have filed lawsuits in multiple states for lack of hepatitis C treatment (Silverman 2016).

When AbbVie came out with a competing drug, Viekira Pak, which was similarly priced to the Gilead offering, pharmacy benefits management firm Express Scripts made an exclusive deal with them, ensuring that all the patients on that plan would receive the newer drug, but at a substantially cheaper price (Humer 2014). This sounds like a winning deal for consumers, right? But the story doesn't quite end there.

In 2016, Merck released Zepatier, another drug to treat hepatitis C, at approximately half the cost of the Gilead and AbbVie options. Efficacy for Zepatier appears to be comparable or even better in some patient groups than its competitors. And though the sticker price for Sovaldi, Harvoni (another Gilead offering), and Viekira Pak could be almost twice that of Zepatier, few patients or insurers are likely paying the full price, as manufacturers often provide rebates that bring the cost down substantially (Atlantic Information Services 2016). But without price transparency, it's impossible to determine which treatment is the most cost-effective.

When Novartis' breakthrough drug, Entresto, for heart failure was approved, the company set a relatively hefty price–$1.25/day per patient. But the company also entered "pay for performance" arrangements with Cigna and Aetna, two large insurers. Under this plan, the insurers will receive rebates that are dependent on real world performance of the drug compared to clinical trials (Aetna) and are linked to hospitalization rates of patients taking the medication (Cigna) (Staton 2016c). Other manufacturers are exploring performance-based payment schemes, too. Amgen has entered into a similar agreement with Harvard Pilgrim Health Care for its *PCSK9* cholesterol drug Repatha and outside of the United States, both Novartis and Johnson & Johnson's Janssen unit have performance-based agreements with the National Institute for Health and Care Excellence in England (Staton 2016c). GlaxoSmithKline has a money-back guarantee for Strimvelis, its $665,000 gene therapy treatment for "bubble boy" disease, a severe autoimmune disorder (Staton 2016b).

This type of haggling between health insurance companies and drug makers was previously unheard of. As costs rose, insurance companies would just raise the cost of premiums. Now, the idea that prices need to be linked to outcomes is catching on (see Chapter 7).

Going forward, data about prices and the effectiveness of different tests and treatments will be essential, and capturing these data is the first step. Currently, data collection is disconnected from the payment mechanism and fails to accurately capture the patient's experience: did the treatment make them healthier? Providers are the ones collecting the data. But insurance companies meanwhile, are using claims data to steer covered members to the highest quality *and lowest priced* providers through restrictive provider networks.

To stay competitive in the future, this data, from how effective a procedure is to how the provider compares to their peers, must also find its way to providers when they need it most, or beforehand. This point is one that Anil Jain, Senior VP and Chief Medical Officer of Explorys, a component of IBM's Watson Health, makes in our interview: "How do you fundamentally change the way a patient is managed—you need to bring [the data and the provider] together. The doctor is usually working with a finite amount of information" (Jain 2017).

Providing the Data for Employers and Patients

The growing need for price and quality transparency in healthcare, especially as patients are moving to high-deductible health plans, has created a fertile environment for entrepreneurs and others to create innovative solutions (see the sidebar *Freeing the Data to Turn Patients into Consumers*). Although healthcare shopping sites existed prior to CMS's release of pricing data for healthcare services, the publicity around prices has informed consumers who stand to benefit from being able to shop wisely for care. And shopping for healthcare means more than just getting a price for a procedure or office visit—it includes shopping for the doctors and hospitals and determining what care is covered by the insurance plan, too.

SIDEBAR: FREEING THE DATA TO TURN PATIENTS INTO CONSUMERS

Lisa Maki

Cofounder and CEO, PokitDok

"The consumer is the wild card in healthcare transparency," says Lisa Maki, cofounder and CEO of healthcare-pricing website PokitDok (Maki 2017). "The big question is whether we can engage them and get them to make better decisions about their care. You can't do that from the top down, by telling them what to do. You must free and connect their data to modern, digital experiences consumers have come to expect."

PokitDok was founded in 2011, with the goal of allowing healthcare consumers "to shop for the best products at the best price, just as they would at an e-commerce site like Zappos" (Roush 2014). The site's prices are not based on claims data or the data on the government's Healthcare Compare website, but instead use the actual "cash rate" that providers charge the uninsured or people with high deductibles. The site currently has prices from more than 1,000 primary care physicians and other independent specialists. Hospital prices, which Maki says are harder to get, will come next.

Whether the patient is uninsured or just has a high deductible, they can get the best rate by using the site, according to Maki. "Consumers are shopping, and they are talking to each other too," she says. "This is convenient and helps people save money." Patients are also interested in quality, but Maki says there isn't enough difference in quality. She points to automobile manufacturing. "All the cars are pretty much safe, and the minute they are deemed unsafe they are off the market," she says. "If something is unsafe, it's not going to be available for long."

Consumers can research the physicians who post prices on PokitDok. And more than 1,000 doctors have already done so (Roush 2014). That information includes where and when they went to college, how many years they studied, and how many procedures they do per year. Doctors can also upload videos and other information to market themselves.

It's still very early days for such "comparison healthcare shopping" sites. Will enough consumers try them? Will they actually be able to use them to cut their costs and find better care? Or will they be overwhelmed by the amount of information and lack of confidence to make healthcare choices on their own?

New companies are starting to access price and quality data and offer it to employers or the public to help guide healthcare purchasing decisions. In December 2015, the start-up Amino gained access to Medicare claims data, information that historically has been restricted to a limited number of researchers (Versel 2015). Amino's goals are to bring price transparency to consumers and self-insured employers, enabling both groups to reduce healthcare costs. The company's physician search lets consumers find providers and see costs based on key variables like their health condition, provider preferences (e.g., male, female), and health insurance coverage. The company recently announced $25 million in Series C venture capitalist funding, supporting expansion of its solutions to the employer and provider market (Baum 2017b).

MediBid is another website that provides information to patients about cash pricing for doctors' services (MediBid 2017). Similar in concept to Lending Tree ("When Banks Compete—You Win!"), patients submit requests based on their needs to MediBid, which contacts doctors and facilities who review the patients' requests and return bids. Patients can select providers based on price, quality, and location, whatever their insurance status (e.g., uninsured or with a high deductible plan). Physicians can also benefit from these websites to get new self-paying patients, sidestepping the administrative hassles of insurance (MediBid 2017).

FAIR Health Consumer is a not-for-profit website designed to help patients better manage their healthcare through data (FAIR Health 2017). Using online and mobile app tools for both medical and dental procedures, FAIR Health allows patients to estimate the cost of services in their region and potential reimbursement for out of network care based on their insurance plan. Uninsured patients can calculate the full market price for healthcare services (FAIR Health 2017).

Jeff Rice's Healthcare Bluebook, described at the beginning of this chapter, has evolved over the years. The company still offers its flagship free online pricing data for consumers, which includes data on everything from hearing aids to hospitals. Patients can determine a fair price, find the nearest facility offering such a price and even print out a contract letter that binds the provider to it. The company now also offers large employers an enterprise solution, which helps employees to get best healthcare at the best price. One of the keys, Rice says, is to be able to distinguish how hospitals perform in various specialties. Insurers can use the site instead of building their own transparency products and providers can work with Healthcare Bluebook to become "Value Certified" and thereby distinguish themselves from competitors.

The company gets data from employers, insurers, and CMS's MedPAR (Medicare Provider and Analysis Review) database, which consolidates Inpatient Hospital or Skilled Nursing Facility claims data from the National Claims History. It includes data on all Medicare patients, including procedures, diagnoses, and diagnosis related group, length of stay, payment amounts, and revenue center charge amounts. "Hospitals have to submit all of their data to the MedPAR database," Rice explains. There is also data from several voluntary quality initiatives available.

Castlight Health is another company focused on offering employers detailed information about costs and quality, as well as health insurance packages that encourage employees to make prudent decisions (Castlight Health 2017). The company offers plans with high deductibles, as well as centers of excellence and reference-based pricing. Employers can send patients to facilities that are rated highly by Castlight for doing specific high-cost procedures, such as transplants or orthopedic surgeries, at a competitive price, and companies can offer to pay a reasonable, market-based price for a procedure. If the employee decides to get the surgery elsewhere at higher expense, they are responsible for the difference.

Leah Binder's organization provides employers with a free report, the Leapfrog Hospital Survey, that grades hospital safety performance. Employers can use the data to let workers know which hospitals have the best safety profiles and use that information to structure their benefits programs, encouraging employees to use the safest and most efficient providers.

There's also evidence that insurers are paying attention to patients' rising healthcare costs and demand for quality data. Aetna's WellMatch price comparison tool allows employees of subscribed companies to search for providers and services. Aetna-covered members can see exactly how much a visit to a doctor will cost them after insurance and what the cost of the service would be for noncovered patients. Quality data are included and is derived from external websites (WellMatch 2017). Cigna's consumer-facing website, myCigna.com (Business Wire 2012), and other insurers offer similar price and quality tools for their members.

Consumer-generated reviews are increasingly important components of quality transparency despite concern that they "don't capture dimensions of care that reflect clinical or objective quality metrics" (Howard and Feyman 2017). Emerging research suggests these concerns may be unfounded or overstated. Overall scores of hospitals based on patient reviews on Yelp, a website better associated with helping consumers find a good restaurant, have been found to correlate well with more objective quality measurements (Howard and Feyman 2017). A 2016 study found that Yelp reviews correlated with some variables on the Hospital Consumer Assessment of Healthcare Providers and Systems survey (Ranard et al. 2016). New research using New York State hospitals and Yelp reviews found the consumer-generated data are "good composite metrics of hospital quality" and are more accessible to patients than other data (Howard and Feyman 2017).

CareDash, a Boston-area company, offers consumers an online forum for physician reviews. The company has more than 30,000 patient-generated reviews and ratings on its website, which can be accessed through mobile devices—a convenience used by more than half its users (Bentley 2017). The company's founder and CEO Ted Chan cites the user-generated data as setting CareDash apart from its competition, since the company won't let providers pay to have negative reviews removed or edited (Bentley 2017; CareDash 2017).

It's too early to say whether these websites and others will succeed in years to come. Will enough consumers try them? Will they be able to use these sites to reduce their healthcare costs and find better quality care? Will they be overwhelmed by the amount of information and a lack of confidence to make healthcare choices on their own? Or, with insurers bringing price and quality tools available to patients on their own, will companies like PokitDok and Healthcare Bluebook be left to serve just the uninsured population?

Future for Consumer Health Pricing and Quality Transparency

It should be clear that healthcare is moving from one of price and quality opacity to a system that enables patients to act like consumers—albeit slowly. We are still a long way from the point at which consumers can efficiently shop for services. As we have tried to present in this chapter, the system is at a relative tipping point, where having the most expensive providers in your network is no longer as beneficial for competition, due to burgeoning national healthcare costs. Everyone involved can see that it's becoming imperative to rein in expenditures and choose cost-effective providers and treatments. The question is whether hospitals, insurers, and patients will all move forward at the same pace, and if not, who will be left behind.

As insurers and employers feel the squeeze of these costs, they are moving employees to high deductible plans and raising premiums. Most of the plans available on the ACA's state exchanges also had high deductibles, and it is unclear what, if anything, will replace them. But it's still of great importance to provide patients with price and quality information. Another new trend is the migration of employers to private exchanges. These are online health insurance sales sites that allow employees to "shop" among a wider range of insurance options. The rub is that employers will provide only a set amount (defined contribution) toward the worker's health insurance purchase. Anything over that will be the employee's responsibility. That means workers will need even more information to help them understand the benefits and limitations to help them distinguish between health insurance policies.

Consumers don't just need information about the prices and quality of healthcare services, but for diagnostics, drugs, and medical devices as well. This type of information is currently hard to come by. What treatments and tests are really worth paying for? Which providers are using them optimally? This is the kind of data that could really empower consumers.

There are potential negative consequences of continued shifting of the healthcare financial burden on patients. Relatively stagnant wages, forcing employees to take on more of the expense of healthcare, could lead to increased medical debt. If patients can't afford their high deductible plans, they may be unable to pay their bills for services rendered, leaving hospitals and providers stuck without reimbursement. This leads to higher charges for everyone else, as providers look to recoup costs, and more medical bankruptcies. Prior to the ACA, medical expenses were the cause of more than 60% of all bankruptcies (*American Journal of Medicine* 2016). With proposed legislation that would reduce the number of people covered by insurance, patients who are uninsured or underinsured will have the highest risk.

Patients may also start delaying or avoiding necessary care to cut healthcare expenses. For patients with chronic conditions, this could be disastrous, forcing them to seek medical treatment that is more expensive and more invasive than preventive medicine would have been.

This type of scenario is already playing out across the country. Elizabeth Price, a woman with a rare genetic disorder, described having to weigh the consequences and pain from delaying medical attention to the costs associated with emergency room visits and possible hospital charges for kidney stones in a 2015 *New York Times* article (Bernard 2015).

As mentioned earlier, including quality data are extremely important. Without quality data, patients will conflate price with quality, as Judith Hibbard wrote in the Catalyst for Payment Reform report (deBrantes and Delbanco 2016). Pushing patients to lower-cost providers and services without demonstrating that the quality is equal or better will undoubtedly result in a backlash, similar to what occurred in the 1980s and 1990s in response to HMOs (Blendon et al. 1998). But quality data doesn't just help patients. Anil Jain of Explorys says the information also lets providers and hospitals know where they stand in relation to their peers. Just having that information can be enough to elicit improvements—similar to the concept of ACS's NSQIP for surgical complications.

More data will become publicly available in the upcoming years. The continued release of the data by government (federal and state) agencies and others (such as large, self-insured employers) to the public is crucial. Insurers, employers, and entrepreneurs must augment those data to help patients, like Michael Shoppens, make smarter and more informed choices.

The ultimate goal? For providers and health systems to use the data to make value-based decisions (see Chapter 7), for payers to use it to set evidence-based coverage policies, and for patients to use the data to choose providers or healthcare products based on both price and quality.

But it's going to take more than just releasing the data to achieve these aims. Most of the data exists in user-specific "silos," and data collected for one purpose, like claims data or health data from electronic health record (EHRs), may not be easily used for other purposes. Information has to be freely accessible and interoperability between company databases are needed for patients (and others) to truly be informed consumers of healthcare.

Providers (both physicians and medical centers) will find it increasingly difficult to hide this information from public view. Companies that embrace data sharing and system interoperability can find it's a competitive advantage. Patients will more often begin to ask questions like "How much will this cost me?" and "Is there a cheaper alternative that works just as well?" And they will expect that their doctors will have a ready answer for them and that they can find the information on their own.

But a change from the status quo to a price- and quality-transparent healthcare system is not going to happen overnight, keeping patients at the losing end of the relationship. It's no wonder that alternatives like medical tourism have continued to garner significant interest among price-conscious patients, like Michael Shopenn and T.R. Reid, who were described at the beginning of this chapter. Medical tourism is big business and it's expected to reach an estimated $32.5 billion by 2019 (Transparency Market Research 2015). What's driving this? Substantial differences in cost from one country to the next for healthcare.

The *New York Times* more recently published an article documenting Freda Moon's experience traveling to Thailand for dental work (Moon 2017). The cost of treatment in the United States for her and her husband's routine care would have exceeded $5,000. So, the couple researched their options and decided to have the dental work performed in Thailand, instead. The bonus: a weeklong vacation for less money than the cost of having the dental work performed in the United States (Moon 2017). Asian countries like Thailand, India, and the Philippines are among those most often traveled to for healthcare due to their low cost and high standards (Transparency Market Research 2015). Until the U.S. healthcare system can reduce costs and provide patients with transparent price and quality data, allowing them to shop around, alternatives like medical tourism will continue to grow.

The system is ripe for disruptive technologies that bring the data to the consumer. Jeff Rice, Lisa Maki, and Leah Binder are just a few of the people looking to inject transparency into opaque healthcare pricing. They and other entrepreneurs are striving to turn the quest for accurate price and quality data into innovative companies, like Healthcare Bluebook.

It's going to take time and education to get more consumers shopping. "We've had two decades of managed care where people were trained to be like sheep," Rice says (Rice 2017). But the days of $10 copays are fast fading, as employers' healthcare costs rise and they shift more healthcare costs to employees with higher deductibles and coinsurance. "People can literally save thousands of dollars if they start shopping for care," he says. Likewise, companies who make those data available should be able to thrive in the new price and quality transparent landscape.

Chapter 7

Value-Based Care: Paying for Results

In the past, doctors ordered things and insurers paid for them. Under the new payment plans being rolled out, providers are going to be sharing more financial risk with payers.

Stan Norton
Vice President and Chief Technology Officer, Humedica

The U.S. healthcare market is worth approximately $2.7 trillion and growing. Several major profit streams currently dominate this market; they include hospitals, drug makers, device makers, and medical specialists. Most of these profit streams are thriving, thanks to the idea that we should do as much for patients as possible, without a lot of discussion about "value," either in terms of price or quality. Patients believe more procedures, more treatments, and more care will give them better outcomes and healthier lives—the more expensive the care is, the better quality it is assumed to be.

But the dialogue is shifting as the nation's capacity to pay for all this "more" starts to wane and outcomes, not just cost and quality, start to take precedence. What new fields and opportunities will emerge as this trend increases? How will the current stakeholders adapt to the new value-based purchasing trend? Will innovative start-ups be able to snatch up big pieces of this lucrative market? Who will be the winners and losers? These are a few key *Moneyball Medicine* questions.

In the last chapter, we outlined how the U.S. healthcare system is slowly embracing price and quality transparency—and that's a step in the right direction for patients. But what providers, medical systems, and insurance companies want is *value*. If you're not sure what that means, you're not alone (Meyer 2017). In a recent nationwide survey, fewer than two-thirds of all participants could describe what avoiding low-value practices (e.g., unnecessary testing or treatments) could mean for patients (Schlesinger and Grob 2017). Certainly, value depends, in part, on price and quality. If one medication costs double the price of another but in every aspect, they are identical, most people would say that the lower priced one is a better value. But measuring value isn't always as simple as comparing prices.

Fifty-one-year-old Bob Mannschreck had long suffered from back pain due to a skiing accident decades earlier. When even standing became difficult and extremely painful, he called for a doctor's appointment (Levey 2014). Here is where Mannschreck's experience at Seattle's Virginia Mason Spine Clinic diverges from that of a typical patient with back pain:

Mannschreck received a same-day appointment, arriving and moving into the exam room without a lengthy stay in the waiting room. Ten minutes later, after a medical assistant had input his medical history and information into the electronic health records (EHR) system, a physical therapist arrived and began to examine Mannschreck and test his mobility. Twenty minutes later, a rehab physician joined him and the physical therapist for an exam and to develop a treatment plan: an anti-inflammatory drug and physical therapy for a likely herniated disk or irritated joint. The remainder of Mannschreck's appointment was spent working on exercises with the physical therapist. He was out the door in 70 minutes (Levey 2014).

Contrast that with a more typical experience: the patient wakes up in pain and calls for an appointment with their primary care provider (PCP), which is scheduled for some time in the future. The PCP might refer the patient to another physician, such as an orthopedist or a neurologist, or to a physical therapist, requiring another appointment to be scheduled in advance. At some point, the patient might undergo an MRI or other radiological test. There is little coordination of care and duplication of efforts is likely (Porter and Lee 2013).

The value of the integrated, patient-centric strategy at Virginia Mason? As reported in a *Harvard Business Review* article, "Compared with regional averages, patients at Virginia Mason's Spine Clinic miss fewer days of work (4.3 versus 9 per episode) and need fewer physical therapy visits (4.4 versus 8.8). In addition, the use of MRI scans to evaluate low back pain has decreased by 23% since the clinic's launch in 2005, even as outcomes have improved." In addition to patient-level benefits, Virginia Mason increased revenue through efficiency and productivity: the clinic added nearly 1,000 new patients seen each year with the same number of staff members and physical space (Porter and Lee 2013).

Patients with breast cancer who undergo lumpectomies at the Mayo Clinic may find their operating room time extended by 20 minutes while surgeons wait for pathology results to come back, before determining if additional tissue needs to be removed (Lee and Kaiser 2016). With each minute in an operating room costing an average of more than $60 (Macario 2010), an extra 20 minutes can add up to a substantial charge for patients and their insurers. Most doctors simply finish the operation and wait a day or two to receive pathology results. If the final report indicates that the surgery didn't catch all the cancer, the patient will find themselves headed back to the operating room days (or weeks) later.

At Mayo Clinic, however, spending 20 minutes waiting for an answer in the middle of surgery eliminated the need for repeat operations approximately 96% of the time (Boughey et al. 2014)— improving patient outcomes and ultimately saving the institution (and patient) time and money.

These are just two examples that highlight why one of the biggest shifts in U.S. healthcare is occurring today—a change in how we pay for care and what patients expect for those costs. It's moving from a "fee-for-service" system to one based on value and outcomes. That means changes in not only how doctors are paid, but what they are paid to do.

A hospital, doctor, or social service that can provide appropriate preventive care for a patient with diabetes can save the healthcare system thousands of dollars over the course of that patient's lifetime, by reducing preventable surgeries and complications (Squires and Bradley 2015). A hospital might find that incorporating simultaneous tissue pathology into breast lumpectomies or restructuring care for patients with back pain can lead to both better patient outcomes *and* improved provider efficiency with the ability to see more patients, which can drive up revenue. Patients benefit by eliminating both the costs and risks from repeat surgery as well as better health outcomes.

Traditionally, doctors and hospitals have billed for each individual service they deliver, in the fee-for-service model that still dominates today. Under this model, the more services that are delivered, the more the doctor or hospital is paid: higher volume equals higher revenue (Dartmouth-Hitchcock 2017). Though not explicitly stated, there is an underlying assumption that the services rendered improve patient outcomes. However, as we will attempt to show in this chapter, misaligned incentives between patients and providers (or hospitals) have often led patients to pay for *more*: more expensive drugs, more procedures and tests, and more invasive care—without substantially improved results.

According to some experts, the fee-for-service system has exacerbated the steep rise in healthcare costs, due to misaligned incentives for providers who are paid for ordering tests and performing procedures, versus care based on the value those tests and procedures provide (Fernandopulle 2015; *Wall Street Journal* 2015). Meanwhile, prices for medical care, drugs, and devices have continued to climb, pushing healthcare costs in the United States to more than $3 trillion (Centers for Disease Control and Prevention 2016b).

But we have reached a tipping point and most experts agree we can't afford this approach anymore—particularly when this method doesn't buy us better outcomes. The United States, by far, spends the most among developed countries, more than 17% of our GDP in 2014, on healthcare (World Bank 2017). The United Kingdom, in contrast, spends about half of that (World Bank 2017).

Yet, for all the expensive care, we don't have better results than other nations. The United States has lower life expectancy at birth than 29 other countries (79.3 years) (World Health Organization 2016), higher infant mortality, and worse management of patients with asthma and diabetes (Peter G. Peterson Foundation 2016). U.S. patients with cystic fibrosis live a decade less than similar patients in Canada (Stephenson et al. 2017). A significantly higher proportion of U.S. adults have multiple chronic illnesses (28%) compared to 12 other high-income countries (Squires 2015).

Additionally, there are substantial disparities between states. The percentage of adults with diabetes, for example, ranges from 6.8% in Colorado to nearly 15% in Mississippi. Massachusetts has the highest percent of adults complying with colorectal screening recommendations (76.4%) compared to Wyoming, which has the lowest (56.5%) (United Health Foundation 2016).

Moreover, even under the Affordable Care Act (ACA), which has provided a record number of Americans with health insurance, many still struggled to access healthcare (Osborn et al. 2016). For example, according to a recent survey, nearly one-third of all American adults and more than 40% of low-income adults went without healthcare in the United States because of costs, while in 10 other high-income countries, the rates ranged from 8% to 31% (Osborn et al. 2016). If the number of Americans with healthcare drops, there will be even fewer "paying customers" for healthcare services.

As healthcare costs continue to rise and the quality of care doesn't match what we are spending, payers and policy makers are trying to shift the fee-for-service system to one that pays for positive performance or *value*. The work involved in this change isn't inconsequential and encompasses nearly every aspect of healthcare. As Jamie Heywood, cofounder of PatientsLikeMe, said in our interview, "[healthcare] almost has designed resistance to improvement" (Heywood 2017).

When providers and hospitals are only paid for the delivery of a service after requiring demonstrated patient improvement or reduction in complications, they will have to not only treat the patient, but also collect measurements that will allow them to prove the patient's health improved or that they were able to prevent complications or hospital readmissions. In short, there must be demonstrable value to the healthcare services rendered.

Michael Porter, professor and founder of the Institute for Strategy and Competitiveness at Harvard Business School, has developed a framework for value-based healthcare (Institute for

Strategy & Competitiveness 2017). In addition to measuring outcomes for every patient, this model includes bundling prices across the entire patient care cycle, integrating medical care around the patient and their condition(s), even across different facilities, and determining the actual costs associated with patient care (Institute for Strategy & Competitiveness 2017).

From a practical standpoint, value-based healthcare requires a new mindset, a re-engineering of the workflow side of medical care, and learning how to leverage large amounts of data to aid clinical decision-making and organizational structure. The process of moving to value-based care entails more than adding new tools and measurements to the existing workflow—it demands thinking about how to deliver care in a different way and having the organizational and technological infrastructure to move on those ideas.

Providers and hospitals will place a greater emphasis on preventive medicine, cost-effective treatments, and evidence-based medicine (see the sidebar *Managing Patients under Risk Contracts*). How will patients see the results of these changes at the health system level? The impacts will vary, but as Bob Mannschreck discovered (see above), it can mean better efficiency, less waiting, and improved care coordination, ultimately resulting in a more optimal level of health. Treatments, procedures, and tests might be reduced or changed in favor of high-value alternatives. Combined with greater price and quality transparency (see Chapter 6), these changes will enable patients to more effectively shop for the healthcare they need and get the outcomes they deserve (Dartmouth-Hitchcock 2017).

New business opportunities will emerge that will be aimed at improving healthcare efficiency, price and quality transparency, and making health data useable. Existing hospitals, insurers, and other health-related groups will have to rethink their business models and collaborate with others to stay competitive and meet the demands of insurers and government. *Effective use of data is what will make all this possible.*

SIDEBAR: MANAGING PATIENTS UNDER RISK CONTRACTS

Stan Norton

Vice President and Chief Technology Officer, Humedica

"Care delivery and reimbursement are heading in a new direction, where providers are going to be sharing more risk. Doctors, for example, will be paid to achieve certain goals among diabetics. If they don't achieve those goals, they'll lose money," says Stan Norton, former Vice President and Chief Technology Officer of Humedica (Norton 2017).

Humedica, which is now part of Optum, provides analytics that work across multiple settings, including hospitals and doctors' offices, to provide better insights into which treatments work or don't work. The company's current network includes data from approximately 30 million patients across almost 40 states. Those data are drawn from electronic health records, medical practice management systems, and claims data.

The idea is to use big data to pull out optimal treatment paradigms and to make sure that individuals or all patients in a certain subgroup (i.e., heart failure or diabetes) get what they need. One of the key hurdles, Norton says, is properly categorizing patients to begin with:

"We [Humedica] have data showing, for example, that some providers underestimate their diabetic population by 20%. And we've seen cases where as many as 50% of the diabetics in a practice aren't identified. We help practices identify these patients by analyzing laboratory and prescription data. Then we go into the clinical data to determine outcomes and evaluate the quality and cost of care being delivered. This is incredibly difficult, because the average electronic medical record has 16 places where you can find the time (when) the patient was admitted, for example. Lab results will also have different reference ranges and use different units, depending on which forms you are looking at."

In the end, it's all about the analytics, the computer power, and the quality of the underlying data. "The big data here is being able to manage 42 million patients under a risk management contract," says Norton. "That's terabytes and terabytes of data, a lot of computers, a lot of standardization, and a lot of normalizing. But if you get it right, it protects the providers and empowers them. It also improves quality while controlling costs, and you can measure both."

Government Initiatives: Medicare's Value-Based Purchasing Programs

As we described previously, the pressure to bring transparency to healthcare costs has been driven by federal programs and spurred entrepreneurs to tackle the challenges of bringing the data to patients (see Chapter 6). A 2012 Institutes of Medicine report, for example, estimated that $1 in $6 spent on healthcare in the United States ($750 billion per year) is unnecessary or outright harmful (Institute of Medicine of the National Academies 2012; Kliff 2012). Unnecessary services and excess administrative costs were the two highest categories contributing to this amount (Kliff 2012).

A further concern is the high rate of medical errors, estimated to kill more than 250,000 patients each year (Makary and Daniel 2016). And though individual patients are unique, across the entire country, that uniqueness isn't enough to justify the substantial variation seen in regional practice differences (Song et al. 2010). That means many more patients are receiving risky and expensive procedures, such as knee replacements or angioplasties, just because they went to a particular facility or live in a particular area, driving up healthcare costs for everyone.

All these worrying statistics have raised a call for more focus on quality and efficiency in our healthcare system. Because Medicare costs account for approximately 20% of all U.S. healthcare spending (Centers for Disease Control and Prevention 2016b), it's not surprising that CMS led the way and developed several programs to improve patient care while reducing unnecessary costs. In fact, this has been a CMS initiative for decades.

Since 1999, Medicare has collected data from hospitals and other healthcare facilities (e.g., nursing homes) on their performance related to certain "quality measures" (Agency for Healthcare Research and Quality 2011). These measurements were essentially proxies for treatment guidelines (i.e., the best practices for treating common conditions such as heart attacks, heart failure, or pneumonia) (Agency for Healthcare Research and Quality 2011). Hospitals were initially encouraged to submit the data voluntarily until 2004, when it became mandatory to do so. Beginning in 2005, data from more than 4,200 hospitals has been made publicly available on the Hospital Compare website (ACH Media 2005; Centers for Medicare & Medicaid Services 2016c).

Data collection was just the first step in moving Medicare toward a value-based purchasing framework. In October 2012, Medicare payments to all hospitals were reduced by 1% to create a funding pool. Those funds were redistributed based on the hospitals' performances on the quality measurements (Robert Wood Johnson Foundation 2012). A range of other data, including on readmissions (see the section *Reportable Outcomes: Readmissions and Medicare Penalties*), is also now collected and made publicly available on the Hospital Compare website.

It took about 10 years to get from the initial data collection to some actual value-based purchasing, but for the last few years Medicare has moved aggressively in this direction. By 2016, the administration had met its goal of tying 30 percent of traditional Medicare payments to new quality- or value-based payments, including alternative payment models such as Accountable Care Organizations (ACOs) or bundled payment arrangements (Centers for Medicare & Medicaid Services 2016a).

ACOs are groups of doctors, hospitals, and other healthcare providers, who joined together with the goal of providing coordinated high-quality care. With bundled payments, healthcare providers receive a single fee for a single episode of care. The idea behind both these approaches is to encourage doctors to be as efficient as possible *and* provide the highest quality care, rather than a high volume of care. The last part of this is particularly important: the goal isn't to restrict necessary care, but to optimize the care provided to achieve the best outcome for the patient at the best value.

ACOs are not the government's first attempt at alternative delivery systems. The Medicare Physician Group Practice Demonstration gave providers bonuses for lowering costs and meeting certain quality targets better than control physicians in the same area (Colla et al. 2012). Although the financial benefits were mixed, for some patient groups the cost savings and readmission rate decreased significantly (Colla et al. 2012). The next milestone will be having 50% more transactions tied to such alternative models by 2018.

Other programs, such as the ACA's Medicare hospital readmissions penalty policy and the Leapfrog Group's hospital safety ratings, are encouraging that process. The goal is to make metrics such as quality and price transparency in healthcare, and to encourage transactions that are based on value, whether it's the insurer, the employer, or the patient making the buying decision. Increasingly, this means penalizing healthcare providers who can't meet certain quality standards, while better rewarding those who can. And this only works if the provider (or health system) has the right data and can use it to make decisions.

It should be apparent that moving away from a fee-for-service-based reimbursement system to a value-based plan involves a complex series of both positive and negative incentives—a "carrot and stick" approach. Leading the way are the providers and health systems that have already adopted (at least to some degree) organizational structures or programs designed to move toward a value-based model.

While the goal is to eventually get most patients involved in making wiser healthcare purchasing choices, the government has so far been leading this charge in a bid to improve the quality and lower the cost of Medicare. Successful initiatives and programs implemented for Medicare patients will ultimately benefit all patients.

Private insurers are also starting to follow suit, and while the vast majority of care is still paid for based on fee-for-service, it's expected that system will be eclipsed by other payment methods by about 2020 (Ellison 2014). Though there are likely to be changes to the ACA, the data gathered by CMS is already being used by insurers and private companies, as described in Chapter 6.

What's unclear is where the tipping point is for value-based purchasing. If the government abandons the value-based care program entirely, will the system continue down the path? Without the incentives or penalties to do so, it's unlikely. Others may pick up the baton, once a preponderance of data indicate value-based reimbursement decreases overall healthcare costs while improving patient outcomes. In short, while the government got the ball rolling, making sure it stays on the value-based path now relies substantially on data and the ability of health systems to recognize how value-based care can give them a competitive advantage.

This shift is a significant disruption to existing establishments. Today, hospitals thrive by doing procedures and admitting as many patients as possible. And to keep as many patients as possible in their overall network, many hospitals have acquired physician practices. But while that can be good business for the hospital and make it substantially easier for patients to have their health data shared between all their healthcare providers, it doesn't necessarily mean the care patients receive is of high value.

Using data from more than 31,000 primary care visits for back pain, headache, and upper respiratory infections (URIs) that took place between 1997 and 2013, Mafi and colleagues compared utilization of low-value services such as certain types of imaging, antibiotic use, and specialist referrals in the different physician practice settings. The researchers found greater usage of low-value CT and MRI imaging and specialist referrals in the hospital-based practices as compared to physician-owned community-based practices, though antibiotic use for URIs was comparable. These results suggest patients may receive more low-value care when primary care physicians are associated with hospital-owned practices (Mafi, Wee, and Davis 2017).

Unlike a product that can be returned to a store for a refund, it's not possible to undo an operation or give back medication that was taken, even if the surgery leads to complications or the medication didn't work. But a novel program from Geisinger Health System demonstrates that it is possible to offer a "money-back guarantee" for healthcare without breaking the bank.

In 2016, Geisinger gave such an offer to all patients: through the ProvenExperience program. An earlier Geisinger program, ProvenCare, held the health system—not the patient—financially responsible if they were readmitted to the hospital with a preventable complication within 90 days of discharge (Ellison 2015). ProvenExperience builds on that foundation. But Geisinger's program was about more than just giving patients a refund for services. They took the opportunity to also gather positive and negative feedback from its patients—information that identified long waits in the emergency department and difficulties in making appointments in some departments (Minemyer 2017a). The benefit of collecting this feedback? Using that information to improve the patient experience, so that over time, fewer patients might report dissatisfaction with their care.

Geisinger is among the few health systems uniquely poised to try out innovative programs, such as ProvenExperience, that move away from the fee-for-service model toward value-based care. Because it is self-insured, that is, the health system also offers health insurance, the incentives of the providers and the payer are more closely aligned.

The approximate cost of the program in the first year was $500,000—an amount not substantially more than the health system was already doling out through other initiatives (Minemyer 2017a). As the nation edges closer to value-based care and away from a fee-for-service model, all health systems are being asked to take on more of the financial risk of treating patients. Implementing ProvenExperience took significant risk for the health system, but they are reaping the rewards by learning where they can improve their processes, which can save them money in the long run.

In the system of tomorrow, doctors and hospitals that can prove they provide the best, high-value care, the most efficiently, will get the most business. That means these systems will be redistributing and/or reorganizing their resources, so that they get better outcomes with fewer interventions, which will all be backed by solid data.

Two new fields are thriving under these demands: practice management and population health. Many firms with healthcare analytics capabilities, such as 3M, Caradigm, Deloitte, IBM, Phillips and others are creating analytics and offering services that will allow hospitals, insurers, and other healthcare-related enterprises to closely track the performance of specific physicians and adjust their business structures as needed. Doctors are given a clear report on where they stand compared to their peers. Did they order many more of a certain test? Were more of their patients readmitted?

On the other side, population health management data shows what a patient population looks like and then tracks the health system's overall performance. The data that is included can come from the patient's health record (ideally across all systems the patient uses), the health system's financial and claims information, such as how much it cost a hospital to treat a particular patient, and, perhaps in the near future, from the patients themselves as data from medical devices or fitness wearables is integrated into the health record.

Many insiders say the current situation is confusing because doctors and hospitals must prepare for the system of the future, while much of their compensation is still based on the fee-for-service system. Adding to the confusion is the uncertainty surrounding the future of the ACA and current value-based initiatives due to a new administration. But experts have been describing U.S. healthcare costs as "unsustainable" for years—under both Republican and Democratic administrations. The availability of all this new data and powerful analytical tools should spur change.

Reportable Outcomes: Readmissions and Medicare Penalties

Bruce Perry was 57 when he was diagnosed with stage Gleason 6 prostate cancer in 2010. He underwent successful surgery, but suffered from complications for nearly a year afterward. Mike Steskal, a 55-year-old Philadelphia-area commodities trader, was also found to have Gleason 6 prostate cancer after an elevated prostate-specific antigen (PSA) test. However, Steskal chose to undergo active surveillance, not surgery. When follow-up PSA tests were normal, his doctor suggested the initial test was high probably due to an infection. "It was pure chance," Steskal said, that his prostate cancer was diagnosed (Kolata 2016).

In December 2009, 19-year-old Alex Halsted went to her local emergency room with severe abdominal pain, worried she might have appendicitis. After a CT scan showed nothing out of the ordinary, she was sent home with a diagnosis of a likely ovarian cyst. After a follow-up at her gynecologist's office and surgical consult the next morning, she was correctly diagnosed with appendicitis and underwent surgery—a delay that could have put her at risk for infection and a ruptured appendix (Branam 2014). A 9-year-old Florida boy had a metal plate placed in the wrong ankle, leading to the filing of complaints with the state (O'Matz 2016).

Misdiagnosis, wrong-site surgery, overdiagnosis, and overtreatment, like the scenarios described above, contribute to health costs and can have real, negative consequences on patients. Dartmouth professor H. Gilbert Welch is among several noted experts who have identified patterns of overdiagnosis and overtreatment of patients with breast, thyroid, and prostate cancer—patients such as Bruce Perry, who might have been followed closely for his cancer, instead of undergoing surgery, and avoided complications for a cancer that may never have become invasive (Esserman et al. 2014; Jung 2016; Welch et al. 2016).

Many patients require more invasive, complicated, and expensive treatment because of a lack of preventive care or getting the wrong care in the first place. For Medicare patients alone, it's estimated that the United States spends about $17 billion per year on avoidable readmissions (Robert Wood Johnson Foundation 2013). And just like the costs associated with various procedures and treatments, readmission rates vary widely among hospitals. For example, readmission rates to children's hospitals for a variety of conditions ranged from 3% to 23% (Berry et al. 2013).

As part of the larger initiative to move Medicare toward value-based reimbursement, CMS began collecting 30-day readmission measures for heart attack, heart failure, and pneumonia patients in 2008, and used the data from 2008 to 2011 to implement the Hospital Readmissions Reduction Program (HRRP) in October 2012 (Consumer Purchaser Alliance 2017). Today, the site contains data on 30-day unplanned readmissions for heart attack, heart failure, pneumonia, hip/knee replacements, chronic obstructive pulmonary disease, and coronary artery bypass graft surgery (Centers for Medicare & Medicaid Services 2015a).

In the HRRP, Medicare payments to hospitals are levied based on the actual number of readmissions compared to the number of expected ones, penalizing hospitals that have high rates of avoidable readmissions. Penalties were eased in, starting at no more than 1% of Medicare payments in 2012, with a maximum 3% in 2014 (Consumer Purchaser Alliance 2017). In the first round of payment penalties, more than 2,200 hospitals lost out on $280 million in Medicare payments due to excessive readmissions (Rau 2012). The number of hospitals failing to curb preventable readmissions grew to more than 2,600 in 2014 (Rau 2014). In 2014, though the average penalty was 0.63%, 39 hospitals were penalized the full 3% of payments (Rau 2014).

There is data suggesting the HRRP has been successful. The program reduced preventable readmissions for Medicare patients by 8% from January 2012 to December 2013, representing 150,000 fewer readmissions (Consumer Purchaser Alliance 2017). And there was no increase in the number of hospitals to be penalized in FY2017 (Rau 2016c). However, the average penalty grew to 0.71%, the highest reached by the program, and is expected to reach $528 million (Rau 2016c). That sounds like a small amount of money, but given that Medicare is the biggest payer for healthcare services in the United States, accounting for 20% of total healthcare spending (Centers for Disease Control and Prevention 2016b), it's a noticeable proportion of most hospitals' budgets (Kaiser Family Foundation 2015).

Readmissions data from more than 2,800 hospitals collected between 2008 and 2015 found hospitals that participated in one or more of the Medicare value-based reforms (Pioneer and Shared Savings ACOs, Bundled Payment for Care, or the Electronic Health Records Incentive Programs) reduced 30-day readmissions for heart failure, pneumonia, and acute myocardial infarction (Ryan 2017; Slabodkin 2017).

According to study coauthor Julia Adler-Milstein, assistant professor at the University of Michigan, "The hospitals that reduced readmissions the most were the ones that chose to participate in all three" (Slabodkin 2017). "There are so many different approaches to reorganizing how we deliver and pay for care," she continues, "We're in a phase where we're sort of trying to experiment with everything at once because we don't really know what the magic combination is that's going to improve quality performance while reducing cost" (Slabodkin 2017).

Faced with the new penalties, a growing number of healthcare facilities are establishing more stringent processes to prevent readmissions. Patients with the highest risk of readmission are also getting more attention through red flagging or hot-spotting. "Flagged" or "spotted" patients are given specialized services that might include a healthcare coordinator visiting them at home, a prescheduled appointment with their primary care physician right after they leave the hospital, or even free medications they might not otherwise be able to afford (Hillis et al. 2016).

They are also taking steps and using creative technologies, such as making discharge instructions clearer and more accessible (i.e., on your smartphone), telehealth, and Internet-connected devices to keep patients recuperating at home safely.

Christine Lemke of Evidation Health explains that some institutions are beginning to send their patients home with connected devices such as scales, blood pressure cuffs, and home ECGs after acute cardiac events (see Chapter 10 for more on this topic). These devices allow healthcare providers to monitor the patient's vital signs, weight, and other parameters after they leave the hospital. Through remote monitoring, if the patient begins to have complications or appears to be at risk of readmission, the physician can intervene, by sending home healthcare services or bringing the patient into the doctor's office. However, this trend is relatively recent, so there is limited data to analyze the effectiveness of these initiatives in recently discharged patients.

And because hospitals have historically been paid more under the fee-for-service model if patients are readmitted, those that work harder to avoid readmissions can lose money in the short term. In the long term, however, hospitals may see increased revenue under value-based schemes because they will be able to manage more patients with the same staffing levels due to increased productivity and efficiency—all the while improving patient outcomes.

As the data becomes public, entrepreneurs, and health organizations can start using it to steer consumers to the best healthcare providers and hospitals with low readmission rates, making up for the loss of revenue from readmissions penalties.

Safety First?

Another area that is under intense focus is safety. Most people don't realize that preventable medical errors are the third-largest cause for deaths in the United States, after heart disease and cancer. Approximately 400,000 people die each year from such errors at a cost to the nation of around $1 trillion each year (McCann 2014). However, until recently it was very difficult for anyone, let alone consumers, to determine which hospitals had the best safety records.

SIDEBAR: IMPORTANCE OF SAFETY DATA

Leah Binder

President and CEO, The Leapfrog Group

Besides employees themselves, no one has a bigger stake in employer-based health insurance than the companies that offer it. Typically, companies pay a much larger share of insurance premiums than workers do, and those premiums have been steadily escalating (Kaiser Family Foundation 2014). The Leapfrog Group has been working since 2000 to help employers get better quality from their healthcare spending.

"Healthcare is a huge issue for employers. It holds tremendous value to our workers, having a major impact on their health and wellbeing. But it is also an enormous cost," says Leah Binder, Leapfrog's president and CEO (Binder 2017).

"Until recently, it has been very difficult to engage employees in helping to improve the quality [of healthcare] and control costs. For example, many consumers think 'more expensive equals better' in healthcare, so they want the more expensive procedure. But study after study has shown there is no correlation between price and quality. And yet, prices vary dramatically, [even] across providers that are within blocks of each other."

But Leapfrog hasn't given up. "We think employers have a huge role in helping their employees become smarter healthcare consumers," Binder says. The group started by focusing on safety, because it saw a huge opportunity there to improve things. It's estimated that approximately 400,000 people are dying each year from preventable errors in U.S. hospitals (James 2013). "Beyond the terrible human trauma and suffering, that's an enormous waste of money," says Binder. "Hospitals are paid for all that avoidable follow-up care. So, instead of paying a hospital $39,000 to treat a preventable infection, for example, why not just prevent the infection, save that money, and create new jobs with it?"

In the era of Big Data, "Doctors are simply not going to get a pass," Binder says. "Forever, they have been saying 'no cookbook medicine' and insisting on autonomy. But the data is there for consumers to make better decisions, and we are trying to get it to them."

In addition to the HRRP, the Hospital-Acquired Condition (HAC) Program attempts to improve patient safety through the reduction of conditions such as hip fractures after surgery, pressure sores, and certain infections, like *Clostridium difficile* (*C. diff*) and methicillin-resistant *Staphylococcus aureus* (MRSA), by reporting the numbers of patients with these conditions at each facility (Sullivan 2013; Centers for Medicare & Medicaid Services 2015b).

Overall, hospital-acquired infections affect an estimated 1.7 million Americans, are responsible for 99,000 deaths, and approximately $20 billion in associated healthcare costs (Centers for Disease Control and Prevention 2017b). According to the latest data from the Centers for Disease Control and Prevention (CDC), there were almost half a million *C. diff* infections in the United States during 2011, and nearly 30,000 of those patients died within 30 days of a diagnosis (Centers for Disease Control and Prevention 2016a). Nearly 56,000 patients contracted healthcare-associated MRSA (Centers for Disease Control and Prevention 2016c).

In the HAC Program, hospitals that perform in the lowest quartile of all hospitals at preventing these conditions are penalized 1% of Medicare payments. CMS estimates the HAC Program saves Medicare $350 million yearly (Centers for Medicare & Medicaid Services 2015b). Other value-based Medicare programs include the End-Stage Renal Disease Quality-Incentive Program targeted to dialysis centers, Skilled Nursing Facility Value-Based Purchasing Program, Home Health Value-Based Purchasing Model, Hospital Value-Based Purchasing Program, and the Physician Value-Based Modifier (Centers for Medicare & Medicaid Services 2016f). Each has a goal of improving patient care while reducing unnecessary care and complications from treatment. The ranking system and dissemination of data on a publicly available website (Hospital Compare) has the added benefit of spurring competition, as hospitals and other facilities work to improve their outcomes.

Medicare's value-based programs are some of the most aggressive efforts the government has ever made to control health costs. Because the programs have been implemented only in the past few years, there is limited data to analyze their impacts on patient outcomes and whether they are, in fact, driving patients to choose healthcare providers and hospitals based on the information.

This is precisely where the explosion of data will have tremendous impact. The penalties have indeed prompted some big changes in how hospitals manage infection control, discharges, follow-ups, and outcomes tracking—a trend that was largely absent prior to the value-based initiatives (Torrieri 2014; Rau 2016a). They have also spurred the launch of multiple new products and start-ups focused on these problems (Kern 2014a). Already, half a dozen mobile apps, such as Propeller Health (for asthma and COPD, see more below), SeamlessMD (for after-surgery care), and HealthPatch MD (for vitals), are targeted at helping providers improve quality of care, including fewer readmissions.

For example, because patient adherence to medication and proper use of medical devices can impact readmission rates as well as patient health, providers are now interested in solutions that can help their patients stay on track. Propeller Health's FDA-cleared platform uses sensors that attach to a patient's inhaler, tracking when the medication is used (Baum 2016c). This kind of information can help a doctor learn if a patient's asthma or COPD (chronic obstructive pulmonary disease) is under control or if they need a different medication—information that can keep their patient out of the hospital. A 2016 study of the effectiveness of Propeller's device found that use of rescue inhalers decreased in a 12-month trial compared to patients receiving standard care and patients with uncontrolled asthma at the study start improved control over their disease (Merchant, Inamdar, and Quade 2016). Another company (Hindsait) has developed an AI-based program that will help doctors decide whether a diagnostic test is actually necessary. Hindsait has partnered with Magellan Health and has plans to pilot its technology with Blue Cross Blue Shield plans (Baum 2016b).

There remains some criticism to the HRRP and the other value-based programs. Hospitals argue that it's hard to define avoidable readmissions. Some patients are much more complicated than others or have more comorbidities, and certain hospitals (e.g., teaching hospitals) get a higher share of those types of patients. A 2015 study published in the *Journal of the American Medical Association* using National Surgical Quality Improvement Program data found patient comorbidities, discharge to some place other than the patient's home (e.g., rehab or skilled nursing facility) and teaching hospital status were associated with higher readmission rates (Merkow et al. 2015). Patients who live alone or have no primary care support are also more likely to be readmitted due to insufficient social and medical support (Robert Wood Johnson Foundation 2013).

The contribution of socioeconomic status to readmission rates has not been fully defined in the United States. However, a 2016 Danish study of more than 25,000 patients undergoing hip surgery found a higher rate of readmission and worse mortality in patients with the lowest income and educational attainment, even when the quality of inpatient care and length of stay were similar (Kristensen et al. 2016). A 2016 Canadian study further compared homeless patients to age-, sex-, and condition-matched low-income controls and found the homeless patients were four times more likely to have a 30-day hospital readmission (Saab et al. 2016).

Although certain cancer hospitals, critical access facilities, some specialized facilities (e.g., psychiatric or rehabilitation), and hospitals in Maryland are exempt from the HRRP penalties (Rau 2014), there remains significant debate over the fairness of the Medicare programs which do not take into account patients' socioeconomic status or the inherent complexities of certain conditions, particularly as the number of hospitals and their penalties increase (Sisson 2015).

Despite these limitations, there is emerging evidence that the HRRP is doing exactly what it was intended to do: improve patient outcomes and reduce healthcare costs. For example, Scripps Mercy Hospital in California, which serves a large disadvantaged population, has faced rising penalties each year of the HRRP. As a consequence, they are developing partnerships with community health centers to establish "medical homes" for at-risk patients to better coordinate patient care (Sisson 2015).

One key point that should be clear is that while bringing value to healthcare can take many forms (such as federally mandated initiatives with penalties and incentives, specialty provider quality improvement programs, or use of connected devices), all require consistent measuring of parameters and subsequent data analysis to make sense of the information. Consequently, healthcare is becoming more similar to other industries that have long adopted a continuous measurement mindset—the "Six Sigma moment" we described in Chapter 1—to achieve better outcomes.

Delivering the Data to Patients and Employers

In 2016, CMS released the Star Rating system, designed to give patients and health consumers an overall picture of the quality of a hospital. Based on the vast amount of data available on the Hospital Compare website, the Star Ratings are designed to make this information easier for patients to understand (Centers for Medicare & Medicaid Services 2016b). Out of the more than 3,600 hospitals rated, only 102 received the top (5 star) rating and 129 hospitals received the lowest (1 star) (Rau 2016b). Interestingly, several well-known hospitals failed to achieve even the average rating, while those at the top included some relatively obscure or highly specialized facilities (Rau 2016b). Because the Star Rating system is based on data included on the Hospital Compare website, criticisms are consistent with those of the individual programs from which it draws its data. With only a single year's ratings released, it's uncertain how popular the Star Rating system will become over time and whether patients will find its information more useful or better than alternatives.

There are numerous competitors to the CMS Star Rating system that have been developed by entrepreneurs in the past few years. They have largely entered the market with a goal of collating the vast amount of data on Hospital Compare with rankings, quality measurements from other organizations, and even patient feedback, and putting it into an easy to understand format for consumers or employers. Healthgrades, for example, uses patient reviews as part of its rating system. However, it has been criticized for allowing people who have never seen a particular doctor to review that doctor, and also because some of the scores are based on very few reviews (Bumpass and Samora 2013).

Leapfrog, a coalition of employers that includes many of the largest companies and organizations in the United States that buy insurance for their employees, has launched one of the most intensive campaigns to bring hospital safety records, and the cost of medical errors to light (Leapfrog Group 2017). The group, which includes companies such as AARP, Boeing, FedEx, and General Motors, supports "informed healthcare decisions" and "high-value" healthcare, or data-driven decisions (Leapfrog Group 2017).

In the summer of 2012, Leapfrog launched its Hospital Safety Score program, which provides a letter-grade (A, B, C, D, or F) rating reflecting how well more than 2,500 U.S. hospitals compare to each other in protecting patients from accidents, infections, injuries, and errors. The rating uses data from the proprietary Leapfrog Hospital Survey, as well as the CDC, CMS, and the American Hospital Association's Annual Survey and Health Information Technology Supplement. A hospital's ultimate score reflects performance on 28 measures. These are all "currently in use by national measurement and reporting programs," according to Leapfrog (Leapfrog Group 2016). The group's methodology has also been published in the *Journal of Patient Safety* (Austin et al. 2014).

The average patient, however, may be more familiar with safety and quality ratings published by *Consumer Reports* and *U.S. News & World Report*, as we described in Chapter 6. *Consumer Reports* issued its first hospital safety ratings in 2012, using data from Hospital Compare, state healthcare reporting sites, and other sources. The magazine rates a facility's safety based on hospital-acquired infections, unnecessary readmissions, mortality, communication about new medication and discharge instructions, and appropriate use of scanning. They also consider readmission data, hospital practices, patients' experiences, and more (*Consumer Reports* 2015).

The rating tools are not yet optimal and have garnered substantial criticisms. For example, using physician survey responses to base a hospital's rating (e.g., *U.S. News & World Report*) instead of objective outcomes data (*U.S. News & World Report* 2016). Just like the data collected by CMS, these rating systems don't consider how different patient populations might be from one hospital to the next. Teaching hospitals, which often have large numbers of complex and low-income patients, are rarely found at the top of hospital rating lists (Rice 2014).

Additionally, critics have pointed out that the ratings don't always agree and that they reach "opposite conclusions about many facilities," a consequence of using different measurements to calculate the rating (HCPro Inc. 2012; Rice 2014; Austin et al. 2015; Beck 2015; Ross 2016). This can confuse patients who don't understand the methodological differences in the rating systems. In fact, a recent analysis of hospital rankings based on four national systems found that *no* hospital was given the highest ranking with all four, and only 10% were consistently rated highly by two methods (Austin et al. 2015).

Some experts have questioned the utility of the ratings to help the patients determine which hospital is best for their needs. Nicholas Osborne at the University of Michigan says that "[the ratings] have become more important for hospital marketing than for actually helping patients find the best care" (Rosenthal 2013d). Professor of healthcare finance J. B. Silvers is even more cynical: "Some hospitals are better at working the numbers than others," he said. "My guess is the safety net hospitals aren't as good at it as richer hospitals" (Ross 2016).

So the question remains: Will patients take the time to check out the safety record of their hospital and will they make decisions about where to receive care based on that information? Research suggests they will. An Altarum Institute study found that patients shown hospital safety scores along with cost information will choose the safer hospitals 97% of the time, regardless of the cost difference (Duke et al. 2014). In England, where prices are consistent, patients provided with information about provider quality and measurements such as waiting time, chose higher-quality providers for elective hip replacement, even if it meant traveling a greater distance and bypassing a local provider of lesser quality (Moscelli et al. 2016).

The key here is getting the information into the hands of the patient/consumer in a format they can understand and find useful. And unlike the United Kingdom, where prices are controlled, paying for value in the United States demands price information to go along with the quality. Competition, innovation, and new ways of looking at data will shape the evolution of websites such as Hospital Compare and Healthgrades, and ranking systems such as Leapfrog Group's and *Consumer Reports*. As we have seen with many other systems like this outside of healthcare, the more the systems are used, the better the data becomes.

Healthcare's Sea of Change

Making this shift to data-driven medical decisions and outcomes-based reimbursement requires major adjustments. Doctors and hospitals have been billing "per procedure" for decades. An entire infrastructure has been built up around this practice, with every aspect of patient care able to be "coded" in some way for billing purposes. According to Jean Balgrosky, founder of Bootstrap Incubation and expert in health information systems, the early precursors to today's EHRs were developed primarily as software to track patient billing and financial information. It was only later that these systems were used for things like electronic prescribing and clinical decision support (Balgrosky 2014). What's worse, very little has been done to track patient outcomes or even to make them measurable until recently, and both price and quality must be taken into consideration.

We've already described in Chapter 6 how difficult it can be to get at healthcare price and quality data. An even bigger challenge is communication between healthcare providers at different facilities. How can hospital administrators justify spending a lot of money to ensure that patients can access their records when visiting competitors? As the move toward value-based care evolves, the most powerful hospitals will likely try to take control of as many nearby facilities as possible, and control the flow of patients among those. An influx of new patients will buffer their institutions' budgets as Medicare penalties mount. Of course, a key issue will be how many of those patients have health coverage, which is a number that could change dramatically over the years.

An increase of mergers and acquisitions isn't necessarily all bad. With this carrot-and-stick approach of penalties and new opportunities moving the system toward value-based reimbursement, hospitals and providers that aren't high quality are likely to be left behind or forced to improve as consumers attempt to choose alternatives. That is good for everyone: individual patients benefit from improved care, populations benefit from overall improved health, employers can see their healthcare cost burdens decrease while their employees' healthcare improve, and institutions benefit financially.

Until healthcare price and quality transparency is the status quo, patients will have to rely on the penalties and incentives that the federal programs provide to weed out poor performing hospitals and draw attention to institutions that succeed. Negative ramifications of these value-based initiatives could include a lack of available healthcare providers in some regions as lower-quality providers and hospitals find CMS penalties and unfavorable ratings bring them to insolvency. Though it's not good for patients (or the economy) to keep institutions open if they can't meet certain standards, there are potential solutions to the problems resulting from hospital closures, including geographic expansion of health systems that are successfully delivering high-value care.

Many Americans are also fervent advocates of privacy. Some have deep concerns that making their medical records easily accessible to healthcare providers will also compromise their privacy. These concerns are just one of the obstacles that have led to a medical system where it is very difficult to share records. However, as we described in Chapter 1, this situation is analogous to online banking. Many of the technological problems have already been addressed and online banking is generally safe and accepted. Patient education and strict guidelines will be key components to making interoperability work.

In addition, many individuals and enterprises have made lots of money under the current U.S. health system, which, as noted earlier, accounts for about $2.7 trillion in spending. Redirecting the flow of that money will be very difficult. No one is going to want to give up their piece of the pie. The U.S. system is unlike other countries that have healthcare systems that are largely controlled by the government (e.g., single-payer) and/or are not-for-profit. Outside of the United States, even when there is competition, there are often regulations that dictate the amount an insurer can raise rates, who they must cover, and what level of services they are required to provide (Paris 2010).

Some market leaders, however, have already started to pioneer truly revolutionary business models that could turn cost-effective care into the next big thing. In 2013, Intermountain Healthcare, a not-for-profit healthcare system in the western United States, announced their partnership with Deloitte Consulting to create ConvergeHEALTH, which combined the hospital system's data and the consulting company's informatics capabilities. As Deloitte's chief innovation officer Andrew Vaz said, "We hope to accelerate the development of what the Institute of Medicine refers to as a 'learning health-care system'" (Intermountain Healthcare 2013).

Because Intermountain has been collecting patient data for nearly 40 years, they have the ability to look at a large number of outcomes, something that researchers can use to find the most cost-effective treatments for patients and best practices for physicians. As Intermountain's chief information officer Marc Probst said, "Research studies that previously might have taken years to complete could be conducted in just a few weeks instead" (Intermountain Healthcare 2013). This is an important point. Instead of having to wait years to follow a patient population to determine their outcomes, Intermountain and Deloitte can leverage the trillions of data points they already have collected.

Since its inception, ConvergeHEALTH has developed several products designed to help hospitals and providers get more out of the data they already have, monitor patient safety, and increase patient engagement (Deloitte 2017). In addition, it has entered into a partnership with pharmaceutical company Allergan to explore outcomes related to specific context, such as respiratory diseases and women's health (Deloitte 2015).

Geisinger Health System is another pioneer in value-based care delivery. Geisinger Health System includes physician practice groups, managed care company (Geisinger Health Plan), and provider facilities across Pennsylvania. It's been named as one of the country's "Most Wired" health systems for 14 consecutive years (Advisory Board 2016a) and has a fully integrated EHR, connecting hospitals, providers, and patients. In 2006, Geisinger implemented the concept of patient-centered medical homes, called the ProvenHealth Navigator (PHN). According to a 2012 paper, "PHN is designed to move resources further 'upstream' in the primary care setting to reduce 'downstream' costs from the highest acuity settings" (Maeng et al. 2012). Geisinger is uniquely positioned to explore the impact of different patient care models because it has access to both claims data (as a payer) and patient outcomes, through the EHR. With a widespread network of providers and facilities, interventions can be tested in a subset of patients or providers, analyzed to determine the financial and patient impacts, and rolled out system-wide or scrapped depending on the results.

This model has demonstrated patients in the PHN were more likely to have used their physician's office for standard care rather than the emergency room (Maeng et al. 2013) and that the medical-home model reduced acute inpatient care (Maeng et al. 2015) and outpatient (Maeng, Sciandra, and Tomcavage 2016) costs.

The idea that treating patients more aggressively earlier in the care cycle can improve patient outcomes and reduce overall costs was tested by Geisinger by "bundling" care for patients with diabetes. Here, the study found that increased professional and outpatient costs, 13% and 9.7%, respectively, were balanced by a significant reduction of nearly 30% in inpatient facility costs and improved patient outcomes (xG Health 2014; Maeng, Yan et al. 2016). And in the Medicaid population covered by Geisinger through the state's expansion using private care organizations, authors found that although prescription drug costs increased, Geisinger's patient-centered medical home approach led to lower-than-expected costs for inpatient, outpatient, and professional care (Maeng, Snyder et al. 2016). If Geisinger's diabetes bundled care program was implemented across the nation, the impact on patients and economic consequences could be substantial.

These studies are certainly impressive and demonstrate that patient care needn't suffer in order to reduce costs. In fact, improved outcomes and lower costs can be the result of targeted, strategic investments based on data.

Geisinger Health System is now spinning out its "optimized care delivery" system, as xG Health, to help other hospital systems and insurers adapt to the new environment (xG Health 2017). But Geisinger's experience isn't likely to be adopted where payers and providers/facilities are playing on different teams. Today, insurers reap most of the rewards when providers are able to increase value. Only when the hospital is also the insurer, do such changes improve the provider's bottom line. This disconnect between the delivery of care and reimbursement will continue to stymie value-based care until the incentives for payers and health systems are aligned. Both want *and need* to reduce overall costs, but health systems can't continue to bear the financial burden of implementing programs, like Geisinger's PHN, unless payers are willing to chip in.

Glen Steele, Chairman of xG Health Solutions and former President and CEO of Geisinger Health System, says that though some groups are aiming to change provider behavior with better incentives, reimbursement is still a "schizophrenic" process with most services paid on the fee-for-service model.

Shifting the bulk of patient care to nonspecialists can be cost-effective, as long as the primary care model can obtain improved outcomes for patients. That's the idea with direct primary care, which companies such as Iora Health are championing. Better primary care, and more careful oversight of the use of specialty care, they argue, can improve health and reduce costs (see Chapter 9).

As Anil Jain, vice president and chief medical officer of Explorys told us, different CEOs are going to have different drives, but all are going to need engagement at the financial level. This is where analytics and technologies such as IBM Watson can identify data-proven, value-based solutions. As mentioned previously, improving the healthcare system relies on constant measuring and data analysis. To find patterns in the data that could point to novel or innovative value-based solutions is challenging, and cognitive computing programs, such as IBM Watson, may provide some answers.

Both Geisinger and Intermountain Health have been pioneers in collecting and tracking data about the connection between treatments and outcomes. They are capitalizing on their early work and beginning to monetize it. As the impetus to move toward value-based care continues, through the need to reduce healthcare costs at the health-system level, and through penalties raised by federal programs such as Medicare, other hospital systems will either become those pioneers' clients, will have to build their own analogous systems, or face being unable to compete in the new environment. Many new biotechnology and healthcare-related companies will emerge in this space, bringing together existing data and new methods to analyze it. Healthcare systems and payers will partner to bring data-driven solutions to life, benefitting patients, providers and facilities, and payers alike.

Future for Value-Based Healthcare Programs

This is just the start, as the unstoppable pressures of healthcare costs and new sources of data converge to reshape the healthcare system—however, much more needs to be done. "We also have challenges on the data management side, around integrating and storing it," says John Glaser, Vice President, Population Health and Global Strategy for Cerner Corporation. "But I think the real innovations ahead will be around the analytics. The issue isn't going to be how much data we can handle, but are we better at collecting and interpreting it?" This will include not only identifying the patients who are at greatest risk of needing health services, but determining which treatment provides the best value. As we've described in this chapter, this is a multifaceted problem, and solutions are likely to be equally complex, require federal incentives, rely on building partnerships with patients, and leverage entrepreneurial innovation.

The federal government has embraced value-based care for years (see the section *Government Initiatives: Medicare's Value-Based Purchasing Programs*). Despite the intent, high-quality analysis of the impacts of value-based purchasing programs has generally been lacking and what has been published has shown mixed results (Farmer and Hochman 2017). For example, some studies have found no improvement in mortality rates for a variety of conditions with value-based payments, while successes have been seen in Britain and with the Blue Cross Alternative Quality Contract (Farmer and Hochman 2017). With a small base of published studies, the overall success or failure of value-based programs to improve patient outcomes or otherwise support the triple aim of healthcare is uncertain. It's also very unclear whether the current U.S. administration will continue to support the regulations that have spurred value-based care in this country. If these regulations are ignored, or outright abandoned, will the trend continue?

This top-down approach hasn't always been well received by patients, providers, or health systems. As one alternative to the government-directed value-based programs, the American Board of Internal Medicine developed a program in partnership with *Consumer Reports* called "Choosing Wisely," in 2012 (American Board of Internal Medicine 2017).

The goal of the initiative is to get buy-in from providers to reduce the number of low-value treatments and tests they order, behaviors that contribute to an estimated $750 billion in unnecessary healthcare spending yearly (Schlesinger and Grob 2017). Improved patient education for value-based healthcare strategies (e.g., avoiding unnecessary antibiotics, more conservative or palliative treatment vs. aggressive treatments) is another goal of the program. California has developed a similar program, Smart Care California, with similar goals to reduce unnecessary tests and procedures. Elective cesarean sections and opioid use among patients with lower-back pain are among its current priorities (Terhune and Kaiser Health News 2017).

A recent study assessed the impact of "framing unnecessary care as waste" and better understanding the public's perception of low-value care across different socioeconomic and racial/ethnic groups using the SelectMD website (Schlesinger and Grob 2017). SelectMD is a physician-choice website from the Better Health Coalition, a nonprofit organization focused on delivering a variety of quality data about healthcare providers to consumers. Using the website, consumers can find local providers based on their use of effective treatments and patient survey results (The Better Health Coalition 2017). Even when study respondents could articulate the benefits to choosing high-value care over low-value options, when using SelectMD less than a third were willing to choose providers who were more conservative in their treatment choices (less low-value care) (Schlesinger and Grob 2017).

The study authors also uncovered an impact of conventional media portrayal of low-value care as waste, fraud, and/or abuse. Patients who associated low-value care as wasteful were "three times as likely to blame providers" compared to those who associated it with health risks (Schlesinger and Grob 2017). Their findings indicate the media should reframe descriptions of value-based care in the context of improving and personalizing the physician–patient relationship and reducing risks and harms to patients (Schlesinger and Grob 2017).

How to calculate the value of specific procedures and treatments continues to be a barrier to moving away from payments based on volume of medical care.

As we described in Chapter 6, there has been significant resistance on the part of public and private payers to reimburse for some high cost drugs. A new treatment for Duchenne muscular dystrophy (DMD), Emflaza (deflazacort), is a case in point. Emflaza is a corticosteroid that has been used for decades, but only recently received FDA approval for DMD under previous owner Marathon Pharma (Sagonowsky 2017a). Marathon also set Emflaza's price at $89,000 before selling off the drug to PTC Therapeutics in a deal worth more than $190 million. Although PTC hasn't yet released Emflaza's new price, Washington State's Health Care Authority published a report indicating prednisone, an older steroid that costs ~$55 yearly, would be its preferred drug for DMD patients instead of Emflaza (Sagonowsky 2017a). In another example where price became a major issue, UniCure gave up on Glybera, the world's first approved gene therapy treatment. The drug is for treatment of a very rare disease—familial lipoprotein lipase deficiency. But the $1 million-plus anticipated price tag clouded its prospects and UniCure is not going to try and renew that approval (Sagonowsky 2017b).

When you consider the lifetime costs of paying for someone with a chronic disease, such as diabetes, or cancer, where new medication costs can reach $150,000 or more (Knox 2017), it's not difficult to see that it makes sense to use a value-based system to determine whether or not to pay for the drugs. But determining the tipping point, identifying the specific patient characteristics (e.g., age, sex, other health conditions) that make a treatment or procedure cost-effective, is complicated and driven by data and advanced analytics. And beyond simply determining whether or not to pay for a specific drug, the data can be used to identify the most effective drug or even what preventive measures can be taken to keep the patient healthy in the first place. We foresee payers and health systems using evidence-based practices and data analytics, including artificial intelligence (AI), to move value-based care forward as penalties continue to rise and there are improved financial incentives to do so.

Changing provider behavior is key to making value-based care successful. Clinical decision support mechanisms, such as alerts that are integrated in an EHR system to warn doctors of potential drug interactions or services that have already been ordered by another provider, are just a few examples where data analytics and bioinformatics can change physician behavior. Successful implementation of these types of interventions requires an EHR with advanced capabilities and interoperability between different EHRs and/or different health systems.

Workforce engagement is the essential element that bridges safety, quality, and patient experience in a value-based healthcare system (Minemyer 2017b). A 2017 report by Press Ganey found a direct association between patient experience and safety. The health systems with the highest patient engagement scores on the Hospital Consumer Assessment of Healthcare Providers and Systems survey were found to have lower spending in the first 30 days of patient care but had higher net margins (Minemyer 2017b). According to James Merlino, president and chief medical officer of Press Ganey's strategic consulting division, "What this demonstrates clearly is that when you focus on the right things for patients, you're not only improving the delivery of care and meeting needs, you're actually doing it in a more cost economical way" (Minemyer 2017b).

Geisinger Health System recently published the initial results of a case study with its nursing staff to adopt structured, evidence-based processes in patient management that are demonstrated to improve patient outcomes (Robel 2017). The patient experience is paramount to Geisinger. In 2015, new CEO David Feinberg announced the ProvenExperience program, where the health system would refund patients if patients were unhappy with their care. This money-back guarantee program made it even more important that the care patients received was consistent across the system's 12 hospital campuses (Robel 2017).

Geisinger developed and implemented a "nursing bundle" across their health system consisting of five practices including hourly rounding on patients, whiteboard use in patient rooms, and bedside shift reports. Importantly, the practices identified by the nursing staff for inclusion in the nursing bundle were *measurable*, a necessary component to track the utility and value of the program (Robel 2017). Preliminary results suggest hourly rounding, bedside shift reporting, and whiteboard updating occurred more frequently after the nursing bundle was implemented (Robel 2017). In addition to providing a more consistent patient experience across the healthcare system, overall patient satisfaction scores improved (Kuhrt 2017b).

Traditionally autonomous, physicians will need to be aware of evidence-based practices, especially where they counter a hospital's established standards of care. We've already seen how evidence has changed provider practices, with fewer men receiving PSA tests and fewer women taking hormone replacement therapy after menopause. Academic consortia and partnerships with industry (e.g., pharmaceutical companies) that explore health-related outcomes in their patient databases can achieve more, and more quickly, thanks to informatics and data analytics. ConvergeHEALTH is just one example where this is taking place, IBM Watson Health is another.

Another critical issue will be whether health consumers can rise to the occasion and play a part in rewarding value-based care, or whether it will be up to insurers and employers to help them make better decisions. For solutions such as patient-centered medical homes to be successful, patients need to see the value of not starting their care at a specialist or acute medical facility. Developing trusted relationships with primary care providers is the first step in this process (Schlesinger and Grob 2017), something that can minimize patient perceptions of primary care doctors as "gatekeepers" or equivocating value-based care with rationing.

How do providers and the medical centers that employ them encourage patients to develop this type of relationship with doctors? First, patient needs will have to be addressed. This means primary care centers will need convenient hours, be easy to access, and be staffed with high-quality providers that can address a wide variety of patient concerns. Meeting patients' needs includes addressing social determinants of health and behavioral health issues (Manos 2017). Second, when patients need to see a specialist, access to their EHRs will be essential to avoid duplication of services and so that the specialist can hand off care back to the primary care provider without difficulty.

With patients paying for higher proportions of their medical care through high-deductible health plans, it should be easier to get them on board—if the data are there for them to identify providers who practice the best quality and highest value-based care for their condition(s).

Encouraging patients to choose providers who eschew low-value care (e.g., redundant or unnecessary tests) will require a multifaceted approach that involves providers, medical systems, and the media to better communicate the benefits of value-based care while avoiding the stigma of healthcare rationing or perception of lesser care. As noted by Schlesinger and Grob, emphasizing the benefits of value-based care (e.g., risk reduction) will reduce conflating low-value solely with fraud, waste, and abuse, and blaming providers for recommending low value care or excessive treatment (Schlesinger and Grob 2017). Better communication from health systems to their catchment area through advertising and outreach programs can make this happen.

Although this chapter has described the movement toward value-based programs largely from a provider- or medical center-centric perspective, other key stakeholders include pharmaceutical companies, medical device manufacturers, and the growing number of digital health companies. They are also under increasing pressure to demonstrate the value for their products, often through clinical trials or other research and clinical studies. These data also have a role helping providers make evidence-driven, value-based decisions for their patients. For example, the information gleaned from a single molecular test, such as whole exome or whole genome sequencing (see Chapter 2), has the potential to reduce or eliminate several other, less informative tests.

Companies that have the data to support the value for their products (medications, tests, or medical devices) will have a tremendous advantage over those that don't. As value-based payments increase, expect to see more providers making decisions about which test to use or which medication to prescribe based on data.

Some of these companies are already embracing value-based reimbursement. Patients with chronic disease(s) that use Noom, a digital health company that provides virtual coaching, won't have to pay unless they reach their health goals (Baum 2016a). Some pharmaceutical companies offer a money-back guarantee if their drug doesn't work (Staton 2016b). Companies that can differentiate themselves from the competition by publishing their data or at least sharing it with providers will find themselves at the forefront of a value-based system.

From patients to providers to healthcare systems, moving away from fee-for-service to value-based care means each stakeholder will be making decisions and acting based on data. For patients, that might mean selecting a hospital for their heart surgery based on data from the Hospital Compare website, and finding the hospital uses remote patient monitoring to keep them healthy once they go home. For providers, preparing for the Medicare Access and CHIP Reauthorization Act (MACRA) and other value-based reimbursement regulations will require greater emphasis on evidence-based medicine *and* collecting the patient outcome data to support it. MACRA replaces prior methodology to update the physician fee schedule with a new program, the Quality Payment Program, which uses two methods to reward value-based care: advanced alternative payment models and merit-based incentive payment systems (Centers for Medicare & Medicaid Services 2016d). Hospitals and other medical centers may undergo an increase in strategic mergers and acquisitions, the creation of ACOs, or structuring of their provider networks into patient-centered medical homes to meet the demands of a value-based reimbursement system.

In the end, value-based payment stands on three pillars: quality, cost, and outcomes, and the three are not mutually exclusive. It is possible—and is already being done—to have high-quality, lower-cost healthcare that demonstrably improves patient outcomes and advances population health—and *Moneyball Medicine* will get us there.

Chapter 8

Data-Driven Drug Discovery and Development

Are pharma companies chemists or data scientists in the future?

Christine Lemke
Cofounder and President of Evidation Health

"She was a 32-year-old aerobics instructor from a Dallas suburb—healthy, college educated, with two young children. Nothing out of the ordinary, except one thing. Her cholesterol was astoundingly low" (Kolata 2013b). That's how *New York Times* reporter Gina Kolata describes the woman whose exceedingly rare genetic mutation helped fuel the race to produce a potentially multibillion-dollar drug.

Such races are common in the pharmaceutical industry, which commands a world market of just over $1 trillion (Deloitte 2016). The industry spends at least $60 billion on research and development (PhRMA 2016), and there are thousands of life science and information technology firms that support that effort. The life sciences informatics market alone has been estimated to be worth $1.7 billion (Grand View Research 2016a). But drug discovery is a highly competitive field where the stakes are high. In 2016, 22 novel drugs were approved in the United States. But that number can vary significantly—45 were approved in 2015 (Hirschler 2017). It's important to note, however, that only 2 out of 10 drugs ever return revenues that match or exceed developers' R&D costs (PhRMA 2016), which averages $2.87 billion for a single drug when all pre- and post-approval required costs are considered (DiMasi, Grabowski, and Hansen 2016). Time is another factor, since it typically takes 10–15 years to develop a drug (PhRMA 2016), though this can also vary substantially.

Failure in pharma or biotech is thus a huge setback; being the first to market, even by months, can be a crucial element in success. New data, analytical tools, and other technologies are increasingly being brought to bear on drug discovery and development in the hopes of bringing new treatments to market faster, and ensuring more of them will be successful.

At the time she was discovered, that aerobics instructor was one of only two people in the entire world documented to have "dazzling" low-density lipoprotein (LDL) levels, as Kolata wrote. The Dallas woman's level was 14, while a woman in Zimbabwe had recorded a 15. Normal adults, meanwhile, have LDL levels of about 100 and people who have abnormally high cholesterol can see those levels reach beyond 300, despite drug therapy and drastic lifestyle changes. And doctors continue to be frustrated that many people with high cholesterol, even those who are on drug therapy, are still dying of heart attacks.

Statins, drugs that lower cholesterol, are the typical treatment for high cholesterol (hypercholesterolemia) and among the biggest sellers of all time. In fact, Lipitor (atorvastin) has garnered lifetime sales of $148.7 billion, making its sales the highest for any drug (Williams 2017). But as we described earlier, many patients who take statins have negative side effects, such as neuropathy, and these can reduce compliance with the medication (see Chapter 2). So any new class of drug that can effectively lower cholesterol levels and reduce outcomes such as strokes, heart attacks, and death, but without the negative side effects (e.g., neuropathy) common with statins, has the potential to be a financial blockbuster (Staton 2015).

Both women turned out to have a double mutation of a gene called *PCSK9*, which quickly became one of the hottest targets in the pharmaceutical industry. "It's just really exciting," one scientist told newsletter *FierceBiotech* of the *PCSK9* drugs, "This is why we all got into biotechnology in the first place" (Garde 2014).

But the story of *PCSK9* and LDL cholesterol began almost a decade earlier.

A family in France with an inherited form of hypercholesterolemia and a history of heart disease was found to have *PCSK9* mutations (Varret et al. 1999; Abifadel et al. 2003). Researchers at the University of Texas Southwestern Medical Center hypothesized that just as some *PCSK9* mutations led to incredibly high levels of LDL cholesterol, others might lead to very low levels. Using data from a large population-based study (the Atherosclerosis Risk in Communities [ARIC] study), the researchers found subjects with certain *PCSK9* mutations had lower LDL cholesterol levels and a concomitant reduction in the risk for coronary artery disease (Cohen et al. 2006). Based on these findings, the researchers combed through their own patient data, looking for a patient that might have inherited two defunct copies of *PCSK9* from their parents (Kolata 2013b). The patient they found was the aerobics instructor.

A dramatic race ensued between Amgen and Sanofi/Regeneron, with the latter pulling ahead using an unusual tactic: Sanofi and Regeneron bought a priority review voucher from BioMarin for $67.5 million (Carroll 2014). BioMarin received the voucher from the FDA following the agency's approval of Vimizim (elosulfase alfa), a drug for Morquio A syndrome, a rare disease that affects approximately 1 in 200,000 people (Gaffney 2014; Children's Hospital of Philadelphia 2017). Such vouchers are part of the agency's Orphan Disease program to accelerate research in rare, or orphan, conditions (see Chapter 5). The voucher cut months off the normal regulatory review for Sanofi/Regeneron's drug. In the race to be the first to bring this new kind of drug to market, that shortcut was considered worth the price of the voucher. In July 2015, Sanofi/Regeneron's alirocumab (Praluent) became the first such treatment approved by the U.S. FDA (U.S. Food & Drug Administration 2015a), followed by approval of Amgen's evolocumab (Repatha) in August of the same year (U.S. Food & Drug Administration 2015b).

The story doesn't quite end there for the newly approved *PCSK9* inhibitors. Deals with pharmacy benefits managers led to exclusive arrangements for both Repatha and Praluent (Phend 2016) and Amgen signed a payment for performance value-based contract with insurer Harvard Pilgrim (Weisman 2015; Cassels 2016). Results from ongoing clinical trials were positive, demonstrating a reduction of heart attacks and strokes in addition to lowering LDL cholesterol levels (Amgen 2017a,b; Kolata 2017; Sabatine et al. 2017).

But despite the hope about the market potential of *PCSK9* inhibitors, and the excellent science that went into this drug, it appears to have been largely hype. Sales have failed to meet analysts' expectations. Prelaunch research suggested the market was worth approximately $10–20 billion per year, with some suggesting even higher potential depending on the patient population (Staton 2015). But the first full quarter sales of *PCSK9* inhibitors reached only $4 million, far below even a more modest $21 million prediction (Cassels 2016). First quarter 2017 sales have improved, though remain far below analysts' expectations (Chen 2017; Gatlin 2017). Pfizer, which was developing its own *PCSK9* inhibitor (bococizumab) and was expected to seek (and receive) FDA approval in 2016/2017 (Staton 2016d), abruptly shuttered its clinical trials and halted development in November 2016 after spending hundreds of millions of dollars, citing the "evolving treatment and market landscape for lipid-lowering agents" (Carroll 2016; Husten 2016).

So why the colossal failure, after so much hope? As STAT's Damian Garde writes, "The problem boils down to doctors who are reluctant to write prescriptions, insurers who are unwilling to pay for them, and drug companies that have failed to understand a fast-changing marketplace" (Garde 2016). The doctors are reluctant because insurers are demanding tedious amounts of paperwork to prescribe the drugs, such as proof a patient failed to respond adequately to at least two other lipid-lowering regimens (e.g., high-dose statin therapy). Insurers are unwilling to pay because they want to see solid outcomes data: do these drugs just lower LDL or do they also actually improve outcomes (e.g., reduce strokes and heart attacks)?

Ongoing and recently concluded clinical trials may start to provide some answers. Results from the FOURIER clinical trial were announced at the 2017 American College of Cardiology meeting and published simultaneously in the *New England Journal of Medicine* (American College of Cardiology 2017; Sabatine et al. 2017). The FOURIER trial included more than 27,000 patients in 49 countries with high cholesterol who were already on statin therapy. Adding the *PCSK9* inhibitor evolocumab to patients' therapy regimens reduced the composite primary outcome of cardiovascular death, myocardial infarction, stroke, coronary revascularization, and hospitalization for unstable angina by a modest 1.5%, but failed to reduce cardiovascular death or all-cause death compared to placebo (Sabatine et al. 2017). Whether this reduction is sufficient to satisfy payers, or that the benefit of the treatment is worth the cost remains to be seen.

But the changing market for drugs may be the biggest factor here. For decades, pharmaceutical companies have operated on the assumption that if they could develop a drug that clearly affects a well-known target, their marketing arms could sell that drug. Insurers offered little resistance. Patient demand could be driven up by direct-to-consumer advertising, and doctors would not resist.

So what changed? Rising healthcare costs and shifting of more of the financial burden of treatment to patients, to start. Clearly, the market still tolerates expensive drugs: multiple hepatitis C drugs are on the market, with prices starting around $55,000 (Graham 2016b). In stark contrast to *PCSK9* inhibitors, the hepatitis C drugs are *cures*. They completely eradicate the deadly virus from the patient's body after treatment. And rare disease treatments can cost more than $400,000 yearly (see Chapter 5). But for *PCSK9* inhibitors, there hasn't yet been a compelling enough reason for insurers to pay for them.

To this day, Amgen and Sanofi/Regeneron are in a continued battle over patent rights. In March 2016, a jury found that Praluent infringed on the Repatha patents (Staton 2016a), paving the way for Amgen to receive some of the Praluent royalties. Although the court ordered Praluent off the market, a federal judge stayed the injunction, allowing Praluent to remain on the market while the companies fight it out in court (Caffrey 2017). No matter who wins the patent case, with a yearly cost of more than $14,000 for this drug, they have an uphill battle proving to patients and doctors that they are a cost-effective treatment for long-term use (Kolata 2017).

The story of *PCSK9* encompasses several of the topics we've covered in the book thus far: value-based care, price and quality, and the role of big data and new technologies in healthcare. It also highlights some of the inherent challenges of drug discovery, such as regulatory and market uncertainties, an ultracompetitive market, and the investments of hundreds of millions of dollars with no guarantee of launching a new drug. In this chapter, we'll show how data-intensive methods are changing drug discovery pipelines and the companies developing them.

Genome Revolution in Pharmacology

The sequencing of the human genome sparked a period many would later refer to as "genome fever" (Shreeve 2005; Finkel 2012). Brand new "genomic data" companies such as Celera, CuraGen, and Incyte Genomics sold pharmaceutical companies subscriptions to their exclusive databases for daunting prices that reached into the hundreds of millions. Dozens of new firms were launched around proprietary software to analyze all this new data. With the stock market peaking, there was a giddy atmosphere, and tech companies that would have normally stuck with the staid and somber image typical to life sciences firms were putting splashy furniture in their waiting rooms and coming up with clever names more suited to dot-com start-ups.

Seeking to uncover the causes of various diseases, laboratories around the world launched massive databases that aimed to compare the newly available "average" genome to the blueprints from people with specific illnesses. There was great hope of sifting through all that genomic data and lifting out the targets for many new billion-dollar drugs.

The genomic big data curve was growing at a remarkable speed and genomics was red hot. The problem was that we still didn't know the best use for these data.

It did not take long for this to lead to disappointment. Genomics-based leads for new drug targets largely failed, and the growing amount of public data available made creating and maintaining proprietary data look less attractive.

Within a few years, the market for genomic databases collapsed, scores of companies went out of business or changed their models drastically. Incyte, for example, abandoned genomics, hired a seasoned pharmaceutical executive and dove straight into traditional (small molecule) drug development (Allen 2005). Realizing their investment in genomic data couldn't be quickly exploited with new drugs on a fast turnaround, big drug companies and investors became skittish. Genomics was no longer a buzzword that could net you generous financial backing.

Suddenly, people and the press were complaining about genome hype and the first part of the genomic era was widely labeled by the press to be a bust (Allen 2005). Perhaps the classic example is Human Genome Sciences (HGS), which was born of the genomic revolution. HGS was founded in 1993 by noted scientist William A. Haseltine as the for-profit partner to a genomics research institute Craig Venter was leading at the time.

Haseltine declared that "Death is a series of preventable diseases," and imagined using the onslaught of genomic data to create a cornucopia of new drugs (Fisher 1999). He said the company had sequence data for 95% of all human genes and would amass a patent portfolio that would essentially make it a "must have" partner for anyone seeking to create genomics-based drugs.

His assertion seemed vindicated early on, as HGS netted over a billion dollars from investors, including big pharmas. Haseltine maintained that HGS's approach "speeds up biological discovery a hundredfold, easily" (Zitner 2000). But by mid-2000, the company's pipeline was running dry, as promising drugs failed in clinical trials and the stock had fallen to about $10 from a one-time high of $241, when it "seemed to epitomize the promise of genomics," as the *New York Times* reported (Pollack 2004). Haseltine left the company, and like many biotechnology start-ups before it, HGS set out to reinvent itself under new leadership.

So, while sequencing the human genome did not provide a list of easy targets for drug companies to start picking off, "They created a quantum leap in biomedical science," Kenneth C. Carter, a former executive at the company, told the *New York Times* (Pollack 2004).

Several years later, in March 2011, HGS and its longtime partner and drug giant GlaxoSmithKline netted FDA approval for belumimab (Benlysta), the first drug to treat lupus (*Pharma Letter* 2011). Based on that achievement, and several other promising treatments in advanced trials, GlaxoSmithKline paid $3 billion for the genomics pioneer in 2012 (Herper 2012). It's not the wave of genomic drugs that was expected from HGS and others. But the use of genetic data "remains one of the most likely ways to improve the lackluster success rates of pharmaceutical research labs," wrote *Forbes* Matthew Herper about that deal (Herper 2012).

Indeed, the genome revolution has started to come of age. Though not at the initial pace anticipated by Haseltine and early genome companies, once sequencing technology evolved to next-generation (and next-next-generation) sequencing methods, the scientific discoveries, such as identification of drug resistance variants in HIV and tuberculosis or the pathways involved in the development of lung cancer, began to flood in and haven't slowed since (Koboldt et al. 2013).

Another key development has been the emergence of companies providing genomics services, including sequencing, analytics, data storage and other services. This has made it possible for a much wider range of companies and organizations to incorporate genomics, thereby helping the field to advance more rapidly.

Geiseinger Health System's MyCode biobank project, carried out in collaboration with the Regeneron Genetics Center, is an early success story of how a clinical center can partner with a genomics service provider. The health system enrolled 150,000 patients/participants by mid-2017 (Allison Branca 2017). And it is not only already being used for patient care, but has identified possible new drug targets, including one related to heart disease. Seven Bridges is providing data analysis and management to multiple Big Data projects, including the Cancer Genomics Cloud and the Million Veteran Program. WuXiNextCODE, meanwhile, offers a global contract genomics platform, and it works with multiple pharma companies and other organizations in the United States and abroad, including Children's Hospital Boston and Genomics England. Their "tool box" now includes artificial intelligence, and has been used to uncover new findings related to rare diseases, autism, cancer, cardiovascular disease and other conditions.

Large-Scale Drug Screening and Virtual Assays: From Millions of Compounds to One

The world of drug design and development has changed substantially in the past several decades as laboratory techniques have improved (e.g., crystallography) and computers make it easy to virtually manipulate molecules. To appreciate just how much techniques like virtual assays and structural modeling are shortening the drug discovery pipeline, it might be helpful to provide an example describing how drugs were developed in the past.

The cancer drug Taxol (paclitaxel) has been used to treat breast, ovarian, and lung cancers for years. The drug is derived from the bark of the Pacific yew tree; samples of the bark were collected in the early 1960s by researchers who were looking for natural substances that could cure cancer (Wani et al. 1971). Nearly 15 years passed before researchers at the National Cancer Institute published studies showing paclitaxel's antitumor activity in a variety of cell line and animal models of cancers (Fuchs and Johnson 1978).

Alongside the *in vitro* (cell-based) and animal experiments (Sternberg et al. 1987; Riondel et al. 1988), scientists were investigating the biological mechanism that made the drug work (Schiff, Fant, and Horwitz 1979; Schiff and Horwitz 1980). But this work was slow-going, and harvesting the bark from the yew was unsustainable in the quantities necessary for cancer treatment. Creating the compound in the lab was complicated, but the first large-scale production of Taxol was finally achieved by

Polysciences, Inc. (Wei 2007). Eventually, chemists discovered a method to produce Taxol by isolating one of its precursor molecules from a more common species of the yew, eliminating the source problem, and a cell culture method was put into use by Bristol-Myers Squibb for production (Wei 2007).

More than 20 years after the initial discovery of paclitaxel, in 1984, the National Cancer Institute began phase I clinical trials of Taxol (Wiernik et al. 1987). Eight years later, in December 1992, Taxol was approved by the FDA for ovarian cancer, and in 1994 for breast cancer treatment (AP 1994).

A 30-year time span from drug discovery (collection of the yew bark) to FDA approval and launch (Wei 2007) was not unusual in the past, and even more recently, it could easily be more than a decade between discovery and the finished drug. The costs of this lengthy process: more than $2 billion (DiMasi, Grabowski, and Hansen 2016). But today, that timeline (and its associated costs) can be dramatically reduced using computers, high-throughput molecular screens, and the analysis of vast amounts of existing data.

High-Throughput Screening: A Case Study

In 1998, Robert Beall, the president and CEO of the Cystic Fibrosis Foundation, approached a small company called Aurora Biosciences, which was cofounded by Roger Tsien, who is now a Nobel Laureate. Tsien had been working on large-scale ways to track the movements of proteins and cell signaling. This approach is called high-throughput screening (HTS), and it can test many compounds simultaneously to see which ones have the desired effect.

HTS is hypothesis-agnostic: scientists don't need to have any insight that a molecule or class of molecules might work against their target. By screening thousands, hundreds of thousands, or even millions of chemicals at once, the hope is to identify a percentage that can be tested more in-depth (Sliwoski et al. 2014). HTS can be combined with computational methods, further reducing the costs associated with performing a large HTS and increasing the potential yield (Sliwoski et al. 2014).

Notably, this method would have a dramatic impact on rare disease research, specifically for cystic fibrosis (CF), which was, like most rare diseases at the time, largely ignored by the pharmaceutical industry. Instead of screening one or a few compounds at a time, the entire process could be turned on its head, so that researchers could winnow down to a few likely drug candidates before beginning even preclinical studies, which are expensive and time-consuming. For rare diseases with very small patient populations and limited financial means for clinical trials, it could mean a drastically reduced timeline to bring new drugs to patients.

Beall's idea was to pay Aurora Biosciences to find compounds that would repair the effects of the mutation and allow chloride to move freely into the cell. He started by giving the company $2 million directly from the Cystic Fibrosis Foundation's own coffers. A year later, he snagged $20 million from the Gates Foundation and added another $17 million from the Cystic Fibrosis Foundation (Groopman 2009). By then, Aurora had devised an effective high-throughput screen and was on its way to using it to test more than a half a million chemical compounds.

But to go from crude drug candidates to a final, approved drug was going to take a lot more money. In 2003, Beall asked one of the Cystic Fibrosis Foundation's staunchest supporters, millionaire businessman Joe O'Donnell (see Chapter 5) to help them raise the additional funds (McGrory 2012). O'Donnell raised $175 million for the project, 2 years ahead of schedule, and in 2012 Vertex Pharmaceuticals (which had acquired Aurora) launched ivacaftor (Kalydeco). It was the first drug to address the fundamental cause of CF, the mutated protein. The drug was initially approved for use in only a very small percentage of CF patients, those ages 6 years and older with the G551D mutation. But the approval was later expanded to include even younger patients and a broader range of mutations, though not the most common CFTR F508 deletion (Vertex 2015).

The investment proved a wise one for the Cystic Fibrosis Foundation for another reason: They were able to recoup their investment and make money by selling their rights to the drug to Royalty Pharma for $3.3 billion (Fidler 2014). The Cystic Fibrosis Foundation had invested a total of about $150 million in the drug by the time the sale was made, reaping them a huge profit they could now plow back into finding more CF drugs. The Foundation is thus again rewriting the rules of drug discovery, thanks to a data-intensive approach and an investment acumen that other nonprofits are hoping to duplicate (Tozzi 2015).

Although the development timeline for Kalydeco was shorter than the three decades it took for Taxol, it still took more than 10 years to bring the drug to market from the initial HTS. A drawback for traditional HTS is the low overall yield of potential drugs (Sliwoski et al. 2014). But computer-aided design methods continue to reduce the lead time between an initial idea for a drug and testing the compound in cell and animal models. Databases of molecules with pharmacokinetic information can be combed through automatically with computers, and structural modeling programs allow scientists to visualize how a compound might physically interact with a protein. Structural modeling programs use three-dimensional representations of molecules that can be manipulated *in silico*. This process is computationally intensive, but can increase the yield of likely drug candidates at a lower cost, compared to traditional HTS (Sliwoski et al. 2014).

These computer-aided design methods have resulted in the ability to "virtually" assess hundreds of thousands of molecules using "libraries," such as PubChem (Wheeler et al. 2006) and DrugBank (Wishart et al. 2006). Information giant Thomson Reuters has developed several databases for life sciences research, including MetaDrug for drug development (Thomson Reuters 2017). Starting with a library of hundreds of thousands of molecules, researchers can now use these computational, virtual assays, to narrow down candidate drugs to a few dozen or fewer. Additionally, these methods can be used to design a novel compound, using known pharmacologic characteristics to guide virtual construction of a molecule (Sliwoski et al. 2014). However, due to a variety of factors, such as proprietary or incomplete databases, virtual assessments don't tell us everything we need to know about a molecule's potential effects. For example, as Eric Topol, director of genomics at the Scripps Research Institute, told us, every drug used to treat heart disease has some sort of pharmacogenomic effect, but there are still many with unknown properties. Continued lab research contributes to our understanding, but unless the data are structured in a way that makes it easy to search (or even find in the first place), the knowledge can remain inaccessible.

This is one reason why pharma companies and others have spent significant resources on building proprietary databases. With these databases, scientists can identify molecules based on where and how they interact with the target molecule. Some even have toxicity and half-life information—which can be helpful when ruling out potential compounds or for pursuing extended-release formulations. For example, p38 MAPK inhibitors, used in cancer treatments, were designed by identifying and modeling fragments of molecules that bound to specific regions of the protein (Cogan et al. 2008; Sliwoski et al. 2014). With the ability to virtually screen thousands of molecules, pharma companies can decide which ones to move to *in vitro* experiments more efficiently, ultimately reducing the time it can take to move from the initial hypothesis to a clinical trial.

Changing Clinical Trials: Study Design and Patient Recruitment

Described previously (see Chapter 3), genomic data are changing how clinical trials are structured. Instead of oncology trials focused on breast or pancreatic cancer, basket trials (where patients are grouped by molecular mutation) are underway for numerous treatments.

Though the trials are in early stages, results from the SUMMIT phase II trial for HER-targeted treatment with neratinib presented at a recent American Association for Cancer Research conference indicate this approach is valid. Across 21 different cancer types, patient responses to neratinib were influenced by both the type of cancer (e.g., bladder or breast cancer) *and* the specific *HER2* and *HER3* mutation (Ashford 2017).

In May 2017, the FDA approved the cancer drug pembroluzimab (Keytruda) for patients with solid tumors with specific genetic mutations. In the FDA's press release, the acting director of the Office of Hematology and Oncology Products Richard Pazdur said, "This is an important first for the cancer community. Until now, the FDA has approved cancer treatments based on where in the body the cancer started—for example, lung or breast cancers. We have now approved a drug based on a tumor's biomarker without regard to the tumor's original location" (U.S. Food & Drug Administration 2017b). The implications of this approval are wide-reaching, as we'll present later in this chapter and later in the book. For clinical trials, it validates the hypothesis behind basket trials, where different cancer types with the same genetic mutation are tested with the same drug, and underscores the importance that molecular testing will play in the future.

But molecular testing is useful for more than just oncology. As described above for cystic fibrosis, eligibility for Kalydeco depends on which specific genomic mutation a patient has. And patients needing a blood thinner might have genetic testing performed first to determine how they are likely to metabolize the drug and help their doctor with dosing (see Chapter 2). As pharma companies look to ensure that drug candidates make it through the development pipeline, there will be further segmentation of the patient population by molecular status. And although large sample sizes are one way of ensuring statistical rigor, there are alternate methods that can be used for smaller populations.

Inevitably, recruiting patients for a trial, which is already challenging due to the myriad inclusion and exclusion criteria and other requirements for participation, will become more complicated, at least in the short term. This will have the effect of limiting the number of potential candidates for a study, but may increase the number of studies reaching completion. Furthermore, having molecular testing as a screening method for study inclusion will result in databases that can be mined for future studies of other drugs, or when the drug maker is seeking approval for a new indication (see the sidebar *Moving from Data to Personalized Treatment*).

So rather than perceiving molecular screening as a barrier to patient participation in trials, entrepreneurs and others are looking at it as an opportunity to make the eligibility process more efficient. The federal government's website, clinicaltrials.gov, is publicly available and patients can search for trials of interest. Some genomic testing companies provide a service to match patients to potential clinical trials based on their test results. Foundation Medicine's patient reports provide doctors and patients with not only information about the genetic mutations in the patient's cancer, but also approved treatments and clinical trials that may be beneficial (Foundation Medicine 2017). Start-up Deep 6 AI uses artificial intelligence methods to analyze patients' clinical information from their EHR record and biomarker data to match them to clinical trials (Deep 6 AI 2017). As with other AI approaches, as Deep 6's system analyzes a greater number of patients and their data, the system improves its accuracy, making it more valuable to other providers.

SIDEBAR: MOVING FROM DATA TO PERSONALIZED TREATMENT

Eric Schadt, PhD

Chair, Genetics and Genomic Sciences, Mount Sinai Health System

"For the people with the right tools, talent and big data, there is a unique opportunity here to do something that's never been done before," says Eric Schadt, Director of the

Icahn Institute for Genomics and Multiscale Biology at Mount Sinai Health System. "And we've positioned ourselves to achieve that" (Schadt 2017).

One of the group's key hires was Jeff Hammerbacher—a classmate of Mark Zuckerberg's from Harvard and the person widely credited with scaling Facebook. "We're setting up a system by which we will be massively scaling parallel biological information, integrating it with clinical data, and able to distill information on the fly," explains Schadt.

He points out that multiple groups are testing cancers for numerous specific genetic mutations, as many as 200 or more. Mount Sinai has done several studies using whole genome sequencing of tumors as well as their RNA, and then mapped that to a network model to see if they can predict the best treatment for a particular tumor.

For several types of cancer, including medullary thyroid (a relatively rare malignancy), Schadt's team and collaborators have genomic data on several hundred tumors. That's terabytes of information about the genetic makeup of these different tumors. "We've analyzed that to find out what's disrupted in a particular tumor that could be driving its growth and spread. Next, we can do a chemogenomic screen to see what drugs that could target these specific disruptions [that] already exist or may be in the pipeline," he says.

Schadt believes that knitting all that together is what could offer patients something new that would go against the traditional pharmaceutical paradigm.

Typically, pharmaceutical companies are looking for a "one-size-fits-all" product—a single pill that treats a common condition such as heart failure, high cholesterol or diabetes, because that nets the biggest returns. But that's not an easy proposition. "The reason 9 out of 10 drugs fail in clinical trials isn't because pharmaceutical companies are stupid," says Schadt. "There are all kinds of things that make this extremely difficult. The advantage of our approach is that whether or not it quickly nets us any better treatments, we're continually learning more about biology and predictive modeling."

Mount Sinai has also partnered with Sage Bionetworks, headed by Stephen Friend, on The Resilience Project. For this project, they are sequencing the whole genomes of people who have mutations that put them at high risk for certain conditions and trying to uncover "second site" mutations and environmental factors that are protective. "After all, we know that many genes can greatly increase risk, but usually not everyone with the gene gets the disease so there must be some factors that keep even those with 'bad genes' from developing disease," Schadt says. This study will help further elucidate what makes a mutation increase risk, and whether other factors can mitigate that.

"I think we should look at Big Data in healthcare like the Hadron super collider project," Schadt says. "It's not just about answering the questions you know; it's about coming up with completely new types of questions." He points out that people today are already coming up with bold new ways of leveraging the digital universe in other fields. "What I see as the culmination of our efforts is precision medicine—building individualized models for each person that map their health course trajectories and, as a result, provide treatment options specifically tuned to the individual," says Schadt.

Getting patients into clinical trials is just one challenge. Many clinical trials fail to reach completion when a treatment fails to demonstrate a benefit or negatively affects patients. Defining "benefit" is of particular concern, since outcomes are often measured by proxy variables. In fact, one of the criticisms of the *PCSK9* clinical trials has been that they didn't really measure a reduction in death by itself, but used a composite endpoint that included myocardial infarction, stroke, and hospitalization for angina instead (Sabatine et al. 2017).

Another issue is that in some diseases patients progress very differently, with some worsening much faster than others, whether or not they take a particular drug. Multiple sclerosis, for example, has several subtypes that progress differently (National Multiple Sclerosis Society 2017). Patient variation makes it very difficult to determine whether a drug is having the desired effect or not. The cTAP Collaborative (see Chapter 5) is trying to address this for Duchenne muscular dystrophy, and finding patients could be categorized based on their 6-minute walk test trajectories (Mercuri et al. 2016), but hopes their findings can be applied to other diseases as well. Other means of objectively measuring gait, such as using Microsoft's Kinect image and depth sensors, could be applied to Duchenne trials, as well as studies for other disorders where movement can be impaired or declines over time (Ťupa et al. 2015). Deep diving into patient data and analyzing what variables are associated with disease progression may lead to improvements in patient recruitment for clinical trials.

Digital health, additional data sources, and unusual study designs might improve the results of clinical trials. This is what real world evidence (RWE) is all about—data collected from real-life experiences of the patient that might be contained in EHRs, billing and claims data, disease registries, or even from wearable fitness devices (see the sidebar *Bringing Patient-Reported Data into Play*) (Brennan 2016). For instance, a patient might *feel* more energetic while on a drug, but the study sponsor is only measuring the average number of steps the patient takes each day. So if the patient doesn't increase their steps, the drug might not appear to be demonstrably improving their health status—even if the patient is slightly more mobile, requires fewer hours of sleep to feel rested, is drinking less caffeine to feel alert, or requires less pain medication for arthritis.

RWE can also be as simple as determining whether a recommended drug actually worked for a patient. Sometimes, a drug works differently in real patients than it does in clinical trials. Although clinical trials are expected to represent the larger patient population, this is not always the case. Furthermore, clinical trials occur in a limited timeframe and some side effects might not be apparent until a patient has been on a medication for a long period of time. SERMO is a peer-to-peer platform for physicians to document how their patients are responding to medications. This website can give providers valuable information on efficacy, safety, and adherence that goes beyond the data gleaned from a clinical trial (SERMO 2017). Flatiron Health is collecting data from oncologists about how their patients respond to particular treatments (see Chapter 1). Massachusetts General Hospital's Center for Assessment Technology and Continuous Health, meanwhile, is amassing data from traditional (i.e., patient records) and nontraditional sources (i.e., smartphones and wearables) to "better define wellness and disease" (Massachusetts General Hospital 2017b).

Capturing real-world patient data are challenging, but has tremendous potential, especially as analytics capabilities improve.

SIDEBAR: BRINGING PATIENT-REPORTED DATA INTO PLAY

Ben Heywood, MBA
Cofounder, President
Jamie Heywood
Cofounder, Chairman
PatientsLikeMe

When it was founded in 2004, PatientsLikeMe was the first of its kind. Born from the grief of two brothers who lost their sibling (Stephen Heywood) to ALS, the company aimed to give patients access to better information about how to treat their conditions, and a stronger voice into research.

"We are trying to engage patients directly in their own healthcare by using the web, communities and online tracking tools. In doing that, we learn about the unmet needs patients have and how well we actually currently measure those in traditional settings. We want to enable individual patients to monitor and measure and drive that data back into the healthcare system," Ben Heywood explains (Heywood 2017). Ben and his brother Jamie have been running the company ever since it started, and they've evolved it over time.

It all started out with the idea of patients sharing their data. "In healthcare, there is still a lot of paternalism with the doctor making all the decisions," Ben explains. But the Heywood brothers believe the best dynamic is a patient and provider working together on the same information set: that eliminates the information asymmetry between the doctor and the patient.

The company has a website where patients can record their personal data and see how it compares to others' experiences. PatientsLikeMe can also do studies using those data, including those that are prospective. The company partners with drug developers and other innovators in the healthcare sectors to push research forward and fund its endeavors.

A key component is being able to accurately measure the right things. "When you give patients tools with which to measure their own health, you begin to look at and understand healthcare in a different way," he says. Jamie adds that, "We've learned tons of surprising things just by connecting patients with information and data."

With Parkinson's patients, for example, they found the patients measure their own health at a much higher frequency than is usually done in a trial. The week-to-week variability is also much bigger than expected, which means a traditional clinical trial is probably not going to be able to account for that variability. That's important information for anyone designing a trial of a drug for Parkinson's.

PatientsLikeMe has now gathered data from more than 500,000 patients with about 2,700 conditions. Some of the larger groups are multiple sclerosis (MS) and fibromyalgia, with over 50,000 MS patients and about 80,000 with fibromyalgia. They also have approximately 10,000 participants with Amyotrophic Lateral Sclerosis (ALS), 16,000 with Parkinson's, and 40,000 with major depressive disorder. As a result, the company may have some of the biggest cohorts available for certain rare diseases. "We're finding that there is value in the data at any scale, but, of course, the larger the dataset the more rigorous research you can do," Ben says.

PatientsLikeMe has also already contributed valuable findings to medicine. They carried out a study of lithium (a drug most often used for bipolar disease) in ALS at a time when some people were convinced it should be used for another condition. "We did a study on PatientsLikeMe with almost 600 people with ALS who reported their symptoms online, and in nine months we had data suggesting it doesn't actually work," Ben says.

This shift to patient-driven research is a big change, and it's going to take time. Of the thousands of branded drugs available, only a handful have been approved based on patient-reported outcomes. "But we believe that we need to collect those patient reported outcomes in parallel with those the physicians are tracking," Ben says. For example, feedback from PatientsLikeMe's multiple sclerosis community suggests patients do not think the drugs they take are impacting the most significant symptoms they deal with. One of the most common endpoints in trials is pathological lesions on the brain, which indicate damage caused by relapses. But what patients care about is being able to walk, having their eyesight, diminishing pain, and reducing bowel problems.

"In the past, researchers have really been doing trials *on* patients, rather than *with* them," Ben says. "We should be educating patients about the discovery process and working with them as partners in it."

PatientsLikeMe's chief goal, Jamie adds, "is to make the patient experience transformatively better." That means answering the question 'How are you?' with all the data available—including that from biology, environmental exposure, behavior, and social issues. "Eventually, we are going to have an Internet of life, that will tell people exactly what they should do today to get and stay healthy for their whole lives," he says.

One major development pushing that objective is PatientsLikeMe's recently announced $100 million deal with iCarbonX. Founded by renowned genomicist Jun Wang, iCarbonX has created a Digital Life Alliance of the world's leading bio, health networking, sequencing, and artificial intelligence (AI) technology and application companies. The alliance will merge biological and patient-generated data with AI technology to instantly detect meaningful signals about health, disease, and aging, and deliver a personalized guide for living a healthy life.

Patient engagement through mobile apps and connected devices could also substantially transform clinical trials. According to John Reites, head of Digital Health Acceleration at Quintiles, mobile health (mHealth) devices give the organizations running the trials "the ability to gather and move patient data in a more efficient manner" (Miseta 2016).

Monitoring clinical trials subjects between visits can be easier using mHealth technology. "For clinical trials, that component is really critical," said Validic cofounder and chief technology officer Drew Schiller. "We now have the capability to drive patient engagement by allowing patients to actively participate in trials by passively collecting data. No longer do they have to worry about filling out forms or diaries on an hourly basis. By just wearing a device or being prompted by an app, they are able to easily participate in a trial. We can now make the trial easier for the patient while collecting more relevant and continuous data," Schiller added (Miseta 2016).

Schiller described a scenario where a new arthritis drug is being tested in a trial. "With a wearable device on a wrist you can get information such as when the patient woke up and how active they were. You could then know if 2 weeks into a trial the patient was more active in the first 90 minutes after waking up. That can tell you a lot about the efficacy of a drug. Without the wearable device, the information might be self-reported, derived through a sleep study in a clinic, or not available at all," he explained (Miseta 2016).

Adding mHealth data has the potential to both improve the quality of patient data and to minimize some of the costs of running a clinical trial. But for now, most pharma companies are watching on the sidelines as predominately academic groups test mHealth integration with clinical studies (Miseta 2016). Success in clinical studies should demonstrate the data originating from connected devices, particularly those which are consumer-oriented, such as fitness trackers, may be satisfactory for the purposes of a clinical trial, and where the information collected could reduce errors or bias in the data. Connected scales, for example, might be helpful where there is concern that study participants may not accurately remember how much they weighed on a particular day, and smartphone-based nutrition apps that take photos of meals to estimate caloric intake might be more accurate than a patient's food diary.

In addition to collecting data more accurately than some patient-reported options currently available, mHealth solutions might also make it easier for patients who live farther from a medical center to participate in clinical trials. For example, if a connected blood pressure cuff can take as accurate a reading as one in a doctor's office, clinical trial sponsors might require fewer on-site visits during a trial and replace them with telemedicine visits and data collected from devices that transmit information wirelessly. This may reduce some of the socioeconomic barriers to participation that continue to plague clinical trials.

New Data Tools for Pharma

Figuring out *how* the drug works is another challenge of drug development that is changing because of data. Instead of testing each new drug and laboriously determining how it works in the lab, researchers can use statistical models to predict the drug's mechanism of action. Scientists have suggested there are three essential properties for data-driven drug discovery: (1) that the statistical models should accurately predict the mechanism of action for drugs with known biological actions; (2) the model should recognize when a drug's predicted mechanism falls outside of known actions; (3) the model should predict the mechanism for new drugs (Pritchard et al. 2013).

This means that given a database of drugs with known biological mechanisms as a training set, machine-learning algorithms should be able to correctly match the drugs to the right mechanism, and know when a drug's predicted mechanism doesn't match, within certain restrictions, known mechanisms. The better the algorithm performs and learns as it is fed more data, the more valuable it will be in drug discovery, where scientists might be trying to find a new drug with a very specific mechanism of action, like might be seen for many rare diseases.

Several companies are using these data-intensive machine learning methods in drug discovery and design. IBM Research was recently granted a patent on machine learning models that predict side effects and disease associations from a variety of drug information databases (Phys.org 2017). Recursion Pharmaceuticals uses a computer software developed at the Broad Institute, a joint venture between Harvard and MIT, that can extract information from images, helping the researchers identify molecules for rare diseases. Recursion's algorithm and imaging platform has already identified more than a dozen potential candidates for rare diseases, with one expected to enter clinical trials within the year (Simonite 2017). As machine learning becomes more commonplace for drug discovery and repurposing, the time involved and costs of bringing a drug to market can decrease substantially.

Understanding a molecule's chemical and pharmacological characteristics is just one part of the drug development puzzle. Despite decades of research, scientists are still discovering new things about human biology and the human response to drugs. It's not altogether unusual for drugs that worked spectacularly in animal models to fail once they start human trials, due to unexpected toxicity, differences between animal and human biology, or even physiological differences between males and females (Allen 2006; Seok et al. 2013; Harris 2017). One company is taking drug development and turning the cell model → animal models → human trials on its head (see the sidebar *Using Data to Understand the Language of Biology*).

SIDEBAR: USING DATA TO UNDERSTAND THE LANGUAGE OF BIOLOGY

Niven R. Narain

CEO, Berg Health

Most pharmaceutical companies start by identifying an unmet need in medical care, and then doing basic research in the laboratory to find promising compounds that could treat a particular disease.

Berg has decided to go in a different direction. "We start with the patient," says Niven R. Narain, the company's CEO (Narain 2017). "Because it turns out we don't know much about individual biology. So we make a deep dive into individual patient biology, and then find correlations that tell us where to start our research programs."

Berg is an artificial intelligence (AI)-based company. They use genomics, proteomics, metabolomics, lipidomics and whatever other data are available to create a data-rich platform that can support modeling and correlation with clinical results. That works through careful study of both patients with specific diseases and a population of healthy, nondisease controls.

Narain is not embarrassed to say theirs is a bioinformatics-intensive approach, even though both AI and bioinformatics have had checkered histories. "AI in medicine started in the 50s, and then died down because of the discovery of DNA, the knockout gene hypothesis, and rise of pathway-driven drug development," he explains. "Bioinformatics made big headway around 2006, but that died down also after the financial crisis of 2008. It wasn't until 2011 when you would hear big pharma people using the term," he explains.

But times have finally changed and today, "Data has become a currency allowing us to understand the language of biology," Narain says. Berg uses patient data to "interrogate" disease states and then figure out which are the most logical targets and which are the most druggable, or practical to pursue.

The company's approach is thus patient-intensive on the front end. "If you make biology too neat and you miss the messiness, you might miss the best targets," he explains.

Modeling is one of the cornerstones of Berg's approach. "You have to know the ontology of the modeling," Narain says. "We use data from clinical records, molecular biology, genetics, demographics and much more to build our models." The company relies on Bayesian algorithms, because "We can then take an unstructured environment, gather our data and then make an unstructured causal inference, which gives us higher confidence in the programs we pick," he explains.

They already have a couple of examples. "We just found a novel drug for Parkinson's after spending two years analyzing tissue fibroblasts (skin cells), urine, blood, and medical records from patients," Narain says. Their work has not just identified a new target, which is called PIG-3 (p53 inducible gene). It has also produced a laboratory model that they can use to test their ideas. "This is the first new target for Parkinson's in 20 years," Narain says.

The target also makes sense. p53 is an important molecular player in cell death. In cancers, it tends to not work well enough, letting too many cells overreproduce and spread. But in Parkinson's it is thought that this molecule may be working too well, and deleting more neurons than is normal.

While their approach is novel, and involves technology that has been deemed overhyped in the past, Narain says they are now getting more positive responses. "Initially, people wanted to know what the 'product' was—what was the drug we were developing," he says. "Now we are getting a lot more interest in the platform. Companies are saying 'we get it now' and they want to know what we are doing and how we are doing it. That's a big switch from the past."

Finding a novel molecule to treat a disorder is not the only aspect of drug discovery that's being changed by data. With the costs associated with bringing a new drug to market in excess of $2.8 billion (DiMasi, Grabowski, and Hansen 2016), and no certainty of success (e.g., the *PCSK9* inhibitor gamble), identifying *new* indications for existing drugs can be a cost-effective option.

This approach involves leveraging the data already collected in earlier clinical trials (even for a very different indication) and combining it with externally collected data, such as from publicly available databases. Isaac Kohane, chair of the Department of Biomedical Informatics at Harvard Medical School has said, "Drug development from scratch is too costly to even begin to address our patients' needs. For any condition, some combination of existing drugs may be an effective treatment. Thanks to the increased public availability of high-quality data sources, we have the opportunity to 'compute' the right drugs at a time scale and cost far below that of drug development" (Fliesler 2016).

Even a single existing drug can sometimes work in a different disease, as the Progeria Research Foundation's progress with lonafarnib, a drug that had been investigated for cancer, shows (see Chapter 5) (Wong and Morse 2012). Mining through existing scientific knowledge is not an insignificant challenge, so often looking for drugs that can be repurposed is hypothesis-driven, to narrow the scope. But some scientists think this method is inefficient with how quickly the amount of data increases and could eliminate promising candidates. As a result, methods are being developed that take into account prior disease, drug, and genetic understanding to identify new areas for drug repurposing (Mullen et al. 2016).

Finding a drug that can be repurposed for another indication is limited by proprietary databases and publication bias, where trials with negative results are less often published. Recently, there has been renewed interest in requiring the publication of all clinical trials data, but without an incentive or regulatory requirement to do so, pharma companies are unlikely to report the results of trials where the drug failed or where the trial was closed prematurely.

Seeing the great promise in drug repurposing, and the lack of incentives, the U.S. government became interested in this issue and in 2012 launched a program called New Therapeutic Uses for Existing Molecules, which was the first initiative of the NIH's National Center for Advancing Translational Sciences (Allison 2012; National Center for Advancing Translational Sciences 2017). The program gives academic researchers access to data on big pharma small molecule drug candidates that were shelved during development.

Though many experts were skeptical about the program, the first companies to join were an impressive list: Pfizer, AstraZeneca, Eli Lilly, Abbott, Bristol-Myers Squibb, GlaxoSmithKline, Janssen, and Sanofi. The first batch of data released was only for 58 compounds, but the vision is for that to grow substantially and researchers will be able to dive into those data and possibly build upon what pharma gathered before the compounds were shelved: but they will be looking at them for different indications than the drug company pursued. The program recently announced that, in collaboration with AstraZeneca and Janssen, it would fund $6 million in new research into drug repurposing (National Center for Advancing Translational Sciences 2017). That project will support partnerships between drug companies and the broader research community.

Meanwhile, tech companies with expertise in managing and analyzing massive amounts of data are finding their skills are in demand in the drug discovery, repurposing, and development realm. IBM Research's patent for machine learning algorithms (described above) can be extended to find new indications for existing drugs (Phys.org 2017). Start-up Healx uses artificial intelligence and vast amounts of biological and pharmacologic data to identify drugs that could be repurposed for rare diseases (Healx 2017). A collaboration between Healx, the University of Insubria (Italy), and the LouLou Foundation identified a drug that they are now testing for CDKL5 deficiency, a rare neurological disorder that affects approximately 1,500 people worldwide. And unlike the long timeframe involved in developing a novel drug, Healx took only 5 months from data curation and evaluation to begin studies in cell lines (Healx 2017).

Palantir, a tech engineering company known more widely for its work with government, legal, and financial companies, recently announced a partnership with Merck. Palantir brings its expertise with data analysis and visualization to mine data from numerous sources, helping Merck better target potential patient populations and decrease the drug development timeline (Chapman 2017). Focusing initially on cancer treatments and services, the companies aim to develop tools that will make drug discovery and delivery more efficient, expanding to other Merck divisions later (Chapman 2017).

Drug Discovery of Tomorrow

The role of massive datasets and advanced analytics is going to drive exponential growth in drug discovery in the upcoming years. "I think drug discovery, in general, is another place where they're putting big [computational] platforms together to analyze genomic data, biology, drug interactions, and chemistry in new ways," says Christine Lemke, president of Evidation Health (Lemke 2017). "Literally, drug pipelines, early drug pipelines are going to explode. They have more compute power, more data and can separate out with more precision new hypotheses about new chemicals and treatments."

If that all pans out, we'll see faster time to market, more targeted clinical trials based on molecular characterization instead of simply the patient's indication, and an increased reliance on data scientists to put it all together. That means traditional pharmaceutical companies are going to face advancing competition from pharma start-ups and tech companies, not just for talent, but for ways to shorten the drug development timeline.

Preclinical studies in animal models can be time-consuming and expensive, particularly if there isn't an appropriate model system that adequately mimics the human disease. For example, creating a mouse model of a disease with multiple genetic mutations could take a year (or even longer) and cost $20,000 per mutation. This is one of the reasons why there has been so much excitement surrounding the gene-editing technique CRISPR. Though many reports have focused on its potential as a therapeutic tool, a growing number of pharmas are using CRISPR for drug discovery, including identification of potential drug targets using high-throughput knockout screens and for preclinical studies (De Almeida 2017).

Traditional drug development roles at pharma companies are evolving. As noted by Lemke at the start of this chapter, data scientists will become an integral part of the drug development team. Even chemists will have to take on more technological skills, like accessing and analyzing large amounts of data from disparate sources, and will need to become adept at communicating and working in large, diverse teams which may include others outside of the company (Lusher et al. 2014). Computer scientists will also find themselves in demand by pharma, as AI and other advanced machine learning techniques are used in both drug design and for repurposing. In short, the world of drug design and development will look a lot more technical and demand people with new sets of skills. Whole new fields are also emerging, such as the microbiome. Each person's microbiome contains trillions of bacteria. Studying those and how they impact disease is a nascent area of research interest that has already produced promising leads. Research suggests, for example, a connection between the neurodegenerative disease Parkinson's, and the composition of the gut microbiome (Hill-Burns et al. 2017).

One likely area of expansion in drug development is the use of cloud technology to solve some of the computational burdens of computer-aided drug design (see Chapter 10 for more on the cloud). As described above, structural modeling programs are computationally intensive. As pharma relies on these methods more for early drug research, both hardware and software demands increase. Cloud-based computing and data storage gives companies the flexibility to scale their computing power based on their evolving needs at the time, instead of what they expect to need in the future.

Big Data is beginning to shape the industry. As described in Chapters 2 and 3, precision medicine and personalized cancer treatments rely on the interpretation of an individual's genome based on massive databases. Diagnostics developers are leading the way with companion and complementary diagnostics: molecular tests that are required or recommended to be performed prior to a treatment being started. For example, Myriad Genetics' BRACAnalysis CDx was recently approved as a complementary diagnostic to identify patients with ovarian cancer who would be most likely to benefit from niraparib (Zejula) treatment (Ray 2017). Although the drug development and diagnostic development timelines are very different, increasing reliance on molecular data for treatment decisions will lead to a greater number of collaborations.

The FDA's approval of Keytruda is just the tip of the iceberg for relationships between molecular diagnostics companies and pharma. Drugs are currently designed for particular cancers or disorders in mind and extending its use to another indication (e.g., cancer type) means undergoing FDA approval again, likely with a new clinical trial. But instead of focusing on creating a drug for a particular cancer or disorder, pharma can begin to structure drug design based on a genomic variant, opening up its use to a much larger patient population, and creating new business opportunities and potential profits for both pharma and diagnostics companies.

But partnerships with myriad organizations and biotech companies may be one of the keys to success in the evolving pharma market. Already, patient advocacy groups, such as the Progeria Research Foundation (PRF) (see Chapter 5) are working with pharma to develop new treatments for rare diseases. With the patient data, samples, and financial backing provided by the PRF, researchers were able to move from gene discovery in 2003 (Eriksson et al. 2003); to identifying an existing compound (lonafarnib); to a clinical trial in 2007; and evidence for a potential treatment by 2012 (Gordon et al. 2012; Ullrich et al. 2013)—an incredibly short timeline when compared with traditional drug discovery. With these successes pointing them towards specific mechanisms, researchers continue to move forward testing new treatments in preclinical studies (Ibrahim et al. 2013).

Some companies, such as Flatiron Health, FDNA, and PatientsLikeMe are using data they've collected to share with pharma or device manufacturers to guide treatment use and development. This is giving them access to the type of RWE or clinical data that so many experts in this field covet, but is so hard to access because of privacy concerns. The key challenge here is making certain that the data are properly de-identified, since there is so much concern about privacy. Patients with serious diseases, however, tend to be more willing to share their data. There will likely be more such businesses based on data access in the future; it remains to be seen whether they can wrest real value from that data.

Nearly every aspect of clinical trials will be impacted by this growing use of data analytics. As described above, molecular testing is being used to determine eligibility for trial inclusion. Consequently, there will be a need for more individuals, companies, and software that can interpret the genomic data and identify which trial is most appropriate for a patient.

Another trend is increased involvement of patients from early on. As was mentioned earlier in this chapter, mHealth is becoming more integrated into the clinical experience and has the potential to improve patient engagement in clinical trials and make data collection easier for study sponsors and clinical research organizations. While pharma has always needed patients to participate in clinical trials, the industry has largely ignored their input in trial design (Sablinski 2014). By utilizing existing data, embracing mHealth solutions, partnering with advocacy organizations and companies such as PatientsLikeMe or Transparency Life Sciences, or even using unique methods such as crowdsourcing (Leiter et al. 2014), pharma companies can better understand the patient's needs and improve patient engagement in clinical trials, especially on issues such as medication adherence. Improving the quality of the data and relevance of study endpoints for patients would undoubtedly be beneficial during the regulatory approval process.

One reason that clinical trials often fail is that patients are noncompliant with study protocols. Not only does this reduce the number of subjects who complete the study, but can impact interpretation of the study data. The extent of noncompliance in clinical trials is shocking: one study of 55 women in a breast cancer study found only slightly more than one-third adhered to all aspects of the study protocol (Li et al. 2000) and an analysis of 100 randomized controlled trials found 98 reported some aspect of nonadherence (Dodd, White, and Williamson 2012). Digital health solutions (see Chapter 10) could have a big impact on monitoring patients for adherence in clinical trials, and they are just beginning to be embraced by pharma.

Nontraditional competition for pharma is already coming from innovative start-ups and existing technology companies. Direct-to-consumer genetic testing company 23&Me secured $115 million from investors as it looked to build an in-house drug development lab (Taylor 2015). Start-up TwoXAR is using deep learning to identify drug candidates based on the data from both public and proprietary datasets. The small company, with fewer than 10 employees, was able to test their method on more than 20 diseases, demonstrating how data and machine learning can make drug discovery a more efficient and lean process (Nanalyze 2016).

In a word, traditional pharma companies will have to become more *agile* to remain competitive and relevant in a $1 trillion-plus landscape that is beginning to see start-ups go from an idea to clinical trials in just a few short years. Embracing data, in new ways, will be the key to making that happen. This means a new way to approach drug design and development that will look more like computer science than the chemistry-based labs of yesterday. New job roles will emerge, largely based on manipulating large datasets, virtual manipulation of molecules, and efficient scanning of databases. It's an exciting time for pharma, driven by data.

Chapter 9

Re-Engineering the Healthcare System

I see tremendous shifts taking place. We are in an era of value re-engineering, where costs have to come down and where companies like CVS and Walmart are looking for new opportunities, and starting to compete with traditional health systems. We need to respond to that new competition now.

Glenn D. Steele

Chairman at xG Health Solutions, Columbia, Maryland, Former President and Chief Executive Officer at Geisinger Health Systems, Danville, Pennsylvania

Somewhere in Cleveland, Ohio, cardiac technician Jim Goldstein is getting ready to start his shifts monitoring patients in the intensive care unit. Screens mounted on the wall broadcast patients' vital signs. "These here are PVCs [premature ventricular contractions]; they're bad things," says Goldstein, as he points to a graph, getting ready to alert the nurse (*The Economist* 2017).

What's unusual about Goldstein's job is that he's not at the hospital, standing feet away from the patient or the nurse. Instead, he and the doctors, nurses, and other technicians monitor patients from a control center, miles from the actual hospital. This kind of remote patient monitoring was unheard of only a few short years ago. But today, the Cleveland Clinic, which runs the site Goldstein works at, and other health systems, are exploring different ways to structure a hospital. These changes include a growing reliance on remote monitoring of patients in the hospital, but could also include monitoring patients at home (*The Economist* 2017).

In previous chapters, we've presented how the ever-growing deluge of data and its analysis are transforming healthcare, improving price and quality transparency, and supporting the transition to value-based reimbursement models. And while data-driven initiatives are beginning to transform both patient care and how providers do their jobs in fairly visible ways (e.g., molecular testing to determine treatment, greater emphasis on evidence-based guidelines and demonstrated patient outcomes), they are also changing how health systems are structured in ways that may not always be publicized or easily noticed by patients.

There are more than 5,500 hospitals in the United States, ranging widely in size and they account for a full one-third of the approximately $3 trillion in U.S. health expenditures (Centers for Medicare & Medicaid Services 2017a). The majority of these hospitals are community-based, nongovernment, and not-for-profit (American Hospital Association 2017). With health costs anticipated to continue rising by about 6% per year for the next decade or so, hospitals, in particular, will have to embrace value-based care and other initiatives designed to reduce financial burdens while maintaining (*and improving*) patient outcomes.

Behind the scenes, mergers, acquisitions, and partnerships of health systems, payers, even pharmaceutical and healthcare tech companies, are occurring at a startling pace (Shinkman 2016), including four proposed hospital system mergers in early 2017 worth more than $1 billion (Barkholz 2017). Despite uncertainty over the eventual approval of these and other mergers (e.g., the proposed merger between Chicago area's Advocate Health Care and NorthShore University HealthSystem was rejected in federal court [Schencker 2017]), the first quarter of 2017 saw more hospital transactions than in the same period the previous year, as health systems seek to gain market share, reduce costs, and increase bargaining power with insurers (Morse 2016; Barkholz 2017; Cryts 2017). Hospitals can also grow by acquiring private practices, such as specialty clinics. In fact, hospital ownership of physician practices grew by 86% between 2012 and 2015 alone (Rappleye 2016).

What's behind the frenzied pace of hospital mergers? According to some experts, increasing costs and evolving payment models play a role. But a report from the industry group, American Hospital Association, found mergers and acquisitions improved the quality of care and expanded services for patients. Notably, operating expenses were reduced 2.5% at the acquired hospitals due to mergers. It appears the growth of hospital mergers is both a response to market forces in a competitive industry and a consequence of value-based care initiatives.

There can be clear advantages for pharmaceutical companies to partner together (e.g., Regeneron and Sanofi) for drug development and to merge or acquire competitors (e.g., Shire's acquisition of Baxalta) to gain market share or expand therapeutic offerings. Similar incentives apply for health systems, provider groups, even long-term care facilities, all of which can gain market share and create efficiencies through mergers. Silicon Valley and venture capitalists are bullish on healthcare, too, investing $1.2 billion into technology-focused health insurance companies in 2015, like start-up Clover Health, a Medicare Advantage contractor, which raised $160 million in a recent Series C funding round (Chapman 2016; MarketWired 2016). In this chapter, we'll show how health systems are leveraging data to restructure their operations, interact differently with patients and providers, and serve as the basis for targeted mergers, acquisitions, and partnerships between both traditional and nontraditional partners. This creates a huge opportunity for health IT companies to step in and help hospitals adjust.

Making Data Work for Patients, Providers, and Health Systems

Today's providers are under significant pressure from patients to stay current with rapidly emerging information on new diagnostic tests (including genetic tests), medications, and other treatments. At the same time, they are trying to care for patients in smaller and smaller appointment windows, while facing changing payment structures and evolving incentives for value-based care. Thus, new methods to improve workflow efficiency are highly desirable and increasingly, they are the result of data analytics or cognitive computing technologies.

As described in previous chapters, the practice of radiology is being dramatically altered by increasing reliance on vast amounts of imaging data and cognitive computing solutions to read images and assist physicians with diagnoses for complex cases. But as Christoph Wald of Lahey Hospital and Medical Center explains below, in addition to patient care, data are also changing how radiology departments themselves are structured.

SIDEBAR: CASE STUDY IN DATA-DRIVEN PROCESS RE-ENGINEERING—LAHEY'S IMAGING DEPARTMENT

Christoph Wald, MD, PhD, MBA

Chairman, Department of Radiology, Lahey Hospital and Medical Center

In the push to control healthcare costs, one of the first areas to come under pressure was also then one of the fastest growing: imaging.

"Right around 2011 or thereabouts, I was getting concerned about how payment reform was going to lead to stricter utilization management in imaging," says Christoph Wald, Chairman of the Department of Radiology at Burlington, Massachusetts-based Lahey Hospital and Medical Center (Wald 2017). "It was clear this was going to have a profound influence on our book of business and with that our staffing and equipment base, and that we were going to have to start collecting systematic data to better justify how we were operating."

At that time, only a small portion of the data Wald needed was being collected. And even those data weren't readily available on demand, nor was it in one place. To adjust, "I needed to know many things: the service line P&L, how technologists' and radiologists' performances compared to their peers', how to systematically track radiation dose for each patient and type of exam, analyze the quality of the work we were doing, assess machine utilization, assess process cycle times for specific exams. How much time would that take?" says Wald.

So they redesigned the back end of their radiology department, to ensure that all processes were captured in a digital and interoperable fashion. They acquired software to provide that interoperability because no one vendor of the component systems was able to offer a complete portfolio, and they began to consolidate the data streams.

The initial effort started in 2012 and reached reasonable maturity by 2015. Now, "Every single transaction in radiology goes into a SQL Server database," he explained. "That includes image metadata, report texts and metadata, quality complaints by radiologists, critical results communication by radiologists with referring physicians, self- and peer-reported errors, resident-overread* scores by staff, agreement versus discrepancy with initial image impressions by emergency room physicians. Everything. And many of these data elements are structured data, except for the user-generated commentary and reporting. We're now pursuing an even more comprehensive method in the latest system, which incorporates imaging machine and process data from the imaging platform

---

* *Overread* means that a staff physician reviews the preliminary report of a physician-in-training (resident) as well as the corresponding images and either makes edits as needed and/or signs off the report. At Lahey, every time this happens a staff physician sends an alphanumerical score and comments expressing agreement or disagreement into a database which is used as a key performance indicator for data-driven resident training guidance.

itself and from the image DICOM headers. That new system promises to give us more insight into the process efficiency at the scanner level."

Today, Wald has a much better idea exactly how his department is operating and can make better-informed critical staffing and other operational decisions. What's more, the quality of their work has improved. "We went from a defect* rate of 8–10% in some modalities to a rate of less than 1%," he says. When urgent results need to be communicated, the department uses a clever combination of clerical assistants with computer-based tracking and reporting software, so doctors who need to get these results can be reached much more quickly. The ease of this new reporting process (three clicks), has improved interactions between radiologists and clinicians.

This data-driven system comes at an opportune time: Lahey opened a brand new emergency department (ED) in early 2017, and it has several times the footprint of the previous facility. Thanks to the hospital's new system, Wald says, "I'm able to estimate how many of which types of exams we will be doing there, since I can see a granular history of exam types by ordering location and patient type."

If, for example, a quarter of the run rate of imaging exams was neurologic, they could then inflate that number by the expected growth predictions provided by the ED leaders and then model whether they would have sufficient staff or if they needed to rebalance the workforce. "I can tell you exactly what percent of ED work is ultrasound, versus CT scans, and how many are body scans versus neurological," he says. The system even catches details about how long each staff member is taking to do specific tasks. "I can break down how long we are taking to do each type of exam, by radiologist, and then I can connect that to collection data and expense estimates to tell whether the contribution margin is net positive or net negative for that exam type and provider combination."

Making this transition was clearly a tall order. Overall, Lahey doctors do 1,400 to 1,600 imaging exams per average business day. Now, many processes have been automated, such as letters with results (e.g., in mammography or lung cancer screening) and reminders for follow-up appointments. In the short time since the Lahey's new electronic health record was introduced, approximately 85,000 patients have signed up for a patient-directed module that allows them to log in and get their results online. They can even schedule telehealth visits and have a face-to-face discussion with their doctor through the system's online portal.

Wald sees many future applications for the new online interactive systems the hospital has invested in. "I can see my colleagues in surgery doing follow-up wound care counseling through the portal, and so saving the patient a trip back to the hospital, because the provider can see how things are healing online. We are also thinking of tying the results from biometric devices, such as health trackers and digital scales, to the system," he says. A patient with congestive heart failure, for example, could be remotely

---

* A *defect* is defined as any deviation from the expected image quality that can interfere with image interpretation: examples include artifacts, whether these results from machine malfunction, patient-related issues such as motion during the imaging exam, issues with the timing of a contrast injection, or operator mistakes such as scanning too much or too little of the body or incorrect use of the imaging machine. Defect reports are databased, sorted by modality, and routed to the appropriate manager for improvement action which may include remediation, additional training of the operator, working with the vendor to adjust/repair/improve the machine, and so on. This is a continuous process.

monitored for rapid weight gain—a sign of fluid retention and a symptom that signals the need for further medical attention.

In the end, Wald says, it took a tremendous effort to get to this point, but he's delighted with the results. "We are now working closely with data scientists for the first time," he says, "and they are working with our physicians to solve problems."

As Wald noted, radiology departments aren't the only hospital divisions that can benefit from leveraging data to improve processes. As mentioned in Chapter 7, research performed in England, where prices are consistent, found patients were more likely to choose higher-quality providers, even if they were less convenient than lower-quality providers (Moscelli et al. 2016). But this research has valuable insights for American health systems, too. If patients would rather choose providers that are considered higher quality, that's an opportunity for hospitals to highlight the quality of their providers—something that can only be done quantitatively with data.

Within a single health system, where costs between providers are likely to be similar, hospitals can use data about individual providers to direct quality improvement programs to providers that may not be performing at the same level as their peers (see the sidebar *Bringing Optimal Guidelines into Daily Medical Practice*). The hypothesis behind this is that "clinical inefficiency in the provision of hospital services occurs when a physician uses a relatively excessive quantity of clinical inputs compared with physicians treating a similar case load and mix of patients" (Chilingerian 1995). Further, objectively measuring the performance of individual providers (e.g., by surgical infection rates or proportion of patients with controlled diabetes) lets hospitals use the data to identify best practices or guidelines for their specific patient population.

NSQIP, described in Chapter 6, is a ranking system used by hospitals to measure the quality of surgical care in a way that can be compared between hospitals (American College of Surgeons 2017). Though physician-level statistics aren't publicly reported, hospitals can parse their data down to individual providers to determine compliance with best practices and to identify doctors who are providing high-quality/high-value care to patients. Individual surgical societies, like the American Association of Endocrine Surgeons and the American Society for Metabolic and Bariatric Surgery, have developed discipline-specific quality improvement programs analogous to NSQIP, capturing measurements that may better reflect their specialists' experience.

Nonsurgical specialties have also developed quality improvement programs (QIPs). The American Congress of Obstetricians and Gynecologists partnered with the American Society of Anesthesiologists to create the Maternal Quality Improvement Program (MQIP) in 2014. Goals of MQIP include "address the variations that currently exist between institutions, to aid in driving care standardization that has been shown to improve outcomes" (American Congress of Obstetricians and Gynecologists 2017).

Getting the necessary data can be one of the barriers to participation in QIPs and has sometimes resulted in the need for dedicated personnel who comb through patient health records to find the right information, such as length of hospital stay. Electronic health records (EHRs) are getting on board to help institutions participate in these and other QIPs by standardizing some data fields and simplifying the reporting process (American Congress of Obstetricians and Gynecologists 2017). As EHR adoption reaches more hospitals, this could change the types of employees needed for QIP tasks by increasing the number of EHR-certified reporting staff (e.g., Epic certified) and bioinformaticians to analyze the data, while concurrently decreasing the staff who currently perform data extraction manually. Over time, increased EHR utilization will mean compliance with the data requirements for QIPs should become easier, and the data captured more useful at the hospital level.

SIDEBAR: BRINGING OPTIMAL GUIDELINES INTO DAILY MEDICAL PRACTICE

Anil Jain, MD, FACP

Cofounder, Senior VP and Chief Medical Officer, Explorys, Inc., an IBM company

"When you are dealing with people's health, no one wants to think about data. Rather they focus on the patient's relationship with their doctor," says Anil Jain, Senior VP and Chief Medical Officer at Explorys (Jain 2017). "So even as the healthcare industry has evolved, we've always kept the patient–doctor relationship at the center."

That approach has good and bad effects, according to Jain. Certainly, no one knows more about the patient's condition than his or her own physician. But medicine moves much more quickly these days, and not everybody keeps up as well. "If we want to do a better job, we need more transparency," Jain says. "We need to know if patients are actually getting the right care by today's standards. Are all providers following the optimal guidelines?" he asks.

Explorys was founded in 2009, based on innovations Jain developed while working as a physician at the Cleveland Clinic. The start-up was acquired in 2015 by IBM, and became part of the IT giant's new Watson Health business unit. That unit represents IBM's major foray into healthcare.

The Watson unit brings the famed computer, which triumphed at Jeopardy, into realms such as drug discovery, patient engagement, and oncology, where it's hoped it's processing prowess will help it answer questions much more quickly and efficiently than mere mortals can. Explorys also takes a data-driven approach, and is focused on improving patient care. It uses patient-level longitudinal data, clinical data from electronic medical records, claims data, and all other available data streams, to help determine optimal standards of care and then determine how well providers are meeting those standards.

While this is a relatively new development, it turns out that physicians can be extremely responsive to quality metrics. "If you just ask doctors how well they think they are doing, not surprisingly most of them think they are performing in the top 10% compared to their peers," Jain says. "But if you have a dashboard that actually ranks them according to how well they are following guidelines, that can be very powerful. Because once they see their ranking it has an impact, and I can tell you that nobody wants to be at the bottom of the list."

But providers aren't just being graded, they are being rewarded for doing well or improving their performance. "By taking a data-driven, quality-focused approach, you can improve not just their performance and quality of patient care, but their reimbursement as well," Jain points out.

The bottom line, he says, is that increasingly, providers need to be able to bring disparate datasets together, and to be able to mine and analyze those data to make the best decisions for their patients. "You need to couple real world data with a true knowledge base if you really want to complete the picture," he says.

So, data are really impacting providers from two different, yet intertwined, perspectives: it is transforming how they interact with patients, from utilizing EHRs with clinical decision support tools to precision medicine, *and* it's changing their clinical workflow. Indeed, as the Cleveland Clinic example at the beginning of this chapter demonstrates, patient monitoring is an area where digital health and data analysis work together to keep patients safer while changing the hospital experience.

Johns Hopkins Hospital in Baltimore, for example, worked with GE Healthcare to outfit a room with flat screens and video capabilities to serve as the hub for managing patient flow in its 1,100-bed facility and offer remote access to specialists for referrals (*The Economist* 2017). And this technology could be further exploited in the future, allowing doctors to respond to referrals remotely or to monitor patients while both doctor and patient are at home. In Chapter 1, we described how some hospitals are starting to embrace remote monitoring as a way to minimize readmissions after certain types of surgeries, like sending home cardiac patients with connected blood pressure cuffs or scales that send data to doctors, alerting them to early complications that, without intervention, could result in a readmission after surgery.

But the technology and data has farther-reaching potential and could be used to keep patients out of the hospital in the first place (see the sidebar *Bringing Health IT to Hospitals*). The Cleveland Clinic and pharmacy chain CVS started a partnership to install telehealth stations bringing the expertise of Cleveland Clinic's doctors to Ohio CVS MinuteClinics (Siwicki 2016). And while patient care is at the heart of using technology in this way, medical centers that embrace this technology may realize infrastructure goals will change, as fewer patients have to come to the hospital and their needs can be met with decentralized care models that include telemedicine, more comprehensive primary care–centric offices, and focused, specialist-based outpatient clinics.

But getting hospitals onboard with the kind of advanced technology that's needed to create systems like Cleveland Clinic's remote patient monitoring can be difficult. Not only is the technology infrastructure incredibly expensive, but interoperability between legacy systems and newer systems can be a substantial barrier. MD Anderson's recent termination of its partnership with IBM Watson is a case in point, with incompatibility between Watson and the medical center's newly implemented Epic EHR cited as one of the reasons for the failure of the venture (Herper 2017b).

SIDEBAR: BRINGING HEALTH IT TO HOSPITALS

John Glaser, PhD
Senior Vice President, Population Health and Global Strategy, Cerner Corp.

"The pure growth in electronic data available about individuals is staggering," says John Glaser, Senior VP of Population Health at health IT giant Cerner Corp., "particularly as electronic health records expand and patients start to contribute to that data through their personal devices" (Glaser 2017). As interoperability improves, and more of these systems can talk to each other, Glaser predicts there will be more and better data sharing and that will push healthcare forward.

The other trend he sees advancing this is the shift in reimbursements. Increasingly, new documentation and quality measures are being required. So the explosion of data is coming from multiple sources. "If you just think of the huge amount of data generated just in the daily provision of care, it's potentially immense," Glaser says.

But of course, it's not just the capture of data but its analysis that matters. IBM's Watson computer is an example of how that's happening. Watson can actually distill information—such as making diagnoses or finding patterns in disease—by analyzing health data.

"I think we're going to see a steady move toward the use of such clinical decision support [CDS] tools in the future," Glaser says. "It's not going to be a dramatic shift, it is more likely to be evolutionary and occurring over years, but more care is going to follow standards of care that are distilled from data, rather than a doctor's own experience."

Doctors are finding that a lot of medicine can be routinized—not things like trauma or mental health, but many other tasks, such as monitoring diabetes or heart failure.

For example, he points to health systems such as Geisinger, Intermountain, and Kaiser Permanente, which have been standardizing how they treat cancer. For the top 20–30 types of cancer genetic testing is now a routine part of treatment and is used to determine if the patient is at risk of the disease or to guide the treatment.

The transition has not been perfectly smooth. Electronic health records, for example, add to the doctor's workload. In the time it takes to sign onto a computer, pick out a drug, and enter the data, the doctor could have easily written a script. "But if we can do this right, the care will be better," Glaser says. And the data gathered won't just be useful to the doctor and the patient. It will be useful to researchers and policy makers too.

"We also have challenges on the data management side," he says. "There are issues around integrating and storing it. But I think the real innovations ahead will be around the analytics." The issue, he explains, isn't going to be how much data a system can handle, but whether people are getting better at collecting and interpreting it.

"Interoperability is the big one of course," Glaser adds. "And we are seeing more discussions about collaboration. But it's not always clear what those groups are trying to do. You hear people talk and they are not speaking from the same page. So while anything that advances the cause is a good thing, we have to be sure that's what's actually going to happen."

Experts like Glaser keep tabs on novel analytics and he says he is encouraged that progressively those tools are solving tougher and tougher problems. "Health IT is a form of guerilla warfare though," he cautions. "There are lots of series of small and medium steps needed to get to the next level. That's why I say it will be a steady advancement of the science and technology, which, over time, will add up to a lot."

Patient interaction with EHR systems can facilitate remote monitoring. As health systems adopt (or upgrade existing) EHRs, a patient portal is increasingly becoming a standard feature. Patient engagement can range from being able to electronically request appointments, to obtaining lab results, to emailing providers about health concerns or questions. Some health systems are taking patient interaction even further, by allowing patients to view portions of their medical records and even updating health histories or noting items they want to discuss at upcoming appointments.

A recently published study evaluated both patient and physician perceptions of having patients in safety-net population type agendas into an EHR prior to their provider visit (Anderson et al. 2017). A safety-net population is typically defined as one where the majority of the population is in the lowest socioeconomic categories and where the patients rely predominantly on social services (e.g., Medicaid, food stamps) to meet their needs. Healthcare utilization in safety-net populations can be quite high, as comorbidities can be common (Hostetter and Klein 2015).

With limited in-person time with providers, it can be difficult for patients to prioritize their health concerns and for physicians to ensure that they have identified all relevant health problems and patients understand treatment plans. In the study by Anderson and colleagues, patients in a safety-net population were able to put into the EHR a list of health issues they wanted to discuss with physicians, prior to their appointment. This allowed patients to consider their health situations deliberately and not feel rushed, as they would otherwise be trying to do the same thing during the appointment. The study's authors found more than 70% of both patients and clinicians felt allowing patients to access the EHR in this way improved communication during the visit and more than 80% of clinicians wanted the process to continue after the study ended (Anderson et al. 2017).

Patient recruitment for clinical trials can also be enhanced through EHR utilization. Some medical centers, such as the Yale-New Haven Health System, are attempting to improve low levels of patient participation in clinical studies by allowing patients to fill out a survey or create a profile that researchers can use to find subjects that fit study criteria (Gruessner 2015). Because patient portals are a relatively new feature of EHR systems, patient recruitment for research studies has been modest, particularly in comparison with other methods like telephone calls, though providers are hopeful this trend will increase over time (Baucom et al. 2014).

Giving patients access to their EHR through patient portals, and analyzing existing utilization management data can change how the health system approaches staffing needs (see the sidebar *Personalizing Patient Services*). If patients can request appointments electronically through the EHR, with increasing patient participation, health systems might find they need fewer customer service personnel to staff telephones. Allowing patients to see their lab and other test results online could reduce the need to mail patients the information. By identifying which patients use the patient portal and analyzing *how* they use it, the health system can target specific patient populations for things like reminders for recommended vaccinations or indication-specific interventions, such as weight-loss clinics.

How patients interact with EHRs is just one aspect of patient use of medical services that can be useful to health systems administrators. Looking at historical claims and billing data, hospitals can determine which patients use the most healthcare services. It's been said that 20% of patients use 80% of services (a derivation of the Pareto Principle). By focusing attention on that 20% of patients, hospitals can find ways to increase efficiencies and minimize care that is redundant, unnecessary, or otherwise not of high value.

SIDEBAR: PERSONALIZING PATIENT SERVICES

Kathryn Teng, MD, MBA, FACP
Physician Executive Director, Adult Health & Wellness Service Line,
MetroHealth Medical Center

Primary care has long been the backbone of medicine, but because these doctors usually make a lot less than their specialist colleagues, it is often overlooked in discussions of cost control and quality. "Many studies over the years have shown that primary care is the key to changing the health cost trajectory. Relying on specialty care is just too expensive," says Kathryn Teng, Director of Adult Health & Wellness at MetroHealth Medical Center (Teng 2017). That realization is bringing new attention to how primary care operates, and new initiatives to redesign it.

MetroHealth is embarking on such a campaign, and theirs is largely data-driven. "We want to deliver personalized services," Teng explains. "Just like a hotel might keep track of your preferences and then adjust their offerings to meet your needs, we're trying to do that for our patients."

Teng's team is collecting and analyzing market research about patients in the region they serve, information from focus groups and surveys, but also a lot of data about how their own patients use services. This is helping the hospital system to reengineer their practices. For example, an analysis of when patients call for appointments and which times they are most likely to request found that relatively few will accept a Friday appointment, and more people skip appointments that have been scheduled far in advance. "However, that only applies to primary care," Teng cautions. "For specialty care, patients are much more flexible and tend to keep their appointments, no matter what day of the week they have been scheduled for."

Urban and suburban patients, she adds, also tend to have different habits. "In the suburbs people are more willing to come in at lunchtime, evening and on Saturdays. But our urban patients usually do not like evening appointments, because of concerns of safety," she says. The overall goal is to reduce "no-show" rates, which have a big impact on a practice's bottom line.

MetroHealth has over 200 primary care physicians (PCPs) and they are spread over more than 20 health clinics and community health centers as well as the main hospital. So another key challenge for Teng's team is helping to make sure patients get care in the most convenient location. "Some people are traveling quite far to reach the hospital," Teng points out. "If we can determine that we have doctors at locations much nearer to them, we can make their experience better and use our staff more efficiently."

Metrics on patient outcomes are another priority. "That is a big change," Teng says. "Before, providers were not being shown this data, but now we give them feedback on how their patient outcomes compare to those of their peers." Comparative data on the volume of patients doctors see is also shared, and in real time. "They always complain 'If I'm behind, I need to know now, not in several months,'" Teng says. "Now we can tell them right away if they are falling behind."

MetroHealth's PCPs tend to be in charge of larger volumes of patients than most such doctors. "Some of our PCPs have panels as large as 3,000, whereas the normal range is about 1,200–1,800," Teng says. A key goal for her team now is to determine which tasks the PCPs are doing now, that a nurse, medical assistant or even a pharmacist could do just as well. "The PCPs are doing a lot of non-physician work," she says. Her team is analyzing data about that, and will soon be rolling out new staffing models.

Another project for the future is to analyze electronic health record data and use that to identify patients at high risk of serious diseases, and help them head off those conditions early. "Unfortunately, there is no financial incentive for that, so it's difficult to justify it financially," she says, echoing many other experts.

Teng points to an initiative they carried out to improve outcomes for patients with high blood pressure. "We had a staff member who was very passionate about this, and she pretty much led the effort and made it happen, with good results," Teng says. "At this point, I think that's what you need—a champion who can make it happen. The current reimbursement system just doesn't support that kind of effort otherwise, although that's exactly what we want to be doing more of."

Evolving Business Model

In Chapter 7, we described how Accountable Care Organizations (ACOs) are one way to offer patients integrated care. Not only do they have the potential to reduce overall healthcare costs for Medicare, but implementing value-based, cost-effective strategies can be financially advantageous for health systems. Through the Medicare Shared Savings Program, there is the potential to receive a portion of the money the healthcare system saves Medicare.

There have been several notable ACO success stories. In the first year of participation (2012/2013), Heartland Regional Medical Center in St. Joseph, Missouri, earned almost $2.9 million through Medicare's Shared Savings Program, one of just 29 organizations sharing $128 million (Kern 2014b). Heritage Provider Network, a California physician group, found success as a Pioneer ACO and is transitioning to a Next Gen ACO (Janjigian 2016). And a paper by McWilliams and colleagues found the ACO model was financially beneficial to CMS even after accounting for the shared savings payments and expected the savings to continue to increase year after year as participation in the ACO program grows (McWilliams et al. 2015). The study also found ACOs with baseline expenses higher than their local competitors found their savings under the ACO plan were greater than those ACOs with below average baseline expenditures (McWilliams et al. 2015). Even when ACO initiatives fail to save money, physicians (and patients) are happy if patient outcomes improve (Kaiser Health News 2015).

But for all of the successes of the Pioneer Model ACOs, there are numerous criticisms that have been lobbed against the model and overall, results of patient outcomes are mixed. One of the most widespread critiques concerns the IT infrastructure needed to implement the ACO model (Blackstone and Fuhr 2016). Many health systems underestimate the cost and time involved in EHR adoption and overestimate their risk management capabilities (Agency for Healthcare Research and Quality 2014). And patients may have several health conditions that make care coordination challenging. Jonathan Gluck, senior executive and corporate counsel at Heritage Provider Network has said, "It's not as easy as it sounds. It sounds simple—let's get all the data, coordinate the care, and we'll save a bunch of money. I don't think people understand the detailed work that is necessary to effectively coordinate the care of an individual who may have a bunch of different chronic conditions. I don't think people appreciated it's really a mindset change that they have to undergo if they want to be successful" (Perna 2013).

Inequities in risk assumption are further difficult to address. Large health systems can better spread their risk across a large patient population, whereas smaller provider networks are less able. Conversely, physician groups might be able to individually achieve ACO goals, but if the ACO they are a part of does not, they won't receive financial awards (Kaiser Health News 2015). And there is some evidence that patients could receive subpar care due to reduced hospital admissions (Blackstone and Fuhr 2016). Nevertheless, CMS has moved on from the Pioneer ACO Model to the Next Gen ACO program in hopes of continuing to achieve the Triple Aim in healthcare: improving the patient care experience, improving population health, and reducing per capita healthcare costs.

There are other ways that healthcare organizations, as businesses, can be structured. Integrated delivery networks (IDNs) are one example. In addition to the hospitals and providers affiliated with Geisinger Health in Pennsylvania, the company also manages its own health plan. Kaiser Permanente, based in California, is another example of an IDN with provider networks and both individual and family plans across the country. Though many IDNs are self-insured, not all are able or willing to take on the financial risk and prefer to contract with existing insurers.

IDNs contrast with the traditional model where providers and hospitals provide services to the patients who have third-party insurance plans, which reimburse providers for the costs of goods and services. This creates a disconnect between the groups providing services and those who are paying for them. Bernard Tyson, CEO of Kaiser Permanente, thinks that misaligned financial incentives are to blame for things like overhospitalization, since healthcare providers and hospitals are incentivized to have "heads in beds" (*The Economist* 2017).

But with a self-insured plan, the payers and the providers are on the same team, and their incentives for keeping patients healthy and reducing costs are aligned. There is no financial benefit and in fact, there is a financial penalty, to ordering unnecessary procedures or for choosing more expensive treatments when a less expensive one will be as good. But this does not imply that providers in self-insured plans withhold expensive care when it is appropriate and will improve overall patient outcomes. In fact, the goal of IDNs (and that of self-insured plans) is to provide value-based care (see the sidebar *Championing Value-Based Care, Realistically*).

In Chapter 6, we presented the debate around paying for Sovaldi and other expensive hepatitis C treatments. These drugs cost more than $70,000 per year and with more than 3 million Americans infected with the virus, the cost for treating all of them would be staggering. But compared with the $500,000 cost for a liver transplant (Transplant Living-UNOS 2017), not to mention the posttransplant, antirejection medicine and other ongoing medical costs, treating hepatitis C with one of these drugs can be cost-effective and dramatically improve patients' lives. But as noted in Chapter 7, finding the tipping point where an intervention, treatment, or procedure becomes cost-effective for a patient based on their particular characteristics requires data analysis. Another key issue is the fact that patients in America often move from one insurer to another. Insurers are skeptical of paying huge sums to cure patients who will then move on to another insurer, though it's unclear just how many patients are switching insurers willingly (i.e., not because of a job change, or insurer leaving the market) (Fisman 2007; Hoadley et al. 2013; Sanger-Katz 2014).

To truly get to value-based care, will mean a change in the way health systems approach patient care. Patient care will become more personalized and precise, as doctors use predictive analytics to head off disease or determine the best medication choice for individual patients. To this end, medical centers with robust informatics departments and established EHR systems will find themselves ahead of the competition, at least initially. Medical centers and provider practices will have to similarly adapt to measuring internal business practices, such as comparing patient outcomes between providers and identifying providers that select low-value procedures or treatments for their patients. Inefficiency, redundancy, and waste can be minimized, but hospitals have to be capturing those data and be willing to act on it. Borrowing ideas from other industries, such as automotive, that have spent the past decades transforming their processes to be more efficient and value-based will be helpful. The Toyota Production System's continuous measurement philosophy is one such example (Toyota 2017).

SIDEBAR: CHAMPIONING VALUE-BASED CARE, REALISTICALLY

Howard R. Grant, MD, JD
President and CEO, Lahey Health

Howard R. Grant sees something seriously wrong with the U.S. health system. "We are spending at least twice as much as any other industrialized country and not getting results on most objective metrics that are nearly as good as countries that spend much less and use fewer resources," says Grant, who is President and CEO of Lahey Health (Grant 2017). "That is my fundamental concern."

Grant came to Lahey from Geisinger Health System, an integrated delivery network (IDN, or system that combines an insurance company with a hospital system). At the time, about half of Geisinger's patients for whom the organization cared were also insured by the health system's own health plan, and that puts the system in a unique position. "When Geisinger health plan expends fewer healthcare resources on those patients, by improving the management of their care, avoiding unnecessary expenses and lowering their total costs of care, the Geisinger system retains those unspent health insurance premium dollars and reinvests in the clinical enterprise," Grant explains. "Typically, if hospitals, physician groups, or health systems lower healthcare costs, an outside insurer gets the reward. That makes it very difficult to justify investments in initiatives that are likely to lower total medical expenses," he points out.

That's left Geisinger and others like it in an enviable position, and they are often lauded as the models for the value-based healthcare system of the future that many contemplate. But what if you lead a hospital that is not directly affiliated with an insurer? How do you achieve similar goals? That is the challenge CEOs such as Grant are taking up.

The rewards of value-based care could be extraordinary. "If we could get just half the people with type 2 diabetes in this country to reach normalized lab results and have healthier lifestyles, we could cut $6 to $7 billion out of U.S. healthcare costs," Grant says. "But doctors and hospitals have historically been paid to treat sick people, to react to illness, and not to invest in strategies to keep patients healthy. It's a system with backward incentives."

That's why Grant wants the country to "migrate to a system were healthcare providers bear the financial responsibility for the care of their patients and have adequate resources to actually make the patients healthier in the long term, not just treat them when they are sick." The change in that direction was jumpstarted under the Affordable Care Act, with new policies such as penalties to providers if patients were readmitted to a hospital shortly after their stay. "But nobody would have expended a major effort and invested resources on the issue without those rules," Grant says. "We need to keep driving people in that direction. It's better for our patients' health and it's better for our country's finances."

He points to one particularly compelling initiative that Lahey started. The hospital's imaging department studied the use of rapid slice CT at low radiation exposure to diagnose lung cancer in a clearly defined population of patients at very high-risk for developing lung cancer. Almost all patients who are diagnosed with lung cancer in the later stages of the illness die. Meanwhile, about 85% who are diagnosed at the earliest stages of the disease survive. So, it made a lot of sense to try this approach, but there just wasn't sufficient evidence and insurers were not reimbursing for such screening. The Lahey team showed how effective early, low-dose screening could be. And now, after some resistance of course, Medicare and some insurers are paying for the procedure.

How is Grant preparing for the future? For one thing, Lahey has just invested about $5 million in predictive analytics. With that software they plan to take on challenges such as type 2 diabetes. "There are 30 million diabetics in the United States today and they account for 10% of U.S. healthcare expenditures," he says. If Lahey's doctors can mine patients' electronic health records to identify those who are at risk of the diseases, but don't yet show signs, they can help some of those patients avoid the disease altogether. "Diabetes is a healthcare tsunami staring us right in the face," Grant says. "We should be mobilizing against it now."

Grant knows the classic obstacles to radical change. Many of the processes in medicine need to be reengineered in order to support a comprehensive approach to population health. For example, you can't expect primary care doctors to see a patient every 15 minutes if you want our caregivers to build relationships that will impact health outcomes. But he's hopeful. "There are a lot of forces moving in the right direction," he says. "There's going to be disruption, but there's also going to be positive change."

The fee-for-service model has been advantageous for a variety of stakeholders, including providers. So, they are among those who are resistant to move toward a value-based payment system. One health system has a novel plan to train providers in a value-based network. California-based Kaiser Permanente is planning to open a medical school in the fall of 2019 (Dietsche 2015; Masunaga 2016a; Kaiser Permanente 2017). The ethos of Kaiser's health system is based on primary care providers as the center of healthcare delivery and the medical school is expected to build on their model. If Kaiser's gamble to start a medical school works, it could lead to a new way of teaching the next generation of doctors.

Shifting the Balance of Power

Due to rising healthcare costs, the United States has been trying alternative provider and health system models for years. Though first tested in a 2005 pilot program, ACOs are now gaining traction as some high-profile health systems find success with the paradigm and the number of ACOs continues to rise (Blackstone and Fuhr 2016). A 2016 release of data from CMS found approximately 29% of participating ACOs earned shared savings in 2015, though experts disagree if the model is truly successful (Introcaso 2016). Currently, private payers hold much of the power in healthcare systems, as they determine coverage policies (i.e., whether or not they will cover a particular treatment or procedure) and what their reimbursement level will be for medical care that falls outside of ACA-mandated essential care. And while providers (health systems and individual clinicians) can negotiate reimbursement, patients are left out of the discussion entirely.

The rise of high deductible health plans is steadily increasing the amount patients have to contribute toward their healthcare, as described in Chapter 6. Generally, patients have little incentive to select low-cost providers and often conflate low cost with low quality (deBrantes and Delbanco 2016). This can put patient demands for the newest technology or unnecessary testing at odds with value-based care. In addition, consolidations between insurers or provider networks can leave patients unable to choose healthcare alternatives, and outside of self-insured and not-for-profit health systems, patients may end up paying more with no market checks to limit price increases (Blackstone and Fuhr 2016).

The growing number of mergers and acquisitions of hospitals and health systems has many experts and regulators concerned. As noted in the beginning of the chapter, a proposed merger of Chicago-area Advocate Health and NorthShore University HealthSystem was blocked by the Federal Trade Commission (FTC) because "the combined entity would operate a majority of the hospitals in the area and control more than 50% of the general acute care inpatient hospital services" (Federal Trade Commission 2017). In an article for the *NEJM Catalyst*, David Balan of the FTC notes that mergers often have negative outcomes for patients in the form of higher prices and reduced quality when the firms that are merging are close competitors (Balan 2016). Even cross-market (distinct geographic area) mergers can lead to price increases of 7%–10% or lower quality care (Dafny, Ho, and Lee 2016).

Hospital mergers can also create efficiencies, reducing costs for the merging firms that can lower prices or improve quality. For example, mergers may decrease the number of different EHRs used by patients' providers, which can lead to improved data sharing and care coordination between providers and reduce redundant procedures (Birkmeyer 2016).

But when these systems become so large as to limit provider choice, the outcome is a lack of a "true market," noted by Elisabeth Rosenthal, medical doctor and senior writer at the *New York Times* in her new book, *The American Sickness: How Healthcare Became Big Business and How You Can*

Take It Back. In a recent interview with RadioBoston, she says that patients aren't always in a position to shop for healthcare, which means they rely on providers for advice (Bruzek and Chakraparti 2017). Patients who are unable to really "shop" for the best value care on their own thus need to work with their providers to do this. Sometimes the providers will have incentives to actually direct their patients to higher-cost facilities. For example, a provider based at a certain hospital may send a patient to that facility's lab. That makes sense practically, but is not always cost effective.

Primary Care Revival?

In primary care, innovation is spurring competition where previously there was none. Primary care has long been one of the fields of medicine with among the lowest reimbursement rates: hence the infamous 15-minutes-or-less consultations and huge patient loads, which are often cited as reasons young doctors are increasingly shying away from this field (Kavilanz 2009). Long ago, PCPs were regarded as the "gatekeepers" in medicine. They were the patient's first contact with the medical system, and the doctors who made sure that only the most appropriate care was delivered. This identity as "gatekeeper" is unfortunate, as it impedes patient (and sometimes specialist) acceptance of the PCP as an *integrated* part of patient care (Krieger 1996). Over time, however, specialists gained more control as they were able to offer more advanced treatments and insurance companies began letting patients see specialists—even without a PCP's referral.

But some PCPs are now offering patients alternative practice models.

Concierge services are where patients pay a flat monthly rate for access to the doctor whenever they need it (Metz 2017). Typically, such services have a relatively high annual fee (more than $1,000 per year), and patients are given virtually unlimited contact with their primary care doctors. There are often other "frills" added in, such as more comprehensive preventive and wellness care, to make the high-fee subscription attractive. But the patient also needs additional comprehensive insurance, such as Medicare or a private policy, since the service only covers primary care. Massachusetts General Hospital and the Mayo Clinic are just two renowned facilities that offer a concierge service (Massachusetts General Hospital 2017a; Mayo Clinic 2017b).

In addition to existing medical centers, numerous start-ups are entering the concierge medicine market, leading to an estimated 12,000 physicians now offering concierge services (Colwell 2016). Though primary care is the focus of most concierge medical groups, Prime Surgeons, a Los Angeles–based group is even piloting the model for certain types of surgeries (Masunaga 2016b). Some, like Silicon Valley–backed Forward and One Medical are putting an emphasis on connected devices and smartphone apps as ways to keep tabs on their patients and help manage outcomes like weight and blood sugar (Tansey 2015; Coren 2017).

Direct primary care is another new model slowly being introduced. It also involves a subscription service, but in this case the monthly fees are usually much lower than for concierge practices, and the emphasis is on cutting unnecessary costs by more closely managing a patient's ongoing health and overseeing where and when they go for specialty care (Huff 2015).

Iora Health (formerly Renaissance Health) is a company that sprang from groundbreaking work with Boeing and others to develop an "intensified chronic care program" to improve patients' health and reduce costs (Milstein et al. 2009). Results from the Boeing pilot program (Iora) showed lower costs and substantially better health outcomes. Iora now operates in eight states and has raised more than $100 million in the past 2 years, adding new investors that support its business model (Pai 2015; Bartlett 2016). Iora's model is to partner with groups such as unions, employers (e.g., Hartford Healthcare), and even health insurance companies like Humana, which have a great interest in lowering health costs (Iora Health 2017). In April 2017, Iora partnered with the state of Massachusetts' Government Insurance Commission to "…provide specialized healthcare to around 2,000 people in an attempt to save the state money" (Bartlett 2017).

Both patients who are dissatisfied with rushed office visits and physicians who are frustrated with large caseloads and insurance requirements might find concierge-style medical services an alluring option (Doherty 2015). Don Sommers, a retired chemical engineer, credits this type of service with saving his leg, after several surgeries failed to remove a clot and doctors had no further treatments to recommend. Sommers turned to San Francisco–based Grand Rounds, a company that works with patients and employers to match patients to top physicians for either primary care or second opinions. Sommers received a second opinion from a doctor who was able to remove the clot, saving Sommers from a potential amputation (Hernandez 2014).

Whether either of these are economically sustainable business models is still unclear, particularly as competition increases from more traditional physician networks. Even financial backing from heavyweights like the Mayo Clinic and the Social+Capital fund weren't enough to prevent concierge start-up Better from failing in 2015, something former CEO Geoff Clapp ascribes to "failing to find an appropriate product market and fundamental misalignment with the investors and strategic partners" (Mack 2016). Turntable Health, a direct primary care service using Iora Health started by a Stanford-trained Zubin Damania and Tony Hsieh, CEO of online shoe store, Zappos, closed after a few years due to "economic challenges of the Las Vegas market," according to Damania (Comstock 2017c; Ventura 2017).

More recently, Seattle-based Qliance also ceased operations, citing a healthcare system that resisted their care delivery model, making "it harder and harder to survive" (Comstock 2017c; Qliance 2017). However, the closing of these alternative care delivery options doesn't mean the direct care model is going away. Samir Qamar, CEO of MedLion, another direct primary care business, said they chose not to rely entirely on venture capital from the beginning and "has found great success in slowly peeling away layers of various markets over several years" (Comstock 2017c).

If the direct primary care model proves unsustainable over time, there are alternatives for patients. Pharmacies, and even grocery stores, are adding additional health services, such as vaccinations and school physicals, to their offerings (see the sidebar *Achieving a New Value-Based Model of Healthcare Delivery*), giving patients some measure of choice. Hospitals need to be aware of that and respond.

SIDEBAR: ACHIEVING A NEW VALUE-BASED MODEL OF HEALTHCARE DELIVERY

Glenn D. Steele, MD, PhD

Chairman, xG Health Solutions

Getting to true value-based care is going to require a profound change in culture, according to Glenn Steele, chairman of start-up xG Health Solutions, which is a spin-off of Geisinger Health Systems. xG is taking a set of proprietary innovative approaches developed at Geisinger, scaling them, and putting them to work for other groups, including the Health Transformation Alliance and EHR vendors, such as Epic and Cerner.

He likes to point to a pivotal project Geisinger carried out while he was leading the system, and which helped them see the potential for a new approach. "About 10 years ago, we set about to manage the health of 30,000 patients with type 2 diabetes in a different way," he explains (Steele 2017). "We decided we would enable our community practitioners and endocrinologists to work together and manage these patients in a more optimal way. The key things we asked were: What are the dozen or so things that should happen to manage these patients in the optimal way? How do we transmit that information to the clinicians? And what are the metrics that will gauge success?"

The first set of metrics, Steele advises, should always be related to performance—what are the providers doing? The second should be functional outcome metrics—how are the patients doing in response? The Geisinger diabetes program also embedded nurses who acted as "concierge care managers" in some of the practices. They could personalize the treatment plan according to the patient's specific needs.

The results were remarkable. "In only 3 years, we dramatically improved the percentage of patients who received best practice level treatment. With that, we saw a significant decrease in the probability of heart attack, stroke, and eye disease [among diabetic patients]," Steele says. The health system is now trying to replicate that approach with more diseases, including COPD, congestive heart failure, and reactive depression.

One of the key things in Geisinger's favor is that this company has an unusual structure, because it combines a health system with a health insurance company. About half of Geisinger's patients are also members of the company's health plan. As a result, if the health system improves quality or efficiency, the company as a whole benefits. Most hospitals don't reap rewards from improvements in their processes. Rather, the insurance companies they contract from profit from those gains. That makes it difficult to make efficiencies a top priority.

Whatever the provider's structure is, the shift from a fee-for-service (i.e., getting paid more for doing more) to a value-based system (i.e., getting paid for outcomes) involves a shift in culture, Steele emphasizes. "To achieve that you need to have strategic aims that resonate with the people providing the care," he says. "We went through that process starting almost 20 years ago. Everyone at Geisinger now knows the company is putting aside anything that hurts patient outcomes, and prioritizing the things that optimize outcomes."

Another key advantage for Geisinger is that they moved to EHRs in the mid-1990s, long before many of their competitors. And since Geisinger has both the clinical and claims data on at least half their patients, they can track utilization and outcomes better than most other hospital systems.

xG Health Solutions is now working to help other health systems achieve this new model of healthcare delivery. "I see tremendous shifts taking place," says Steele. "We are in an era of value re-engineering, where costs have to come down and where companies like CVS and Walmart are looking for new opportunities, and starting to compete with traditional health systems. We need to respond to that new competition now."

Having good data, Steele thinks, will make a big difference for any organization. "The more you use the data, the more the process improves," he says. "It is never perfect, and we are always modifying it, but at Geisinger, it's already a vastly improved system than it was before." Others, he believes, can achieve the same types of results.

Building the Health System of the Future

So, what does the health system of the future look like? Will hospitals become more like "air traffic control centers" where people sit "in a room full of screens and phones," like Toby Cosgrove, head of the Cleveland Clinic, has said? (*The Economist* 2017) Will the vast quantities of data that are now being collected and analyzed really help health systems achieve the "Triple Aim?" How will the relationships between stakeholders change? Below, we have made some predictions.

Hospitals will put an emphasis on improving efficiency and consolidating. As costs are increasingly shifted to the government and consumers, price sensitivity is becoming an issue and there is a growing emphasis on paying for quality care and good outcomes rather than paying per service rendered (i.e., "fee-for-service").

These trends are putting pressure on hospital budgets. One result of this is that hospital administrators are scrambling to do what other industries have been doing for years—optimize their operations. That means measuring things so they know what they need to improve and where they are not getting sufficient return on their investment. It's the Six Sigma* moment for healthcare. With quality measures, outcomes, and population health becoming more important, hospitals will also be looking for ways to show that they are providing optimal care, and improving the health of the communities they serve.

Achieving that requires a keen focus on process improvement. You cannot improve what you cannot measure, so healthcare providers are investing in software, databases, and systems that will give them the data required to determine where they need to make cuts and where they should invest. Hospitals are even looking outside the healthcare industry for direction, such as the automotive industry's Toyota Production System, which focuses on continuous improvement, standardization, and measurement to deliver high-value vehicles (Toyota 2017). Look for changes across the hospital operations landscape. Administrators will be scrutinizing everything from office processes to surgeries to identify high-value practices. As a result, it's inevitable that job roles will evolve and staffing needs will change. Employees, including providers, will need to learn new skills to stay relevant in a data-driven environment.

Hospitals also have to be willing to let the data drive process change, sometimes leading them in unexpected or new directions, rather than trying to force insights to fit within existing frameworks. For example, Virginia Mason Medical Center redesigned their care delivery process for patients with lower back pain in response to potential exclusion from an Aetna provider network. The hospital used Aetna-provided claims data to analyze provider practices and identify low-value services, ultimately creating a patient-centric care delivery model (described in Chapter 7) for lower back pain that increased productivity while reducing unnecessary treatments (Pham et al. 2007). Non-emergency medical assets are another area of substantial inefficiency and waste. Cohealo cofounder and CEO Mark Slaughter has said, "Everyone ends up owning the exact same things." The Boston-based company aims to fix that by letting hospitals within geographic regions share high-cost, low-use equipment (Verel 2014).

The Mayo Clinic has used data to cut costs within its health system and maintain and improve patient outcomes. Mayo, already considered one of the top hospitals in the world, is proof that even high-performing institutions can find new insights from data. For example, before becoming CEO, neurologist John Noseworthy led an investigation to identify areas that Mayo needed to overhaul to remain competitive in the future. As a result, in the past several years, the hospital has revamped care delivery for children with complex breathing and swallowing problems, expanded the role of nurses in the management of patients with epilepsy, and reconfigured cardiac surgical care for patients by standardizing equipment and procedures (Winslow 2017).

Due to ever-increasing financial pressures on hospitals and health systems, it is almost certain that the pace of mergers, acquisitions, and partnerships will not slow in the foreseeable

---

* Six Sigma is a business approach that encourages meticulous measurement and evaluation of processes to achieve optimal efficiency (http://www.isixsigma.com/new-to-six-sigma/getting-started/what-six-sigma/).

future. There is simply too much potential cost savings and ability to increase market share for health systems not to consider mergers and acquisitions of competitors. Here is where the push to value-based care becomes much more important. But proposals will be under scrutiny from regulators and will have to demonstrate patients will not suffer from higher prices or lower quality.

Payers also need to reinvent themselves. As the growth of the healthcare expenditures slows, competitors, such as hospitals and insurance companies, will start to cannibalize each other. Hospitals, which are burdened by reduced payments, penalties from quality improvement programs and other federal initiatives, and continued increases in healthcare costs, can find it difficult to achieve value-based outcomes when any financial benefit for doing so goes to a third party. Consequently, self-insured health systems, such as Pennsylvania's Geisinger Health, are the biggest competitor to traditional payers today, because they reap the benefits of innovative programs, keeping cost savings within the system where they can be reinvested.

Already hospitals, including Boston's Partners Healthcare, Northern Virginia's Innova Health Systems, Geisinger Health, and Northern California's Sutter Health, are offering their own health plans (i.e., insurance). For Sutter the move allows the hospital to "develop closer more direct partnerships with employers and patients," the new plan's CEO Steve Nolte said in a press release (Sutter Health 2013). It gives them more data and more control. And as discussed earlier in this chapter, IDNs can better align the financial incentives for keeping patients healthy by focusing on value-based care and innovations that support that goal. By keeping the financial profits of such initiatives within the health system, hospitals can reinvest in further innovation.

The entire stand-alone insurance industry is in a state of change. Mergers and acquisitions of other insurers are ongoing. Others have started to buy up hospitals systems. Highmark, for example, acquired the five-hospital West Penn Allegheny Health System (Mathews 2011), with plans to establish one of the largest integrated delivery systems in the country. Data will be crucial for them to both run these facilities and provide optimal care.

Aetna's CEO, meanwhile, has described his organization as a "health IT company with an insurance component" (Chase 2012). Because they have the claims data, he argues, insurance companies can figure out what a health system really needs to look like to fit a particular community's needs. Aetna International is doing just that for China's Binhai region, which aims to be that country's Silicon Valley. Aetna has helped to build the healthcare infrastructure and the technology platform there (Aetna 2014a). More recently, the CMO of insurer Humana said he does not think his company as much as an insurer as "an IT company who is helping us with the data that we need in order to deal with our population heath tools" (Sweeney 2017a).

Employers will try harder to reduce their health costs, or shift out of providing healthcare coverage entirely. While the growth in health costs has slowed, the trend is still unsustainable. Developed as a way to attract workers in the face of wage controls, U.S. businesses are now viewing health costs associated with employer-based insurance plans as a major burden. This puts them at a disadvantage globally, since we have the highest health costs in the developed world. Health costs are also unpredictable and hard to manage; CEOs wait with dread to find out what the next year's health costs will be. Small companies suffer even more than large ones. The prices for their policies are usually higher, and costs are even more difficult for them to manage.

The clearest trend here has been the shift to greater cost sharing for employees with work-based health plans. High deductible health plans are increasingly common and will continue to be. But we also expect to see many more businesses shift to a defined contribution model for health plans: the company will pay a set amount toward premiums, and employees who want expensive plans will pay the difference themselves.

There's also been a noticeable shift to private insurance exchanges, where employers provide a fixed contribution to the costs of premiums, but employees shop for their own care. An Accenture Consulting report predicts that by 2018, more than 40 million people will get their insurance through private exchanges (Kalish 2014).

Further, we expect that businesses will start looking at healthcare much more strategically. A greater number of them will offer plans with narrow networks, or even start contracting directly with specific hospital systems for certain common and high cost procedures (e.g., transplants and hip replacements). This approach, often referred to as "Centers of Excellence," can help businesses control costs, since they can set fee limits up front. Concierge medical service companies, like Grand Rounds, that help match patients with high-quality providers can also help employers point their employees in the direction of value-based care.

We may begin to see more big businesses actually move their offices to communities with more affordable health systems—or help to create them in their current environment. Boeing, Costco, and Starbucks have pressured health systems to improve their care delivery processes and reduce the costs of healthcare, using business strategies, such as Six Sigma or other continuous improvement frameworks (Levey 2014). What data employers and patients use and how they use it will be critical however. For example, providing price data without quality data is not that useful. And quality data are difficult to arrive at. Is the best surgeon the one who does the most procedures? Some experts believe "over diagnosis" is actually a big problem in the U.S., and that the best measure is doctors who correctly diagnose their patients most of the time, and who seldom need to repeat procedures. Compiling that kind of data will be more challenging, but essential, and successes at places such as Geisinger, Kaiser, Virginia Mason, and others demonstrate that it can be done.

But for all the benefits of employer-based healthcare plans, they may have outlived their utility. Analysts have concluded that these benefits help to keep wages relatively stagnant even in the face of shifting more of the costs onto workers (Herman and Livingston 2016). A single-payer system could benefit both employers and workers, as suggested by Warren Buffet's comments supporting a single-payer system at a Berkshire Hathaway shareholder meeting (Olen 2017). Employees would find they have increased mobility and could change jobs without consideration of their health insurance and wages would rise. This in turn could further spur increased innovation, as workers don't feel tied to a job because of health insurance. Employers would also benefit from a single-payer system. Though their tax benefits are substantial, rising healthcare costs are a major pain point and employees are finding it difficult to bear higher deductibles. Getting out of the healthcare business would free up revenue for other projects or employee wages.

Patients will become price-sensitive and more engaged in own care. In the past, patients equated high prices with higher value. After all, a higher-priced procedure must be better, right? And if someone else is paying the entire bill, why not just go with that provider? But now with high deductible plans, narrow networks, more quality data being released, and an explosion in care provided in alternative settings (such as urgent care clinics, or via telemedicine), patients are starting to be more price sensitive. Today, purchasing insurance with an unaffordable deductible or going to an out-of-network hospital can bankrupt someone.

Patients on health insurance exchanges and those choosing Medicare Advantage plans are finding their choices diminished as payers pull out due to higher than expected costs. Wellmark Blue Cross Blue Shield pointed to $12 million annual costs for a single member and financial losses as the reason for leaving Iowa's marketplace (Small 2017). Wellmark's departure from the Iowa exchanges left Minnesota-based Medica with monopolies in the Iowa and Nebraska exchanges, reducing consumer choice and price competition (Snowbeck 2017). One potential solution is the formation of a "virtual high-risk pool" that could work across state lines to minimize the impacts of members that require expensive treatments, an idea supported by Medica (Snowbeck 2017). However, analysis performed by the Kaiser Family Foundation about the impacts of pre-ACA, state-run, high-risk pools and the temporary federal high-risk pool (Pre-Existing Condition Insurance Program) for people with preexisting conditions found the subsidies to cover the deficit between premiums and claims substantial (Pollitz 2017), so it's uncertain that a new high-risk pool program would attain desired healthcare savings in this population.

Substantial change is needed in how care is delivered. Concierge health services and direct primary care services have the potential to become a significant player, at least for primary healthcare, as they can compete with traditional provider networks on quality, service, and price transparency. However, their services are relatively limited and patients typically still need another form of insurance, which will be barriers to more widespread adoption.

Data about provider prices are also starting to trickle out. But it's still difficult to determine what the real cost is, since insurers negotiate prices with each provider. And, the crucial data patients are missing is about the quality of care. Despite the rapid migration to HDHPs, which was supposed to encourage shopping for healthcare, patients still have little access to quality data.

Many new companies are also forming around the idea of engaging patients in their care. Wellness coaches and care coordinators are helping patients to address social, practical and behavioral problems that are keeping them from getting optimal outcomes. If a patient can't get to the clinic, for example, their health will suffer. And someone with asthma can't get better if their home is full of mold and contaminants. Just having someone on staff (but not a doctor) that can arrange for that ride or find a better living situation can improve outcomes.

Wearable devices and digital health could significantly change how providers monitor, treat, and engage with patients. There has also been a significant uptick in the number of mobile and wearable devices available that will let patients monitor their health more closely, from fitness trackers to more medically relevant devices like connected blood pressure cuffs or ECGs. Until now, most of these devices and their corresponding apps were only useful to consumers themselves and not generally adopted into clinical care, but as we will describe in the next chapter, better integration of digital health data into EHRs will start to change how providers measure how their patients are doing.

The healthcare system is in a state of flux from ever-increasing costs, price, and quality opacity, and penalties from federal quality initiatives are leaving hospitals and providers bearing the brunt of these pressures. This upheaval is driving innovation in every aspect of the industry in ways that these institutions and providers can take advantage of—if they choose. How far the system can be transformed will rely on the willingness of the stakeholders to move toward a value-based system and engage in continuous improvement and measurement initiatives. It won't be sufficient to simply measure a process or an outcome—real change will arise from the transformation that arises as health systems use those data to develop new ways, value-based methods, of delivering care. If most of this innovation and change happens, we'll have a completely different healthcare system within 5–10 years. For that to occur, we'll need to keep pressing for greater transparency (especially more public data), better means of measuring quality, better processes to ensure care standards are optimal and are transferred to other institutions. If all that continues to happen, we can reduce costs, improve quality and make sure that more patients are receiving optimal care at a reasonable price.

Chapter 10

Digital Health: Moving from Sci-Fi Fantasy to a New Healthcare Reality

These extraordinary accomplishments, from dissecting and defining DNA to creating such pervasive electronic technologies that immediately and intimately connect most individuals around the world, have unwittingly set up a profound digital disruption of medicine.

Eric Topol, MD
The Creative Destruction of Medicine, *Basic Books, 2012*

Working at a "nondescript office in Palo Alto," a secret team of Apple employees are toiling on a noninvasive, continuous blood glucose monitor to help people with diabetes better control their disease (Farr 2017a). Apparently, this was a project Steve Jobs himself came up with, and it could thrust the tech giant deeper into the healthcare field. Already there are indications that the company has hired consultants to navigate the FDA approval process and claims that "clinical sites" are trialing the device in the San Francisco Bay area (Cooper 2017). But Apple isn't alone. Dozens of companies, both traditional healthcare businesses and nontraditional start-ups, are now looking at digital health as an entry into the profitable healthcare market.

The sci-fi fantasies of yesterday are starting to be realized and health systems are embracing digital technology in ways never before seen—all of which is leading to a dramatic transformation of healthcare. Connected devices, such as scales or blood pressure cuffs, which help monitor patients remotely, are now targeting the profitable consumer market. And provider-oriented devices are getting smaller and smarter: the Qualcomm XPrize contest recently announced the winning team that developed a Star Trek–like tricorder, able to diagnose multiple health conditions, such as diabetes, sleep apnea, pneumonia, and a urinary tract infection (Diguilio 2017) with a palm-sized device. Start-ups are exploring new ways to improve outcomes and help providers care for patients using a growing number of digital health devices, smartphone-enabled apps, and technologies like artificial intelligence.

Digital health is transforming how patients and employers shop for healthcare, how providers and medical systems market themselves, and how payers are tackling rising healthcare costs. It's a market already worth over $80 billion and expected to reach more than $379 billion by 2024 (Global Market Insights 2016). A record number of digital health start-ups emerged in 2016, and while total funding was down, investors were still bullish on the field: more than 500 digital health companies grabbed $8 billion in funding (Tecco 2017). And the global cognitive computing market value is expected to grow from an estimated $738.5 million in 2014 to nearly $2.5 billion by 2022 (Grand View Research 2016b). As a result, interest and innovation in these areas are still growing, with many ripe opportunities including interoperability, wearables, and AI, as described in this chapter.

Dawn of Digital Health

More than 15 years ago, the article "Digital Health Care—The Convergence of Health Care and the Internet" was published in the *Journal of Ambulatory Care Management* by Seth Frank, formerly a vice president at A.G. Edwards and currently vice president at Allscripts Healthcare Solutions. In the article, Frank categorized digital health companies into three main areas: commerce, connectivity, and content, and envisioned digital health solutions that would help consumers make informed decisions, provide information, and ultimately lower health costs by empowering consumers. He also saw digital health opportunities as a way to develop a sense of community amongst patients and to promote health and well-being (Frank 2000).

Since that article was published, others have followed Frank's lead, expanding and clarifying what (and what does not) constitute digital health. Rock Health, a venture fund dedicated to healthcare and digital technologies, describes this field as the "intersection between healthcare and technology; and not solely in medicine, but across healthcare, including wellness and administration" (Gandhi 2017). For the purposes of this chapter, we'll also use a broader definition of digital health, because as we've presented in examples throughout this book, digital health and Big Data are already transforming every aspect of healthcare, for all stakeholders.

It's no secret that the amount of healthcare data are increasing annually. With data driving everything from precision medicine and drug development, to price transparency and value-based reimbursement, it's easy to get caught up in the idea that all of healthcare's problems could be solved if we just had more data.

But having data by itself isn't sufficient to enable the kinds of changes we've described in previous chapters, and several experts have cautioned about the hype surrounding Big Data and its limitations. Indeed, "Big data are worthless in a vacuum. Its potential value is unlocked only when leveraged to drive decision making" (Gandomi and Haider 2015). For example, "A lot of data has been gathered by sequencing cancer genomes, but it is not properly aggregated yet," says Eric Topol. "The holdup isn't necessarily the analytics, it's the willingness of different centers to work together and administrative hurdles such as Institutional Review Boards, privacy, etc."

Certainly, the kind of complex analytics being used today in these pursuits require amounts of data that would have been almost incomprehensible even a decade ago. But to gain meaningful insights from the data deluge necessitates the information be structured in a way that allows analysis. Even more importantly, the data being collected should be the *right* data for the situation, and they must also be in the *right format or structure* to enable the kinds of outcomes-based analyses needed for adoption of new technologies/procedures. Otherwise, the value of the data are lost (Beckers 2017; Wang, Azad, and Rajan 2017). Data needed to bring price transparency to hospital procedures for patients isn't the same kind of information needed by clinicians to predict which patients are at risk for cardiovascular disease. Digital health, cloud, and AI solutions make generating, structuring, and aggregating the data into useable formats feasible (Beckers 2017).

Embracing the Cloud

Another big driver of digital health is "the cloud." Cloud-based computing has taken off in the past few years as a means to maximize the computing power needed for advanced analytics and data storage that healthcare systems, hospitals, and researchers need. In fact, according to a 2016 HIMSS Analytics survey of healthcare IT executives, 84% reported using cloud-based solutions as part of their IT operations (HIMSS Analytics 2016a).

So what exactly is "the cloud"?

According to technology pioneer IBM, cloud computing is "the delivery of on-demand computing resources—everything from applications to data centers—over the internet on a pay-for-use basis" (IBM 2016). Companies can host their own private clouds or use a public or hybrid cloud to manage data and application. Benefits of cloud computing are that it facilitates data sharing and is secure. On-demand use of specialized staff, routinely updated software and platforms to fight against cyber-attacks, and data centralization are key benefits of cloud services. Furthermore, cloud services are easily scalable (up or down, depending on the needs of the company) and this, in turn, can reduce the financial burden for companies since they only pay for the services/storage they use and don't pay for the upfront costs or maintenance of creating their own IT infrastructure (IBM 2016).

These benefits are behind a growing number of healthcare organizations moving their IT operations to the cloud, leading to a market forecast for healthcare cloud services of $9.5 billion by 2020 (McCarthy 2015). For instance, the USMD Health System, created after the merger of three Texas-based health systems in 2012, has been moving their IT operations to Amazon's cloud in order to consolidate and centralize IT functions (Butler 2016). And researchers at Mount Sinai Icahn School of Medicine studying breast and ovarian cancer can analyze more than 100 terabytes of data using a cloud-based platform—a feat that wouldn't be possible without the cloud-based service, according to one of the researchers (Ratchinsky 2016).

But for all the benefits of the cloud, security is one area of concern, due to the need to keep identifying patient information and sensitive health information private to comply with HIPAA regulations. A 2015 cyber-attack on an Indiana-based medical software company and its cloud service shot ripples through the healthcare system as patient names, addresses, Social Security numbers, and personal health records were compromised (Guccione 2015) and cyber-attacks on healthcare records skyrocketed in 2016 to 93 major attacks, up from 57 in 2015 (Sheridan 2016). In a high-profile case, Emory Healthcare's Brain Health Center fell victim to a ransomware attack in 2016, after a third-party database was compromised (Dietsche 2017). But many of the attacks are a consequence of failing "to adopt basic safeguards like anti-malware tools, firewalls, and encryption," according to a 2016 HIMSS Cyber Security report (HIMSS Analytics 2016b), so moving to cloud-based services, where these security measures are applied and routinely updated, may actually result in stronger security for healthcare systems.

Improving Clinical Workflow

Digital health is contributing an ever-increasing amount of information that can straddle many healthcare domains and be useful to stakeholders with very different goals. Companies such as

Philips are pushing the boundaries of technology for healthcare with imaging and patient monitoring systems. As microprocessors and sensors shrink in size and improve their abilities to capture data accurately, digital health data from both commercial and consumer-oriented devices will become more widely accepted and integrated within healthcare systems. Digital health is starting to change how existing data are collected and interpreted, making the process more user friendly and reducing costs.

Incorporating massive amounts of data into a physician's clinical workflow is not an easy task. Systems that automate the process and help the provider interpret the information will become ever more valuable. As described in Chapters 2 and 3, radiology is at the forefront of this data-driven revolution, in part thanks to advances in cognitive computing solutions that can scan through thousands of images faster than humans, and sometimes with better accuracy. Pathology is another field that could be transformed by digital technologies (see the sidebar *Paving the Way for Digital Pathology*), but there are substantial regulatory and infrastructure barriers that will have to be addressed before we see widespread adoption.

SIDEBAR: PAVING THE WAY FOR DIGITAL PATHOLOGY

Mark Boguski, MD, PhD
Chief Medical Officer for Precision Medicine, Inspirata, Inc.

Pathologists have always provided and helped interpret the test results that their clinical counterparts in clinical care rely upon to optimally manage their patients. So it's not surprising that pathologists need to be at the forefront of data-driven medicine. The key question is, how to best achieve this?

"Approximately 500 clinical laboratory tests are currently in use," says Mark Boguski, Chief Medical Officer for Precision Medicine at Inspirata, Inc. (Boguski 2017). Many of these tests have been in use for decades. However, some big leaps have occurred in specific areas, particularly cancer diagnosis.

One challenge is reproducibility. "We can measure all these different analytes on a single chip, but is the result reliable enough to trigger a serious clinical action?" he asks. For many of the newer tests, he says, "We are still in the proof of concept stage."

Even genotyping, which is now extremely common, is still not being used to its maximum advantage. "I had myself genotyped and my own primary care doctor said 'Great, but what should I do with that?'" Boguski says. In 2009, he pioneered an educational program that teaches pathology residents at hospitals about genomics. The doctors-in-training were all genotyped and then learned about interpreting the results. The program, which is now called Training Residents in Genomics, included experts in medical education, molecular pathology, and clinical genetics, who develop teaching tools, and promote genomic pathology education.

Now, Boguski is focused on Inspirata, which aims to bring pathology for cancer diagnosis into the digital age. Inspirata makes anatomic and molecular pathology workflows faster and more efficient, the company also facilitates whole slide imaging, image analytics, prognostic and predictive assays, remote consultations, and tumor boards—a process by which multiple experts access a particular malignancy.

"Pathology has been doing things the old fashioned way for a long time," he says. "We carefully examine tissue and then painstakingly analyze it through a microscope." But if those images were all digitized, pathologists and researchers could get a lot more use out of them and would herald the age of computational pathology.

"It will relieve tedious aspects of routine pathologic diagnosis, lead to better repro-ducibility and consistency, and allow us to apply new algorithms to exploit big data," Boguski says. In some ways, the task ahead is daunting. "Any cancer center will be gen-erating petabytes of data once they commit to the analog-to-digital shift in pathology," he adds.

Boguski sees three key barriers to the dawn of digital pathology. The first is regulatory. The microscope, he points out, was "grandfathered" into the FDA approval process since it had already been around for so long. Digital imaging requires a separate approval process. But that barrier is already being broken, when Philips received FDA approval in April 2017 to market its IntelliSite Pathology Solution for diagnostic use. This is the first whole slide imaging (WSI) system to receive such clearance, and was approved via De Novo classification, a regulatory pathway for devices of a new type with low- to moderate-risk that are not substantially equivalent to an already legally marketed device (U.S. Food & Drug Administration 2017a).

A second barrier is cost. "It is already expensive to retrofit your lab," he explains. "You need to get scanners and some other new equipment." But likely, it will be a big com-petitive advantage once a group has made that transition.

Finally, there is the age-old problem of change management. "People are not used to seeing millions of data points," he says, "but new algorithms and software tools we're developing will not only empower them, but also make them more efficient. Change will come once these advantages are experienced."

As a result, he sees big changes coming to the field of pathology. "The software will be so good that most pathologists still won't need to be techno-savvy," he says. "But there will be tremendous opportunities, both in the clinic and in research, for those who are."

Getting the right data, at the right time, for the right problem is the goal. For physicians and researchers, that will increasingly mean new software and other tools to help them analyze patient data, such as radiology images and lab results, using predictive and real-time analytics so that the information can have the greatest impact on patients. In the meantime, patients are adopting fitness trackers and other wearable technologies that generate incredible amounts of data at a rapid pace.

Digital Biomarkers: Wearables and Wireless for Tracking Patients

According to the NIH, a biomarker is "a characteristic that is objectively measured and evaluated as an indicator of normal biological processes, pathogenic processes, or pharmacologic responses to a therapeutic intervention" (Biomarkers Definitions Working Group 2001). Typical biomarkers include sex, gender, age, and lab results, such as a blood calcium level. With the rise of genomic testing, genetic variants and protein expression levels are also considered biomarkers. However, considering other types of data that can be indicators, but that fall outside of traditional thinking, it is more precise to use the term "digital biomarker" for "consumer-generated physiological and behavioral measures collected through connected digital tools that can be used to explain, influ-ence and/or predict health-related outcomes" while excluding some types of patient-reported data, like those collected through surveys (Wang, Azad, and Rajan 2017).

Digital biomarkers are what make the fourth "P" in 4P medicine possible (see the sidebar *Applying Systems Medicine to Wellness and Disease*) and are changing disease management in the process. They enable patients to be more participatory in their healthcare and in clinical research by collecting information that can be used in much the same way as traditional biomarkers. For example, Novartis has suggested adding remote patient monitoring of vital signs (e.g., weight) for patients taking certain heart medications, potentially allowing doctors to monitor more completely whether a medication is working or not, and giving them a chance to intervene before more serious complications arise (Roland 2015). And several digital health companies have entered the diabetes space, with smartphone-based apps that provide coaching as well as glucose monitoring (Baum 2017a; Comstock 2017a). A recently published study finds that adolescents, in particular, are receptive to mHealth interventions that monitor their disease control and inform treatment decisions (Kitsiou et al. 2017). Digital biomarkers face considerable barriers to be seen as useful by providers and payers for healthcare, but they can play a substantial role in a systems medicine approach to healthcare, as described by Leroy Hood.

SIDEBAR: APPLYING SYSTEMS MEDICINE TO WELLNESS AND DISEASE

Leroy Hood, MD, PhD

President and Cofounder, Institute for Systems Biology

"What we need is a systems medicine way of thinking," says Leroy Hood, President and Cofounder of the Institute for Systems Biology (Hood 2017). "You need the genome, the proteome, the transcriptome and more." The genome, Hood points out, may be the blueprint, but it is the proteins that execute functions in the body. Understanding the relationships between the genome and the proteome, and everything in between, is therefore crucial.

"I think the new medicine will be predictive, preventive, personalized and participatory (P4 medicine). All of this depends on the applications and technologies of systems medicine and the explosion of big data and its analytics," Hood says. P4 medicine leads to the realization that healthcare has two major thrusts—wellness and disease, he adds. His group has recently carried out a year-long experiment with 108 individuals to employ "dense, dynamic, personal data clouds to identify the actionable possibilities that allow individuals to either optimize their wellness or avoid disease." They have termed this approach the quantification of "scientific wellness."

He also believes there is a crucial need to bring an understanding of P4 medicine and scientific wellness to consumers. "Many physicians are conservative and reluctant to adopt new ideas," he says. "It is patients, at least in part, who will need to drive the real change catalyzed by scientific wellness." This trend is already evident in the quantified-self movement. Some patients are using multiple digital gadgets to gather information about dozens of parameters. In many cases they don't know when these gadgets should be talking them. Often, the patients are pushing their doctors to keep up with them.

In 10 years, Hood predicts, every patient will be surrounded by a virtual cloud of billions of data points. These will include molecular, clinical, and social network data, but also expand to predict things such as cellular interactions and even social networks. The key will be how to integrate all of these types of data into models that make predictions for each individual about how to optimize their health and wellness.

A key challenge is that there is an enormous signal-to-noise problem with big datasets. "You cannot solve that problem just by getting more data and using machine learning.

Data space in biology is infinite, hence one must employ biological domain expertise to deal with the noise and identify the probable regions of signal," Hood says.

One dramatic example is the search for blood biomarkers. Millions of dollars have been spent on this search, but most of those biomarkers have never been successfully moved to clinical practice. About 95% are simply noise, and not relevant to diagnosis or treatment of disease. "I believe it will take a systems approach to find the ones that are relevant," Hood says. "So we are pioneering at Integrated Diagnostics—a company I cofounded about 10 years ago, a systems strategy, to find useful markers."

Integrated Diagnostics (Indi) developed the Xpresys Lung marker, which helps physicians distinguish benign from neoplastic pulmonary lung nodules and thus avoid unnecessary surgeries that cost the healthcare system billions of dollars a year. This is a protein expression test using 13 blood biomarkers that can distinguish whether a nodule is malignant or benign. "We looked at more than 350 potential blood markers to identify this set. This will not only help patients avoid unnecessary biopsies, which are painful and can have serious side effects, but will also help reduce healthcare costs by avoiding unnecessary tests and surgical treatments," Hood says.

While this is just one small step forward, Hood is optimistic about the field. "I think proteomics will create the next wave of diagnostic and predictive tests," he says. "There is still a lot of skepticism, but we are making real progress and I believe it will become a leading edge of diagnostic biomedicine."

Rock Health, the digital health-focused venture firm mentioned earlier, developed a classification system for digital biomarkers based on the novelty of both measurement and insight. For example, as described in a recent report, continuous blood pressure monitoring (a novel measurement) could be used to predict the risk of a heart attack (a known insight) or to predict depression (a novel insight). Similarly, discrete blood pressure data (a known measurement) could be used to predict the risk of heart attack or predict depression (Wang, Azad, and Rajan 2017).

While much of today's healthcare research focuses on the use of known measurements for both novel and known insights, digital biomarkers, which fall into the "novel" measurement category, are only just now beginning to be considered accurate or valuable enough to inform patient management or clinical research. For example, researchers at the University of Southern California are testing the use of wearable devices to fill in the time between provider visits for cancer patients in one study, part of the Cancer Moonshot program (Vuong 2016). Study co-lead researcher Peter Kuhn said in an interview for the University's newspaper, "The more than 30,000 minutes between visits are a missed opportunity. Technology can be leveraged to fill this gap and provide a comprehensive picture" (Vuong 2016).

Filling the data gap for clinical trials is just one of many problems digital biomarkers can solve. Another is improving the quality and utility of data collected for trials. For example, a study might currently have participants fill out a food diary, to keep a record of the quantity of food consumed daily. But this type of data can be prone to error from over- and underestimation. Instead of the food diary, researchers might find incorporating a smartphone app that takes a picture of a meal and calculates the number of likely calories is more accurate. Alternatively, a wearable tracker like Healbe's GoBe2, that measures calorie intake using an impedance sensor, could provide valuable data.

A team of researchers from the University of California Davis are testing the GoBe2 device over the next 5 years. Sara Schaefer, associate director of children's health at the Foods for Health Institute at UC Davis told a reporter for the online news site MobiHealthNews, "We know it's actually a consumer device, not a scientific research device, so we are interested in using it to see how it could be applied to scientific research" (Mack 2017b). The accuracy of the data coming from wearable devices is something that impedes their use in research and the clinic. But as Christine Lemke of Evidation Health told us, it may not be necessary to have the data for an individual data point be accurate if it can reliably capture trends in the overall data.

California-based Evidation Health partners with academic researchers and healthcare companies to assess digital biomarkers for clinical research and development (Evidation Health 2017). They are unusual among digital health companies in that they actively publish and present their work at scientific conferences and in peer-reviewed journals. The company also works with stakeholders across the healthcare industry, including pharma and payers.

Using a digital platform that aggregates users' fitness activities, Evidation found users who were the most adherent to food tracking lost an additional 0.63% of their body weight over a 2-year period than those users who logged their food with low frequency (Pourzanjani, Quisel, and Foschini 2016). When the researchers looked at patient-level data, the results became even more impressive, with +2.74% body weight lost per month during the times patients consistently tracked their weight. The authors suggest adherence to exercise, weight, and food tracking could be leveraged for "large-scale, personalized intervention strategies" (Pourzanjani, Quisel, and Foschini 2016). In a study presented at the 2016 Neural Information Processing Systems meeting, Evidation researchers found that day-level activity and minute-level sleep data from fitness trackers improved the predictive performance of classification of patients with mental health or nervous system disorders (Quisel 2016).

Research such as the studies described above could have significant clinical importance in the future, if the system continues to improve its predictive abilities to identify patients who have chronic disorders with the addition of other digital biomarkers, such as heart rate or blood pressure, captured by activity trackers. For example, physicians could use this information to target interventions, for example, counseling or medication, to patients when the composite data indicates they have become depressed or have developed sleep apnea. Even more useful would be if patients could upload their fitness and health tracker data into their electronic health record (EHR) that used a clinical decision support system: if the system alerts the doctor to a condition, they could reach out to the patient even before the patient might think there is a potential problem.

Evidation is also working with researchers at Harvard Medical School and Brigham and Women's Hospital to develop a mobile app to improve patient adherence with blood pressure medication. The MediSAFE-BP trial will prospectively study more than 400 patients and evaluate the impact of the mobile app on blood pressure and medication adherence (Morawski et al. 2017). Studies like this are essential to demonstrate digital health devices and software have clinical utility and are the first step in gathering the necessary data to support reimbursement from payers.

Previously, we noted that digital health devices have the potential to transform clinical trials, but uncertainties about their accuracy and off-target data contributing to statistical "noise" are significant limitations (see Chapter 2). Verily (previously Google Life Sciences) recently launched Study Watch, a smartwatch developed specifically for use in clinical trials that may address some of these concerns. With a simple user interface and long battery life, the device is meant to unobtrusively collect a wide variety of physiological and environmental data that can be shared with researchers with minimal input from the user. Verily will be using the Study Watch in the Baseline Study, a 10,000-person observational study designed to capture data that can help researchers better understand the transition from a healthy state to disease (Mack 2017c; Reuters Editorial 2017). In addition to the Baseline Study, Verily is using the Study Watch on the Personalized Parkinson's Project with researchers in the Netherlands to track the symptoms of the disease (Donders Institute 2016).

Furthermore, Apple continues to work with researchers with its ResearchKit and CareKit frameworks. These platforms offer developers an opportunity to create innovative mobile apps for the iPhone and Apple Watch that support both medical research and clinical studies (ResearchKit) as well as personal health (CareKit) (Apple 2017).

In the few years that ResearchKit has been available, researchers at major medical centers like the University of Rochester, Duke University, and Johns Hopkins University have created mobile apps for Parkinson's disease, autism, and epilepsy, respectively. For Parkinson's patients, an iPhone app can monitor disease progression in between twice-yearly doctor visits, giving the physician a more comprehensive look at how the patient is faring (Farr 2016). Other institutions are targeting postpartum depression, melanoma, diabetes, postsurgical care, and chronic disease management with ResearchKit and CareKit (Apple 2017). And by creating a standardized technological platform, Apple can maintain some measure of interoperability between the apps and other aspects of the operating system.

Barriers for Digital Biomarkers

As noted in Chapter 8, patient recruitment for clinical trials is low. But patient participation in research studies for digital biomarkers isn't likely to be similar. Companies, such as Transparency Life Sciences (TLS), help to increase patient engagement in clinical trials by incorporating their opinions in study design, so that pharma studies assess outcomes that matter to the patients. Clinical trials run by TLS use digital devices to capture patient information which is then shared with researchers in a HIPAA-compliant manner (Transparency Life Sciences 2017). According to a Rock Health survey about digital health adoption by consumers, the vast majority of respondents indicated a willingness to share their data if it meant receiving better care from their provider and nearly 60% indicated they would be willing to contribute to medical research (Gandhi and Wang 2015). This is an improvement over the REMOTE study, a phase 4 trial of a drug for overactive bladder (Orri et al. 2014). In REMOTE, more than 5,000 patients registered via a website, but only 18 were randomized to treatment after satisfactorily passing medical screening and other inclusion criteria.

Interest in alternative recruitment methods continues to increase with awareness that traditional patient recruitment strategies may not be as effective for a growing, digitally savvy population. Importantly, virtual recruitment methods aren't constrained by geography and can lead to a more diverse study population. Apple's ResearchKit (described in Chapter 1) is used by a variety of digital health companies to perform research studies using Apple products (Research Kit 2017). In 7 months, MyHeart Counts smartphone app recruited nearly 49,000 patients from all 50 U.S. states for a study about cardiovascular disease risk (McConnell et al. 2017). ResearchKit recruitment has been valuable for rare disease research, too. Sarcoidosis is a rare, inflammatory disease that can affect multiple organs. Investigators from Penn Medicine launched a smartphone app using ResearchKit in January 2017. Within 2 months, more than 700 patients had downloaded the app and more than half were participating in the study (Research Kit 2017).

While digital biomarkers will have a growing impact on clinical research in the upcoming years, how patients and their doctors respond to the data may be of greater importance. Research from One Drop found patients who used their smartphone app lowered their A1c level, an important measure of overall glucose control in patients with type 2 diabetes, nearly 0.7% during a usage period of 2–12 months (Dachis 2017). As mentioned previously, importing digital biomarker data into EHR systems could enable clinicians to tailor patient recommendations based on the information. A patient with type 2 diabetes whose blood sugar isn't under control might be counseled to increase their exercise and improve nutrition. If the patient is already doing those things and has uploaded their exercise and nutrition information for the provider to view, the doctor might instead determine a change in medication dose is more appropriate.

However, until digital biomarkers can be easily merged with EHRs or other stakeholder's data systems (e.g., payers' claims data) and there are robust methods to interpret the data and thus, make reimbursement decisions, policy recommendations, or clinical decisions with the information, patients are the ones most likely to benefit from the consumer-oriented devices and smartphone apps.

Another barrier is likely to come from regulators as they will want to see comparisons between digital biomarkers and existing measurements. As the Rock Health report notes, "Before regulatory approval, the digital biomarker will need to be supported by evidence that demonstrates its specificity, sensitivity, and positive and negative predictive values." Comparisons to existing standards will be needed, but Rock Health cautions that the current "gold standard" may not be an appropriate comparison for digital biomarkers (Wang, Azad, and Rajan 2017).

This last point will be a difficult one to overcome for digital biomarkers, despite evidence that "gold standard" tests for some conditions have low positive predictive values and are marked by variability in performance. An anecdote relayed by David Shaywitz, Chief Medical Officer of DNAnexus, highlights in a *Forbes* blog post the difficulty a molecular diagnostics company had with a new genetic test for thyroid nodules (Shaywitz 2014).

Thyroid nodules are fairly common, but the vast majority are benign. However, to rule out malignancy, the American Thyroid Association recommends fine needle aspiration (FNA) of the nodule; however, there are several known limitations, including substantial variability between clinicians for nodules classified as "indeterminate" or ambiguous, the potential that the biopsy may miss the area with cancer, and the inability to collect enough cells for analysis (Zhang and Lin 2016). This was the problem the new test sought to address: reducing the number of repeat biopsies from ambiguous lesions.

Shaywitz writes, "While the performance characteristics of the new diagnostic test were closely scrutinized, as you'd expect (and hope), the so-called gold standard in the field against which they were compared turned out to be anything but" (Shaywitz 2014).

As technology continues to improve, many newly developed tests are likely to face the challenge of being compared to an older, less accurate test that's considered the "gold standard." However, digital biomarkers, particularly those which are derived from consumer-oriented devices, are likely to face the most difficulty, given their perception as nonclinically relevant. Furthermore, unlike many diagnostics that can obtain FDA clearance though the 510(k) pathway by demonstrating a new test is essentially equivalent to an existing one on the market, digital biomarker devices are likely to require individual approval due to inconsistencies between devices (Cadmus-Bertram et al. 2017), even in the same category (like wrist-worn fitness trackers) (Wang, Azad, and Rajan 2017). Thus, devices that capture digital biomarkers and digital health apps would be wise to consider early in their development process what type of evidence would demonstrate the usefulness of their product.

The need for companies to consider the utility of their biomarker-based product is not unlike the situation for developers of *in vitro diagnostics* (IVDs). As I described in my book, *Commercializing Novel IVDs: A Comprehensive Manual for Success*, health technology assessments are an essential component for manufacturers seeking positive payer coverage decisions (Glorikian 2017). From the beginning stages of design ideation, it's important that IVD developers consider how clinical trials will need to be structured to provide necessary analytical and clinical validity and clinical utility data. This type of evidence is *exactly* what digital health companies should be thinking about for their products.

Commerce: Putting the Data Together to Enable Business

Over the past several years, numerous entrepreneurs have formed start-ups that focus on aggregating data in a way that facilitates the commercial aspects of healthcare in this data-driven reality. For example, Healthcare Bluebook and PokitDok, described in Chapter 2, were created to provide price and quality information to consumers and employers so that they could make better-informed decisions about where to obtain healthcare services. Incorporating patient-contributed data to these and similar websites/mobile platforms, including ZocDoc and HealthGrades, will further refine their data and increase its utility.

According to Paul Sonnier, who tracks this field, social media is a key component to digital health and is essential to engaging the patient in healthcare behavior (Sonnier 2017). A recent report from the Manhattan Institute, a think tank focused on market forces in a variety of public and private sectors like healthcare and education, found reviews posted on Yelp correlated with objective quality measurements for New York State hospitals. Generally, hospitals with good Yelp reviews were found to have fewer preventable readmissions. The report's authors make recommendations for the continued use of crowdsourcing or "hackathons" to find additional ways social media patient reviews/scores could be used for non-English speaking or vulnerable populations.

Incorporating social media reviews into existing price/quality databases may be technically challenging or involve complex partnerships, particularly when a mix of for-profit and not-for-profit entities are involved. Ultimately though, doing so would be beneficial to the consumer/patient. Collaborations between diverse companies will depend on their willingness to share data and the interoperability of their systems to do so.

Most connected devices, particularly those targeted at the consumer market like fitness trackers, are typically out-of-pocket expenses. A key deficit in the digital health market is getting buy-in from payers for reimbursement. Emerging evidence suggests they can have real impacts on users' healthcare-related outcomes, including weight loss (Pourzanjani, Quisel, and Foschini 2016) and medication adherence (Propeller Health 2016; Smits 2016). There have also been several widely publicized cases of a fitness tracker alerting the user to dangerous heart rate anomalies (see Chapter 2). But aside from case reports and company white papers, gathering the pertinent data and performing the necessary analysis to demonstrate the impact on patient outcomes has been lacking in the past and remains a barrier for reimbursement.

So far, few digital health start-ups are presenting evidence for their products. One Drop offers a subscription-based service for patients with type 2 diabetes to help them manage their glucose levels using mobile apps and a connected glucose monitor. They presented data at a recent conference on improved glucose control of patients using their system (Dachis 2017). But most digital health companies aren't following in Evidation's and One Drop's footsteps with publishing their data. This is a necessary step for companies desiring positive coverage determination and reimbursement from insurers.

Insurers are also exploring the use of digital health. Aetna has taken the lead by subsidizing the cost of Apple Watches for some of its insured members. In addition, the insurance giant will be developing apps that help members with medication use and insurance planning (King 2016). Presumably, the data collected through the apps will allow Aetna to better target members with products that will help keep them healthy.

Digital health commerce also relies on the literal bringing together of data. In fact, data interoperability and import/export capabilities are essential to making digital health ventures successful. As with banking, security is also a critical component to healthcare data sharing. Several companies, such as Rosetta Health, have formed to help companies and medical centers navigate this challenge. Rosetta is an organization that offers cloud-based IT solutions that help connect every part of the healthcare continuum, to provide a seamless transition for all healthcare data while keeping patients' data secure. This is a tall order, in a field that puts such a priority on privacy and has many proprietary data sources as healthcare, so Rosetta worked with the Office of the National Coordinator to ensure their products met legislated and industry standards (Rosetta Health 2017).

Key issues, specifically for digital biomarkers, but more generally for both healthcare and IT, are getting the systems to talk to each other and breaking down existing data silos (Wang, Azad, and Rajan 2017). Existing data infrastructure is designed with each end user and data type in mind, with no regard for how other stakeholders might value this information.

For example, payers focus on claims data, while providers use clinical data such as lab results and imaging, and pharmaceutical companies are interested in data from clinical trials. Separate from each of those is the growing digital footprint of consumers, something that could be valuable for all stakeholders. How to make these diverse data types interoperable is an ongoing challenge in the absence of cross-system data standards. According to Buff Colchagoff, CEO of Rosetta Health, many digital health start-ups fail because of data issues (HIT Consultant 2017). If the data from a start-up's mobile app can't integrate with the existing software its customers use, it's unlikely the start-up will be very successful, unless it has sufficient financial backing to maintain solvency while it works to solve the data problem.

Even large, well-established organizations can find themselves with data interoperability problems. MD Anderson Cancer Center, in Texas, recently made headlines for its announcement that it was stopping a highly publicized program to bring IBM Watson technology to the center (Herper 2017a). During the development of the Watson project, MD Anderson switched to a new EHR system. An audit of the project found "the Watson product doesn't work with the new Epic system, and must be revamped in order to be re-tested" (Herper 2017b). As we'll describe below, blockchain technology, the technology underlying Bitcoin currency, may solve some of the data interoperability and IT issues in healthcare (see the section *Blockchain: Straddling the Gap between Commerce and Connectivity*).

AI and Cognitive Computing: Generating Novel Insights through Analytics

Although consumers are becoming more comfortable with the idea of AI delivering healthcare information to them on demand (when they perceive a *benefit*), it's unclear if they will respond as positively when the technology identifies them as high risk for a disease like diabetes and suggests a weight-loss regimen or dietary changes. And patients aren't the only ones that may find themselves at odds with the new technology.

Artificial intelligence (AI) and cognitive computing are technical terms now being used to describe a wide variety of software and methods for analyzing complex data. Kris Hammond, a professor of Computer Science at Northwestern University and cofounder and Chief Scientist at Narrative Science, notes that even people working in the field argue about what AI is and what it is not (Hammond 2016).

According to the Turing Archive for the History of Computing, AI is "the science of making computers do things that require intelligence when done by humans" and has focused on five main aspects of intelligence: "learning, reasoning, problem-solving, perception, and language-understanding" (Copeland 2000). So while AI has long been the stuff of science fiction, the reality is that using this broad definition, the technology takes many forms and is already starting to be used in diverse applications like Netflix recommendations, Amazon's Alexa, and Google Photos

(Evans 2017). Taken to its *fullest* capabilities, we define AI as control over other computers without any intervention or action by humans. Cognitive computing, deep learning, are components of, but not always synonymous with, AI.

Cognitive computing, which is how IBM describes its Watson solution, is probably most aligned to what the general public thinks of as AI. But according to VDC Research analyst Steve Hoffenberg, cognitive computing and AI differ in how they would approach a task, such as sifting through medical records and published data to determine the best therapy. "In an artificial intelligence system, the system would have told the doctor which course of action to take based on its analysis. In cognitive computing, the system provides information to help the doctor decide" (Evans 2017). In this book, cognitive computing describes techniques that require some level of human input and is not prescriptive in its output, meaning the result of a problem approached with cognitive computing methods would be suggestive and not definitive.

Together with others in the field, Kris Hammond developed a "Periodic Table of AI" that identifies the technologies that fall under this broad "AI" definition. From top-to-bottom and left-to-right in the table, the technologies become more complex, ending at "control," defined as "The intelligent control of other machines that doesn't require any manipulation or action in the physical world (e.g., automated trading)." But other technologies included in the Periodic Table of AI are less complex and include speech and facial recognition, decision making, and text extraction, which rely on machine learning to identify patterns (Hammond 2016).

As Hammond and others have noted, what *specifically* constitutes AI is still debatable (Hammond 2016; Shaywitz 2017) and some have argued that the term is now virtually meaningless (Bogost 2017). As a result, AI's relative success or failure, to date and in the future, is thus based upon what is included in its definition.

Standardizing Clinical Guidelines

Clinical guidelines are typically a blend of both scientific evidence and expert opinion. Consequently, there's potential for guidelines to be inherently biased (Huston 2017). The discrepancy between the evidence-based guidelines of the United States Preventive Services Task Force (USPSTF) and the practices of gynecologists and internal medicine doctors for screening mammography for breast cancer is a case in point. Although the USPSTF recommends mammography beginning at age 50, the majority of providers in a recent survey screened patients at age 40 (Corbelli et al. 2014).

As clinical decision support systems become more sophisticated, incorporating AI and cognitive computing technologies, they will be able to make finer distinctions among diagnoses and treatment plans for patients. Here, the difference between AI and cognitive computing, at least as defined by Steve Hoffenberg, would be noticeable: a cognitive computing decision support system would provide the physician with the evidence supporting mammography at age 50 and reference the guidelines. An AI decision support system might not allow a physician to enter the orders for a mammogram that fall outside of the recommended guidelines without being overridden.

Identifying differences in potential patient management between providers and AI-derived decisions has the potential to improve patient outcomes and contribute to value-based care. For example, a provider is likely to base a patient's risk for cardiovascular events according to multiple risk factors. In fact, patient management guidelines developed by the American College of Cardiology (ACC)/American Heart Association (AHA) take into account eight risk factors, like smoking or having diabetes, when determining a patient's risk for having a cardiovascular event in the next 10 years.

A test of four different machine learning algorithms (random forest, logistic regression, gradient boosting, and neural networks) compared to the ACC/AHA guidelines found the computational strategies better predicted cardiovascular events with fewer false positives. Of note, the algorithms included severe mental illness and taking oral corticosteroids as risk factors, but not diabetes, which is included in the ACC/AHA guidelines (Huston 2017). Confirming additional risk factors could lead to a change in the existing guidelines that could save patient lives by identifying who is likely to develop a cardiovascular event.

Some companies are betting that making AI/cognitive computing systems seem more personal or human can make it easier for patients to share personal information or follow their provider's instructions. Following a hospitalization, having patients adhere to medication or other regimens can keep readmission rates down. Sensely, a healthcare technology company, has developed an AI virtual nurse, "Molly," that providers can customize to give patients recommendations for a variety of chronic conditions like diabetes and congestive heart failure (Sensely 2017). The company has developed a platform that follows patients from hospital discharge through the convalescence period, sending clinicians alerts if the patient's risk of readmission or other adverse event increases or fails to decrease over time. The provider can then connect with the patient via telemedicine (video calls) or by having them come to the office for an unscheduled visit (Sensely 2017).

AI/cognitive computing can also be used where a large amount of data needs to be analyzed to obtain a composite score and make recommendations. EnsoData, a digital health company, received FDA clearance for its EnsoSleep sleep analysis software. Using advanced analytics, EnsoSleep interprets sleep data with algorithms, automatically scoring data from sleep monitoring devices. With this software, clinicians who study sleep disorders can perform sleep studies more efficiently, decreasing the amount of time needed to interpret patient results, ultimately leading to lower costs and a better patient experience (Mack 2017a).

Although we've described several examples of AI/cognitive computing being used in healthcare today, there are some who feel the technology hasn't quite reached prime time (Shaywitz 2017). This may be a fair assessment, if you define AI very narrowly. And some analysts have suggested the evidence is lacking to show that AI/cognitive computing solutions can perform better than humans at certain tasks, like assessing radiology images (Mack 2017a). In addition, some of the applications straddle the line between research and clinical, something noted in our interview with Keith Elliston in Chapter 2, which challenges us (and others) to consistently identify solutions that have a clinical focus but may be currently implemented as research or pilot clinical studies.

Regardless of how AI and cognitive computing are defined, there is no doubt that the technology is attracting interest from diverse stakeholders for a widely variety of healthcare problems. There is clearly room for growth in the field which can serve to improve the quality of applications through competition. The FDA recently announced that it is creating a digital health unit that may help to clarify and address some of the challenges facing these technologies.

Blockchain: Straddling the Gap between Commerce and Connectivity

One of the key challenges in digitizing healthcare is linking together data from disparate sources. Blockchain is an encryption method that the healthcare industry is starting to embrace. It's an electronic database, but with special features that make it very secure and ideal for data-sharing situations (Crowe 2016). That's key for healthcare, which suffers from interoperability woes and a lack of data sharing. As Micah Winkelspecht, founder and CEO of blockchain start-up Gem, has said of patient medical records, "There is a major push toward a patient-centric focus in healthcare, yet your data is stored all over the place in kind of a Frankenstein concoction of records with very little interoperability of file formats between systems" (Raths 2016).

In the financial industry, blockchain technology supports Bitcoin, a type of "cryptocurrency," and is expected to dramatically change the way and how quickly financial transactions can be settled, leading to significant cost savings and reduced employee requirements (Crowe 2016). But blockchain is not the same thing as Bitcoin—it might be easier to think of blockchain as Bitcoin's "operating system." Just as an operating system lets a computer do different tasks, blockchain can be used for more than just financial transactions like Bitcoin.

As described above, blockchain is like an electronic database that is "distributed and immutable" (Das 2017). This means that each record is written only once and then becomes read-only, ensuring that the interaction can't be edited or deleted. Consider a hospital's EHR system. It is also a database (or likely many databases) that contains patient-identifying information, insurance and claims data, laboratory results, and provider notes from patient encounters. A single patient's record needs to be accessed by a variety of individuals, each of whom might add something to the record. Each time someone accesses the record, there's opportunity for something to go wrong or for misuse, so hospitals limit who has access (and what they can access) to EHR systems.

In a blockchain system, each time someone interacts with the EHR, a permanent record is made of that information and it builds on the previous interaction (creating a "chain"). Because each interaction is linked to the one before it, the system is very secure and there's a measure of transparency to the process. Each interaction is recorded and because the data are spread out over all of the records in the chain, it takes a concerted effort (and a lot of computational resources) by a large percentage of users (~1/3) to hack the system (Lin 2017).

So how can blockchain transform healthcare? The opportunities touch on nearly every aspect of the field: EHRs can be made more secure, genomic data can be kept private, claims and billing can be made more efficient (Lin 2017). With so much potential, it's unsurprising that the federal government is looking at ways blockchain can be used for healthcare. A 2016 competition by the Department of Health and Human Services' Office of the National Coordinator for Health Information Technology yielded 15 winning entries and many more submissions on this topic (CCC Innovation Center 2017). A few of the proposed applications for sharing medical records, improving the medical claims process, making population health research less expensive and more efficient, and reducing healthcare fraud are described below.

Some of the entries described blockchain frameworks or solutions to interoperability problems and data-sharing issues between EHRs and other systems. Here, barriers to data-sharing could be reduced and patients could have any and all interactions with healthcare providers chronologically tracked in a single, but widely distributed, database (Brodersen 2016; Conn 2016; Shrier 2016). Importantly, while the overall database might contain all of a patient's data, access to particular components could be assigned as needed. Brodersen and colleagues described a situation where a patient might want to keep the information from a visit with a specialist withheld from their primary physician, even though the patient and both providers are all on the same chain (Brodersen 2016).

The implications of a blockchain system enabling such a system are profound, but not novel. In 2008, Google launched Google Health, a central repository for patients' health information (Rao 2011). Prescriptions, family and personal medical histories, and medical records could be uploaded to the platform, giving each person complete control over (at least some of) their health information and allowing them to share the data with providers. In today's increasingly patient-centric environment, this type of data access and control is desired by many, but in 2012, Google closed down Google Health, citing an inability to "translate that limited usage into widespread adoption in the daily health routines of millions of people" (Google 2011).

The current fractured healthcare system means most patients are likely to have multiple EHRs with limited data-sharing between them. Blockchain solutions could enable a universal, single record for every patient. New providers could be added to the chain when a person moved or changed providers and existing data access permissions for old providers could be removed. This type of system wouldn't replace existing EHRs, but could work with them to "enable seamless access to historic and real-time patient data" (Das 2017).

In related submissions, multiple researchers proposed blockchain solutions to enable clinical research (Ekblaw 2016; Linn 2016). Though replete with clinical data, using EHRs to perform clinical research is difficult, in part because of their inability to "manage multi-institutional, life time medical records" (Ekblaw 2016). As with the white papers from Brodersen and Shrier, researchers see blockchain as a way to address current system interoperability problems (Ekblaw 2016; Linn 2016). These proposed solutions could be used for population health research by connecting patients to health data from all provider encounters, even across multiple health systems, even adding data from fitness trackers and other patient-generated health data. The researchers envision the systems reducing the resources (i.e., time, financial, human) needed to recruit large populations for long-term clinical and observational studies (Ekblaw 2016; Linn 2016).

Other entries to the competition involved the use of blockchain to minimize security problems and fraud (Brodersen 2016; Culver 2016; Shrier 2016). It's been estimated that healthcare fraud costs the United States between $68 billion and $230 billion annually (Blue Cross Blue Shield of Michigan 2017). One way to reduce healthcare fraud is to ensure patient identification is accurate. By setting up a trusted identification method, like a PIN (personal identification number) that is required every time a healthcare "transaction" takes place, it "adds to the chain as a form of continuous identity authentication" (Brodersen 2016) and improves data integrity (Krawiec 2016). Different encryption infrastructures may further improve the security of blockchain technology (Shrier 2016). Here, the financial industry's experience with blockchain security might provide valuable insights for the healthcare field.

The claims process is fundamentally at the center of healthcare transactions, connecting providers, health plans, the government and others with the healthcare system (Culver 2016; Yip 2016). But this process is notoriously slow, and patients and providers alike express frustration and mistrust over the speed and accuracy at which claims are processed (Culver 2016). Using blockchain, Culver envisions a process that could adjudicate claims in near real time, as patient eligibility information, pertinent health data, and payer requirements could be placed on the same chain (Culver 2016). This is analogous to using blockchain technologies in the financial sector to speed up transactions (Stafford 2016). As with this application for financial purposes, in addition to the stated purpose of improving the accuracy and efficiency of the claims process, blockchain systems could reduce potential fraud and misuse.

Blockchain technology presents tremendous opportunity for existing tech companies and for start-ups alike. PokitDok created a blockchain platform (DokChain) for its customers. PokitDok CEO Ted Tanner said, "Telehealth could be the killer app on blockchain" (Conn 2016). Technology companies are using their prowess to move into the healthcare space. IBM Watson is working with the FDA to explore ways in which blockchain can be used to share healthcare data from a variety of sources, from EHRs and genomic data to real-world evidence collected by wearable devices to support public health research (Mearian 2017). Alphabet's (formerly Google) DeepMind group will use technology such as blockchain to build "Verifiable Data Audit," a tool that will enable medical centers to see exactly who accesses healthcare records and for what purpose (Condliffe 2017). With pilot programs ongoing in England, the company hopes to find ways to deal with the problem of fragmented medical records, a goal that will demonstrate DeepMind's ability to securely aggregate data across multiple databases and structures (Condliffe 2017).

Start-ups Gem and Hashed Health are among the growing number of emerging companies focusing on the application of blockchain for healthcare. California-based Gem initially focused on developing an application program interface for Bitcoin, but turned its attention on healthcare in 2016 with a proof-of-concept project with Capital One for claims management and is now partnering with Philips Blockchain Lab (Raths 2016; Das 2017). The company closed more than $7 million in Series A funding in 2016 (*Business Wire* 2016b). Nashville start-up Hashed Health raised $1.8 million in funding for its technology consortium to explore blockchain-based health-care projects (Pennic 2017).

Despite the enormous potential for blockchain technology to transform both the commercial aspects of healthcare and how patients, providers, payers, and others interact with increasing amounts of health data, there are notable limitations that remain. Regulatory and legal barriers, such as mandatory reporting and HIPAA compliance, are among these challenges (Brodersen 2016; Krawiec 2016). Potential scalability issues affect computational requirements and speed, and maintaining security of the technological infrastructure is no small matter (Brodersen 2016; Krawiec 2016; Linn 2016). Furthermore, the costs associated with implementing blockchain may be substantial and without incentives from the NIH or clear financial benefits to do so, participation may be lacking or slow to start (Krawiec 2016).

Digital Healthcare of Tomorrow

So, what do we anticipate will happen in the next several years? How do we see digital health evolving?

As AI continues to mature, expect more healthcare uses to pop up. Initially, there will likely be many AI failures, but once AI processes are optimized and costs decline, innovation will follow (Hosanagar and Saxena 2017). Jeroen Tas of Philips thinks AI will eventually save patient lives (Tas 2017). We're on the cusp of this now with oncology-focused uses of IBM Watson and Alphabet's DeepMind, but the potential of this technology extends far beyond saving individual cancer patients.

Wearable technology and the data it generates will integrate with EHR systems easily, giving providers a more comprehensive look at how their patient is doing 365 days a year, not just when they are in the office. AI and cognitive computing algorithms will use this and other health data to alert doctors when a patient is at risk for developing a disease and recommendations for patient management will be based on these data.

Digital health solutions will augment and replace traditional pharmaceuticals, such as online clinic Virta's goal to use telemedicine, texting, AI, and connected devices to reduce type 2 diabetes (Sweeney 2017b). Companies such as Propeller Health are already inking deals with pharma, but expect to see more of this as payers and providers find value in digital health solutions and begin to pay for them (Farr 2017b).

Patient participation in clinical trials and medical research will increase because wearable devices and virtual visits can reduce the need to go into an office frequently. Clinical trials will be more likely to go to completion and after-market launch serious problems will be reduced, as patient eligibility will depend on molecular and digital data (Satell 2017). How trials are structured will change as the current "gold standard" of randomized controlled trials are pushed aside for newer study designs that take into account patient-generated data and real world evidence (Wang, Azad, and Rajan 2017).

Blockchain and similar technologies will facilitate data-sharing, improve interoperability, and maintain privacy and security for health and financial data. Patients will find their EHRs can follow them when they move between health systems, across the country or just across town.

As in every other aspect of our lives, digital technologies are becoming much more common in healthcare. Will they revolutionize the field? The question is open. Some see great potential for these technologies, broadly; others see them as having very specific uses, such as helping patients with serious chronic diseases avoid hospitalizations, or keeping track of medical appointments. In healthcare, a key issue with digital technologies is often patient engagement. If the patient isn't responsive, no amount of beeps or alerts will help. People tire of online games fairly quickly; it's not surprising if they tire of healthcare gadgets too. Still, the momentum of this field is unquestionable, and many new opportunities for breakthroughs and new businesses are likely.

Conclusion: The Next-Generation Healthcare Landscape

The new healthcare business paradigm is to measure → optimize → transform.

Harry Glorikian and Malorye Allison Branca

Before Michael Lewis published *Moneyball*, the idea that analyzing massive amounts of data could help pick a better baseball team than the wisdom of experts seemed laughable. Well, until the 2002 Oakland Athletics (A's) did just that and finished in first place in the American League West division after winning a startling 20 consecutive games (Bahr 2015). Notably, the A's success came while the owners spent a fraction of the amount on team salaries as their competitors, fielding more "no-name" free agents after they lost some big stars (Lewis 2004).

We're now seeing the same basic idea Lewis described (use data and statistical analysis to get higher value results) applied to diverse industries, from employment to sales, even agriculture (Horowitz 2013).

With healthcare costs spiraling out of control, the healthcare industry is beginning to take advantage of *Moneyball* techniques, too. Global trends, such as the growing epidemic of chronic diseases, a demographic shift to an older population, and increasing life expectancies are just some of the drivers behind the increased costs and demand for healthcare services.

Additionally, in the United States, the healthcare insurance market has undergone dramatic transformation in the past decade. The Affordable Care Act (ACA) increased the number of patients with health insurance and specified essential coverage (at least temporarily), further growing demand for healthcare services. A majority of the population has seen their healthcare plans evolve to become high-deductible plans, shifting even more of the financial burden of care onto the patient. That seems like a trend that will continue. This has all occurred in an opaque system, where patients struggle to understand their health insurance plans and can't consistently (or adequately) shop for healthcare at the lowest cost and highest quality.

Meanwhile, providers and health systems are under pressure to improve patient outcomes, all while reducing costs, serving a greater number of patients, and integrating growing amounts of data into clinical practice. Pharmaceutical companies are finding traditional processes of drug development, clinical trials, and sales/marketing have to change in today's increasingly more price-sensitive market. And entrepreneurs are developing potentially disruptive innovative, consumer-facing devices, but can be stymied by a lack of reimbursement by payers and slow uptake by providers.

This environment is where *Moneyball Medicine* can, and is starting to, make a difference. From payers to providers to patients, pharmaceutical companies to tech start-ups, we've attempted to highlight current challenges facing these stakeholders, present some ways *Moneyball Medicine* can help, point to ways entrepreneurs are turning these challenges into opportunities, and describe how roles may change in this evolving landscape.

In Chapter 6, we described how data are enabling price and quality comparisons for providers, hospitals, and even lab tests, drugs, and medical devices. The federal government was a key player in early efforts to release this type of data, which caused journalists and healthcare analysts to call out startling cost differences between hospitals, even in the same cities. In addition to the government, a growing cadre of entrepreneurs have been developing unique programs and software to make shopping for healthcare easier for patients and for employers that offer insurance plans to their employees.

As we noted previously, patients will often conflate price with quality. Though it can be difficult to quantify "quality," the federal government and physicians' societies have been attempting to do that through a variety of quality improvement programs and rating systems. Websites that bring both metrics together can, and should, do more to highlight high-value providers and hospitals. Bringing price and quality transparency to lab tests, drugs, and medical devices will undoubtedly be just as challenging, since manufacturers strike individual contracts with medical centers and labs, similar to the way doctors do with hospitals, and those data are rarely made publicly available. Resistance also comes from hospitals and providers, unwilling to publicize the contracts they have negotiated with payers and who challenge the feasibility of giving patients upfront pricing. But maintaining secrecy around price and quality for these items will reach a point where it is no longer a competitive advantage to do so.

Value is a difficult concept for people to understand, particularly when it comes to healthcare. If you were to ask someone to compare the value of one car to that of another, the individual would probably consider the purchase prices of the cars, the annual fuel costs and other costs of ownership over a period of time, and the expected lifetimes of the vehicles. If two vehicles had the same purchase price and expected lifetimes, but one had an annual cost of ownership that was double that of the other, it would be easy to say which car is a better value.

But ascribing value to healthcare services and products isn't as simple. What if you didn't even need the service that was recommended? Should you pay many times more for service from a hospital that is "highly rated," if you don't understand the rating systems? What if the hospital is "highly rated," but also has high rates of errors or hospital-acquired infections? These types of questions have made moving from a "fee-for-service" payment model to one based on value incredibly challenging. You can't just choose healthcare based on the lowest cost and highest quality measurements. Quality measurements are currently just beginning to be used, and are highly contested. Patient outcomes are rarely quantified, let alone taken into account.

Still, data and innovative thinking can lead to better processes, as other industries have demonstrated. The Toyota Production System, used by the auto maker to standardize processes and increase efficiency, is one model (Toyota 2017). We presented such an example in Chapter 7, describing how Mayo Clinic was able to eliminate the need for repeat breast cancer surgeries approximately 96% of the time by pausing in the middle of the operation to wait for pathology results before finishing the surgery (Boughey et al. 2014). Though the additional time in the OR can make for a more slightly more expensive upfront surgery, there is tremendous value to the patient (less likely to need a repeat surgery days or weeks later) and to the hospital (able to see a greater number of patients for primary surgery because there are fewer repeat ones).

Patient outcomes can be an integral part of determining when procedures or treatments are unnecessary. A recent study (Siemieniuk et al. 2017) found that the world's most common orthopedic procedure (knee arthroscopy, sometimes referred to as "keyhole" surgery) "is frequently a waste of time and money and should almost never be performed on patients with degenerative knee disease" (Ross 2017). Performed more than 2 million times each year, the study's lead author said "Clinical trials have shown that keyhole surgery doesn't help people suffering from arthritis of the knees any more than mild painkillers, physical therapy or weight loss" (Thompson 2017).

Not many payers, or patients for that matter, will want to pay thousands of dollars for a painful surgery that has been deemed ineffective. But how many patients would second-guess a doctor who prescribed such surgery? Even assuming patients can effectively shop for the best quality surgeon at the least expensive cost for keyhole surgery, it wouldn't be *value*-based if it was unnecessary in the first place, and the same end result could have been obtained with nonsurgical methods. More such studies are likely to come out spurring more data collection and more pushback against waste, inefficiency, and high prices. But the business case can be made for value-based care and its emphasis on measurable patient outcomes. In addition to avoiding penalties from failing to meet federal quality metrics, health systems that take the initiative in these early stages of transition may find financial benefit and the increased market share from innovative programs, such as Geisinger's money-back guarantee. After all, if Geisinger can confidently offer patients such a program, why can't other health systems?

Moving to a value-based care model has meant hospitals and providers are looking more closely at preventive care—how can they do something now for a patient that will keep the patient healthier in the long run? This means better communication and collaboration between primary care providers and specialists and new organizational structures such as integrated delivery networks and accountable care organizations. It can also mean developing unusual alliances between health systems and other groups or considering non-medical interventions. Some physicians are even promoting the idea of "prescribing" subsidized housing or vegetables for certain patients with chronic conditions (Brody 2014; Moses and Davis 2015).

Hospitals are doing more analysis of their clinical workflows and providers, using these data to help them restructure departments, reduce errors, and become more efficient. In Chapter 7, we described how Virginia Mason restructured their spine clinic with the result that patients can be seen and a multidisciplinary care team can begin treatment the same day the patient calls for an appointment. One consequence of this patient-centered clinic? The hospital can see more patients yearly with the same physician staffing and space constraints because efficiency has increased (Porter and Lee 2013).

The practice of medicine has long been individualized, as doctors treat patients based on their own knowledge and experiences. Clinical guidelines developed largely by physician organizations or government entities have attempted to standardize some practices, with varying degrees of success. But hospitals and medical practices are beginning to act more like businesses in other industries by using self-measurement to continually optimize their processes. We've described it as the "Six Sigma moment" of healthcare, in reference to the Six Sigma technique. Programs such as the National Surgical Quality Improvement Program (NSQIP) and similar specialty-specific programs, described in earlier chapters, are one way of getting hospitals to collect data for quality improvement and to identify providers who aren't performing adequately. Here, robust IT infrastructure will give health systems an edge, since those systems will have the ability to collect the necessary data to determine what programs reduce costs *and* improve patient outcomes.

One big question is whether the federal government will continue to push value-based care. Currently a variety of programs with incentives and penalties exist, but value-based care has yet to reach a critical mass nationally beyond those initiatives. Continued data collection on patient outcomes under such initiatives that clearly demonstrates value-based care can both lower healthcare costs and improve patient outcomes will make it easier for stakeholders to demand more providers and hospitals move to this structure. It could be the government, insurance companies, or even patients who drive this demand (and will likely be a combination of all three), but experts agree that this single trend—value-based care—could be the biggest disruptor in healthcare for decades and one way to attain lower healthcare costs without sacrificing patient outcomes.

At the patient level, Big Data, analytics, and related technologies are having big impact.

Advances in technology have reduced the costs of genetic sequencing so that the price of whole exome sequencing and whole genome sequencing are nearing $1,000. Sequencing pioneer Illumina claims it will soon have the capability to bring that cost down to $100 (Keshavan 2017). That's a far cry from the almost $3 billion it took to sequence the first human genome for the Human Genome Project in 2003 (National Human Genome Research Institute 2016). The sharp cost reductions in sequencing has led to explosive growth in the genetic testing industry, and as the technology has continued to improve, innovative methods such as liquid biopsy are shaping what cancer care, in particular, will look like in the years to come. But the success of precision medicine for this and other diseases relies on the continued discovery and sharing of variant information. For Big Data to really work in precision medicine, researchers must establish clear links between variants and clinical outcomes, for diagnostics and for drugs.

Several leading academic medical centers are using genetic and genomic data to choose which medication to give a patient, to avoid adverse effects of some drugs (pharmacogenetics), and to predict a patient's likelihood of developing cancer, which allows the patient to take prophylactic measures, such as having a double mastectomy to avoid breast cancer. This last point is important and ties into our earlier observation about the value of preventive care. If a test can predict, to a high degree, the likelihood of a given cancer (or other disorder) developing, and an intervention can be given, the value of that test is substantial. In the increasingly competitive and financially driven diagnostics landscape, manufacturers will be under tremendous pressure in the upcoming years to produce evidence of value and clinical utility. Here, in particular, is where continued clinical research that can demonstrate improved outcomes and reduced costs will be essential to sway insurance companies to pay for more of these tests.

Precision medicine is also getting a boost from advanced computer science techniques such as clinical decision support (CDS) systems and AI. CDS systems can be built into electronic health record (EHR) systems or can be stand-alone software. Older versions of CDS were not much better than flow charts, giving providers a roadmap for managing patients. But many CDS systems today, particularly those that are built into EHR systems, use natural language processing and other advanced methods, and can alert physicians to potential drug interactions or adverse events, recommend treatment options, or identify patients for a particular intervention.

But for all the potential benefits of CDS systems, many health systems, hospitals, and providers still have only rudimentary EHRs that meet only the bare minimum for technical capabilities and interoperability. Improving the IT infrastructure is an expensive undertaking that may be beyond the reach of some, leaving them at risk of falling behind competitors, but as patient demand for more personalized treatment, or precision medicine, grows, health systems and providers must find a way to keep up with IT advances. This is where the benefits of cloud computing (Chapter 10) can minimize the financial burdens on an organization while providing a system that can grow and contract to meet its changing needs.

Other companies, such as Philips, are developing AI-based radiology systems that can scan patient images and alert physicians to which images, or areas of images, to focus their attention on. IBM Watson and Alphabet's DeepMind are using AI and cognitive computing techniques to help doctors confirm patient diagnoses and tell the difference between cancerous and noncancerous skin lesions, respectively. These systems generally exist outside the EHR and integration with various EHR platforms is currently highly variable. Interoperability will be key for further adoption of these systems. Although there have been widely publicized examples in using these (and other AI-based methods) in patient care, such as to diagnose a patient's rare form of cancer, AI in healthcare is still a young field, and there is much progress to be made before it becomes widely used.

Digital health technologies are proliferating, such as smartphone-based apps that collect digital biomarkers and transformative technologies, such as a TriCorder, that was developed for the XPrize and can diagnose a variety of diseases with a handheld device and a smartphone (Comstock 2017b). But digital devices could face a slow climb to adoption, at least for clinical care, where reimbursement by insurers may be difficult to come by and providers are unsure of their accuracy. The most important task for companies in this industry is to clearly identify the *value* their product provides by analyzing the data that comes from their use. Doing this, and publicizing it, will be essential to garner buy-in from health systems, providers, and payers.

Prenatal testing is another area that is in the midst of a transformation, brought on by noninvasive prenatal tests (NIPTs). "Over the last few years, non-invasive prenatal testing has evolved at a particularly explosive rate," says Vance Vanier, a venture capitalist and former executive at a NIPT start-up (Chapter 4).

Once relegated to high-risk patients, NIPTs are now being offered to nearly all pregnant women, early in their pregnancies. Although NIPTs currently detect risk of only a few genetic disorders, patients who undergo assisted reproductive techniques like *in vitro* fertilization have the potential to test the embryo for many more genetic mutations before implantation. This means parents can find out about not only chromosomal abnormalities, but also whether or not the embryo carries a *BRCA1* mutation, for example, and would be at high risk for developing breast and ovarian cancer later in life. Gene editing techniques, such as CRISPR, are being refined and tested. In the future, it may be possible to offer parents a choice to fix a mutation.

As with precision medicine and oncology, the prenatal testing industry relies on accurate interpretation of the data these tests provide. As NIPT manufacturers build up their databases, they must compete in an increasingly crowded field. By touting the number of disorders they can screen for and the predictive values of their tests, companies can set themselves apart from the competition.

The rare disease community has largely embraced the benefits of data-sharing and technology. The maturation of the genomic sequencing industry and data analytics have helped researchers identify the causes of many previously unknown disorders, which in turn has led to targets for new and existing drugs. Social media allows researchers and patients to find others with similar disorders, impacting how quickly clinical studies can accrue subjects and fostering a sense of community for patients.

As we learned in Chapter 5, patients with rare diseases want to share their data for research, but also want to be viewed as partners and to maintain some control over research decisions, an observation that is equally pertinent for patients with more common disorders. Patient advocacy groups are increasingly helping to fund targeted, disease-specific research. Now, digital health devices and platforms are giving patients the opportunity to remain engaged in research and provide valuable data for researchers and physicians.

Data analysis and computational modeling are transforming drug development. Instead of the decade (or more) it takes to bring a drug to market, pharma is now performing virtual assays to narrow down potential compounds before beginning costly and time-consuming preclinical trials. But despite even such advances, drug development is still a very high risk venture, as shown by the example of the *PCSK9* inhibitors (Chapter 8). The twin necessities of efficacy and safety must always be satisfied. But now, cost-effectiveness will also become a growing concern, so companies will have to consider the value their drugs provide much more carefully as they estimate the market potential.

This opens an opportunity for precision medicine to better identify patients who are more likely to benefit from a particular drug and reduce the potential for serious adverse events that could halt a study. Genomic testing will play an ever larger part in eligibility criteria in the future, but precision medicine can also encompass environmental exposures, socioeconomic variables, or digital biomarkers that predict how a patient will respond to a treatment or whether they will be adherent to therapy. Identifying those variables will be nearly impossible without the ability to leverage clinical data from EHRs and other databases.

Future of *Moneyball Medicine*

So what do we anticipate will happen in the next several years? How will data analytics, emerging technologies, and novel business models come together to change the healthcare industry? The role of technology in healthcare will continue to increase, creating new opportunities for innovation, but also changing the landscape of care. Automation of processes will eliminate some positions while creating others, and numerous job functions are likely to change.

Probably the biggest observable shifts will be a greater emphasis on standards, whether they are related to quality or efficiency, and increasing integration of data scientists into the healthcare mix. As Christoph Wald, Lahey's Chair of Radiology, told us, "We are now working closely with data scientists for the first time" (Chapter 9). Likewise, Flatiron Health's cofounder Zach Weinberg says "a lot of our [software] engineers spend time consulting our oncologists, and the doctors also feel comfortable going to the engineers and saying 'hey, could we do this?'" (Chapter 1).

Business models will continue to evolve due to market and regulatory pressures. Mergers, acquisitions, and strategic partnerships will become more commonplace as companies struggle to remain relevant, increase efficiency, and expand their markets. Most recently, there were rumors that Amazon would go into the pharmacy business (Weise 2017). Imagine how they might start using data to increase their sales in this area. Likely, a growing number of new healthcare deals will be between nontraditional partners, such as a digital device company partnering with a drug company to improve treatment adherence, or a genetic test manufacturer working with a health system to identify patients at risk for developing cancer.

Here are a few big-picture projections:

Value-Based Care Will Reach a Tipping Point

Particularly if federal and state governments continue to push for it, value-based care will become a major trend. It's clear that the old way (i.e., fee-for-service) of doing things is unsustainable and finding an alternative is an economic imperative. The effects of rising healthcare costs have been most pronounced in the United States, where prices are higher and the cost of healthcare routinely rises faster than GDP. However, nations and employers worldwide are being pummeled by health costs. A 2017 survey found that medical insurers projected the cost of healthcare benefits would rise 7.8% globally this year, an increase from 7.3% in 2016. Larger cost increases were projected in nearly all regions around the world, with Latin America seeing the largest increases, but Africa and the Middle East also seeing big rises in benefits costs (HR Specialist 2017). Employers and government administrators alike all around the world are looking for solutions to this problem, from restricting patient care to putting price controls on new drugs.

So who will move first? Will buyers demand lower prices and higher quality service, or will agile enterprises offer such services before their competitors do? Complying with current mandates can be viewed as onerous, particularly for health systems that lag behind others in being able to measure the necessary quality metrics and for small systems with limited budgets. As a result, many healthcare facilities are just biding their time, operating "business as usual" unless they have a juicy carrot or a big stick above their heads. But others are looking at this as an opportunity to invest in homegrown solutions, try innovative and/or unconventional methods, or develop breakthrough new tools that truly improve quality, efficiency, and the patient experience. Hospitals that stand on the sidelines may find themselves unable to move quickly enough when they decide to transform their processes to remain competitive.

Even hospitals that are objectively performing well can benefit from adopting a continuous improvement mindset. The Mayo Clinic, arguably one of the top hospitals in the United States, saw payment reform, declining revenues, and other changes on the horizon in 2008, when it undertook an evaluation of its preparedness for the future. This endeavor, called the Mayo Clinic 2020 Initiative, has involved more than 400 projects to find areas where workflows could be restructured. Some of the results have been remarkable, for example, in care for pediatric patients with complex feeding, breathing, and swallowing disorders. Providers were able to reduce the average time to diagnosis from 210 to 4 days (Winslow 2017).

The biggest barrier to value-based care lies squarely with the providers and health systems tasked with delivering care. Moving away from a fee-for-service model is a paradigm shift of immense proportions. Particularly for providers and health systems that have been successful under the old model, this new mindset can be threatening. This is an understandable concern when you have been well-paid by how much you can bill or by how many things you do for patients. The hesitation and backlash to value-based care by providers is compounded by a system that has been slow to determine the value that should be given to a procedure, device, or lab test. Even when a provider is fully on board with value-based care, how can they calculate the value from preventive care that prevents the need for more specialized, expensive care 6 months, 1 year, or even further into the future?

In addition, the benefits for making clinical practice and operational changes are not going substantially to the providers or health systems, but instead to the insurers who have less to reimburse. In a fiscally challenging environment where providers are still largely paid based on the number of procedures they bill, it can be difficult to justify changing practice methods when it will reduce the number of billable procedures and thus, reimbursement from payers in the short-term. Hospital systems, such as Geisinger, that also have an insurance arm illustrate the dilemma and benefit to being self-insured.

As Lahey Health's Howard Grant, formerly of Geisinger, told us (Chapter 9), "When Geisinger health plan expends fewer health care resources on those patients [who are also insured by Geisinger], by improving the management of their care, avoiding unnecessary expenses and lowering their total costs of care, the Geisinger system retains those unspent health insurance premium dollars and reinvests in the clinical enterprise. Typically, if hospitals, physician groups, or health systems lower healthcare costs, an outside insurer gets the reward. That makes it very difficult to justify investments in initiatives that are likely to lower total medical expenses" (Grant 2017).

These problems are not insurmountable. Some health systems, including Intermountain Health, Kaiser Permanente, and the Mayo Clinic have salary-based payment models for their physicians. Notably, these are considered some of the most reputable and efficient health systems in the country. But they are also rare outliers with respect to their compensation schemes. The vast majority of hospitals still reward doctors based on how much they do, and certain specialists make far more than others (Peckham 2016). Getting health systems (and providers) on board with salaries instead of billing-based compensation structures could be a key piece to the value-based care solution, but it will clearly be an uphill battle. The shift from getting paid more to do more, to getting paid for doing better, may not be an easy one for some. Finding innovative solutions to assign values to services that are not easily billable or are undervalued will be critical.

Continued release of price and quality data for providers and hospitals is another way to support value-based care. As we've described, making these data publicly available can help patients (and employers) better shop for healthcare services. But even providers and hospitals can benefit from measuring what they charge for procedures. When the Mayo Clinic undertook their dramatic overhaul, described in a *Wall Street Journal* article, an internal report found substantial variation between surgeons' average cost per case—nearly a twofold variation between some providers. Mayo used this information to help them standardize the brand of heart valve used in surgery, a key driver of the cost differential (Winslow 2017). The role of the government in this process would be essential. Federal and state authorities could require additional outcomes measurements be released publicly. Over time, this will also encourage competition by providers and hospitals for patients, and force providers to demonstrate their care leads to improved outcomes at lower costs.

Expansion of current alternative models, such as accountable care organizations (ACOs) and integrated delivery networks (IDNs), could continue to push value-based care under the current health insurance structure. These organizational structures can help to better align providers' goals to value-based care. Self-insured health systems are another way this can be accomplished. As we described in Chapter 9, there are some important advantages to hospitals who have their own health plans: most importantly, they will directly reap the rewards of their efficiency, rather than just passing those dollars directly to the insurer. This keeps the financial benefits of value-based care within the health system, to be reinvested in new solutions and initiatives and for direct patient care.

Decentralization of health services through grocery store vaccinations, pharmacy urgent care clinics, and telehealth platforms can give patients essential value-based care and also serve as competition to traditional healthcare providers. Technology will play a substantial role in decentralization of services. Meanwhile, concierge providers and direct primary care companies offer competition, but until more patients are enrolled in these programs, it could be difficult for these companies to expand beyond the perception they are "boutique" providers. However, we're already seeing the start of health systems partnering with alternative healthcare providers. A recent partnership between pharmacy giant CVS and the Cleveland Clinic will bring the hospitals' providers to CVS Minute Clinics via telemedicine (Siwicki 2016). We expect to see additional health systems collaborate with pharmacies and supermarkets to maintain market share and expand offerings to patients.

Though payers have joined the chorus to complain about the rise in healthcare costs, along with the government and employers, they can be the forces driving the transition to value-based care. But to make it happen, they will need to consider new forms of evidence, such as real-world evidence or digital biomarkers, to show how newer technologies, including digital health and genomic testing, can improve patient outcomes. When insurers fail to reimburse for new technologies, it is sometimes the fault of manufacturers that have largely kept any data pertaining to the use of their products private. There may also be institutional barriers that prevent doctors from ordering these tests and devices. But these stakeholders have an opportunity to turn this problem around, particularly if they work together to demonstrate improved outcomes in patient populations *and* publish their findings. Data sharing and interoperability would play a key role to making this happen.

Healthcare Will become More Participatory

Leroy Hood noted that the healthcare of tomorrow will be "4P Medicine," not only predictive and focused on preventive care, but personalized and participatory (see Chapter 10). We're already seeing patients become more active participants in their healthcare through the "quantified self" movement, as patients log their food consumption with apps such as MyFitnessPal and track their steps with fitness trackers like Fitbit or Apple Watch. Patients are already starting to embrace digital technology, such as smartphone apps for glucose monitoring that lower A1c levels in patients with diabetes (Dachis 2017) and platforms like Apple's ResearchKit is testing how digital biomarkers can be used for clinical trials and patient care (Research Kit 2017). Though little of the data or digital biomarkers collected by these devices and programs is being integrated into the EHR *currently* and thus, is not being used to provide insight on the user's health and wellness, we expect this will change in the upcoming years and digital health could be a driving force for patient participation.

Interoperability and emerging standards, such as FHIR (fast healthcare interoperability resources), will continue to erode existing barriers to data sharing. That will make it easier for digital biomarkers to find their way into a patient's clinical record and for patient records from different health systems to be shared. Again, the federal government can play a role in accelerating this process by mandating adoption of a single standard, but in the absence of such a rule, progress is certain to continue, albeit more slowly as industry tries to do this.

Patients with rare diseases can be particularly highly engaged and financially supportive of clinical research and drug development through patient advocacy groups, such as the Progeria Research Foundation and the Cystic Fibrosis Foundation. For these patients, the role of social media will be a driving force for continued identification of fellow sufferers of rare conditions. Growing their numbers is especially important, because it helps fuel research, awareness, and fundraising.

Increased patient participation will impact clinical trials design, broadly, and increase the amount of real-world evidence (RWE) available for an intervention after clinical trials are over. Already, groups such as PatientsLikeMe and Transparency Life Sciences are working with patients to gather insight on the outcomes that are clinically meaningful to *them* and to incorporate digital health data.

Participation in clinical trials for certain conditions, such as cancer, is often low, and for rare diseases, patients may be spread out across the country and the world. Pharmaceutical companies and device manufacturers that make it easier for patients to participate in trials through virtual recruitment methods (Kumar 2016) and telehealth or other remote monitoring methods may achieve improved enrollment and retention while also demonstrating the value of these techniques. Importantly, pharma and device manufacturers will need to account for longer-term impacts of their products on the patient population. Getting a product to launch will be the *start* of continued patient monitoring through digital health devices. This presents an opportunity for entrepreneurs to partner with drug and device manufacturers to create applications that capture important patient data such as adherence and other aspects of patient use that aren't typically identified during a short-term clinical trial.

The value of market and business opportunities for digital health entrepreneurs will continue to grow. As more of these devices and programs are tested in clinical trials and observational studies and data analysis can correlate digital biomarkers with clinical outcomes, providers will be less hesitant to incorporate the data alongside more traditional measurements.

Expert Data Analysis Will Start Driving Healthcare

Data are becoming cheaper than ever to capture, and with that, the competitive advantages of keeping data proprietary are slowly eroding. As this trend continues, the biggest advantages will go to those who can capture and analyze data expertly themselves *and* who find the best collaborators to work with. Existing data will be looked at in new ways, by different researchers, and novel insights will be made, driving the formation of new companies and nontraditional partnerships between companies.

Researchers funded by certain federal grants are already required to deposit some data into publicly available databases (such as dbGAP for genetic and phenotypic data), but we anticipate industry will start to recognize the advantages of releasing their data, too. More shared databases will be developed, likely initiated by the government or by very large, well-known companies working together, since interoperability and data standards would have to be determined, and there are privacy and security issues for patient data.

But rather than limiting research, data sharing will spur innovation and competition, since everyone would have access to the same information. Consider the consequences of the federal government's release of geographic information system (GIS) data: multiple companies developed apps to help drivers get from Point A to Point B, and social media platforms such as Yelp were created to help users find local restaurants (and other businesses). These in turn spurred further innovation, such as ride-sharing and food delivery businesses. The same can happen in healthcare, but it will take a data-sharing initiative on a massive scale to happen.

Winners and Losers

Who are the winners of the healthcare industry of tomorrow? Here are our predicted winners:

- Companies and providers that embrace methods such as Agile Transformation and Six Sigma to improve their business processes and patient care will best be able to respond to evolving market and scientific pressures.
- Entrepreneurs and innovative thought leaders who develop or use breakthrough digital health and emerging technologies, such as AI, or just novel business models to solve healthcare problems.
- Integrated delivery networks, self-insured health systems, and others that can take the lead on innovative programs or organizational structures that support value-based care.
- Technology companies that work to develop data standards that enable interoperability, from EHR companies to those involved in digital health.

There will also be losers in this new healthcare ecosystem. Some hospitals and other health facilities will collapse if they are unable to adapt to the changes we've outlined in this book. Others will lose out if they hold on too tight and too long to the fee-for-service payment model, or try to maintain their old workflows, even in the face of new insights and evidence to the contrary. Healthcare costs are growing more rapidly than the global economy and the old method of paying for care exacerbates the problem. Insights gathered from Big Data can change this.

Companies, including health systems, that continue to lag behind in adopting IT infrastructure and mechanisms to collect and analyze massive amounts of patient and operational data will find it increasingly difficult to compete in the future. *The new healthcare business paradigm is measure → optimize → transform.* If companies aren't measuring how they are performing and how they compare to others, they can't use the data to change practices. This holds true for providers as well as others, including large pharma companies and medical centers. Patients are beginning to expect more personalized, precise, participatory clinical care—those who can't deliver on that will be left behind by companies that can.

If most of this innovation and change happens, we'll have a completely different healthcare system within 5–10 years. But for that to occur, we must keep pressing for greater transparency (especially more public data), better means of measuring quality, and better processes to ensure interoperability. If these pieces fall in place, we can reduce costs, improve quality, and make sure that more patients are receiving optimal care at a reasonable price.

The key is that every professional should be constantly analyzing the data in their field, and asking questions such as:

- What data are relevant to my work now? Which is the most relevant data? What type of data will be most important tomorrow?
- How have the data in my field evolved? How much of it is being digitized? At what point of data maturity is my field?
- How can I add value to those data? Or, how can I use it to increase the value of the services I provide?
- How feasible is that? And what is the estimated return on investment for the effort required?

Moneyball Medicine is here and companies in the healthcare industry (and those that want to be) need to decide if they will embrace it or remain on the sidelines, finding themselves increasingly irrelevant. It's just beginning, but moving fast. Once anything is digitized, it can be measured and analyzed, and the results can be astonishing—big new markets emerge, time to diagnoses are dramatically accelerated, previously unknown diseases are discovered, new cures are found, patients get breakthrough treatments that improve and extend six their lives. Some established companies thrive, some die, and brand new businesses are established. Those who keep up with the field's evolution will be tomorrow's healthcare leaders, forging a new landscape where quality, cost, and outcomes are transparent and change is data- and technology-fueled.

Glossary

Accountable Care Organization (ACO): Groups of doctors, hospitals, and other healthcare providers, who joined together with the goal of providing coordinated high-quality care (Centers for Medicare & Medicaid Services 2017a).

Affordable Care Act (ACA): A comprehensive U.S. healthcare reform act that was passed in 2010 by the Obama administration (HealthCare.gov 2017).

Algorithm: A step-by-step procedure for solving a problem or accomplishing some end, especially by a computer (Merriam-Webster 2017).

Artificial intelligence: The science of making computers do things that require intelligence when done by humans. This field has focused on five main aspects of intelligence: learning, reasoning, problem-solving, perception, and language-understanding (Copeland 2000).

Biobank: A collection of biological material and the associated data and information stored in an organized system, for a population or a large subset of a population (OECD Statistics Directorate 2007).

Bioinformatics: The collection, classification, storage, and analysis of biochemical and biological information using computers especially as applied to molecular genetics and genomics (Merriam-Webster 2017).

Big Data: A large volume of data, which can be either structured or unstructured.

Biomarker: Objective indications of a medical state that can be measured accurately and reproducibly. These stand in contrast to medical symptoms, which are limited to those indications of health or illness perceived by patients themselves (Strimbu and Tavel 2010).

Biorepository: A facility that collects, catalogs, and stores samples of biological material, such as urine, blood, tissue, cells, DNA, RNA, and protein from humans, animals, or plants for laboratory research. If the samples are from people, medical information may also be stored along with a written consent to use the samples in laboratory studies (National Cancer Institute 2017b).

Blockchain: A way to structure data and the foundation of cryptocurrencies such as Bitcoin. It consists of concatenated transaction blocks and allows competitors to share a digital ledger across a network of computers without a central authority. No single party can tamper with the records (Hackett 2016).

Centers of Excellence: Medical facilities, typically hospitals, that provide verifiably high-quality care for specific procedures that are high cost (e.g., hip and knee replacements). The facilities offer a single "bundled" price for the procedure, and employers will pay for their employees to travel there and sometimes cover any additional copays or deductibles. The idea is that by getting "guaranteed" quality care, overall costs will be lower (Pacific Business Group on Health 2017).

Chemogenomic screen: A chemogenomic library is a collection of selective small-molecule pharmacological agents, and a hit from such a set in a phenotypic screen suggests that the annotated target or targets of that pharmacological agent may be involved in perturbing the observable phenotype (Jones and Bunnage 2017).

Clinical Decision Support (CDS): Provides healthcare providers and patients with guidance on the most appropriate care. Such tools include computerized alerts and reminders to care providers and patients, clinical guidelines, condition-specific order sets, focused patient data reports and summaries, documentation templates, diagnostic support, and contextually relevant reference information, among other tools (HealthIT.gov 2013).

Cognitive computing: A term often used interchangeably with AI, describing computer software or systems that have the capability to adapt to changing inputs and learn.

Digital biomarker: Consumer-generated physiological and behavioral measures collected through connected digital tools that can be used to explain, influence and/or predict health-related outcomes, while excluding some types of patient-reported data, like those collected through surveys (Wang, Azad, and Rajan 2017).

Direct primary care: An alternative primary care model in which the patients, or their employers, pay a monthly fee to the doctor and there is no insurance involved. The patient receives the majority of their care from their primary care physician (PCP), and their associates, who may include health coaches. The PCP acts as a gatekeeper, providing the patient as much care as they can and trying to avoid unnecessary expensive services.

Evidence-based medicine: Evidence-based medicine is defined as the incorporation of systematic research into the provider's clinical decision-making process (Sackett and Rosenberg 1995).

Gene fusion: A mutation where chromosomes that have broken apart are reassembled incorrectly. The result is a "fused" gene, often affecting cell signaling, growth, or other critical aspects of cellular function (Mertens et al. 2015).

Genetic testing: Testing that seeks to identify mutations in a single gene or multiple genes.

Genomic testing: Testing that goes across an organism's entire genome. Exome sequencing and whole genome sequencing are genomic tests.

High deductible health plan (HDPH): A plan with a higher deductible than a traditional insurance plan. The monthly premium is usually lower, but patients pay more out-of-pocket (a deductible) before the insurance company starts to pay its share (HealthCare.gov 2017).

High-throughput screening: A drug discovery approach that tracks proteins and cell signaling. Many compounds can be simultaneously tested to see which ones have the desired effect.

HIPAA: The HIPAA Privacy Rule created national standards to protect individuals' medical records and other personal health information. Individuals, organizations, and agencies that meet the definition of a *covered entity* under HIPAA must comply with the Rules' requirements to protect the privacy and security of health information and must provide individuals with certain rights with respect to their health information (Department of Health & Human Services 2015).

HITECH: The Health Information Technology for Economic and Clinical Health Act, enacted as part of the American Recovery and Reinvestment Act of 2009, promotes the adoption and meaningful use of health information technology. Subtitle D of the HITECH Act addresses the privacy and security concerns associated with the electronic transmission of health information, in part, through several provisions that strengthen the civil and criminal enforcement of the HIPAA rules (Department of Health & Human Services 2014).

Integrated Delivery Network (IDN): Vertically integrated health services networks that include physicians, hospitals, and post-acute services that provide care across the continuum for patients in a targeted geographic region. Many IDNs (but not all) may be self-insured health systems, while others may contract with existing insurers (Xu 2015).

Interoperability: The ability to access a patient's, or one's own, healthcare information from different sources, ideally with little delay.

Machine learning: A method of data analysis that automates analytical model building. Using algorithms that iteratively learn from data, machine learning allows computers to progressively improve their analytical capabilities (SAS 2017).

MACRA (Medicare Access and CHIP Reauthorization Act): This new act replaces the old Medicare reimbursement schedule with a new pay-for-performance program that's focused on quality, value, and accountability (Centers for Medicare & Medicaid Services 2016d).

Molecular profiling: Genetic or genomic testing that is performed on a cancer tumor and may include other biomarkers (Ness 2013).

Next-generation sequencing (NGS): NGS, massively parallel, or deep sequencing are related terms that describe a DNA sequencing technology which has revolutionized genomic research. Using NGS an entire human genome can be sequenced within a single day. In contrast, the previous Sanger sequencing technology, used to decipher the human genome, required over a decade to deliver the final draft (Behjati and Tarpey 2013).

Pharmacogenomics: The study of how genes affect a person's response to drugs. This field combines pharmacology (the science of drugs) and genomics (the study of genes and their functions) to develop effective, safe medications and doses that will be tailored to a person's genetic makeup (Genetics Home Reference 2017f).

Proteome/Proteomics: The proteome is the entire complement of proteins produced by an organism or a cellular system under particular circumstances. Proteomics is the study of a specific proteome, including information on protein abundances, their variations and modifications, along with their interacting partners and networks (National Cancer Institute 2017d).

Self-insured health systems: Health systems that create their own insurance plan, underwriting all of the financial risk to provide care to members. Many self-insured health systems are also IDNs.

Terabyte: 1024 gigabytes or 1,099,511,627,776 bytes; *also*: one trillion bytes. A byte is a unit of computer information or data-storage capacity that consists of a group of eight bits and that is used specially to represent an alphanumeric character (Merriam-Webster 2017).

Transcriptome: The study of the transcriptome—the complete set of RNA transcripts produced by the genome, under specific circumstances or in a specific cell—using high-throughput methods, such as microarray analysis. Comparison of transcriptomes allows identification of genes differentially expressed in distinct cell populations, or in response to different treatments (Nature.com 2017).

Variant (genetic variant): An alteration in the most common, or reference, DNA nucleotide sequence. In other words, a variant deviates from what is commonly found at that spot in the genome. The term variant can be used to describe an alteration that is benign, pathogenic, or of unknown significance. The term variant is increasingly being used in place of the term mutation.

References

Abramson, R. 2017. Overview of Targeted Therapies for Cancer. *My Cancer Genome* (last modified April 28, 2017).

Abifadel, M., M. Varret, J. P. Rabes, D. Allard, K. Ouguerram, M. Devillers, C. Cruaud et al. 2003. Mutations in PCSK9 Cause Autosomal Dominant Hypercholesterolemia. *Nat Genet* 34, no. 2: 154–6. doi: 10.1038/ng1161.

ACH Media. 2005. Compare Quality Measures with 4,200 Other Hospitals (accessed January 30, 2017).

ActiveHealth Management. 2017. Creating Better Health Outcomes, http://www.activehealth.com/results (accessed February 21, 2017).

Adams, Ben. 2016. CRISPR Therapeutics Raises a $56M IPO, But Patent Battles, Potential Stock Drops Loom. *FierceBiotech*.

Advisory Board, AMA Survey. 2015. Physician Satisfaction with EHR Systems Has Plummeted.

Advisory Board. 2016a. 364 Hospitals, Health Systems Named as Nation's "Most Wired" Organizations (accessed February 4, 2017).

Advisory Board. 2016b. The First-Ever CMS Overall Hospital Quality Star Ratings Are Out: See How Hospitals Fared on Our Map. https://www.advisory.com/daily-briefing/2016/07/28/cms-star-rating (last modified July 28, 2016, accessed January 20, 2017).

Aetna. 2014a. Aetna International & Starr Companies Launch UltraCare Health Plan Enabling Expatriates and Chinese Nationals to Benefit from Global Health Coverage. *The Health Section*: Aetna.

Aetna. 2014b. Aetna to Acquire Insurance Exchange Technology Provider Bswift. *The Health Section*: Aetna.

Aetna. 2016. Making Electronic Health Records Talk to Each Other (accessed January 24, 2017).

Agarwal, A., L. C. Sayres, M. K. Cho, R. Cook-Deegan, and S. Chandrasekharan. 2013. Commercial Landscape of Noninvasive Prenatal Testing in the United States. *Prenat Diagn* 33, no. 6: 521–31. doi: 10.1002/pd.4101.

Agency for Healthcare Research and Quality. 2011. 2011 National Healthcare Quality and Disparities Reports (accessed March 3, 2017).

Agency for Healthcare Research and Quality. 2014. The State of Accountable Care Organizations: AHRQ Health Care Innovations Exchange. U.S. Dept. of Health & Human Services. https://innovations.ahrq.gov/perspectives/state-accountable-care-organizations (last modified March 26, 2014, accessed April 15, 2017).

AHIP Center for Policy and Research. 2015. 2015 Census of Health Savings Account: High Deductible Health Plans. https://www.ahip.org/2015-census-of-health-savings-account-high-deductible-health-plans/ (last modified November 11, 2015, accessed January 17, 2017).

AliveCor. 2017. *AliveCor*. https://www.alivecor.com/ (accessed March 21, 2017).

Allen, Arthur. 2005. Why Genetics Is So Far a Boondoggle (accessed May 4, 2017).

Allen, Arthur. 2006. "Of Mice or Men": The Problems with Animal Testing (accessed May 4, 2017).

Allison, M. 2012. NCATS Launches Drug Repurposing Program. *Nat Biotechnol* 30, no. 7: 571–2. doi: 10.1038/nbt0712-571a.

American Association for Cancer Research. 2015. Targets and Cancer Therapeutics. American Association for Cancer Research, Boston, MA.

American Association for Cancer Research. 2017. AACR Project GENIE. http://www.aacr.org/Research/Research/Pages/aacr-project-genie.aspx (accessed May 30, 2017). WS3CxRPyvdR.

American Board of Internal Medicine. 2017. Choosing Wisely: Promoting Conversations between Providers and Patients. http://www.choosingwisely.org/ (accessed April 24, 2017).

American Cancer Society. 2017. Immune Checkpoint Inhibitors to Treat Cancer. https://www.cancer.org/treatment/treatments-and-side-effects/treatment-types/immunotherapy/immune-checkpoint-inhibitors.html (last modified February 3, 2017, accessed March 6, 2017).

American College of Cardiology. 2017. FOURIER: Evolocumab Significantly Reduces Risk of Cardiovascular Events. American College of Cardiology.

American College of Emergency Physicians. 2017. EMTALA//ACEP. American College of Emergency Physicians. https://www.acep.org/news-media-top-banner/emtala/.

American College of Physicians. 2016. Internists Say Cost Sharing, Particularly Deductibles, May Cause Patients to Forgo or Delay Care. ACP Newsroom: American College of Physicians.

American College of Surgeons. 2017. ACS National Surgical Quality Improvement Program. American College of Surgeons. https://www.facs.org/quality-programs/acs-nsqip (accessed January 21, 2017).

American Congress of Obstetricians and Gynecologists. 2017. Maternal Quality Improvement Program (MQIP): ACOG. http://www.acog.org/About-ACOG/ACOG-Departments/Patient-Safety-and-Quality-Improvement/Maternal-Quality-Improvement-Program (accessed August 5, 2017).

American Heart Association. 2017. Welcome: AHA Precision Medicine Platform. https://precision.heart.org (accessed February 14, 2017).

American Hospital Association. 2017. Fast Facts on U.S. Hospitals. AHA Hospitals. http://www.aha.org/research/rc/stat-studies/fast-facts.shtml.

American Journal of Medicine. 2016. Under #ACA, Medical Bankruptcy Continues. *American Journal of Medicine*, 2016-01-12. http://amjmed.org/under-aca-medical-bankruptcy-continues/ (accessed March 15, 2017).

Amgen. 2017a. Amgen Announces Repatha Evolocumab Significantly Reduced the Risk of Cardiovascular Events in FOURIER Outcomes Study. Amgen.

Amgen. 2017b. Landmark Outcomes Study Shows That Repatha Evolocumab Decreases LDLC to Unprecedented Low Levels and Reduces Risk of Cardiovascular Events with No New Safety Issues. Amgen.

Amicus Therapeutics. 2011. Amicus Therapeutics Announces John F. Crowley to Return as Chairman and Chief Executive Officer. NASDAQ:FOLD.

Amland, R. C., and K. E. Hahn-Cover. 2016. Clinical Decision Support for Early Recognition of Sepsis. *Am J Med Qual* 31, vol. 2: 103–10. doi: 10.1177/1062860614557636.

Anderson, M. O., S. L. Jackson, N. V. Oster, S. Peacock, J. D. Walker, G. Y. Chen, and J. G. Elmore. 2017. Patients Typing Their Own Visit Agendas into an Electronic Medical Record: Pilot in a Safety-Net Clinic. *Ann Fam Med* 15, vol. 2: 158–61. doi: 10.1370/afm.2036.

Andrews, Michelle. 2015. Prisons and Jails Forcing Inmates to Cover Some Medical Care Costs. *Kaiser Health News* (accessed January 24, 2017).

AP. 1994. New Version of Taxol Is Approved by FDA. *New York Times* (December). http://www.nytimes.com/1994/12/13/science/new-version-of-taxol-is-approved-by-fda.html (accessed April 4, 2017).

Apple. 2016. Apple & Nike Launch Apple Watch Nike+.

Apple. 2017. ResearchKit and CareKit. http://www.apple.com/researchkit/ (accessed April 20, 2017).

Arcedi Biotech. 2016. News and Notes from PNDx 2016 (Diagnostics World News): ARCEDI BIOTECH ApS. http://arcedi.com/news-and-notes-from-pndx-2016-diagnostics-world-news/ (last modified December 6, 2016, accessed May 28, 2017).

Aristizabal, P., J. Singer, R. Cooper, K. J. Wells, J. Nodora, M. Milburn, S. Gahagan, D. E. Schiff, and M. E. Martinez. 2015. Participation in Pediatric Oncology Research Protocols: Racial/Ethnic, Language and Age-Based Disparities. *Pediatr Blood Cancer* 62, vol. 8: 1337–44. doi: 10.1002/pbc.25472.

Ashford, Molika. 2017. HER2 Mutant Basket Trial Confirms Drug Response Depends on Mutation, Cancer Type (accessed April 4, 2017).

Atlantic Information Services. 2016. Merck's New Zepatier May Cause Pricing, Formulary Shakeup in Hepatitis C. *Drug Benefit News* (February).

Attia, Z. I., C. V. DeSimone, J. J. Dillon, Y. Sapir, V. K. Somers, J. L. Dugan, C. J. Bruce et al. 2016. Novel Bloodless Potassium Determination Using a Signal-Processed Single-Lead ECG. *J Am Heart Assoc* 5, vol. 1. doi: 10.1161/jaha.115.002746.

Austin, D. A. and T. L. Hungerford. 2009. The Market Structure of the Health Insurance Industry. Ed. Congressional Research Service.

Austin, J. M., G. D'Andrea, J. D. Birkmeyer, L. L. Leape, A. Milstein, P. J. Pronovost, P. S. Romano, S. J. Singer, T. J. Vogus, and R. M. Wachter. 2014. Safety in Numbers: The Development of Leapfrog's Composite Patient Safety Score for U.S. Hospitals. *J Patient Saf* 10, vol. 1: 64–71. doi: 10.1097/PTS .0b013e3182952644.

Austin, J. M., A. K. Jha, P. S. Romano, S. J. Singer, T. J. Vogus, R. M. Wachter, and P. J. Pronovost. 2015. National Hospital Ratings Systems Share Few Common Scores and May Generate Confusion Instead of Clarity. *Health Aff (Millwood)* 34, vol. 3: 423–30. doi: 10.1377/hlthaff.2014.0201.

Bach, Peter B., Leonard B. Saltz, and Robert E. Wittes. 2012. In Cancer Care, Cost Matters. *New York Times* (October). https://www.nytimes.com/2012/10/15/opinion/a-hospital-says-no-to-an-11000-a-month-cancer -drug.html.

Bahr, Chris. 2015. Flashback: Hatteberg's Walk-Off HR Extends A's Win Streak to 20. *Fox Sports* (accessed April 9, 2015).

Bailey, A. M., Y. Mao, J. Zeng, V. Holla, A. Johnson, L. Brusco, K. Chen, J. Mendelsohn, M. J. Routbort, G. B. Mills et al. 2014. Implementation of Biomarker-Driven Cancer Therapy: Existing Tools and Remaining Gaps. *Discov Med* 17, vol. 92: 101–14.

Balan, David J. 2016. Hospital Mergers That Don't Happen (accessed May 5, 2017).

Balgrosky, J. A. 2014. *Essentials of Health Information Systems and Technology.* Jones & Bartlett Learning.

Barker, Garry. 2015. How My Apple Watch Saved My Life. *Sydney Morning Herald* (November). http:// www.smh.com.au/digital-life/macman/how-my-apple-watch-saved-my-life-20150903-gje4ce.html (accessed February 17, 2017).

Barkholz, Dave. 2017. Hospital Mega-Mergers Hit Fast and Furious in Q1 (accessed May 4, 2017).

Barrangou, R., C. Fremaux, H. Deveau, M. Richards, P. Boyaval, S. Moineau, D. A. Romero, and P. Horvath. 2007. CRISPR Provides Acquired Resistance against Viruses in Prokaryotes. *Science* 315, vol. 5819: 1709–12. doi: 10.1126/science.1138140.

Bartlett, Jessica. 2016. Boston Health Care Company Iora Health Raises $75M to Add Doctor Sites. *Boston Business Journal* (accessed May 4, 2017).

Bartlett, Jessica. 2017. State Employee Health Insurer GIC to Partner with For-Profit Iora Health. *Boston Business Journal* (accessed May 4, 2017).

Barua, S., R. Greenwald, J. Grebely, G. J. Dore, T. Swan, and L. E. Taylor. 2015. Restrictions for Medicaid Reimbursement of Sofosbuvir for the Treatment of Hepatitis C Virus Infection in the United States. *Ann Intern Med* 163, vol. 3: 215–23. doi: 10.7326/m15-0406.

Baucom, R., J. Ousley, B. Poulose, S. T. Rosenbloom, and G. P. Jackson. 2014. Case Report: Patient Portal versus Telephone Recruitment for a Surgical Research Study. *Appl Clin Inform* 5, vol. 4: 1005–14. doi: 10 .4338/aci-2014-07-cr-0059.

Baum, Stephanie. 2015. Clinical Decision Support Start-Up Collaborates with Epic, Allscripts to Better Connect Clinical Guidelines and EMRs (accessed February 17, 2017).

Baum, Stephanie. 2016a. Digital Health Coach Provider Noom Shifts Model to Embrace Outcomes-Based Pricing (accessed January 30, 2017).

Baum, Stephanie. 2016b. Magellan Health Adopts Hindsait Tech Using AI to Approve, Reject Diagnostic Tests (accessed January 30, 2017).

Baum, Stephanie. 2016c. Propeller Health Adds Spirometry through Licensing Deal with Italian Device Manufacturer MIR. MedCityNews.com. http://medcitynews.com/2016/12/propeller-health-adds-spi rometry/ (last modified December 1, 2016, accessed January 16, 2017).

Baum, Stephanie. 2017a. From Real Estate to Healthcare: Trulia Cofounder's New Health IT Venture Takes on Type 2 Diabetes (Updated) (accessed March 9, 2017).

Baum, Stephanie. 2017b. With $25M Fundraise, Amino Launches Price Transparency Services for Employers, Providers (accessed April 19, 2017).

Baylor, Scott & White Hospital. 2017. Baylor Health Care System History. http://www.baylorhealth.com /About/Pages/Timeline.aspx (last modified 2016, accessed January 20, 2017).

Beasley, Deena. 2017. The Cost of Cancer: New Drugs Show Success at a Steep Price (accessed April 19, 2017).

Beck, Melinda. 2015. What Are the Best Hospitals? Rankings Disagree. http://www.wsj.com/articles/what-are -the-best-hospitals-rankings-disagree-1425330348 (March 2, 2015, accessed January 30, 2017).

Beckers, Fabien. 2017. The Future of Healthcare Is Cognitive (accessed April 19, 2017).

Behjati, S., and P. S. Tarpey. 2013. What Is Next Generation Sequencing? *Arch Dis Child Educ Pract Ed* 98, vol. 6: 236–8. doi: 10.1136/archdischild-2013-304340.

Benner, Katie. 2016. Roche Leads a $175 Million Investment in Flatiron Health. *New York Times* (January). https://bits.blogs.nytimes.com/2016/01/06/roche-leads-a-175-million-investment-in-flatiron-health/?_r=0.

Bentley, Chris. 2017. Cambridge Doctor Review Company Announces New Funding as ACA Fight Looms (accessed February 9, 2017).

Berg, J. S., P. B. Agrawal, D. B. Bailey, Jr., A. H. Beggs, S. E. Brenner, A. M. Brower, J. A. Cakici et al. 2017. Newborn Sequencing in Genomic Medicine and Public Health. *Pediatrics* 139, vol. 2. doi: 10.1542/peds.2016-2252.

Berkrot, Bill, and Deena Beasley. 2014. U.S. Lawmakers Want Gilead to Explain Sovaldi's Hefty Price (accessed January 17, 2017).

Bernard, Tara Siegel. 2015. Health Premiums Rise More Slowly, But Workers Shoulder More of Cost. *New York Times* (January).

Bernstein, Nina. 2013. New York State Hospital Data Exposes Big Markups, and Odd Bargains. *New York Times* (December). https://www.nytimes.com/2013/12/10/nyregion/new-york-state-hospital-cost-data -expose-big-markups-and-odd-bargains.html (accessed January 21, 2017).

Berry, J. G., S. L. Toomey, A. M. Zaslavsky, A. K. Jha, M. M. Nakamura, D. J. Klein, J. Y. Feng et al. 2013. Pediatric Readmission Prevalence and Variability across Hospitals. *JAMA* 309, vol. 4: 372–80. doi: 10.1001/jama.2012.188351.

The Better Health Coalition. 2017. SelectMD. http://selectmd.org/?uid=0a8706&p=primer&arm=a1 (accessed June 2, 2017).

Bianchi, D. W., D. Chudova, A. J. Sehnert, S. Bhatt, K. Murray, T. L. Prosen, J. E. Garber et al. 2015. Noninvasive Prenatal Testing and Incidental Detection of Occult Maternal Malignancies. *JAMA* 314, vol. 2: 162–9. doi: 10.1001/jama.2015.7120.

Bianchi, D. W., R. L. Parker, J. Wentworth, R. Madankumar, C. Saffer, A. F. Das, J. A. Craig et al. 2014. DNA Sequencing versus Standard Prenatal Aneuploidy Screening. *N Engl J Med* 370, vol. 9: 799–808. doi: 10.1056/NEJMoa1311037.

Binder, Leah. Personal interview with authors. April 11, 2017.

Biomarkers Definitions Working Group. 2001. Biomarkers and Surrogate Endpoints: Preferred Definitions and Conceptual Framework. *Clin Pharmacol Ther* 69, vol. 3: 89–95. doi: 10.1067/mcp.2001.113989.

Bird, Julie. 2013. CMS Releases Hospital Price-Comparison Data. FierceHealthcare. http://www.fiercehealth care.com/finance/cms-releases-hospital-price-comparison-data (last modified May 8, 2013, accessed January 16, 2017).

Birkmeyer, John D. 2016. Why Health Care Mergers Can Be Good for Patients (accessed May 4, 2017).

Blackstone, E. A., and J. P. Fuhr. 2016. The Economics of Medicare Accountable Care Organizations. *Am Health Drug Benefits* 9, vol. 1: 11–9.

Blendon, R. J., M. Brodie, J. M. Benson, D. E. Altman, L. Levitt, T. Hoff, and L. Hugick. 1998. Understanding the Managed Care Backlash. *Health Aff (Millwood)* 17, vol. 4: 80–94.

Blue Cross Blue Shield of Michigan. 2017. Fraud Statistics. http://www.bcbsm.com/health-care-fraud /fraud-statistics.html (accessed May 10, 2017).

Bodian, D. L., E. Klein, R. K. Iyer, W. S. Wong, P. Kothiyal, D. Stauffer, K. C. Huddleston et al. 2016. Utility of Whole-Genome Sequencing for Detection of Newborn Screening Disorders in a Population Cohort of 1,696 Neonates. *Genet Med* 18, vol. 3: 221–30. doi: 10.1038/gim.2015.111.

Boffa, D. J., R. P. Graf, M. C. Salazar, J. Hoag, D. Lu, R. Krupa, J. Louw et al. 2017. Cellular Expression of PD-L1 in the Peripheral Blood of Lung Cancer Patients Is Associated with Worse Survival. *Cancer Epidemiol Biomarkers Prev.* doi: 10.1158/1055-9965.epi-17-0120.

Bogost, Ian. 2017. "Artificial Intelligence" Has become Meaningless.

Boguski, Mark. Personal interview with authors, April 18, 2017.

Bologna, Jamie, and Meghna Chakrabarti. 2017. The Impact of Financial Instability on Cancer (accessed March 1, 2017).

Bonnington, Christina. 2014. Apple Debuts OS X Yosemite, iOS 8, and Tons of New Developer Tools (accessed January 26, 2017).

Boughey, J. C., T. J. Hieken, J. W. Jakub, A. C. Degnim, C. S. Grant, D. R. Farley, K. M. Thomsen, J. B. Osborn, G. L. Keeney, and E. B. Habermann. 2014. Impact of Analysis of Frozen-Section Margin on Reoperation Rates in Women Undergoing Lumpectomy for Breast Cancer: Evaluation of the National Surgical Quality Improvement Program Data. *Surgery* 156, vol. 1: 190–7. doi: 10.1016/j.surg.2014.03.025.

Boye, Shannon, Michael Stefanidakis, Rina Mepani, Maxwell Skor, Sebastian Gloskowski, Joy Horng, Kevin T. McCullough et al. 2017. Efficient In Vivo Gene Editing of Inherited Retinal Disease Genes in Mice and Non-Human Primates. Presentation, American Society of Gene & Cell Therapy, Washington, DC, May 13, 2017.

Branam, Ian. 2014. A Test Is a Useful Tool, But Can Lead to "Premature" Diagnosis (accessed February 2, 2017).

Branca, Malorye A. 2017. Geisinger's MyCode Genomics Data Brings Power to Precision Medicine and Research. *Clinical OMICs*, July/August 2017: 40–42.

Branca, Malorye A. 2017. How the Orphan Drug Act Changed the Development Landscape. T08:00:00 (accessed April 10, 2017).

Breckenridge, A., J. K. Aronson, T. F. Blaschke, D. Hartman, C. C. Peck, and B. Vrijens. 2017. Poor Medication Adherence in Clinical Trials: Consequences and Solutions. *Nat Rev Drug Discov* 16, vol. 3: 149–150. doi: 10.1038/nrd.2017.1.

Brennan, Zachary. 2016. FDA Says Real-World Evidence Could Generate "Incorrect or Unreliable Conclusions."

Brixner, D., E. Biltaji, A. Bress, S. Unni, X. Ye, T. Mamiya, K. Ashcraft, and J. Biskupiak. 2016. The Effect of Pharmacogenetic Profiling with a Clinical Decision Support Tool on Healthcare Resource Utilization and Estimated Costs in the Elderly Exposed to Polypharmacy. *J Med Econ* 19, vol. 3: 213–28. doi: 10.3111/13696998.2015.1110160.

Broad Institute. 2017. Questions and Answers About CRISPR. Broad Institute. https://www.broadinstitute.org/what-broad/areas-focus/project-spotlight/questions-and-answers-about-crispr (accessed May 15, 2017).

Brodersen, C., B. Kalis, C. Leong, E. Mitchell, E. Pupo, and A. Truscott. 2016. Blockchain: Securing a New Health Interoperability Experience. Accenture LLP.

Brody, Jane E. 2002. Personal Health; Statins: Miracles for Some, Menace for a Few. *New York Times* (December). https://www.nytimes.com/2002/12/10/health/personal-health-statins-miracles-for-some-menace-for-a-few.html (accessed February 19, 2017).

Brody, Jane E. 2014. Prescribing Vegetables, Not Pills. *New York Times* (December). http://well.blogs.nytimes.com/2014/12/01/prescribing-vegetables-not-pills/ (accessed January 30, 2017).

Bruzek, Alison, and Meghna Chakraparti. 2017. "An American Sickness" Diagnoses Our Health Care System (accessed April 12, 2017).

Bumpass, D. B., and J. B. Samora. 2013. Understanding Online Physician Ratings (accessed January 30, 2017).

Burwell, S. M., S. VanRoekel, T. Park, and D. J. Mancini. 2012. M-13-13—Memorandum for the Heads of Executive Departments and Agencies. Project Open Data.

Business Wire. 2012. Cigna Provides Highly Accurate Prices for 200+ Procedures and Health Professional Quality Information to Its U.S. Customers (accessed March 14, 2017).

Business Wire. 2014. Altos Solutions Acquired by Big Data Leader Flatiron Health (accessed May 9, 2014).

Business Wire. 2016a. cTAP Announces Two Research Publications Categorizing and Predicting Disease Progression in Duchenne Muscular Dystrophy (accessed April 5, 2017).

Business Wire. 2016b. Gem Leads Blockchain Investment for 2016 Securing $7.1M in Series A Funding (accessed January 6, 2016).

Business Wire. 2017. Illumina Introduces the NovaSeq Series—A New Architecture Designed to Usher in the $100 Genome.

Butler, Brandon. 2016. Why This Hospital Is Moving to Amazon's Cloud (accessed May 8, 2017).

Cadmus-Bertram, L., R. Gangnon, E. J. Wirkus, K. M. Thraen-Borowski, and J. Gorzelitz-Liebhauser. 2017. The Accuracy of Heart Rate Monitoring by Some Wrist-Worn Activity Trackers. *Ann Intern Med* 166, vol. 8: 610–12. doi: 10.7326/l16-0353.

Caffrey, Mary. 2017. Praluent to Stay on Market While Patent Feud Continues in Court (accessed April 3, 2017).

California Institute for Regenerative Medicine. 2016. Stem Cell Agency Focuses Almost $38 Million on Colorectal Cancer, a Deadly Childhood Disorder and High Blood Pressure in the Lungs. California's Stem Cell Agency.

Callaway, Ewen. 2016. Second Chinese Team Reports Gene Editing in Human Embryos. *Nature News.* doi:10.1038/nature.2016.19718.

Cao, K., C. D. Blair, D. A. Faddah, J. E. Kieckhaefer, M. Olive, M. R. Erdos, E. G. Nabel, and F. S. Collins. 2011. Progerin and Telomere Dysfunction Collaborate to Trigger Cellular Senescence in Normal Human Fibroblasts. *J Clin Invest* 121, vol. 7: 2833–44. doi: 10.1172/jci43578.

Capell, B. C., B. E. Tlougan, and S. J. Orlow. 2009. From the Rarest to the Most Common: Insights from Progeroid Syndromes into Skin Cancer and Aging. *J Invest Dermatol* 129, vol. 10: 2340–50. doi: 10.1038/jid.2009.103.

Captain, Sean. 2016. Paging Dr. Robot: The Coming AI Health Care Boom (accessed April 25, 2017).

Caraballo, Pedro J., Lucy S. Hodge, Suzette J. Bielinski, A. Keith Stewart, Gianrico Farrugia, Cloann G. Schultz, Carolyn R. Rohrer-Vitek et al. 2016. Multidisciplinary Model to Implement Pharmacogenomics at the Point of Care. *Genetics in Medicine.* doi: doi:10.1038/gim.2016.120.

CareDash. 2017. CareDash About—A Better Way to Find Doctors You Can Trust. CareDash, https://www.caredash.com/about (accessed April 23, 2017).

Carroll, John. 2014. Sanofi, Regeneron Pay $67M for a Shortcut in the Blockbuster PCSK9 Race with Amgen. FierceBiotech (accessed March 31, 2017).

Carroll, John. 2015. Big Science: Upstart Gritstone Bags $102M to Go After a New Immuno-Oncology Target. FierceBiotech (accessed April 30, 2017).

Carroll, John. 2016. Pfizer Dumps a Fading Pipeline Star, Giving Up on Its PCSK9 Drug Bococizumab (accessed April 3, 2017).

Carter, Jennifer. Personal interview with authors, April 11, 2017.

Cassels, Alan. 2016. Enthusiasm for PCSK9 Inhibitors to Lower LDL Cholesterol Is Premature (accessed April 3, 2017).

Castlight Health. 2017. Castlight Health. http://www.castlighthealth.com/ (last modified 2017, accessed January 21, 2017).

CCC Innovation Center. 2017. View Winners. https://www.cccinnovationcenter.com/challenges/block-chain-challenge/view-winners/ (accessed April 21, 2017).

Center for Drug Evaluation and Research, and U.S. Food & Drug Administration. 2017. Approved Drugs—Hematology/Oncology (Cancer) Approvals & Safety Notifications. U.S. Dept. of Health & Human Services. https://www.fda.gov/drugs/informationondrugs/approveddrugs/ucm279174.htm (last modified May 26, 2017, accessed May 31, 2017).

Center for Drug Evaluation and Research, and U.S. Food and Drug Administration. 2017. Genomics—Table of Pharmacogenomic Biomarkers in Drug Labeling. https://www.fda.gov/drugs/sciencere search/researchareas/pharmacogenetics/ucm083378.htm (last modified November 7, 2016, accessed February 9, 2017).

Centers for Disease Control and Prevention. 2015. Hepatitis C Information. Centers for Disease Control and Prevention. https://www.cdc.gov/hepatitis/hcv/ (last modified May 31, 2015, accessed January 27, 2017).

Centers for Disease Control and Prevention. 2016a. Clostridium Difficile Infection. https://www.cdc.gov/hai/organisms/cdiff/cdiff_infect.html (last modified March 1, 2016, accessed February 3, 2017).

Centers for Disease Control and Prevention. 2016b. FastStats—Health Expenditures. https://www.cdc.gov/nchs/fastats/health-expenditures.htm (last modified October 7, 2016, accessed January 31, 2017).

Centers for Disease Control and Prevention. 2016c. MRSA Tracking. https://www.cdc.gov/mrsa/tracking/(last modified April 13, 2016, accessed February 3, 2017).

Centers for Disease Control and Prevention. 2016d. Understanding Literacy & Numeracy. https://www.cdc.gov/healthliteracy/learn/understandingliteracy.html (last modified December 19, 2016, accessed January 21, 2017).

Centers for Disease Control and Prevention. 2017a. FastStats—Electronic Medical Records/Electronic Health Records (EMRS/EHRS). Centers for Disease Control and Prevention. https://www.cdc.gov/nchs/fastats/electronic-medical-records.htm (last modified January 18, 2017, accessed January 25, 2017).

Centers for Disease Control and Prevention. 2017b. Preventing Healthcare-Associated Infections (accessed February 3, 2017).

Centers for Medicare & Medicaid Services. 2014. Historic Release of Data Gives Consumers Unprecedented Transparency on the Medical Services Physicians Provide and How Much They Are Paid.

Centers for Medicare & Medicaid Services. 2015a. Hospital Readmission Reduction Program. https://www.cms.gov/Medicare/Quality-Initiatives-Patient-Assessment-Instruments/Value-Based-Programs/HRRP/Hospital-Readmission-Reduction-Program.html (last modified September 28, 2015, accessed February 2, 2017).

Centers for Medicare & Medicaid Services. 2015b. Hospital-Acquired Conditions (HAC) Reduction Program. https://www.cms.gov/Medicare/Quality-Initiatives-Patient-Assessment-Instruments/Value-Based-Programs/HAC/Hospital-Acquired-Conditions.html (last modified November 25, 2015, accessed February 2, 2017).

Centers for Medicare & Medicaid Services. 2016a. Better Care. Smarter Spending. Healthier People: Improving Quality and Paying for What Works. https://www.cms.gov/Newsroom/Media ReleaseDatabase/Fact-sheets/2016-Fact-sheets-items/2016-03-03-2.html (last modified March 3, 2016, accessed January 30, 2017).

Centers for Medicare & Medicaid Services. 2016b. First Release of the Overall Hospital Quality Star Rating on Hospital Compare.

Centers for Medicare & Medicaid Services. 2016c. Hospital Quality Initiative | Hospital Compare. https://www.cms.gov/Medicare/Quality-Initiatives-Patient-Assessment-Instruments/HospitalQualityInits/HospitalCompare.html (last modified October 19, 2016, accessed January 30, 2017).

Centers for Medicare & Medicaid Services. 2016d. Medicare Program; Merit-Based Incentive Payment System (MIPS) and Alternative Payment Model (APM) Incentive under the Physician Fee Schedule, and Criteria for Physician-Focused Payment Models. Federal Register.

Centers for Medicare & Medicaid Services. 2016e. National Health Accounts Historical. https://www.cms.gov/research-statistics-data-and-systems/statistics-trends-and-reports/nationalhealthexpenddata/nationalhealthaccountshistorical.html (last modified December 6, 2016, accessed June 9, 2017).

Centers for Medicare & Medicaid Services. 2016f. Value-Based Programs. https://www.cms.gov/Medicare/Quality-Initiatives-Patient-Assessment-Instruments/Value-Based-Programs/Value-Based-Programs.html (last modified April 21, 2016, accessed February 1, 2017).

Centers for Medicare & Medicaid Services. 2017a. Accountable Care Organizations (ACO)—Centers for Medicare & Medicaid Services. https://www.cms.gov/Medicare/Medicare-Fee-for-Service-Payment/ACO/index.html?redirect=/aco (last modified May 12, 2017).

Centers for Medicare & Medicaid Services. 2017b. FastStats—Health Expenditures. https://www.cdc.gov/nchs/fastats/health-expenditures.htm (last modified January 20, 2017).

Centers for Medicare & Medicaid Services. 2017c. Health Care Coverage Options for Incarcerated People.

Centers for Medicare & Medicaid Services. 2017d. National Health Accounts Projected. https://www.cms.gov/Research-Statistics-Data-and-Systems/Statistics-Trends-and-Reports/NationalHealthExpendData/NationalHealthAccountsProjected.html (last modified February 15, 2017, accessed March 14, 2017).

Centerwall, W. R., R. F. Chinnock, and A. Pusavat. 1960. Phenylketonuria: Screening Programs and Testing Methods. *Am J Public Health Nations Health* 50: 1667–77.

CG Life. 2017. Rare Diseases: The Role of Social Media in Patient Recruitment. *CG Life*. https://cglife.com/blog/rare-diseases-role-social-media-patient-recruitment.

Cha, Ariana Eunjung. 2016. $250 Million, 300 Scientists and 40 Labs: Sean Parker's Revolutionary Project to "Solve" Cancer. *Washington Post* (March). https://www.washingtonpost.com/news/to-your-health/wp/2016/04/13/250-million-300-scientists-and-40-labs-sean-parkers-revolutionary-project-to-solve-cancer/.

Chapman, Lizette. 2016. Silicon Valley Is Trying to Reinvent Health Care, Starting in New Jersey (accessed May 4, 2017).

Chapman, Lizette. 2017. Germany's Merck Taps Palantir for Big Data Health Initiative (accessed January 23, 2017).

Chapman, P. B., A. Hauschild, C. Robert, J. B. Haanen, P. Ascierto, J. Larkin, R. Dummer et al. 2011. Improved Survival with Vemurafenib in Melanoma with BRAF V600E Mutation. *N Engl J Med* 364, vol. 26: 2507–16. doi: 10.1056/NEJMoa1103782.

Charles, Dustin, Meghan Gabriel, and Michael F. Furukawa. 2014. Adoption of Electronic Health Record Systems among U.S. Non-Federal Acute Care Hospitals. Office of the National Coordinator for Health Information Technology, 2008–2013.

Chase, Dave. 2011. Why Google Health Really Failed—It's about the Money.

Chase, Dave. 2012. Aetna's Remarkable Reinvention Underway (accessed January 24, 2017).

Chen, Caroline. 2017. New Cholesterol Drug Falls Short as Sales Driver for Amgen. T20:08:17.176Z (accessed April 26, 2017).

Chen, M. S., Jr., P. N. Lara, J. H. Dang, D. A. Paterniti, and K. Kelly. 2014. Twenty Years Post-NIH Revitalization Act: Enhancing Minority Participation in Clinical Trials (Empact): Laying the Groundwork for Improving Minority Clinical Trial Accrual: Renewing the Case for Enhancing Minority Participation in Cancer Clinical Trials. *Cancer* 120, Suppl 7: 1091–6. doi: 10.1002/cncr.28575.

Chen, R., G. I. Mias, J. Li-Pook-Than, L. Jiang, H. Y. Lam, E. Miriami, K. J. Karczewski et al. 2012. Personal Omics Profiling Reveals Dynamic Molecular and Medical Phenotypes. *Cell* 148, vol. 6: 1293–307. doi: 10.1016/J.cell.2012.02.009.

Chen, S., J. Zhao, L. Cui, and Y. Liu. 2017. Urinary Circulating DNA Detection for Dynamic Tracking of EGFR Mutations for NSCLC Patients Treated with EGFR-TKIs. *Clin Transl Oncol* 19, vol. 3: 332–40. Doi: 10.1007/S12094-016-1534-9.

Children's Hospital of Philadelphia. 2017. Morquio Syndrome. T1753-04:00. http://www.chop.edu/conditions-diseases/morquio-syndrome (last modified March 15, 2014, accessed May 4, 2017).

Chilingerian, Jon A. 1995. Evaluating Physician Efficiency in Hospitals: A Multivariate Analysis of Best Practices. *European Journal of Operational Research* 80, vol. 3: 548–74.

Chiu, R. W., K. C. Chan, Y. Gao, V. Y. Lau, W. Zheng, T. Y. Leung, C. H. Foo et al. 2008. Noninvasive Prenatal Diagnosis of Fetal Chromosomal Aneuploidy by Massively Parallel Genomic Sequencing of DNA in Maternal Plasma. *Proc Natl Acad Sci USA* 105, vol. 51: 20458–63. doi: 10.1073/pnas.0810641105.

Choi, M., U. I. Scholl, W. Ji, T. Liu, I. R. Tikhonova, P. Zumbo, A. Nayir et al. 2009. Genetic Diagnosis by Whole Exome Capture and Massively Parallel DNA Sequencing. *Proc Natl Acad Sci USA* 106, vol. 45: 19096–101. doi: 10.1073/pnas.0910672106.

Choy, K. W., Y. K. Kwok, Y. K. Cheng, K. M. Wong, H. K. Wong, K. O. Leung, K. W. Suen et al. 2014. Diagnostic Accuracy of the Bacs-on-Beads Assay versus Karyotyping for Prenatal Detection of Chromosomal Abnormalities: A Retrospective Consecutive Case Series. *BJOG* 121, vol. 10: 1245–52. doi: 10.1111/1471-0528.12873.

ClinicalTrials.gov. 2017. The Circulating Cell-Free Genome Atlas Study. https://clinicaltrials.gov/ct2/show/NCT02889978 (accessed April 28, 2017).

Cogan, D. A., R. Aungst, E. C. Breinlinger, T. Fadra, D. R. Goldberg, M. H. Hao, R. Kroe et al. 2008. Structure-Based Design and Subsequent Optimization of 2-tolyl-(1,2,3-triazol-1-yl-4-carboxamide) Inhibitors of p38 MAP Kinase. *Bioorg Med Chem Lett* 18, vol. 11: 3251–5. doi: 10.1016/j.bmcl.2008.04.043.

Cohen, J. C., E. Boerwinkle, T. H. Mosley, Jr., and H. H. Hobbs. 2006. Sequence Variations in PCSK9, Low LDL, and Protection against Coronary Heart Disease. *N Engl J Med* 354, vol. 12: 1264–72. doi: 10.1056/NEJMoa054013.

Cohen, P. A., N. Flowers, S. Tong, N. Hannan, M. D. Pertile, and L. Hui. 2016. Abnormal Plasma DNA Profiles in Early Ovarian Cancer Using a Non-Invasive Prenatal Testing Platform: Implications for Cancer Screening. *BMC Med* 14, vol. 1: 126. doi: 10.1186/s12916-016-0667-6.

Colla, C. H., D. E. Wennberg, E. Meara, J. S. Skinner, D. Gottlieb, V. A. Lewis, C. M. Snyder, and E. S. Fisher. 2012. Spending Differences Associated with the Medicare Physician Group Practice Demonstration. *JAMA* 308, vol. 10: 1015–23. doi: 10.1001/2012.jama.10812.

Collins, Francis S., and Harold Varmus. 2015. A New Initiative on Precision Medicine. http://dx.doi .org/10.1056/NEJMp1500523. doi: NJ201502263720901.

Collins, Sara R., Petra W. Rasmussen, Michelle M. Doty, and Sophie Beutel. 2014. Too High a Price: Out-of-Pocket Health Care Costs in the United States. The Commonwealth Fund.

Colwell, Janet. 2016. Concierge Medicine Is Growing (accessed May 6, 2017).

CombiMatrix. 2016. Preimplantation Genetic Diagnosis (PGD). http://combimatrix.com/providers/pgd (last modified March 24, 2016, accessed May 25, 2017).

The Commonwealth Fund. 2016. New 11-Country Health Care Survey: U.S. Adults Skip Care Due to Costs, Struggle Financially, and Have the Worst Health. The Commonwealth Fund.

Compton-Phillips, Amy, and NEJM Catalyst. 2017. Care Redesign Survey: What Data Can Really Do for Health Care (accessed March 13, 2017).

Comstock, Jonah. 2014. Joslin, Glooko Add Activity Tracker Data to Their HypoMap Diabetes Management System (accessed February 17, 2017).

Comstock, Jonah. 2017a. CMS Issues Coverage Criteria, Billing Codes for Therapeutic CGMs (accessed March 24, 2017).

Comstock, Jonah. 2017b. The Qualcomm Tricorder X Prize Has Its Winner, But Work on Tricorders Will Continue (accessed April 13, 2017).

Comstock, Jonah. 2017c. Two Direct Primary Care Clinics Close, Calling Model's Viability into Question (accessed June 1, 2017).

Concert Genetics. 2017a. The Current Landscape of Genetic Testing: An Up-to-Date Overview of Market Size, Market Growth, and the Practical Challenges of the Clinical Workflow.

Concert Genetics. 2017b. GeneSource. https://www.nextgxdx.com/genesource (accessed January 17, 2017).

Condliffe, Jamie. 2017. DeepMind's New Blockchain-Style System Will Track Health-Care Records. *MIT Technology Review* (accessed April 21, 2017).

Condon, Stephanie. 2016. New Watson-Powered Service Aimed at Advancing Precision Cancer Treatments. ZDNet (accessed March 6, 2017).

Cong, L., F. A. Ran, D. Cox, S. Lin, R. Barretto, N. Habib, P. D. Hsu, X. Wu et al. 2013. Multiplex Genome Engineering Using CRISPR/Cas Systems. *Science* 339, vol. 6121: 819–23. doi: 10.1126/science .1231143.

Conn, Joseph. 2016. Could Blockchain Help Cure Health IT's Security Woes? (accessed November 5, 2016).

Consumer Purchaser Alliance. 2017. Fact Sheet: Hospital Readmissions Reduction Program. http://www .consumerpurchaser.org/files/Readmissions_Reduction_FactSheet.pdf (accessed February 2, 2017).

Consumer Reports. 2015. How We Rate Hospitals. *Consumer Reports*. http://www.consumerreports.org /cro/2012/10/how-we-rate-hospitals/index.htm (last modified June 1, 2015, accessed January 30, 2017).

Cooper, Charlie. 2015. Cancer Drugs Fund: Life-Extending Drugs to Be Denied to NHS Patients. *Independent* (accessed January 24, 2017).

Cooper, Daniel. 2017. A Future Apple Watch Could Be Essential for Diabetics (accessed May 8, 2017).

Copeland, B. J. 2000. What Is AI? AlanTuring.net. http://www.alanturing.net/turing_archive/pages /Reference Articles/What is AI.html (accessed May 16, 2017).

Corbelli, J., S. Borrero, R. Bonnema, M. McNamara, K. Kraemer, D. Rubio, I. Karpov, and M. McNeil. 2014. Physician Adherence to U.S. Preventive Services Task Force Mammography Guidelines. *Womens Health Issues* 24, vol. 3: e313–9. doi: 10.1016/j.whi.2014.03.003.

Coren, Michael J. 2017. A Futuristic Doctor's Office in San Francisco Aims to Create a New Operating System for Health Care (accessed May 5, 2017).

Cowley, Stacy. 2013. Doctors Blast Ethics of $100,000 Cancer Drugs (accessed March 2, 2017).

CRISPR Therapeutics. 2017. Our Pipeline. http://www.crisprtx.com/our-programs/our-pipeline.php (accessed May 15, 2017).

Crowe, Portia. 2016. There Is a "Game Changer" Technology on Wall Street and People Keep Confusing It with Bitcoin (accessed April 20, 2017).

Cryts, Aine. 2017. Healthcare Mergers and Acquisitions: What Payers, Providers Will Do in 2017. *Managed Healthcare Executive*. doi: http://managedhealthcareexecutive.modernmedicine.com/node/432919 (accessed May 4, 2017).

Culver, K. 2016. Blockchain Technologies: A Whitepaper Discussing How the Claims Process Can Be Improved.

Cutting, G. R. 2015. Cystic Fibrosis Genetics: From Molecular Understanding to Clinical Application. *Nat Rev Genet* 16, vol. 1: 45–56. doi: 10.1038/nrg3849.

Cyranoski, David, and Sara Reardon. 2015. Chinese Scientists Genetically Modify Human Embryos. *Nature News.* doi:10.1038/nature.2015.17378.

Dachis, Jeff; Chandra Osborn, David Rodbard, and Brian Huddleston. 2017. One Drop Mobile App Users Report Improved Glycemic Control. Annual Meeting & Scientific Sessions of the Society of Behavioral Medicine, San Diego, CA.

Dafny, Leemore, Kate Ho, and Robin S. Lee. 2016. The Price Effects of Cross-Market Hospital Mergers. National Bureau of Economic Research.

Daley, Beth. 2014. Oversold and Misunderstood (accessed March 7, 2017).

Dana-Farber Cancer Institute. 2014. Precision Medicine for Lung Cancer Marks Tenth Anniversary. Dana-Farber Cancer Institute: Boston, MA. http://www.dana-farber.org/Newsroom/News-Releases/Precision -medicine-for-lung-cancer-marks-tenth-anniversary.aspx (last modified April 23, 2014, accessed March 1, 2017).

Dartmouth-Hitchcock. 2017. What Is Value-Based Care? http://www.dartmouth-hitchcock.org/about_dh /what_is_value_based_care.html (accessed January 31, 2017).

Das, Reenita. 2017. Does Blockchain Have a Place in Healthcare? (accessed May 10, 2017).

Davies, Kevin. 2010. John Crowley Relives His Extraordinary Measures to Combat Pompe Disease.

Davila, M. L., I. Riviere, X. Wang, S. Bartido, J. Park, K. Curran, S. S. Chung et al. 2014. Efficacy and Toxicity Management of 19-28z CAR T Cell Therapy in B Cell Acute Lymphoblastic Leukemia. *Sci Transl Med* 6, vol. 224: 224ra25. doi: 10.1126/scitranslmed.3008226.

Davis, Karen, Kristof Stremikis, David Squires, Cathy Schoen. 2014. Mirror, Mirror on the Wall: How the Performance of the U.S. Health Care System Compares Internationally. The Commonwealth Fund.

Davis, Nicola. 2017. AI System as Good as Experts at Recognising Skin Cancers, Say Researchers. *Guardian* (January). http://www.theguardian.com/technology/2017/jan/25/ai-artificial-intelligence-recognise-skin -cancers (accessed January 30, 2017).

De Almeida, Melanie. 2017. How the CRISPR-Cas9 System is Redefining Drug Discovery (accessed May 23, 2017).

de Crescenzo, Neil. Personal interview with authors, April 11, 2017.

De Jong, A., W. J. Dondorp, C. E. M. de Die-Smulders, S. G. M. Frints, and Gmwr de Wert. 2010. Non-Invasive Prenatal Testing: Ethical Issues Explored. *Eur J Hum Genet* 18, vol. 3: 272–7. doi: 10.1038 /ejhg.2009.203.

De Ravin, S. S., L. Li, X. Wu, U. Choi, C. Allen, S. Koontz, J. Lee et al. 2017. CRISPR-Cas9 Gene Repair of Hematopoietic Stem Cells from Patients with X-linked Chronic Granulomatous Disease. *Sci Transl Med* 9, vol. 372. doi: 10.1126/scitranslmed.aah3480.

DeBrantes, Francois, and Suzanne Delbanco. 2016. 2016 Report Card on State Price Transparency. Catalyst for Payment Reform.

Deep 6 AI. 2017. How Deep 6 AI's Patient-Trial Matching Software Works. Deep 6 AI. https://deep6.ai /how-it-works/ (accessed May 24, 2017).

Deloitte. 2015. ConvergeHEALTH by Deloitte and Intermountain Healthcare Expand Real World Evidence Collaboration with Allergan to Focus on Women's Health. PRNewswire.

Deloitte. 2016. 2016 Global Life Sciences Outlook: Moving Forward with Cautious Optimism.

Deloitte. 2017. Life Science Solutions: Perspectives, Insights and Analysis—ConvergeHEALTH. DeloitteUS. https://www2.deloitte.com/us/en/pages/consulting/topics/life-sciences-convergehealth.html (accessed February 4, 2017).

DeloitteUK. 2017. Primary Care Today and Tomorrow. DeloitteUK. https://www2.deloitte.com/uk/en/pages /life-sciences-and-healthcare/articles/primary-care-today-and-tomorrow.html (accessed January 20, 2017).

Dennis, Carina. 2012. The Rise of the "Narciss-ome." *Nature.* doi: 10.1038/nature.2012.10240 (accessed February 15, 2017).

Denniston, Lyle. 2013. Opinion Recap: No Patent on Natural Gene Work. *SCOTUSblog* (June). http:// www.scotusblog.com/2013/06/opinion-recap-no-patent-on-natural-gene-work/.

Department of Health (U.K.), and Earl Howe. 2012. Government Opens Up Data to Benefit Patients and GPs. GOV.UK.

Department of Health & Human Services. 2014. Health IT Rules and Regulations. HealthIT.gov. https://www.healthit.gov/policy-researchers-implementers/health-it-legislation-and-regulations (last modified September 25, 2014).

Department of Health & Human Services. 2015. HIPAA for Professionals. https://www.hhs.gov/hipaa/for-professionals/index.html (last modified September 10, 2015).

Department of Health & Human Services. 2017a. Quality Payment Program Home Page. https://qpp.cms.gov/ (last modified September 10, 2015).

Department of Health & Human Services. 2017b. Read the Affordable Care Act, Health Care Law. https://www.healthcare.gov/where-can-i-read-the-affordable-care-act/ (accessed June 9, 2017).

Dickson, Ben. 2017. How Artificial Intelligence Is Revolutionizing Healthcare (accessed April 17, 2017).

Dietsche, Erin. 2015. 10 Things to Know about Kaiser Permanente School of Medicine.

Dietsche, Erin. 2017. Alleged Ransomware Attack Affects Emory Healthcare Patients (accessed May 8, 2017).

Diguilio, Sarah. 2017. These ER Docs Invented a Real Star Trek Tricorder.

DiMasi, J. A., H. G. Grabowski, and R. W. Hansen. 2016. Innovation in the Pharmaceutical Industry: New Estimates of R&D Costs. *J Health Econ* 47: 20–33. doi: 10.1016/j.jhealeco.2016.01.012.

Dodd, Susanna, Ian R. White, and Paula Williamson. 2012. Nonadherence to Treatment Protocol in Published Randomised Controlled Trials: A Review. *Trials* 13, vol. 1: 84. doi: 10.1186/1745-6215-13-84.

Doherty, R. 2015. Assessing the Patient Care Implications of "Concierge" and Other Direct Patient Contracting Practices: A Policy Position Paper from the American College of Physicians. *Ann Intern Med* 163, vol. 12: 949–52. doi: 10.7326/m15-0366.

Donders Institute. 2016. Parkinson's Cohort Study Kicks Off.

Doroshow, James H. 2017. Update: NCI Formulary & NCI-MATCH Trial.

Druker, Brian. 2017. A Better Way to Treat Cancer: Understanding Tumors. *Fortune Magazine* (accessed March 2, 2017).

Duffy, Tom, and Gemma Mullin. 2016. Teen's Life Saved by Fitbit after Device Detects Potentially Fatal Heart Condition. *The Mirror* (January). http://www.mirror.co.uk/news/uk-news/teens-life-saved-fitbit-after-7154991 (accessed February 17, 2017).

Dugan, Andrew. 2017. Cost Still Delays Healthcare for about One in Three in U.S. (accessed January 24, 2017).

Duke, C. C., B. Smith, W. Lynch, and M. Slover. 2014. The Effects of Hospital Safety Scores, Total Price, Out-of-Pocket Cost, and Household Income on Consumers' Self-reported Choice of Hospitals. *J Patient Saf.* doi: 10.1097/pts.0000000000000146.

The Economist. 2017. A Prescription for the Future: How Hospitals Could Be Rebuilt, Better Than Before. *The Economist* (April).

Editas Medicine. 2017. Our Programs. http://www.editasmedicine.com/pipeline (accessed May 15, 2017).

Ehrich, M., C. Deciu, T. Zwiefelhofer, J. A. Tynan, L. Cagasan, R. Tim, V. Lu et al. 2011. Noninvasive Detection of Fetal Trisomy 21 by Sequencing of DNA in Maternal Blood: A Study in a Clinical Setting. *Am J Obstet Gynecol* 204, vol. 3: 205.e1–11. doi: 10.1016/j.ajog.2010.12.060.

Ekblaw, A., A. Azaria, J. Halamka, and A. Lippman. 2016. A Case Study for Blockchain in Healthcare: "MedRec" Prototype for Electronic Health Records and Medical Research Data. MIT Media Lab: Beth Israel Deaconess Medical Center.

Elliott, L. S., J. C. Henderson, M. B. Neradilek, N. A. Moyer, K. C. Ashcraft, and R. K. Thirumaran. 2017. Clinical Impact of Pharmacogenetic Profiling with a Clinical Decision Support Tool in Polypharmacy Home Health Patients: A Prospective Pilot Randomized Controlled Trial. *PLoS One* 12, vol. 2. doi: 10.1371/journal.pone.0170905.

Ellison, Ayla. 2014. New Reimbursement Models to Eclipse Fee-for-Service by 2020 (accessed January 30, 2017).

Ellison, Ayla. 2015. Geisinger's Money-Back Guarantee is about More Than Refunds.

Elliston, Keith. Personal interview with authors, April 12, 2017.

Eltoukhy, Helmy. Personal interview with authors, April 12, 2017.

eMERGE Network. 2017. Welcome to eMerge > Collaborate. https://emerge.mc.vanderbilt.edu/ (accessed January 24, 2017).

Emerick, Tom. Personal interview with authors, April 11, 2017.

Endo, Akira. 2010. A Historical Perspective on the Discovery of Statins. *Proceedings of the Japan Academy, Series B Physical and Biological Sciences* 86, vol. 5: 484–93. doi: 10.2183/pjab.86.484.

Eriksson, M., W. T. Brown, L. B. Gordon, M. W. Glynn, J. Singer, L. Scott, M. R. Erdos et al. 2003. Recurrent De Novo Point Mutations in Lamin A Cause Hutchinson-Gilford Progeria Syndrome. *Nature* 423, vol. 6937: 293–8. doi: 10.1038/nature01629.

Esserman, L. J., I. M. Thompson, B. Reid, P. Nelson, D. F. Ransohoff, H. G. Welch, S. Hwang et al. 2014. Addressing Overdiagnosis and Overtreatment in Cancer: A Prescription for Change. *Lancet Oncol* 15, vol. 6: e234–42. doi: 10.1016/s1470-2045(13)70598-9.

Evaluate. 2017. EP Vantage PD-1/PD-L1 Combination Therapies. http://info.evaluategroup.com/PD1 -EPV.html.

Evangelidou, P., A. Alexandrou, M. Moutafi, M. Ioannides, P. Antoniou, G. Koumbaris, I. Kallikas, V. Velissariou, C. Sismani, and P. C. Patsalis. 2013. Implementation of High Resolution Whole Genome Array CGH in the Prenatal Clinical Setting: Advantages, Challenges, and Review of the Literature. *Biomed Res Int.* doi: 10.1155/2013/346762.

Evans, Dean. 2017. Cognitive Computing vs. Artificial Intelligence: What's the Difference? iQ UK (accessed March 31, 2017).

Evidation Health. 2017. Evidation Health—About. http://www.evidation.com/about/ (accessed May 8, 2017).

FAIR Health. 2017. FH Consumer Cost Lookup. https://fairhealthconsumer.org/ (accessed January 16, 2017).

Fan, H. C., Y. J. Blumenfeld, U. Chitkara, L. Hudgins, and S. R. Quake. 2008. Noninvasive Diagnosis of Fetal Aneuploidy by Shotgun Sequencing DNA from Maternal Blood. *Proc Natl Acad Sci USA* 105, vol. 42: 16266–71. doi: 10.1073/pnas.0808319105.

Fan, H. C., W. Gu, J. Wang, Y. J. Blumenfeld, Y. Y. El-Sayed, and S. R. Quake. 2012. Non invasive Prenatal Measurement of the Fetal Genome. *Nature* 487, vol. 7407: 320–4. doi: 10.1038/nature11251.

Farkona, S., E. P. Diamandis, and I. M. Blasutig. 2016. Cancer Immunotherapy: The Beginning of the End of Cancer? *BMC Med* 14: 73. doi: 10.1186/s12916-016-0623-5.

Farmer, Jessica, and Michael Hochman. 2017. Disruptions or Distractions: Learning from the Best in Value-Based Payment. Medpage Today (accessed April 19, 2017).

Farr, Christina. 2016. Apple Is Researching How iPhones Can Be Used to Monitor Parkinson's Patients (accessed November 16, 2016).

Farr, Christina. 2017a. Apple Has a Secret Team Working on the Holy Grail for Treating Diabetes (accessed September 5, 2017).

Farr, Christina. 2017b. Can "Digital Therapeutics" Be as Good as Drugs? *MIT Technology Review* (accessed April 17, 2017).

Federal Trade Commission. 2017. Advocate Health Care Network, Advocate Health and Hospitals Corporation, NorthShore University HealthSystem, In the Matter of Federal Trade Commission. https://www.ftc.gov/enforcement/cases-proceedings/141-0231/advocate-health-care-network-advocate -health-hospitals (last modified March 20, 2017, accessed May 5, 2017).

Fernandez, G., E. S. Spatz, C. Jablecki, and P. S. Phillips. 2011. Statin Myopathy: A Common Dilemma Not Reflected in Clinical Trials. *Cleveland Clinic Journal of Medicine* 78, vol. 6: 393–403. doi: 10.3949/ccjm.78a.10073.

Fernandopulle, Rushika. 2015. Breaking the Fee-for-Service Addiction: Let's Move to a Comprehensive Primary Care Payment Model. *Health Affairs Blog.* http://healthaffairs.org/blog/2015/08/17/breaking -the-fee-for-service-addiction-lets-move-to-a-comprehensive-primary-care-payment-model/.

Feyman, Yevgeniy. 2017. Don't Be Fooled: Patients Can Shop for Healthcare. *The Apothecary.* http://www .forbes.com/sites/theapothecary/2016/03/18/dont-be-fooled-patients-can-shop-for-healthcare/.

Fidler, Ben. 2014. CF Foundation Cashes Out on Kalydeco in $3.3B Sale to Royalty Pharma. *Xconomy* (accessed April 4, 2017).

Fine, Sean, Andrea Nix Fine. 2013. *Life According to Sam.* HBO Documentary Films.

Finkel, Elizabeth. 2012. *The Genome Generation.* Melbourne University Publishing.

Fisher, Lawrence M. 1999. The Race to Cash in on the Genetic Code. *New York Times* (August). https:// www.nytimes.com/1999/08/29/business/the-race-to-cash-in-on-the-genetic-code.html.

Fisman, Ray. 2007. The Bad Economics of Switching Health-Care Plans.

Flaherty, K. T., I. Puzanov, K. B. Kim, A. Ribas, G. A. McArthur, J. A. Sosman, P. J. O'Dwyer, R. J. Lee, J. F. Grippo, K. Nolop, and P. B. Chapman. 2010. Inhibition of Mutated, Activated BRAF in Metastatic Melanoma. *N Engl J Med* 363, vol. 9: 809–19. doi: 10.1056/NEJMoa1002011.

Fliesler, Nancy. 2016. Creating a Blueprint for Rare Disease Medicine. *Vector.* https://vector.childrens hospital.org/2016/02/creating-a-blueprint-for-rare-disease-medicine/.

FlowHealth. 2017. Flow Health Home Page. https://flowhealth.com/ (accessed March 21, 2017).

Fluegen, G., A. Avivar-Valderas, Y. Wang, M. R. Padgen, J. K. Williams, A. R. Nobre, V. Calvo et al. 2017. Phenotypic Heterogeneity of Disseminated Tumour Cells Is Preset by Primary Tumour Hypoxic Microenvironments. *Nat Cell Biol.* doi: 10.1038/ncb3465.

Fojo, T., S. Mailankody, and A. Lo. 2014. Unintended Consequences of Expensive Cancer Therapeutics—The Pursuit of Marginal Indications and a Me-Too Mentality That Stifles Innovation and Creativity: The John Conley Lecture. *JAMA Otolaryngol Head Neck Surg* 140, vol. 12: 1225–36. doi: 10.1001/jamaoto.2014.1570.

Fost, Dan. 2017. Catalyst for Cures: UCSF Program Gives Hope to People with Rare Diseases. Clinical & Translational Science Institute. http://ctsi.ucsf.edu/news/catalyst-cures-ucsf-program-gives-hope-people -rare-diseases (accessed April 11, 2017).

Foundation Medicine. 2014. Foundation Medicine Partners with EmergingMed to Offer Clinical Trial Navigation Services for Physicians and Patients. NASDAQ:FMI.

Foundation Medicine. 2017. FoundationOne. https://www.foundationmedicine.com/genomic-testing (accessed April 6, 2017).

Fox, Susannah. 2011. Peer-to-Peer Health Care. Pew Research Center.

Frank, S. R. 2000. Digital Health Care—The Convergence of Health Care and the Internet. *J Ambul Care Manage* 23, vol. 2: 8–17.

Fred Hutchinson Cancer Research Center. 2013. Leading Cancer Research Centers Team Up to Launch Biotech Startup Focused on Cancer Immunotherapy.

Fuchs, D. A., and R. K. Johnson. 1978. Cytologic Evidence that Taxol, an Antineoplastic Agent from Taxus Brevifolia, Acts as a Mitotic Spindle Poison. *Cancer Treat Rep* 62, vol. 8: 1219–22.

Gaffney, Alexander. 2014. First Pediatric Priority Review Voucher Goes Up for Sale, Fetching $67M (accessed May 1, 2017).

Galluzzi, L., and E. Lugli. 2013. Cancer Immunotherapy Turns Viral. *Oncoimmunology* 2, vol. 4: e24802. doi: 10.4161/onci.24802.

Ganda, O. P., and J. Mitri. 2016. Current Consensus and Controversies in Guidelines for Lipid and Hypertension Management in Diabetes. *Curr Cardiol Rep* 18, vol. 11: 114. doi: 10.1007 /s11886-016-0790-1.

Gandhi, Malay. 2017. What Digital Health Is (and Isn't). Rock Health. https://rockhealth.com/what -digital-health-is-and-isnt/.

Gandhi, Malay, and Teresa Wang. 2015. Digital Health Consumer Adoption. Rock Health.

Gandomi, Amir, and Murtaza Haider. 2015. Beyond the Hype: Big Data Concepts, Methods, and Analytics. *International Journal of Information Management* 35, vol. 2: 137–44. doi: 10.1016/j .ijinfomgt.2014.10.007.

Garde, Damian. 2014. Tomorrow's Cardio Blockbusters: Inside "The Next Big Leap" in Controlling Cholesterol. FierceBiotech (accessed March 31, 2017).

Garde, Damian. 2016. These Pricey Cholesterol Drugs Aren't Selling. And That Has the Biotech Industry Sweating. *STAT* (accessed May 3, 2017).

Garde, Damian, and Meghana Keshavan. 2016. Two Patient Deaths Halt Trial of Juno's New Approach to Treating Cancer (accessed March 6, 2017).

Gatlin, Allison. 2017. Regeneron Pops On "Better-Than-Feared" Eye. Cholesterol Drug Sales (accessed May 4, 2017).

Geddes, Linda. 2013. First Baby Born after Full Genetic Screening of Embryos (accessed March 8, 2017).

Geisinger Health Plan. 2014. Whole Exome Sequencing. In *Medical Benefit Policy*: Geisinger Health Plan. https://www.geisinger.org//media/OneGeisinger/Files/Policy%20PDFs/MP/251-300/MP280%20 Whole%20Exome%20Sequencing.ashx?la=en (accessed May 23, 2017).

Gelbman, Dekel. Personal interview with authors, April 11, 2017.

Genetic Alliance. 2017a. Genetic Alliance Registry & Biobank. http://www.biobank.org/ (accessed August 4, 2017).

Genetic Alliance. 2017b. PEER: Platform for Engaging Everyone Responsibly. http://www.peerplatform .org/ (accessed August 4, 2017).

Genetics Home Reference. 2012. Cystic Fibrosis. https://www.ncbi.nlm.nih.gov/pubmed/ (accessed May 3, 2017).

Genetics Home Reference. 2016. Pompe Disease. https://ghr.nlm.nih.gov/condition/pompe-disease (last modified February 2016, accessed May 22, 2017).

Genetics Home Reference. 2017a. Pantothenate Kinase-Associated Neurodegeneration. https://www.ncbi .nlm.nih.gov/pubmed/ (last modified March 21, 2017, accessed March 24, 2017).

Genetics Home Reference. 2017b. Phenylketonuria. https://ghr.nlm.nih.gov/condition/phenylketonuria (last modified February 1, 2012, accessed March 11, 2017).

Genetics Home Reference. 2017c. Pseudoxanthoma Elasticum. https://www.ncbi.nlm.nih.gov/pubmed /(last modified January 2015, accessed March 29, 2017).

Genetics Home Reference. 2017d. Trisomy 18. https://ghr.nlm.nih.gov/condition/trisomy-18 (accessed March 8, 2017).

Genetics Home Reference. 2017e. What Are Single Nucleotide Polymorphisms (SNPs)? U.S. National Library of Medicine. https://www.ncbi.nlm.nih.gov/pubmed/ (accessed March 28, 2017).

Genetics Home Reference. 2017f. What Is Pharmacogenomics? National Library of Medicine, https://ghr .nlm.nih.gov/primer/genomicresearch/pharmacogenomics (last modified June 6, 2017).

Genzyme. 2009. Key Milestones in Genzyme's Effort to Develop Myozyme, the First and Only Approved Treatment for Pompe Disease.

Giles, M. E., L. Murphy, N. Krstic, C. Sullivan, S. S. Hashmi, and B. Stevens. 2017. Prenatal cfDNA Screening Results Indicative of Maternal Neoplasm: Survey of Current Practice and Management Needs. *Prenat Diagn* 37, vol. 2: 126–32. doi: 10.1002/pd.4973.

Glance, David. 2015. Your Phone and Watch Could Warn You of Deadly Heart Problems. So Why Don't They? (accessed February 17, 2017).

Glaser, John. Personal interview with authors, May 4, 2017.

Global Genes. 2017. RARE Diseases: Facts and Statistics. http://globalgenes.org/rare-diseases-facts-statistics/ (last modified January 1, 2012).

Global Market Insights. 2016. Digital Health Market Size to Exceed $379bn by 2024. Global Market Insights.

Global Market Insights Inc. 2017. Precision Medicine Market Size to Exceed $87 Billion by 2023: Global Market Insights Inc. Global Market Insights.

Glooko. 2017. Glooko—Type 1 & 2 Diabetes Remote Monitoring Software. https//www.glooko.com/ (accessed February 17, 2017).

Glorikian, Harry. 2017. *Commercializing Novel IVDs: A Comprehensive Manual for Success*. Needham, MA: Insight Pharma Reports.

Goemans, N., M. Vanden Hauwe, J. Signorovitch, E. Swallow, and J. Song. 2016. Individualized Prediction of Changes in 6-Minute Walk Distance for Patients with Duchenne Muscular Dystrophy. *PLoS One* 11, vol. 10: e0164684. doi: 10.1371/journal.pone.0164684.

Goldbaum, Ellen. 2016. New Smartphone App Makes It Easy to Find—And Enroll In—Clinical Trials. University of Buffalo.

Goodman, Alice. 2016. One-Third of Patients With Advanced Melanoma Survive at Least 5 Years after Nivolumab Treatment. *The ASCO Post* (accessed March 6, 2017).

Google. 2011. An Update on Google Health and Google PowerMeter. *Google* (June). https://googleblog .blogspot.com/2011/06/update-on-google-health-and-google.html.

Gordon, L. B., W. T. Brown, and F. S. Collins. 1993. Hutchinson-Gilford Progeria Syndrome. In *GeneReviews(R)*, Ed. by R. A. Pagon, M. P. Adam, H. H. Ardinger, S. E. Wallace, A. Amemiya, L. J. H. Bean, T. D. Bird et al. Seattle, WA: University of Washington.

Gordon, L. B., M. E. Kleinman, J. Massaro, R. B. D'Agostino, Sr., H. Shappell, M. Gerhard-Herman, L. B. Smoot et al. 2016. Clinical Trial of the Protein Farnesylation Inhibitors Lonafarnib, Pravastatin, and Zoledronic Acid in Children with Hutchinson-Gilford Progeria Syndrome. *Circulation* 134, vol. 2: 114–25. doi:10.1161/circulationaha.116.022188.

Gordon, L. B., M. E. Kleinman, D. T. Miller, D. S. Neuberg, A. Giobbie-Hurder, M. Gerhard-Herman, L. B. Smoot et al. 2012. Clinical Trial of a Farnesyltransferase Inhibitor in Children with Hutchinson-Gilford Progeria Syndrome. *Proc Natl Acad Sci USA* 109, vol. 41: 16666–71. doi: 10.1073/pnas.1202529109.

Gori, Jennifer. 2017. CRISPR-Mediated Editing of Hematopoietic Stem Cells for the Treatment of Beta-Hemoglobinopathies. American Society of Gene & Cell Therapy, Washington, DC, May 11, 2017.

Graham, John. 2016a. Artificial Intelligence, Machine Learning, and the FDA.

Graham, Judith. 2016b. Medicaid, Private Insurers begin to Lift Curbs on Pricey Hepatitis C Drugs (accessed July 5, 2016).

Grand View Research. 2015. mHealth Market Is Expected to Reach $49.12 Billion by 2020. Grand View Research, Inc.

Grand View Research. 2016a. Drug Discovery Informatics Market. Industry Report, 2022. Grand View Research, Inc.

Grand View Research. 2016b. Healthcare Cognitive Computing Market Size Report, 2022. Grand View Research, Inc.

Grand View Research. 2016c. Liquid Biopsy Market Size to Reach $5.96 Billion by 2030. Grand View Research, Inc.

Grand View Research. 2016d. Non-Invasive Prenatal Testing Market Size. NIPT Industry Report, 2025. Grand View Research, Inc. http://www.grandviewresearch.com/industry-analysis/noninvasive-prenatal-testing-market (accessed March 8, 2017).

Grant, Howard. Personal interview with authors, April 11, 2017.

Green, Emma. 2016. Should Women Be Able to Abort a Fetus Just Because It's Female? (accessed March 11, 2017).

Gregg, A. R., S. J. Gross, R. G. Best, K. G. Monaghan, K. Bajaj, B. G. Skotko, B. H. Thompson, and M. S. Watson. 2013. ACMG Statement on Noninvasive Prenatal Screening for Fetal Aneuploidy. *Genet Med* 15, vol. 5: 395–8. doi: 10.1038/gim.2013.29.

Groopman, Jerome. 2009. Open Channels. *New Yorker* (May).

Gruessner, Vera. 2015. Yale Patient Portal Enhances Clinical Study Recruitment (accessed May 4, 2017).

Guccione, Darren. 2015. Is the Cloud Safe for Healthcare? (accessed May 8, 2017).

Gulshan, V., L. Peng, M. Coram, M. C. Stumpe, D. Wu, A. Narayanaswamy, S. Venugopalan et al. 2016. Development and Validation of a Deep Learning Algorithm for Detection of Diabetic Retinopathy in Retinal Fundus Photographs. *JAMA* 316, vol. 22: 2402–410. doi: 10.1001/jama.2016.17216.

Guo, J., C. M. Kelton, and J. J. Guo. 2012. Recent Developments, Utilization, and Spending Trends for Pompe Disease Therapies. *Am Health Drug Benefits* 5, vol. 3: 182–9.

Guzowski, Stephanie. 2015. The Lure of Rare Disease Drugs (accessed November 19, 2015).

Hackett, Robert. 2016. What Is Blockchain? *Fortune Tech* (May). http://fortune.com/2016/05/23/blockchain-definition/.

Hall, Stephen S. 2016. The Cancer Lottery: Precision Oncology Might Save Your Life, or It Might Do Nothing (accessed February 6, 2017).

Hamilton, Jon. 2012. Experimental Drug Is First to Help Kids with Premature-Aging Disease (accessed March 27).

Hammond, Kris. 2016. The Periodic Table of AI. Xprize. http://ai.xprize.org/news/periodic-table-of-ai (last modified December 14, 2016).

Hancock, Jay. 2013. More High-Deductible Plan Members Can't Pay Hospital Bills (accessed January 24, 2017).

Harmon, Amy. 2010. New Drugs Stir Debate on Rules of Clinical Trials. *New York Times* (September). https://www.nytimes.com/2010/09/19/health/research/19trial.html (accessed February 6, 2017).

Harris, Richard. 2017. Drugs That Work in Mice Often Fail When Tried in People (accessed May 4, 2017).

Hay, Timothy. 2014. Google Ventures Leads $130M Round for Big Data Medical Software Company Flatiron Health. *Wall Street Journal* (May). https://blogs.wsj.com/venturecapital/2014/05/07/google-ventures-leads-130m-round-for-big-data-medical-software-company-flatiron-health/.

HCPro Inc. 2012. *Consumer Reports* Launches First Hospital Safety Ratings. http://www.hcpro.com (accessed January 30, 2017).

Health Care Cost Institute. 2016. 2015 Health Care Cost and Utilization Report. Health Care Cost Institute.

Health Design Plus. 2017. Lowe's Centers of Excellence Program. http://www.hdplus.com/clients/lowes/lowesHipsandknees.php (accessed March 14, 2017).

HealthCare.gov. 2017. Affordable Care Act (ACA)—HealthCare.gov Glossary. https://www.healthcare.gov/glossary/affordable-care-act/.

HealthIT.gov. 2013. What Is Clinical Decision Support (CDS)? https://www.healthit.gov/policy-researchers-implementers/clinical-decision-support-cds (last modified January 15, 2013).

Healx. 2017. Advancing Treatments for Rare Diseases. https://healx.io/ (accessed May 24, 2017).

Heger, Monica. 2016. Sequenom Files Patent Infringement Suit against Ariosa, Others in Australia (accessed April 29, 2017).

Henig, Robin Marantz. 2005. Racing with Sam. *New York Times* (January). https://www.nytimes.com/2005/01/30/magazine/racing-with-sam.html (accessed March 28, 2017).

Herman, Bob. 2014. High-Deductible Plans Dominate Next Open Enrollment (accessed March 14, 2017).

Herman, Bob, and Shelby Livingston. 2016. Skimpier Employer Coverage May Accelerate under Trump Administration. *Modern Healthcare.*

Hernandez, Daniela. 2014. Startups Make On-Demand and Concierge Healthcare Reasonable for the Rest of Us (accessed May 5, 2017).

Hernandez, Daniela. 2017. Hospital Stumbles in Bid to Teach a Computer to Treat Cancer. *Wall Street Journal* (March). https://www.wsj.com/articles/hospital-stumbles-in-bid-to-teach-a-computer-to-treat-cancer-1488969011.

Herper, Matthew. 2011. The First Child Saved by DNA Sequencing. *Forbes* (accessed March 26, 2017).

Herper, Matthew. 2012. Three Lessons from GlaxoSmithKline's Purchase of Human Genome Sciences.

Herper, Matthew. 2017a. Illumina Adds IBM Watson to DNA Test for Cancer Patients (accessed January 23, 2017).

Herper, Matthew. 2017b. MD Anderson Benches IBM Watson in Setback for Artificial Intelligence in Medicine (accessed February 19, 2017).

Heywood, Ben. Personal interview with authors, April 12, 2017.

Heywood, Jamie. Personal interview with auhors, April 12, 2017.

Hill-Burns, E. M., J. W. Debelius, J. T. Morton, W. T. Wissemann, M. R. Lewis, Z. D. Wallen, S. D. Peddada et al. 2017. Parkinson's Disease and Parkinson's Disease Medications Have Distinct Signatures of the Gut Microbiome. *Mov Disord* 32, vol. 5: 739–49. doi: 10.1002/mds.26942.

Hillis, R., M. Brenner, P. J. Larkin, D. Cawley, and M. Connolly. 2016. The Role of Care Coordinator for Children with Complex Care Needs: A Systematic Review. *Int J Integr Care* 16, vol. 2. doi: 10.5334/ijic.2250.

Hillman, S. C., S. Pretlove, A. Coomarasamy, D. J. McMullan, E. V. Davison, E. R. Maher, and M. D. Kilby. 2011. Additional Information from Array Comparative Genomic Hybridization Technology Over Conventional Karyotyping in Prenatal Diagnosis: A Systematic Review and Meta-Analysis. *Ultrasound Obstet Gynecol* 37, vol. 1: 6–14. doi: 10.1002/uog.7754.

HIMSS Analytics. 2016a. 2016 HIMSS Analytics Cloud Survey.

HIMSS Analytics. 2016b. 2016 HIMSS Cybersecurity Survey.

Hirschler, Ben. 2017. New Drug Approvals Fall to Six-Year Low in 2016 (accessed January 2, 2017).

HIT Consultant. 2016. VA, Flow Health to Build AI-Powered Med Knowledge Graph for Veterans (accessed February 6, 2017).

HIT Consultant. 2017. Why Data Block Is the Leading Cause of Death for Digital Health Startups. HIT Consultant (accessed April 20, 2017).

Hoadley, Jack, Elizabeth Hargrave, Laura Summer, Juliette Cubanski, and Tricia Neuman. 2013. To Switch or Not to Switch: Are Medicare Beneficiaries Switching Drug Plans to Save Money?

Honore, P. M., R. Jacobs, I. Hendrickx, E. De Waele, J. Van Gorp, J. De Regt, and H. D. Spapen. 2017. Statins and the Kidney: Friend or Foe? *Blood Purif* 43, vol. 1–3: 91–6. doi: 10.1159/000453577.

Hood, Leroy. Personal interview with authors, April 12, 2017.

Hoos, A., and C. Britten. 2012. The Immuno-oncology Framework: Enabling a New Era of Cancer Therapy. *Oncoimmunology* 1, vol. 3: 334–9. doi: 10.4161/onci.19268.

Horowitz, Alan S. 2013. Let's Play Moneyball: 5 Industries That Should Bet on Data Analytics.

Hosanagar, Kartik, and Apoorv Saxena. 2017. The First Wave of Corporate AI Is Doomed to Fail (accessed April 19, 2017).

Hostetter, Martha, and Sarah Klein. 2015. In Focus: Innovating Care Delivery in the Safety Net.

Howard, Paul, and Yevgeniy Feyman. 2017. Yelp for Health: Using the Wisdom of Crowds to Find High-Quality Hospitals. Manhattan Institute.

HR Specialist. 2017. Employer-Provided Health Costs Rising Worldwide.

Huff, C. 2015. Direct Primary Care: Concierge Care for the Masses. *Health Aff (Millwood)* 34, vol. 12: 2016–9. doi: 10.1377/hlthaff.2015.1281.

Hughes, Lisa. 2017. Amazing Allison: A Young "Pioneer" and the Boston Doctors Who Saved Her (accessed February 3, 2017).

Hughes, Virginia. 2015. Pregnant Women Are Finding Out They Have Cancer from a Genetic Test of Their Babies.

Hui, W. W., P. Jiang, Y. K. Tong, W. S. Lee, Y. K. Cheng, M. I. New, R. A. Kadir et al. 2017. Universal Haplotype-Based Noninvasive Prenatal Testing for Single Gene Diseases. *Clin Chem* 63, vol. 2: 513–24. doi: 10.1373/clinchem.2016.268375.

Humer, Caroline. 2014. Express Scripts Drops Gilead Hep C Drugs for Cheaper AbbVie Rival (accessed January 17, 2017).

Husten, Larry. 2015. Precision Medicine Approaches Peak Hype (accessed April 25, 2017).

Husten, Larry. 2016. Pfizer Ends Development of Its PCSK9 Inhibitor (accessed April 3, 2017).

Huston, Matthew. 2017. Self-Taught Artificial Intelligence Beats Doctors at Predicting Heart Attacks. *Science* (accessed April 17, 2017).

Hyett, J. A., G. Gardener, T. Stojilkovic-Mikic, K. M. Finning, P. G. Martin, C. H. Rodeck, and L. S. Chitty. 2005. Reduction in Diagnostic and Therapeutic Interventions by Non-Invasive Determination of Fetal Sex in Early Pregnancy. *Prenat Diagn* 25, vol. 12: 1111–6. doi: 10.1002/pd.1284.

Hyman, D. M., I. Puzanov, V. Subbiah, J. E. Faris, I. Chau, J. Y. Blay, J. Wolf et al. 2015. Vemurafenib in Multiple Nonmelanoma Cancers with BRAF V600 Mutations. *N Engl J Med* 373, vol. 8: 726–36. doi: 10.1056/NEJMoa1502309.

Iannuzzi, M. C., M. Dean, M. L. Drumm, N. Hidaka, J. L. Cole, A. Perry, C. Stewart, B. Gerrard, and F. S. Collins. 1989. Isolation of Additional Polymorphic Clones from the Cystic Fibrosis Region, Using Chromosome Jumping from D7S8. *Am J Hum Genet* 44, vol. 5: 695–703.

IBM. 2016. IBM—What Is Cloud Computing? https://www.ibm.com/cloud-computing/learn-more/what-is-cloud-computing/ (last modified October 17, 2016, accessed May 8, 2017).

IBM Watson. 2016. IBM Watson Health—Genomics.

IBM Watson. 2017. IBM Watson for Oncology.

Ibrahim, M. X., V. I. Sayin, M. K. Akula, M. Liu, L. G. Fong, S. G. Young, and M. O. Bergo. 2013. Targeting Isoprenylcysteine Methylation Ameliorates Disease in a Mouse Model of Progeria. *Science* 340, vol. 6138: 1330–3. doi: 10.1126/science.1238880.

IMS Health. 2016. IMS Health Study: Global Market for Cancer Treatments Grows to $107 Billion in 2015, Fueled by Record Level of Innovation. QuintilesIMS.

Institute for Strategy & Competitiveness. 2017. Value-Based Health Care Delivery—Institute for Strategy and Competitiveness. Harvard Business School. http://www.isc.hbs.edu/health-care/vbhcd/pages/default.aspx (accessed January 31, 2017).

Institute of Medicine. 2010. *A National Cancer Clinical Trials System for the 21st Century: Reinvigorating the NCI Cooperative Group Program*. Washington, DC: National Academies Press (U.S.).

Institute of Medicine of the National Academies. 2012. Best Care at Lower Cost: The Path to Continuously Learning Health Care in America.

Intellia Therapeutics. 2017. R&D Pipeline: Looking Ahead. http://www.intelliatx.com/pipeline/ (accessed May 15, 2017).

Intermountain Healthcare. 2013. Intermountain Deloitte Forge Alliance Around Big Data and Analytics.

Introcaso, David. 2016. ACO Performance Year Three: What Happened and What Does It Mean? *The Health Care Blog*. http://thehealthcareblog.com/blog/2016/10/01/aco-performance-year-three-what-happened-and-what-does-it-mean/.

Iora Health. 2017. About Us. http://www.iorahealth.com/about-us/ (accessed May 3, 2017).

Jackson, K. L., M. Mbagwu, J. A. Pacheco, A. S. Baldridge, D. J. Viox, J. G. Linneman, S. K. Shukla et al. 2016. Performance of an Electronic Health Record-Based Phenotype Algorithm to Identify Community Associated Methicillin-Resistant *Staphylococcus aureus* Cases and Controls for Genetic Association Studies. *BMC Infect Dis* 16, vol. 1: 684. doi: 10.1186/s12879-016-2020-2.

Jain, Anil. Personal interview with authors, April 11, 2017.

James, J. T. 2013. A New, Evidence-Based Estimate of Patient Harms Associated with Hospital Care. *J Patient Saf* 9, vol. 3: 122–8. doi: 10.1097/PTS.0b013e3182948a69.

Janjigian, Janet. 2016. Heritage California ACO to Transition to Next Gen ACO. Heritage Provider Network.

Jarvis, Lisa M. 2013. Orphans Find a Home. *Chemical & Engineering News* 91, vol. 19.

Jha, Saurabh, and Eric J. Topol. 2016. Adapting to Artificial Intelligence: Radiologists and Pathologists as Information Specialists. *JAMA* 316, vol. 22: 2353–354. doi: 10.1001/jama.2016.17438.

Jones, L. H., and M. E. Bunnage. 2017. Applications of Chemogenomic Library Screening in Drug Discovery. *Nat Rev Drug Discov* 16, vol. 4: 285–96. doi: 10.1038/nrd.2016.244.

Jung, M. 2016. Breast, Prostate, and Thyroid Cancer Screening Tests and Overdiagnosis. *Curr Probl Cancer.* doi: 10.1016/j.currproblcancer.2016.11.006.

Kaiser Family Foundation. 2014. Employer-Sponsored Family Health Premiums Rise 3 Percent in 2014. The Henry J. Kaiser Family Foundation.

Kaiser Family Foundation. 2015. The Facts on Medicare Spending and Financing.

Kaiser Health News. 2015. Are Medicare ACOs Working? Experts Disagree (accessed April 12, 2017).

Kaiser Permanente. 2017. Kaiser Permanente School of Medicine. https://schoolofmedicine.kaiserpermanente.org/ (accessed May 31, 2017).

Kalia, S. S., K. Adelman, S. J. Bale, W. K. Chung, C. Eng, J. P. Evans, G. E. Herman et al. 2017. Recommendations for Reporting of Secondary Findings in Clinical Exome and Genome Sequencing, 2016 Update (ACMG SF v2.0): A Policy Statement of the American College of Medical Genetics and Genomics. *Genet Med* 19, vol. 2: 249–55. doi: 10.1038/gim.2016.190.

Kalish, Brian M. 2014. The Year in Exchanges: Where Private Exchanges Go from Here (accessed April 5, 2017).

Karachaliou, N., C. Mayo-de-las-Casas, M. A. Molina-Vila, and R. Rosell. 2015. Real-Time Liquid Biopsies become a Reality in Cancer Treatment. *Ann Transl Med* 3, vol. 3. doi: 10.3978/j.issn.2305-5839.2015.01.16.

Kavilanz, Parija B. 2009. Family Doctors: An Endangered Breed (accessed May 4, 2017).

Kelland, L. R., V. Smith, M. Valenti, L. Patterson, P. A. Clarke, S. Detre, D. End et al. 2001. Preclinical Antitumor Activity and Pharmacodynamic Studies with the Farnesyl Protein Transferase Inhibitor R115777 in Human Breast Cancer. *Clin Cancer Res* 7, vol. 11: 3544–50.

Kelly, Susan, and Bill Berkrot. 2015. Express Scripts Sees Opportunity to Lower Cancer Treatment Cost (accessed April 30, 2017).

Kern, Christine. 2014a. 6 Apps That Can Reduce Readmissions (accessed January 30, 2017).

Kern, Christine. 2014b. ACO Success Stories (accessed April 12, 2017).

Keshavan, Meghana. 2017. Illumina Says It Can Deliver a $100 Genome—Soon. 01-09T18:23:33-04:00.

Khoury, Muin J. 2016. The Shift from Personalized Medicine to Precision Medicine and Precision Public Health: Words Matter! *Genetics and Health Impact Blog* (April). https://blogs.cdc.gov/genomics/2016/04/21/shift/.

Kim, H. J., C. H. Kim, S. M. Lee, S. A. Choe, J. Y. Lee, B. C. Jee, D. Hwang, and K. C. Kim. 2012. Outcomes of Preimplantation Genetic Diagnosis Using Either Zona Drilling with Acidified Tyrode's Solution or Partial Zona Dissection. *Clin Exp Reprod Med* 39, vol. 3: 118–24. doi: 10.5653/cerm.2012.39.3.118.

King, Hope. 2016. Aetna Insurance Will Subsidize the Apple Watch (accessed April 19, 2017).

Kitsiou, S., G. Pare, M. Jaana, and B. Gerber. 2017. Effectiveness of mHealth Interventions for Patients with Diabetes: An Overview of Systematic Reviews. *PLoS One* 12, vol. 3: e0173160. doi: 10.1371/journal.pone.0173160.

Kitzman, J. O., M. W. Snyder, M. Ventura, A. P. Lewis, R. Qiu, L. E. Simmons, H. S. Gammill et al. 2012. Noninvasive Whole-Genome Sequencing of a Human Fetus. *Sci Transl Med* 4, vol. 137: 137ra76. doi: 10.1126/scitranslmed.3004323.

Kliff, Sarah. 2012. We Spend $750 Billion on Unnecessary Health Care: Two Charts Explain Why (accessed January 30, 2017).

Kliff, Sarah, and Dan Keating. 2013. One Hospital Charges $8,000—Another, $38,000. *Wonkblog* (January). https://www.washingtonpost.com/news/wonk/wp/2013/05/08/one-hospital-charges-8000-another-38000/.

Knapton, Sarah. 2017. Every Child with Cancer to Have Tumour DNA Sequenced to Find Best Treatment. *Telegraph* (March). http://www.telegraph.co.uk/science/2017/03/26/every-child-cancer-have-tumour-dna-sequenced-find-best-treatment/ (accessed March 27, 2017).

Knight, Will. 2016. An AI Ophthalmologist Shows How Machine Learning May Transform Medicine (accessed February 6, 2017).

Knox, Richard. 2017. As Cancer Drugs' Prices Skyrocket, Experts Worry about Burden on Patients, Health Systems (accessed March 1, 2017).

Koboldt, D. C., K. M. Steinberg, D. E. Larson, R. K. Wilson, and E. Mardis. 2013. The Next-Generation Sequencing Revolution and Its Impact on Genomics. *Cell* 155, vol. 1: 27–38. doi: 10.1016/j.cell.2013.09.006.

Kocher, Bob, and Bryan Roberts. 2014. Why So Many New Tech Companies Are Getting into Health Care (accessed January 24, 2017).

Kolata, Gina. 2013a. The Human Genome Project, Then and Now. *New York Times* (April). https://www.nytimes.com/2013/04/16/science/the-human-genome-project-then-and-now.html.

Kolata, Gina. 2013b. Rare Mutation Ignites Race for Cholesterol Drug. *New York Times* (September). https://www.nytimes.com/2013/07/10/health/rare-mutation-prompts-race-for-cholesterol-drug.html (accessed March 31, 2017).

Kolata, Gina. 2017. Cholesterol-Slashing Drug Can Protect High-Risk Heart Patients, Study Finds. *New York Times* (March). https://www.nytimes.com/2017/03/17/health/cholesterol-drugs-repatha-amgen-pcsk9-inhibitors.html?_r=1 (accessed March 31, 2017).

Kolata, Gina. 2016. More Men with Early Prostate Cancer Are Choosing to Avoid Treatment. *New York Times* (May). https://www.nytimes.com/2016/05/25/health/prostate-cancer-active-surveillance-surgery-radiation.html?_r=0 (accessed February 2, 2017).

Kolvraa, S., R. Singh, E. A. Normand, S. Qdaisat, I. B. van den Veyver, L. Jackson, L. Hatt et al. 2016. Genome-Wide Copy Number Analysis on DNA from Fetal Cells Isolated from the Blood of Pregnant Women. *Prenat Diagn* 36, vol. 12: 1127–1134. doi: 10.1002/pd.4948.

Konrad, C. V., R. Murali, B. A. Varghese, and R. Nair. 2017. The Role of Cancer Stem Cells in Tumor Heterogeneity and Resistance to Therapy. *Can J Physiol Pharmacol* 95, vol. 1: 1–15. doi: 10.1139/cjpp-2016-0079.

Kort, D. H., G. Chia, N. R. Treff, A. J. Tanaka, T. Xing, L. B. Vensand, S. Micucci et al. 2016. Human Embryos Commonly Form Abnormal Nuclei During Development: A Mechanism of DNA Damage, Embryonic Aneuploidy, and Developmental Arrest. *Hum Reprod* 31, vol. 2: 312–23. doi: 10.1093/humrep/dev281.

Krawiec, R. J., D. Barr, K. Killmeyer, M. Filipova, A. Nesbit, A. Israel, F. Quarre, K. Fedosva, L. Tsai. 2016. Blockchain: Opportunities for Health Care. Deloitte Consulting LLP.

Krieger, Lloyd M. 1996. Make Gatekeepers True Integrators of Patient Care. *Managed Care*, 1996-04-01T.

Kristensen, P. K., T. M. Thillemann, A. B. Pedersen, K. Soballe, and S. P. Johnsen. 2016. Socioeconomic Inequality in Clinical Outcome Among Hip Fracture Patients: A Nationwide Cohort Study. *Osteoporos Int*. doi: 10.1007/s00198-016-3853-7.

Kruszka, P., Y. A. Addissie, D. E. McGinn, A. R. Porras, E. Biggs, M. Share, T. B. Crowley et al. 2017. 22q11.2 Deletion Syndrome in Diverse Populations. *Am J Med Genet A* 173, vol. 4: 879–88. doi: 10.1002/ajmg.a.38199.

Kuderer, N. M., K. A. Burton, S. Blau, A. L. Rose, S. Parker, G. H. Lyman, and C. A. Blau. 2016. Comparison of 2 Commercially Available Next-Generation Sequencing Platforms in Oncology. *JAMA Oncol*. doi: 10.1001/jamaoncol.2016.4983.

Kuhrt, Matt. 2017a. Cleveland Clinic, Atrius Use Cognitive Computing to Fight Physician Burnout FierceHealthcare.

Kuhrt, Matt. 2017b. Geisinger's Nursing Bundle Improves Consistency, Quality of Patient Experience. FierceHealthcare (accessed April 18, 2017).

Kumar, Shefali, Leslie Oley, and Jessie Juusola. 2016. Efficiency of Virtual Recruitment Methods for Broad and Specific Study Populations. http://www.evidation.com/assets/research/efficiency-of-virtual -recruitment-methods-for-broad-and-specific-study-populations.pdf.

Kwan, A., and J. M. Puck. 2015. History and Current Status of Newborn Screening for Severe Combined Immunodeficiency. *Semin Perinatol* 39, vol. 3: 194–205. doi: 10.1053/j.semperi.2015.03.004.

Lamkin, Paul. 2017. Wearable Tech Market to Be Worth $34 Billion By 2020 (accessed February 17, 2017).

Landi, Heather. 2016. Cleveland Clinic, IBM Collaborating to Build Population Health, Value-Based Care Models. Linkis.com (accessed February 14, 2017).

Langreth, Robert, and Cynthia Koons. 2015. Investors Bet $100,000 Cancer Drug Prices Are Here to Stay. 13:25:00-0700.

Lash, Alex. 2016. Stanford Spins Out Immunotherapy Work Funded by CIRM's Millions. Xconomy (accessed April 30, 2017).

Leapfrog Group. 2016. Home: Hospital Safety Grade. http://www.hospitalsafetygrade.org/ (accessed January 30, 2017).

Leapfrog Group. 2017. Data Users. http://www.leapfroggroup.org/data-users (last modified October 16, 2015, accessed January 30, 2017).

Lee, Thomas H., and Laura S. Kaiser. 2016. Turning Value-Based Health Care into a Real Business Model. NEJM Catalyst (accessed January 31, 2017).

Leiter, A., T. Sablinski, M. Diefenbach, M. Foster, A. Greenberg, J. Holland, W. K. Oh, and M. D. Galsky. 2014. Use of Crowdsourcing for Cancer Clinical Trial Development. *J Natl Cancer Inst* 106, vol. 10. doi: 10.1093/jnci/dju258.

Lemke, Christine. Personal interview with authors, April 12, 2017.

Leslie, Nancy, and Laurie Bailey. 2017. Pompe Disease. doi: https://www.ncbi.nlm.nih.gov/books /NBK1261/.

Levey, Noam N. 2014. Where Employers Use Quality Control to Shape Healthcare. *Los Angeles Times* (December). http://www.latimes.com/business/healthcare/la-na-healthcare-employer-leadership-20141215 -story.html.

Lewis, Michael. 2004. *Moneyball: The Art of Winning an Unfair Game.* W.W. Norton & Company.

Li, B. D. L., W. A. Brown, F. L. Ampil, G. V. Burton, H. Yu, and J. C. McDonald. 2000. Patient Compliance Is Critical for Equivalent Clinical Outcomes for Breast Cancer Treated by Breast-Conservation Therapy. *Ann Surg* 231, vol. 6: 883–9.

Li, X., J. Dunn, D. Salins, G. Zhou, W. Zhou, S. M. Schussler-Fiorenza Rose, D. Perelman et al. 2017. Digital Health: Tracking Physiomes and Activity Using Wearable Biosensors Reveals Useful Health-Related Information. *PLoS Biol* 15, vol. 1: e2001402. doi: 10.1371/journal.pbio.2001402.

Lichtenstein, Marc. 2017. Health Insurance from Invention to Innovation: A History of the Blue Cross and Blue Shield Companies. Blue Cross Blue Shield. https://www.bcbs.com/node/982 (accessed January 20, 2017).

Liebman, Michael. Personal interview with authors, April 11, 2017.

Lin, Patrick. 2017. Blockchain: The Missing Link between Genomics and Privacy? (accessed May 9, 2017).

Linn, L. and M. Koo. 2016. Blockchain for Health Data and Its Potential Use in Health IT and Health Care Related Research.

Lo, Y. M., N. Corbetta, P. F. Chamberlain, V. Rai, I. L. Sargent, C. W. Redman, and J. S. Wainscoat. 1997. Presence of Fetal DNA in Maternal Plasma and Serum. *Lancet* 350, vol. 9076: 485–7. doi: 10.1016 /s0140-6736(97)02174-0.

Loew, Brian. 2011. The SCAD Ladies Stand Up Stories of Patient Empowerment.

Lusher, S. J., R. McGuire, R. C. van Schaik, C. D. Nicholson, and J. de Vlieg. 2014. Data-Driven Medicinal Chemistry in the Era of Big Data. *Drug Discov Today* 19, vol. 7: 859–68. doi: 10.1016/j .drudis.2013.12.004.

Macario, A. 2010. What Does One Minute of Operating Room Time Cost? *J Clin Anesth* 22, vol. 4: 233–6. doi: 10.1016/j.jclinane.2010.02.003.

Mack, Heather. 2016. Geoff Clapp Offers Post-Mortem on His Mayo-Backed Consumer Health Startup, Better (accessed May 4, 2017).

Mack, Heather. 2017a. EnsoData Receives FDA Clearance for Sleep Analysis Software (accessed April 17, 2017).

Mack, Heather. 2017b. UC Davis Taps Healbe to Validate Caloric Intake-Tracking Wearable Band (accessed May 8, 2017).

Mack, Heather. 2017c. Verily Introduces Health-Tracking Study Watch for Use in Clinical Research (accessed April 17, 2017).

Madhusoodanan, Jyoti. 2017. The Challenges of Rare-Disease Research. *Scientist Magazine* (September) (accessed May 1, 2017).

Maeng, D. D., D. E. Davis, J. Tomcavage, T. R. Graf, and K. M. Procopio. 2013. Improving Patient Experience by Transforming Primary Care: Evidence from Geisinger's Patient-Centered Medical Homes. *Popul Health Manag* 16, vol. 3: 157–63. doi: 10.1089/pop.2012.0048.

Maeng, D. D., J. Graham, T. R. Graf, J. N. Liberman, N. B. Dermes, J. Tomcavage, D. E. Davis, F. J. Bloom, and G. D. Steele, Jr. 2012. Reducing Long-Term Cost by Transforming Primary Care: Evidence from Geisinger's Medical Home Model. *Am J Manag Care* 18, vol. 3: 149–55.

Maeng, D. D., N. Khan, J. Tomcavage, T. R. Graf, D. E. Davis, and G. D. Steele. 2015. Reduced Acute Inpatient Care Was Largest Savings Component of Geisinger Health System's Patient-Centered Medical Home. *Health Aff (Millwood)* 34, vol. 4: 636–44. doi: 10.1377/hlthaff.2014.0855.

Maeng, D. D., J. P. Sciandra, and J. F. Tomcavage. 2016. The Impact of a Regional Patient-Centered Medical Home Initiative on Cost of Care among Commercially Insured Population in the U.S. *Risk Manag Healthc Policy* 9: 67–74. doi: 10.2147/rmhp.s102826.

Maeng, D. D., S. R. Snyder, C. Baumgart, A. L. Minnich, J. F. Tomcavage, and T. R. Graf. 2016. Medicaid Managed Care in an Integrated Health Care Delivery System: Lessons from Geisinger's Early Experience. *Popul Health Manag* 19, vol. 4: 257–63. doi: 10.1089/pop.2015.0079.

Maeng, D. D., X. Yan, T. R. Graf, and G. D. Steele, Jr. 2016. Value of Primary Care Diabetes Management: Long-Term Cost Impacts. *Am J Manag Care* 22, vol. 3: e88–94.

Mafi, John N., Christina C. Wee, and Roger B. Davis. 2017. Association of Primary Care Practice Location and Ownership with the Provision of Low-Value Care in the United States. *JAMA Internal Medicine.* doi: 10.1001/jamainternmed.2017.0410.

Makary, M. A., and M. Daniel. 2016. Medical Error—The Third Leading Cause of Death in the U.S. *Bmj* 353: i2139. doi: 10.1136/bmj.i2139.

Maki, Lisa. Personal interview with authors, April 11, 2017.

Manning, M., and L. Hudgins. 2010. Array-Based Technology and Recommendations for Utilization in Medical Genetics Practice for Detection of Chromosomal Abnormalities. *Genet Med* 12, vol. 11: 742–5. doi: 10.1097/GIM.0b013e3181f8baad.

Manos, Diana. 2017. Social Determinants: A Must for Value-Based Care and Population Health (accessed March 14, 2017).

Marabelle, A., B. Routy, J. Michels, G. Kroemer, and L. Zitvogel. 2016. Prime Time for Immune-Checkpoint Targeted Therapy at ASCO 2015. *Oncoimmunology* 5, vol. 3: e1068494. doi: 10.1080/2162402x.2015.1068494.

Marcus, Amy Dockser. 2011. Citizen Scientists. *Wall Street Journal* (December). https://www.wsj.com/articles/SB10001424052970204621904577014330551132036.

MarketWired. 2016. Clover Health Raises $160 Million Series C Funding Round. MarketWired.

Markland, Joe. 2014. Aetna Buys Bswift: Why Benefit Brokers Must Pay Attention (accessed January 24, 2017).

Maron, Dina Fine. 2016. A Very Personal Problem. *Scientific American* (May).

Marr, Bernard. 2015. How Big Data Is Changing Insurance Forever. *Forbes.*

Marr, Bernard. 2017. First FDA Approval for Clinical Cloud-Based Deep Learning in Healthcare (accessed January 23, 2017).

Martin, M. A., J. M. Hoffman, R. R. Freimuth, T. E. Klein, B. J. Dong, M. Pirmohamed, J. K. Hicks, M. R. Wilkinson, D. W. Haas, and D. L. Kroetz. 2014. Clinical Pharmacogenetics Implementation Consortium Guidelines for HLA-B Genotype and Abacavir Dosing: 2014 Update. *Clin Pharmacol Ther* 95, vol. 5: 499–500. doi: 10.1038/clpt.2014.38.

Mascalzoni, D., A. Paradiso, and M. Hansson. 2014. Rare Disease Research: Breaking the Privacy Barrier. *Appl Transl Genom* 3, vol. 2: 23–9. doi: 10.1016/j.atg.2014.04.003.

Masic, I., M. Miokovic, and B. Muhamedagic. 2008. Evidence-Based Medicine—New Approaches and Challenges. *Acta Inform Med* 16, vol. 4: 219–25. doi: 10.5455/aim.2008.16.219-225.

Mason, David. 2016. Health Catalyst Launches Open Source Machine Learning: Healthcare.ai. https://www.healthcatalyst.com/news/health-catalyst-launches-open-source-machine-learning-healthcare-ai/(accessed January 24, 2017).

Massachusetts General Hospital. 2017a. Concierge Medicine. Boston, MA. http://www.massgeneral.org/concierge-medicine/?display=overview (accessed May 4, 2017).

Massachusetts General Hospital. 2017b. Our Research—CATCH. Boston, MA. http://www.massgeneral.org/catch/our-research/ (accessed May 24, 2017).

Masunaga, Samantha. 2016a. Kaiser Permanente's New Medical School Will Be in Pasadena. *Los Angeles Times* (March). http://www.latimes.com/business/la-fi-kaiser-medical-school-20160310-story.html.

Masunaga, Samantha. 2016b. L.A. Startup Looks to Extend Concierge Medicine to Surgery. *Los Angeles Times* (June). http://www.latimes.com/business/la-fi-concierge-surgery-20160615-snap-story.html (accessed May 4, 2017).

Mathews, Anna Wilde. 2011. Insurer's Cost-Cut Plan: Buy Hospitals (accessed April 5, 2017).

Mayo Clinic. 2017a. About: Spontaneous Coronary Artery Dissection (SCAD). Mayo Clinic. http://www.mayo.edu/research/centers-programs/spontaneous-coronary-artery-dissection-scad/about/about (accessed March 29, 2017).

Mayo Clinic. 2017b. Medallion Program (accessed May 3, 2017).

McCann, Erin. 2014. Deaths by Medical Mistakes Hit Records (accessed January 30, 2017).

McCarthy, Jack. 2015. Hospitals to Triple Use of Cloud Services (accessed May 8, 2017).

McCarthy, Jack. 2016. Community Medical Centers Integrate Clinical Decision Support with Epic EHR (accessed February 21, 2017).

McConnell, M. V., A. Shcherbina, A. Pavlovic, J. R. Homburger, R. L. Goldfeder, D. Waggot, M. K. Cho et al. Feasibility of Obtaining Measures of Lifestyle from a Smartphone App: The MyHeart Counts Cardiovascular Health Study. *JAMA Cardiol* 2, vol. 1: 67–76. doi: 10.1001/jamacardio.2016.4395.

McGee, Marianne Kolbasuk. 2011. 5 Reasons Why Google Health Failed.

McGrory, Brian. 2012. Driven by Loss, Father Inspires Tireless Pursuit of a Cure. *Boston Globe* (February). http://archive.boston.com/news/local/massachusetts/articles/2012/02/09/joeys_long_legacy/.

McWilliams, J. Michael, Michael E. Chernew, Bruce E. Landon, and Aaron L. Schwartz. 2015. Performance Differences in Year 1 of Pioneer Accountable Care Organizations. http://dx.doi.org/10.1056/NEJMsa1414929. doi: NJ201505143722009.

Mearian, Lucas. 2017. IBM Watson, FDA to Explore Blockchain for Secure Patient Data Exchange (accessed January 23, 2017).

MediBid. 2017. Home. https://www.medibid.com/ (accessed January 22, 2017).

Medium. 2016. German Hospital Turns to Watson to Diagnose Rare Diseases (accessed March 29, 2017).

Medtronic. 2016. Medtronic and Fitbit Partner to Integrate Health and Activity Data into New CGM Solution for Simplified Type 2 Diabetes Management. Medtronic.

Meier, Barry, Jo Craven McGinty, and Julie Creswell. 2013. Hospital Billing Varies Wildly, U.S. Data Shows. *New York Times* (May). http://www.nytimes.com/2013/05/08/business/hospital-billing-varies-wildly-us-data-shows.html (accessed January 17, 2017).

Meldrum, Pete. Personal interview with authors, May 4, 2017.

Memorial Sloan Kettering Cancer Center. 2011. Treating Rare Cancers (accessed January 24, 2017).

Merchant, R. K., R. Inamdar, and R. C. Quade. 2016. Effectiveness of Population Health Management Using the Propeller Health Asthma Platform: A Randomized Clinical Trial. *J Allergy Clin Immunol Pract* 4, vol. 3: 455–63. doi: 10.1016/j.jaip.2015.11.022.

Mercom Capital Group. 2015. Executive Summary Healthcare IT Funding and M&A 2014 Fourth Quarter and Annual Report.

Mercuri, E., J. E. Signorovitch, E. Swallow, J. Song, and S. J. Ward. 2016. Categorizing Natural History Trajectories of Ambulatory Function Measured by the 6-minute Walk Distance in Patients with Duchenne Muscular Dystrophy. *Neuromuscul Disord* 26, vol. 9: 576–83. doi: 10.1016/j.nmd.2016.05.016.

Merkow, R. P., M. H. Ju, J. W. Chung, B. L. Hall, M. E. Cohen, M. V. Williams, T. C. Tsai, C. Y. Ko, and K. Y. Bilimoria. 2015. Underlying Reasons Associated with Hospital Readmission Following Surgery in the United States. *JAMA* 313, vol. 5: 483–95. doi: 10.1001/jama.2014.18614.

Merriam-Webster. 2017. https://www.merriam-webster.com/.

Mertens, F., B. Johansson, T. Fioretos, and F. Mitelman. 2015. The Emerging Complexity of Gene Fusions in Cancer. *Nat Rev Cancer* 15, vol. 6: 371–81. doi: 10.1038/nrc3947.

Messner, D. A., J. Al Naber, P. Koay, R. Cook-Deegan, M. Majumder, G. Javitt, P. Deverka et al. 2016. Barriers to Clinical Adoption of Next Generation Sequencing: Perspectives of a Policy Delphi Panel. *Applied Translational Genomics* 10: 19–24. doi: 10.1016/j.atg.2016.05.004.

Metcalf, Robert. Personal interview with authors, April 11, 2017.

Metz, Rachel. 2017. For $149 a Month, the Doctor Will See You as Often as You Want (accessed January 23, 2017).

Meyer, Denise L. 2017. Public Puzzled about Value in Health Care But Open to Change, Study Finds. Yale School of Public Health (accessed March 23, 2017).

Meyer, Erin. 2012. Social Media a Godsend for Those with Rare Diseases. *Chicago Tribune* (June). http://articles.chicagotribune.com/2012-06-12/news/ct-met-medical-social-networking-20120612_1_rare-diseases-social-media-social-networks (accessed March 29, 2017).

Might, M., and M. Wilsey. 2014. The Shifting Model in Clinical Diagnostics: How Next-Generation Sequencing and Families Are Altering the Way Rare Diseases Are Discovered, Studied, and Treated. *Genet Med* 16, vol. 10: 736–7. doi: 10.1038/gim.2014.23.

Might, Matt. 2012. Hunting Down My Son's Killer. *Matt Might*. http://matt.might.net/articles/my-sons-killer/.

Miller, Harold D. 2009. NRHI Healthcare Payment Reform Series Better Ways to Pay for Health Care. Network for Regional Healthcare Improvement.

Milstein, Arnold, Pranav P. Kothari, Rushika Fernandopulle, and Theresa Helle. 2009. Are Higher-Value Care Models Replicable? (accessed May 4, 2017).

Minemyer, Paige. 2017a. Lessons from the First Year of Geisinger's Money-Back Guarantee. FierceHealthcare.

Minemyer, Paige. 2017b. Press Ganey Report Links Patient Experience and Patient Safety. FierceHealthcare (accessed April 3, 2017).

Miseta, Ed. 2016. Can Digital Health Data Integration Lower the Cost of Drug Development? (accessed March 31, 2017).

Mnookin, Seth. 2014. Fighting a One-of-a-Kind Disease (accessed March 27, 2017).

Molteni, Megan. 2017. Medicine Is Going Digital. The FDA Is Racing to Catch Up.

Mom, Mitchell, and Ashlee Adams. 2016. Digital Health Funding 2016 Midyear Review. Rock Health. https://rockhealth.com/reports/digital-health-funding-2016-midyear-review/ (accessed January 24, 2017).

Monegain, Bernie. 2014. Interoperability: Now Geisinger Has an App for That (accessed March 14, 2017).

Monegain, Bernie. 2015. Boston Children's, IBM Watson Take on Rare Diseases (accessed March 29, 2017).

Moon, Freda. 2017. A Family Adventure in Medical Tourism. *New York Times* (March) (accessed March 15, 2017).

Moran, Jessica Mulvihill. 2016. A Father's Mission: How One Man Developed a Drug to Save the Lives of His Children. *Fox News*. doi: 507f53f9-4cd0-4258-8fdb-bd57030357bf.

Morawski, K., R. Ghazinouri, A. Krumme, J. McDonough, E. Durfee, L. Oley, N. Mohta, J. Juusola, and N. K. Choudhry. 2017. Rationale and Design of the Medication Adherence Improvement Support App for Engagement-Blood Pressure (MedISAFE-BP) trial. *Am Heart J* 186: 40–47. doi: 10.1016/j.ahj.2016.11.007.

Morris, Z. S., S. Wooding, and J. Grant. 2011. The Answer Is 17 Years, What Is the Question: Understanding Time Lags in Translational Research. *J R Soc Med* 104, vol. 12: 510–20. doi: 10.1258/jrsm.2011.110180.

Morse, Susan. 2016. New Report Sheds Doubt on Whether Hospital Mergers Save Money (accessed May 4, 2017).

Moscelli, G., L. Siciliani, N. Gutacker, and H. Gravelle. 2016. Location, Quality and Choice of Hospital: Evidence from England 2002–2013. *Reg Sci Urban Econ* 60: 112–24. doi: 10.1016/j.regsciurbeco.2016.07.001.

Moses, Kathy, and Rachel Davis. 2015. Housing Is a Prescription for Better Health.

Mullen, J., S. J. Cockell, P. Woollard, and A. Wipat. 2016. An Integrated Data Driven Approach to Drug Repositioning Using Gene-Disease Associations. *PLoS One* 11, vol. 5: e0155811. doi: 10.1371/journal.pone.0155811.

Mullin, Emily. 2017. When Even Genome Sequencing Doesn't Give a Diagnosis. *MIT Technology Review* (accessed April 22, 2017).

Murphy, Kenneth M., Paul Travers, and Mark Walport. 2007. *Janeway's Immunobiology*. Garland Science.

Murthy, V. H., H. M. Krumholz, and C. P. Gross. 2004. Participation in Cancer Clinical Trials: Race-, Sex-, and Age-Based Disparities. *JAMA* 291, vol. 22: 2720–6. doi: 10.1001/jama.291.22.2720.

Nanalyze. 2016. 4 Companies Using Deep Learning for Drug Discovery (accessed April 4, 2017).

Narain, Niven. Personal interview with authors, April 11, 2017.

National Academies. 2012. Transformation of Health System Needed to Improve Care and Reduce Costs. National Academies of Sciences, Engineering, Medicine.

National Cancer Institute. 2015. Tumor Markers. https://www.cancer.gov/about-cancer/diagnosis-staging /diagnosis/tumor-markers-fact-sheet (last modified November 4, 2015, accessed March 5, 2017).

National Cancer Institute. 2017a. Cancer Statistics. https://www.cancer.gov/about-cancer/understanding /statistics (last modified March 22, 2017, accessed June 7, 2017).

National Cancer Institute. 2017b. Definition of Biorepository—NCI Dictionary of Cancer Terms. https:// www.cancer.gov/publications/dictionaries/cancer-terms?cdrid=561323.

National Cancer Institute. 2017c. NCI-Molecular Analysis for Therapy Choice (NCI-MATCH) Trial. National Institutes of Health. https://www.cancer.gov/about-cancer/treatment/clinical-trials/nci-sup ported/nci-match (accessed January 24, 2017).

National Cancer Institute. 2017d. What Is Proteomics?—Office of Cancer Clinical Proteomics Research. https://proteomics.cancer.gov/whatisproteomics.

National Center for Advancing Translational Sciences. 2016. FAQs about Rare Diseases: Genetic and Rare Diseases Information Center. https://rarediseases.info.nih.gov/diseases/pages/31/faqs-about-rare-diseases (last modified August 11, 2016, accessed May 22, 2017).

National Center for Advancing Translational Sciences. 2017. Funding Opportunities for Repurposing Existing Drugs. https://www.ncbi.nlm.nih.gov/pubmed/ (last modified February 21, 2017, accessed May 24, 2017).

National Center for Health Statistics. 2016. Health, United States, 2015: With Special Feature on Racial and Ethnic Health Disparities. Hyattsville, MD.

National Center for Veterans Analysis and Statistics. 2016. Department of Veterans Affairs Statistics at a Glance. Ed. by U.S. Department of Veterans Affairs.

National Human Genome Research Institute. 2016. The Cost of Sequencing a Human Genome. National Institutes of Health https://www.genome.gov/27565109/The-Cost-of-Sequencing-a-Human-Genome (accessed June 9, 2017).

National Institutes of Health. 2017. Genomic Sequencing for Childhood Risk and Newborn Illness. ClinicalTrials.gov. https://clinicaltrials.gov/ct2/show/NCT02422511 (accessed March 11, 2017).

National Multiple Sclerosis Society. 2017. Types of MS. http://www.nationalmssociety.org/What-is-MS /Types-of-MS (accessed May 3, 2017).

National Newborn Screening & Global Resource Center. 2017. Newborn Screening. http://genes-r-us.uthscsa .edu/resources/consumer/statemap.htm (last modified November 3, 2014, accessed March 24, 2017).

National Organization for Rare Disorders. 2015. Congenital Disorders of Glycosylation (accessed March 29, 2017).

Nature.com. 2017. Transcriptomics. *Nature*. https://www.nature.com/subjects/transcriptomics.

Need, A. C., V. Shashi, Y. Hitomi, K. Schoch, K. V. Shianna, M. T. McDonald, M. H. Meisler, and D. B. Goldstein. 2012. Clinical Application of Exome Sequencing in Undiagnosed Genetic Conditions. *J Med Genet* 49, vol. 6: 353–61. doi: 10.1136/jmedgenet-2012-100819.

Ness, Sheryl M. 2013. Molecular Profiling: Personalizing Your Cancer Treatment. Mayo Clinic. http://www .mayoclinic.org/diseases-conditions/cancer/expert-blog/molecular-profiling/bgp-20056382 (last modified July 3, 2013, accessed April 27, 2017).

Network for Excellence in Health Innovation. 2015. Real-World Evidence: A New Era for Health Care Innovation.

New England Journal of Medicine. 2017. Home: The SPRINT Data Analysis Challenge. https://challenge .nejm.org/groups/sprint-data-analysis-challenge/pages/home (accessed February 17, 2017).

Newman, S. K., R. K. Jayanthan, G. W. Mitchell, J. A. Carreras Tartak, M. P. Croglio, A. Suarez, A. Y. Liu, B. M. Razzo, E. Oyeniran, J. R. Ruth, and D. C. Fajgenbaum. 2015. Taking Control of Castleman Disease: Leveraging Precision Medicine Technologies to Accelerate Rare Disease Research. *Yale J Biol Med* 88, vol. 4: 383–8.

Ng, Alfred. 2016. IBM's Watson Gives Proper Diagnosis after Doctors Were Stumped. *New York Daily News*, 2016-08-07T14:47:16-0400. http://www.nydailynews.com/news/world/ibm-watson-proper-diagno sis-doctors-stumped-article-1.2741857 (accessed March 6, 2017).

Nicholas Volker One in a Billion Foundation. 2017. One in a Billion: Our History. http://www.oneinabillionic .com/our-history/ (accessed April 30, 2017).

Noah, Timothy. 2007. A Short History of Health Care (accessed January 17, 2017).

Norton, Stan. Personal interview with authors, April 12, 2017.

Nowogrodzki, Anna. 2015. Prenatal Blood Tests Can Also Detect Cancer in Pregnant Women.

O'Connor, Clare. 2008. Fluorescence In Situ Hybridization (FISH). *Nature Education* 1, vol. 1: 171.

O'Matz, Megan. 2016. Limb-Lengthening Doctor Faces State Complaint. *Sun Sentinel* (March). http://www .sun-sentinel.com/local/palm-beach/fl-doctor-dror-paley-20160318-story.html (accessed February 2, 2017).

OECD Statistics Directorate. 2007. OECD Glossary of Statistical Terms: Biobank Definition. https://stats .oecd.org/glossary/detail.asp?ID=7220 (last modified July 23, 2007).

Office on Women's Health, and U.S. Department of Health and Human Services. 2017. Prenatal Care and Tests. https://www.womenshealth.gov/pregnancy/youre-pregnant-now-what/prenatal-care-and-tests (last modified February 1, 2017, accessed March 8, 2017).

Olen, Helaine. 2017. Why Won't More American Corporations Support Single-Payer Health Care? *The Nation*. T09:39:09-04:00 (accessed May 22, 2017).

Ong, Kimberley. 2013. For the Love of Snakes, Online Ads & Cancer Cures: Invite Media's Nat Turner (W'08) Turns a Page after >$80M Google Exit. *Wharton Journal* (accessed January 24, 2017).

Orelli, Brian. 2017. BioMarin Pharmaceutical Inc. Logs a Combined Blockbuster—The Motley Fool.

Organisation for Economic Co-operation and Development (OECD). 2017. Health, Health Expenditure. http://www.oecd.org/health/health-expenditure.htm (accessed January 24, 2017).

Orri, M., C. H. Lipset, B. P. Jacobs, A. J. Costello, and S. R. Cummings. 2014. Web-Based Trial to Evaluate the Efficacy and Safety of Tolterodine ER 4 mg in Participants with Overactive Bladder: REMOTE Trial. *Contemp Clin Trials* 38, vol. 2: 190–7. doi: 10.1016/j.cct.2014.04.009.

Osborn, R., D. Squires, M. M. Doty, D. O. Sarnak, and E. C. Schneider. 2016. In New Survey of Eleven Countries, U.S. Adults Still Struggle with Access to and Affordability of Health Care. *Health Aff (Millwood)* 35 vol. 12: 2327–36. doi: 10.1377/hlthaff.2016.1088.

Ossola, Alexandra. 2017. Betting on the First Disease to Be Treated by Gene Editing (accessed March 15, 2017).

Pacific Business Group on Health. 2017. Employers Centers of Excellence Network. http://www.pbgh.org/ecen.

Paez, J. G., P. A. Janne, J. C. Lee, S. Tracy, H. Greulich, S. Gabriel, P. Herman, F. J. Kaye, N. Lindeman, T. J. Boggon, K. Naoki, H. Sasaki, Y. Fujii, M. J. Eck, W. R. Sellers, B. E. Johnson, and M. Meyerson. 2004. EGFR Mutations in Lung Cancer: Correlation With Clinical Response to Gefitinib Therapy. *Science* 304, vol. 5676: 1497–500. doi: 10.1126/science.1099314.

Pai, Aditi. 2015. Iora Health Raises $28M to Expand its Digital Health-Enabled, Primary Care Practices (accessed May 4, 2017).

Palabindala, V., A. Pamarthy, and N. R. Jonnalagadda. 2016. Adoption of Electronic Health Records and Barriers. *J Community Hosp Intern Med Perspect*.

Palladino, Valentina. 2016. ER Docs Get Heart Rate Info from Fitbit, Save Patient's Life (accessed February 17, 2017).

Pallardy, Carrie. 2016. Epic to Integrate Pharmacogentic Testing Clinical Decision Support System into EHRs (accessed February 20, 2017).

Palomaki, G. E., E. M. Kloza, G. M. Lambert-Messerlian, J. E. Haddow, L. M. Neveux, M. Ehrich, D. van den Boom et al. 2011. DNA Sequencing of Maternal Plasma to Detect Down Syndrome: An International Clinical Validation Study. *Genet Med* 13, vol. 11: 913–20. doi: 10.1097/GIM.0b013e3182368a0e.

Paris, V.; Devaux, M.; Wei, L. 2010. Health Systems Institutional Characteristics: A Survey of 29 OECD Countries. OECD *Health Working Papers*, 50. Paris.

Park, S., J. Y. Hur, K. Y. Lee, J. C. Lee, J. K. Rho, S. H. Shin, and C. M. Choi. 2017. Assessment of EGFR Mutation Status Using Cell-Free DNA from Bronchoalveolar Lavage Fluid. *Clin Chem Lab Med*. doi: 10.1515/cclm-2016-0302.

Park, S. Y., I. A. Jang, M. A. Lee, Y. J. Kim, S. H. Chun, and M. H. Park. 2016. Screening for Chromosomal Abnormalities Using Combined Test in the First Trimester of Pregnancy. *Obstet Gynecol Sci* 59, vol. 5: 357–66. doi: 10.5468/ogs.2016.59.5.357.

Parker Institute for Cancer Immunotherapy. 2017. Parker Institute for Cancer Immunotherapy, Bristol-Myers Squibb and the Cancer-Parker Institute for Cancer Immunotherapy.

Parmar, Arundhati. 2017. Will the Rise of the Machines Imperil Radiologists? (accessed January 23, 2017).

Pasley, Jessica. 2017. Non-Invasive Prenatal Screening's Popularity on Rise. *Reporter* (January). https://news.vanderbilt.edu/2017/01/12/non-invasive-prenatal-screenings-popularity-on-rise/.

Patel, C. J., N. Pho, M. McDuffie, J. Easton-Marks, C. Kothari, I. S. Kohane, and P. Avillach. 2016a. A Database of Human Exposomes and Phenomes from the U.S. National Health and Nutrition Examination Survey. *Sci Data* 3: 160096. doi: 10.1038/sdata.2016.96.

Patel, N. H., H. K. Bhadarka, K. B. Patel, S. N. Vaniawala, A. Acharya, P. N. Mukhopadhyaya, and N. R. Sodagar. 2016b. Embryo Genome Profiling by Single-Cell Sequencing for Successful Preimplantation Genetic Diagnosis in a Family Harboring COL4A1 c.1537G>A; p.G513S Mutation. *J Hum Reprod Sci* 9, vol. 3: 200–6. doi: 10.4103/0974-1208.192072.

Patient-Centered Primary Care Collaborative. 2017. Defining the Medical Home. https://www.pcpcc.org/about/medical-home (accessed January 24, 2017).

PatientsLikeMe. 2017. About Us. https://www.patientslikeme.com/about (accessed May 2, 2017).

Peckham, Carol. 2016. Medscape Physician Compensation Report 2016.

Peikoff, Kira. 2014. Fearing Punishment for Bad Genes. *New York Times* (April). https://www.nytimes.com/2014/04/08/science/fearing-punishment-for-bad-genes.html.

Pellini, Michael. Personal interview with authors, April 12, 2017.

Pennic, Jasmine. 2017. Healthcare Blockchain Startup Hashed Health Lands Nearly $2M in Funding (accessed February 16, 2017).

Perna, Gabriel. 2013. Digging Deeper: Lessons from an ACO Success Story. *Healthcare Informatics* (October). https://www.healthcare-informatics.com/blogs/gabriel-perna/digging-deeper-lessons-aco-success-story.

Peter G. Peterson Foundation. 2016. International Ranking—Health Outcomes. http://www.pgpf.org/chart-archive/0011_health-outcomes (accessed February 1, 2017).

Pew Charitable Trusts. 2014. State Prison Health Care Spending.

Pham, H. H., P. B. Ginsburg, K. McKenzie, and A. Milstein. 2007. Redesigning Care Delivery in Response to a High-Performance Network: The Virginia Mason Medical Center. *Health Aff (Millwood)* 26, vol. 4: w532-44. doi: 10.1377/hlthaff.26.4.w532.

Pharmaceutical-technology.com. 2016. The World's Most Sold Cancer Drugs in 2015. http://www.pharmaceutical-technology.com/features/featurethe-worlds-most-sold-cancer-drugs-in-2015-4852126/ (last modified March 31, 2016, accessed March 5, 2017).

The Pharma Letter. 2011. GlaxoSmithKline/HGS Lupus Drug Benlysta Cleared by U.S. FDA (accessed April 5, 2017).

PharmaVoice. 2017. Focus on Rare Diseases. *PharmaVOICE*.

Phend, Crystal. 2016. Update: PCSK9 Inhibitors Hit the Market (accessed April 3, 2017).

Philips. 2017. Illumeo: Adaptive Intelligence in Radiology PACS. Philips Healthcare. http://www.usa.philips.com/healthcare/product/HC881040/illumeo (accessed May 30, 2017).

PhRMA. 2015. 836 Medicines and Vaccines in Development to Treat Cancer.

PhRMA. 2016. 2016 Profile Biopharmaceutical Research Industry.

Phys.org. 2017. Machine Learning Models for Drug Discovery.

Pol, J., G. Kroemer, and L. Galluzzi. 2016. First Oncolytic Virus Approved for Melanoma Immunotherapy. *Oncoimmunology* 5, vol. 1: e1115641. doi: 10.1080/2162402x.2015.1115641.

Pollack, Andrew. 2004. TECHNOLOGY: Human Genome Sciences Faces Shift in Leadership and Focus. *New York Times* (March). https://www.nytimes.com/2004/03/25/business/technology-human-genome-sciences-faces-shift-in-leadership-and-focus.html (accessed April 5, 2017).

Pollitz, Karen. 2017. High-Risk Pools for Uninsurable Individuals.

Porter, Michael E., and Thomas H. Lee. 2013. The Strategy That Will Fix Health Care (accessed January 24, 2017).

Potter, Wendell. 2015. Why Hospitals Mark Up Prices by 1,000 Percent. *Newsweek* (June).

Pourzanjani, A., T. Quisel, and L. Foschini. 2016. Adherent Use of Digital Health Trackers Is Associated with Weight Loss. *PLoS One* 11, vol. 4: e0152504. doi: 10.1371/journal.pone.0152504.

Preston, Juliet. 2017. From Grail to Freenome, Liquid Biopsies Seize the Day (accessed March 1, 2017).

Pricewaterhouse, Cooper. 2015. New Entrants are Disrupting the U.S. $9.59 Trillion Global Healthcare Market, Says PwC. PwC.

Pritchard, J. R., P. M. Bruno, M. T. Hemann, and D. A. Lauffenburger. 2013. Predicting Cancer Drug Mechanisms of Action Using Molecular Network Signatures. *Mol Biosyst* 9, vol. 7: 1604–19. doi: 10.1039/c2mb25459j.

Progeria Research Foundation. 2012. Progeria Takes Center Stage at Prestigious TEDMED Meeting. http://www.progeriaresearch.org/tedmed-meeting.html (accessed March 27, 2017).

Progeria Research Foundation. 2016. Find the Other 150. http://www.progeriaresearch.org/find-the -other-150/ (last modified December 1, 2016, accessed March 27, 2017).

Progeria Research Foundation. 2017a. The PRF Cell & Tissue Bank. http://www.progeriaresearch.org /cell_tissue_bank/ (accessed March 28, 2017).

Progeria Research Foundation. 2017b. Progeria Clinical Trials. http://www.progeriaresearch.org/clinical _trial.html (accessed March 29 2017).

Propeller Health. 2016. Propeller Health and Boehringer Ingelheim Announce New Partnership Focused on Improving Adherence and Care Management for People Living with COPD and Asthma. Propeller Health.

PXE International. 2004. U.S. Patent Office Issues First Gene Patent to Patient Advocacy Group. PXE International.

Qliance. 2017. Primary Care & Urgent Care Access. Qliance. http://qliance.com/.

Quisel, Tom, David Kale, and Luca Foschini. 2016. Intra-day Activity Better Predicts Chronic Conditions (last modified 2016).

Radiology Quality Institute. 2012. Diagnostic Accuracy in Radiology: Defining a Literature-Based Benchmark. Radiology Quality Institute.

Ramsey, L. B., S. G. Johnson, K. E. Caudle, C. E. Haidar, D. Voora, R. A. Wilke, W. D. Maxwell et al. 2014. The Clinical Pharmacogenetics Implementation Consortium Guideline for SLCO1B1 and Simvastatin-Induced Myopathy: 2014 Update. *Clin Pharmacol Ther* 96, vol. 4: 423–8. doi: 10.1038 /clpt.2014.125.

Ramsey, Lydia. 2017. The FDA and a $1.2 Billion Startup Are Analyzing How Drugs Are Used After Approval—And It Could One Day Change How We Treat Cancer (accessed June 2, 2017).

Ranard, B. L., R. M. Werner, T. Antanavicius, H. A. Schwartz, R. J. Smith, Z. F. Meisel, D. A. Asch, L. H. Ungar, and R. M. Merchant. 2016. Yelp Reviews of Hospital Care Can Supplement and Inform Traditional Surveys of the Patient Experience of Care. *Health Aff (Millwood)* 35, vol. 4: 697–705. doi: 10.1377/hlthaff.2015.1030.

Rao, Leena. 2011. Google Shuts Down Medical Records and Health Data Platform. 11:35:14 (accessed June 24, 2011).

Rappleye, Emily. 2016. Hospital Ownership of Physician Practices Up 86%.

Ratchinsky, Karin. 2016. Why the Healthcare Industry's Move to Cloud Computing Is Accelerating (accessed May 8, 2017).

Raths, David. 2016. Does Blockchain Have a Future in Healthcare? My Interview with Gem CEO Micah Winkelspecht. *Healthcare Blogs.*

Raths, David. 2017. Up and Comers 2016: Flatiron Health: Ex-Google Employees Take on the Oncology Informatics Market. *Healthcare Informatics Magazine* (accessed January 24, 2017).

Rau, Jordan. 2012. Medicare to Penalize 2,217 Hospitals for Excess Readmissions (accessed January 30, 2017).

Rau, Jordan. 2014. Medicare Fines 2,610 Hospitals in Third Round of Readmission Penalties. Kaiser Health News. http://khn.org/news/medicare-readmissions-penalties-2015/ (last modified October 2, 2014, accessed January 30, 2017).

Rau, Jordan. 2016a. 769 Hospitals Hit as CMS Expands Penalties to Infection Control (accessed January 23, 2017).

Rau, Jordan. 2016b. Many Well-Known Hospitals Fail to Score 5 Stars in Medicare's New Ratings (accessed February 2, 2017).

Rau, Jordan. 2016c. Medicare's Readmission Penalties Hit New High (accessed February 2, 2017).

Ray, Turna. 2017. FDA Approves Myriad Genetics' BRACAnalysis as Complementary Dx for New PARP Inhibitor (accessed March 28, 2017).

Razavi, H., A. C. ElKhoury, E. Elbasha, C. Estes, K. Pasini, T. Poynard, and R. Kumar. 2013. Chronic Hepatitis C Virus (HCV) Disease Burden and Cost in the United States. *Hepatology* 57, vol. 6: 2164-70. doi: 10.1002/hep.26218.

Redberg, Rita F. 2011. Squandering Medicare's Money. *New York Times* (May). https://www.nytimes .com/2011/05/26/opinion/26redberg.html (accessed January 24, 2017).

Reid, T. R. 2009. *The Healing of America: A Global Quest for Better, Cheaper, and Fairer Healthcare.* Penguin.

Reinstein, E. 2015. Challenges of Using Next Generation Sequencing in Newborn Screening. *Genet Res (Camb)* 97: e21. doi: 10.1017/s0016672315000178.

Research Kit. 2017. Rare Disease Research with ResearchKit. *Research Kit.* http://researchkit.org/blog.html (accessed March 29, 2017).

Reuters Editorial. 2017. Alphabet's Verily Unit Launches Study to Track Health Data (accessed April 19, 2017).

Ribeil, J. A., S. Hacein-Bey-Abina, E. Payen, A. Magnani, M. Semeraro, E. Magrin, L. Caccavelli et al. 2017. Gene Therapy in a Patient with Sickle Cell Disease. *N Engl J Med* 376, vol. 9: 848–55. doi: 10.1056 /NEJMoa1609677.

Rice, Jeff. Personal interview with authors, May 31, 2017.

Rice, Sabriya. 2014. Experts Question Hospital Raters' Methods (accessed January 30, 2017).

Richtel, Matt. 2016. Immune System, Unleashed by Cancer Therapies, Can Attack Organs. *New York Times* (December). https://www.nytimes.com/2016/12/03/health/immunotherapy-cancer.html?_r=0 (accessed December 3, 2016).

Riondel, J., M. Jacrot, M. F. Nissou, F. Picot, H. Beriel, C. Mouriquand, and P. Potier. 1988. Antineoplastic Activity of Two Taxol Derivatives on an Ovarian Tumor Xenografted into Nude Mice. *Anticancer Res* 8, vol. 3: 387–90.

Robel, Susan M, and Denise A. Venditti. 2017. Using a "Nursing Bundle" to Achieve Consistent Patient Experiences across a Multi-Hospital System (accessed April 13, 2017).

Robert Wood Johnson Foundation. 2012. How Does Medicare Value-Based Purchasing Work?

Robert Wood Johnson Foundation. 2013. The Revolving Door: A Report on U.S. Hospital Readmissions.

Roche. 2006. Plexxikon and Roche Enter Partnership to Develop Targeted Cancer Therapeutic Medicine PLX4032.

Roche. 2011. FDA approves Zelboraf (Vemurafenib) and Companion Diagnostic for BRAF Mutation-Positive Metastatic Melanoma, a Deadly Form of Skin Cancer.

Rohaidi, Nurfilzah. 2016. IBM's Watson Detected Rare Leukemia in Just 10 Minutes (accessed March 6, 2017).

Roland, Denise. 2015. Novartis Looking at Ways to Win Over Cost-Concerned Health Insurers. *Wall Street Journal* (July). http://www.wsj.com/articles/novartis-looking-at-ways-to-win-over-cost-concerned -health-insurers-1436522314 (accessed April 5, 2017).

Rosenberg, Tina. 2016. Shopping for Health Care: A Fledgling Craft. *Opinionator.*

Rosenthal, Elisabeth. 2013a. American Way of Birth, Costliest in the World. *New York Times* (June). http://www.nytimes.com/2013/07/01/health/american-way-of-birth-costliest-in-the-world .html?pagewanted=all.

Rosenthal, Elisabeth. 2013b. As Hospital Prices Soar, a Stitch Tops $500. *New York Times* (December). http://www.nytimes.com/2013/12/03/health/as-hospital-costs-soar-single-stitch-tops-500 .html?pagewanted=all.

Rosenthal, Elisabeth. 2013c. Colonoscopies Explain Why U.S. Leads the World in Health Expenditures. *New York Times* (June). http://www.nytimes.com/2013/06/02/health/colonoscopies-explain-why-us -leads-the-world-in-health-expenditures.html?pagewanted=all.

Rosenthal, Elisabeth. 2013d. The Hype Over Hospital Rankings. *New York Times* (July). https://www .nytimes.com/2013/07/28/sunday-review/the-hype-over-hospital-rankings.html (accessed January 30, 2017).

Rosenthal, Elisabeth. 2013e. In Need of a New Hip, But Priced Out of the U.S., *New York Times* (August). http://www.nytimes.com/2013/08/04/health/for-medical-tourists-simple-math.html?pagewanted=all.

Rosenthal, Elisabeth. 2013f. The Soaring Cost of a Simple Breath. *New York Times* (October). http://www.nytimes.com/2013/10/13/us/the-soaring-cost-of-a-simple-breath.html?pagewanted=all.

Rosenthal, Elisabeth. 2014a. Even Small Medical Advances Can Mean Big Jumps in Bills. *New York Times* (April).

Rosenthal, Elisabeth. 2014b. Patients' Costs Skyrocket; Specialists' Incomes Soar. *New York Times* (January).

Rosenthal, Elisabeth. 2014c. The Price of Prevention: Vaccine Costs Are Soaring. *New York Times* (July). https://www.nytimes.com/2014/07/03/health/Vaccine-Costs-Soaring-Paying-Till-It-Hurts.html.

Rosetta Health. 2017. Connecting a Whole World of Healthcare. http://rosettahealth.com/.

Ross, Casey. 2016. Why Hospital Ratings Should Be Looked at with a Grain of Salt (accessed January 30, 2017).

Ross, Casey. 2017. This Orthopedic Surgery Is the World's Most Common. But Patients Rarely Benefit, a Panel Says. T19:57:49-04:00 (accessed May 10, 2017).

Rothman, Frank G. 2014. A Mother's Mission. *Brown Alumni Magazine* (January/February 2014) (accessed April 3, 2017).

Roush, Wade. 2014. PokitDok CEO's Radical Idea: Transparent Pricing in Primary Care. Xconomy (accessed January 17, 2017).

Rudner, J., C. McDougall, V. Sailam, M. Smith, and A. Sacchetti. 2016. Interrogation of Patient Smartphone Activity Tracker to Assist Arrhythmia Management. *Ann Emerg Med* 68, vol. 3: 292–4. doi: 10.1016/j.annemergmed.2016.02.039.

Ryan, Andrew M., Sam Krinsky, Julia Adler-Milstein, Cheryl L. Damberg, Kristin A. Maurer, and John M. Hollingsworth. 2017. Association Between Hospitals' Engagement in Value-Based Reforms and Readmission Reduction in the Hospital Readmission Reduction Program. *JAMA Intern Med.* doi: 10.1001/jamainternmed.2017.0518.

Saab, D., R. Nisenbaum, I. Dhalla, and S. W. Hwang. 2016. Hospital Readmissions in a Community-Based Sample of Homeless Adults: A Matched-Cohort Study. *J Gen Intern Med* 31, vol. 9: 1011–8. doi: 10.1007/s11606-016-3680-8.

Sabatine, M. S., R. P. Giugliano, A. C. Keech, N. Honarpour, S. D. Wiviott, S. A. Murphy, J. F. Kuder, H. Wang, T. Liu, S. M. Wasserman, P. S. Sever, and T. R. Pedersen. 2017. Evolocumab and Clinical Outcomes in Patients with Cardiovascular Disease. *N Engl J Med.* doi: 10.1056/NEJMoa1615664.

Sablinski, T. 2014. Opening Up Clinical Study Design to the Long Tail. *Sci Transl Med* 6, vol. 256: 256ed19. doi: 10.1126/scitranslmed.3009116.

Sackett, D. L., and W. M. Rosenberg. 1995. The Need for Evidence-Based Medicine. *J R Soc Med* 88, vol. 11: 620–4.

Saey, Tina Hesman. 2014. Rare Disease Sets Mom's Research Agenda (accessed March 27, 2017).

Sagonowsky, Eric. 2017a. Payer Snubs PTC's Emflaza, Signaling Pricing Trouble Ahead of Launch FiercePharma (accessed April 14, 2017).

Sagonowsky, Eric. 2017b. With Its Launch Fizzling Out, UniQure Gives Up on $1M+ Gene Therapy Glybera. FiercePharma.

Sahni, Nikhil, Anauraag Chigurupati, Bob Kocher, and David M Cutler. 2015. How the U.S. Can Reduce Waste in Health Care Spending by $1 Trillion (accessed January 26, 2017).

Sanger-Katz, Margot. 2014. Why Most People Won't Shop again for Health Insurance. *New York Times* (December). https://www.nytimes.com/2014/12/12/upshot/why-most-people-wont-shop-again-for-health-insurance.html?.

Sanofi-Aventis Groupe. 2017. Sanofi Delivers 2016 Sales and Business EPS(1) Growth at CER(2) Paris Stock Exchange: SAN.

Sarkar, P. K., and R. A. Shinton. 2001. Hutchinson-Guilford Progeria Syndrome. *Postgrad Med J* 77, vol. 907: 312–7.

SAS. 2017. Machine Learning: What It Is and Why It Matters. https://www.sas.com/en_us/insights/analytics/machine-learning.html.

Satell, Greg. 2017. How Big Data and Analytics Are Helping Us Unlock Opportunity in the Most Unlikely Places (accessed April 19, 2017).

Sathian, Sanjena. 2013. The New 21st Century House Call. *Boston Globe* (July). https://www.bostonglobe .com/lifestyle/health-wellness/2013/07/28/century-house-call/tdupWvOQI6b3dKdKcEgdGM /story.html (accessed February 16, 2017).

Saunders, C. J., N. A. Miller, S. E. Soden, D. L. Dinwiddie, A. Noll, N. A. Alnadi, N. Andraws et al. 2012. Rapid Whole-Genome Sequencing for Genetic Disease Diagnosis in Neonatal Intensive Care Units. *Sci Transl Med* 4, vol. 154: 154ra135. doi: 10.1126/scitranslmed.3004041.

Saunders, Carol. 2017. Newborn Screening in the Age of Genomics: Innovation versus Evidence. AACC.org (accessed March 24, 2017).

Scandinavian Simvastatin Survival Study Group. 1994. Randomised Trial of Cholesterol Lowering in 4444 Patients with Coronary Heart Disease: The Scandinavian Simvastatin Survival Study (4S). *Lancet* 344, vol. 8934: 1383–9.

Schadendorf, D., F. S. Hodi, C. Robert, J. S. Weber, K. Margolin, O. Hamid, D. Patt, T. T. Chen, D. M. Berman, and J. D. Wolchok. 2015. Pooled Analysis of Long-Term Survival Data from Phase II and Phase III Trials of Ipilimumab in Unresectable or Metastatic Melanoma. *J Clin Oncol* 33, vol. 17: 1889–94. doi: 10.1200/jco.2014.56.2736.

Schadt, Eric. Personal interview with authors, April 12, 2017.

Schattner, Elaine. 2017. In Bold Move, FDA Approves Cancer Drug for Any Advanced Tumor with Genetic Changes.

Schencker, Lisa. 2017. NorthShore, Advocate Drop Merger Plan after Judge's Ruling. *Chicago Tribune* (March). http://www.chicagotribune.com/business/ct-advocate-northshore-merger-decision-0308-biz -20170307-story.html (accessed May 4, 2017).

Schiff, P. B., J. Fant, and S. B. Horwitz. 1979. Promotion of Microtubule Assembly In Vitro by Taxol. *Nature* 277, vol. 5698: 665–7.

Schiff, P. B., and S. B. Horwitz. 1980. Taxol Stabilizes Microtubules in Mouse Fibroblast Bells. *Proc Natl Acad Sci USA* 77, vol. 3: 1561–5.

Schlesinger, M., and R. Grob. 2017. Treating, Fast and Slow: Americans' Understanding of and Responses to Low-Value Care. *Milbank Q* 95 vol. 1: 70–116. doi: 10.1111/1468-0009.12246.

Sehgal, A. R. 2010. The Role of Reputation in *U.S. News & World Report's* Rankings of the Top 50 American Hospitals. *Ann Intern Med* 152, vol. 8: 521–5. doi: 10.7326/0003-4819-152-8-201004200-00009.

Sehnert, A. J., B. Rhees, D. Comstock, E. de Feo, G. Heilek, J. Burke, and R. P. Rava. 2011. Optimal Detection of Fetal Chromosomal Abnormalities by Massively Parallel DNA Sequencing of Cell-Free Fetal DNA from Maternal Blood. *Clin Chem* 57, vol. 7: 1042–9. doi: 10.1373/clinchem.2011.165910.

Sensely. 2017. How Are You Feeling Today? http://www.sensely.com/ (accessed April 21, 2017).

Seok, J., H. S. Warren, A. G. Cuenca, M. N. Mindrinos, H. V. Baker, W. Xu, D. R. Richards et al. 2013. Genomic Responses in Mouse Models Poorly Mimic Human Inflammatory Diseases. *Proc Natl Acad Sci USA* 110, vol. 9: 3507–12. doi: 10.1073/pnas.1222878110.

Sequenom. 2013. Sequenom CMM Achieves Milestone of 100,000 MaterniT21™ Plus Tests Processed. Sequenom.

SERMO. 2017. Press Releases. SERMO.

Sertkaya, A., H. H. Wong, A. Jessup, and T. Beleche. 2016. Key Cost Drivers of Pharmaceutical Clinical Trials in the United States. *Clin Trials* 13, vol. 2: 117–26. doi: 10.1177/1740774515625964.

Shahine, L. K., L. Marshall, J. D. Lamb, and L. R. Hickok. 2016. Higher Rates of Aneuploidy in Blastocysts and Higher Risk of No Embryo Transfer in Recurrent Pregnancy Loss Patients with Diminished Ovarian Reserve Undergoing In Vitro Fertilization. *Fertil Steril* 106, vol. 5: 1124–128. doi: 10.1016/j .fertnstert.2016.06.016.

Shaw, Kenna Mills. Personal interview with authors, April 12, 2017.

Shaywitz, David. 2014. Creating the Data-Inhaling Health Clinic of the Future.

Shaywitz, David. 2017. Why AI and Healthcare Must Learn to Play Together.

Shepherd, J., S. M. Cobbe, I. Ford, C. G. Isles, A. R. Lorimer, P. W. MacFarlane, J. H. McKillop, and C. J. Packard. 1995. Prevention of Coronary Heart Disease with Pravastatin in Men with Hypercholesterolemia. West of Scotland Coronary Prevention Study Group. *N Engl J Med* 333, vol. 20: 1301–7. doi: 10.1056/nejm199511163332001.

Sheridan, Kelly. 2016. Major Cyberattacks on Healthcare Grew 63% in 2016 (accessed May 8, 2017).

Shinkman, Ron. 2016. A Look Back at Hospital Mergers and Acquisitions in 2016. FierceHealthcare (accessed May 4, 2017).

Shontell, Alyson. 2012. After Making Millions, Two 20-Somethings Have Founded a Startup to Help Fight Cancer (accessed January 24, 2017).

Shreeve, James. 2005. *The Genome War: How Craig Venter Tried to Capture the Code of Life and Save the World*. Ballantine Books.

Shrier, A. A., A. Chang, N. Diakun-thibault, L. Forni, F. Landa, J. Mayo, R. van Riezen, and T. Hardjono. 2016. Blockchain and Health IT: Algorithms, Privacy, and Data. MIT Experimental Learning and MIT Connection Science.

Siemieniuk, R. A. C., I. A. Harris, T. Agoritsas, R. W. Poolman, R. Brignardello-Petersen, S. Van de Velde, R. Buchbinder et al. 2017. Arthroscopic Surgery for Degenerative Knee Arthritis and Meniscal Tears: A Clinical Practice Guideline. *Bmj* 357: j1982. doi: 10.1136/bmj.j1982.

Silverman, Ed. 2016. Less Than 1 Percent of State Prisoners with Hepatitis C Get Treated due to Cost of Drugs (accessed January 21, 2017).

Simonite, Tom. 2017. Machine Vision Helps Spot New Drug Treatments. *MIT Technology Review*.

Sisson, Paul. 2015. Readmissions Bleed Cash from 11 SD Hospitals. *San Diego Tribune* (August). http://www.sandiegouniontribune.com/news/health/sdut-readmission-penalties-san-diego-2015aug04-htmlstory.html (accessed February 3, 2017).

Siwicki, Bill. 2016. Cleveland Clinic and CVS Strike Deal to Deploy American Well Telemedicine Platform (accessed May 4, 2017).

Siwicki, Bill. 2017. Machine Learning 101: The Healthcare Opportunities Are Endless (accessed April 19, 2017).

Slabodkin, Greg. 2015. IBM Completes $1Billion Acquisition of Merge Healthcare (accessed April 28, 2017).

Slabodkin, Greg. 2017. Voluntary Value-Based Reforms Help Reduce Hospital Readmissions.

Sliwoski, G., S. Kothiwale, J. Meiler, and E. W. Lowe. 2014. Computational Methods in Drug Discovery. *Pharmacol Rev* 66, vol. 1: 334–95. doi: 10.1124/pr.112.007336.

Small, Leslie. 2017. The Case of the $12Million Member: High-Cost Enrollee Sheds Light on Health Insurers' ACA Exchange Woes. FierceHealthcare.

Smith, M. E., S. C. Sanderson, K. B. Brothers, M. F. Myers, J. McCormick, S. Aufox, M. J. Shrubsole et al. 2016. Conducting a Large, Multi-Site Survey about Patients' Views on Broad Consent: Challenges and Solutions. *BMC Med Res Methodol* 16, vol. 1: 162. doi: 10.1186/s12874-016-0263-7.

Smits, Tine, Elderik Kranen, and Heriburt Baldus. 2016. Medido, a Smart Medication Dispensing Solution, Shows High Rates of Medication Adherence and Potential to Reduce Cost of Care. Philips Lifeline.

Snowbeck, Christopher. 2017. As Health Insurers Drop Out, Medica Gains Unwanted Monopolies. *Star Tribune* (June). http://www.startribune.com/as-health-insurers-drop-out-medica-gains-unwanted-monopolies/425830563/.

Solomon, Lori. 2016. Genetic Test Registry Finds Growth of Oncology, NGS-Based Tests.

Song, Y., J. Skinner, J. Bynum, J. Sutherland, J. E. Wennberg, and E. S. Fisher. 2010. Regional Variations in Diagnostic Practices. *N Engl J Med* 363, vol. 1: 45–53. doi: 10.1056/NEJMsa0910881.

Sonnier, Paul. 2017. My Definition of Digital Health. http://storyofdigitalhealth.com/definition/ (accessed April 14, 2017).

Speights, Keith. 2017. The 7 Most Expensive Prescription Drugs in the World.

Squires, D., and C. Anderson. 2015. U.S. Health Care from a Global Perspective: Spending, Use of Services, Prices, and Health in 13 Countries. The Commonwealth Fund.

Squires, David, and Elizabeth Bradley. 2015. Maybe We Could Have Bought Him a Good Pair of Shoes: Why Peer Nations Spend Less on Health Care but Stay Healthier. Ed. by Sandy Hausman: The Commonwealth Fund.

St Sauver, J. L., S. J. Bielinski, J. E. Olson, E. J. Bell, M. E. Mc Gree, D. J. Jacobson, J. B. McCormick et al. 2016. Integrating Pharmacogenomics into Clinical Practice: Promise vs. Reality. *Am J Med* 129, vol. 10: 1093–1099.e1. doi: 10.1016/j.amjmed.2016.04.009.

Stafford, Philip. 2016. Banks Struggle to Make Blockchain Fast and Secure (accessed May 10, 2017).

Stanford Health Care. 2017. Pharmacogenomics–Individualized Drug Therapy. https://stanfordhealthcare.org/medical-clinics/center-personalized-wellness/pharmacogenomics.html (accessed February 20, 2017).

Staton, Tracy. 2015. Say What? CVS Health Execs Figure PCSK9 Meds to Cost Up to $150B. FiercePharma (accessed March 31, 2017).

Staton, Tracy. 2016a. Amgen Prevails in High-Stakes PCSK9 Patent Fight with Sanofi, Regeneron FiercePharma (accessed April 3, 2017).

Staton, Tracy. 2016b. GSK Inks Money-Back Guarantee on $665K Strimvelis, Blazing a Trail for Gene-Therapy Pricing. FiercePharma (accessed March 13, 2017).

Staton, Tracy. 2016c. Novartis Defies Naysayers with Newfangled Pay-for-Performance Deals on Entresto. FiercePharma (accessed January 21, 2017).

Staton, Tracy. 2016d. Pfizer's Bococizumab May Hit the PCSK9 Market Just in Time. FiercePharma (accessed March 31, 2017).

Steele, Glenn D. Personal interview with authors, April 11, 2017.

Stephenson, A. L., J. Sykes, S. Stanojevic, B. S. Quon, B. C. Marshall, K. Petren, J. Ostrenga, A. K. Fink, A. Elbert, and C. H. Goss. 2017. Survival Comparison of Patients With Cystic Fibrosis in Canada and the United States: A Population-Based Cohort Study. *Ann Intern Med*. doi: 10.7326/m16-0858.

Sternberg, C. N., P. P. Sordillo, E. Cheng, Y. J. Chuang, and D. Niedzwiecki. 1987. Evaluation of New Anti-Cancer Agents against Human Pancreatic Carcinomas in Nude Mice. *Am J Clin Oncol* 10, vol. 3: 219–21.

Stewart, Dava. 2016. More Insurers Willing to Cover Whole Exome Sequencing (WES) in a Trend That Creates New Opportunities for Clinical Pathology Laboratories to Add Value. Dark Daily.

Stockton, Nick. 2016. Everything You Need to Know about the Theranos Saga So Far.

Stone, Judy. 2015. Social Media Is a Lifeline for Patients with Rare Diseases (accessed March 28, 2017).

Strafford, J. C. 2012. Genetic Testing for Lynch Syndrome, an Inherited Cancer of the Bowel, Endometrium, and Ovary. *Rev Obstet Gynecol* 5, vol. 1: 42–9.

Strimbu, K., and J. A. Tavel. 2010. What Are Biomarkers? *Curr Opin HIV AIDS* 5, vol. 6: 463–6. doi: 10.1097/COH.0b013e32833ed177.

Stynes, Tess. 2011. Alexion to Acquire Enobia Pharma for Up to $1.08 Billion. *Wall Street Journal* (December). https://www.wsj.com/articles/SB10001424052970204720204577127020174878512.

Sugerman, Deborah Tolmach. 2013. Centers of Excellence. *JAMA* 310, vol. 9: 994–994. doi: 10.1001/jama.2013.277345.

Sullivan, Katie. 2013. Hospital Compare Now Shows How Hospitals Deal with *C. diff* and MRSA. FierceHealthcare (accessed January 30, 2017).

Sun, L., Q. Wu, S. W. Jiang, Y. Yan, X. Wang, J. Zhang, Y. Liu, L. Yao, Y. Ma, and L. Wang. 2015. Prenatal Diagnosis of Central Nervous System Anomalies by High-Resolution Chromosomal Microarray Analysis. *Biomed Res Int* 2015: 426379. doi: 10.1155/2015/426379.

Sunderam, S., D. M. Kissin, S. B. Crawford, S. G. Folger, D. J. Jamieson, L. Warner, and W. D. Barfield. 2017. Assisted Reproductive Technology Surveillance—United States, 2014. *MMWR Surveill Summ* 66, vol. 6: 1–24. doi: 10.15585/mmwr.ss6606a1.

Sutter Health. 2013. Sutter Health Unveils Name of New Health Plan.

Svenstrup, D., H. L. Jørgensen, and O. Winther. 2015. Rare Disease Diagnosis: A Review of Web Search, Social Media and Large-Scale Data-Mining Approaches. *Rare Dis* 3, vol. 1. doi: 10.1080/21675511.2015.1083145.

Sweeney, Evan. 2017a. Humana CMO Explains Why the Insurer Sees Itself as a Data Analytics Company 'More Than Anything Else. FierceHealthcare.

Sweeney, Evan. 2017b. Replacing Pills with Apps: How Digital Health Is Becoming Pharma's Newest Competitor. FierceHealthcare (accessed April 18, 2017).

Swisher, Kara. 2017. Recode Decode. *Recode Decode*, edited by Kara Swisher.

Taimen, P., K. Pfleghaar, T. Shimi, D. Moller, K. Ben-Harush, M. R. Erdos, S. A. Adam et al. 2009. A Progeria Mutation Reveals Functions for Lamin A in Nuclear Assembly, Architecture, and Chromosome Organization. *Proc Natl Acad Sci USA* 106, vol. 49: 20788–93. doi: 10.1073/pnas.0911895106.

Tang, L., Y. Zeng, H. Du, M. Gong, J. Peng, B. Zhang, M. Lei, F. Zhao, W. Wang, X. Li, and J. Liu. 2017. CRISPR/Cas9-Mediated Gene Editing in Human Zygotes Using Cas9 Protein. *Mol Genet Genomics*. doi: 10.1007/s00438-017-1299-z.

Tansey, Bernadette. 2015. One Medical Raises $65 Million to Expand "Concierge" Doctor Network. Xconomy (accessed May 4, 2017).

Tara, F., M. Lotfalizadeh, and S. Moeindarbari. 2016. The Effect of Diagnostic Amniocentesis and Its Complications on Early Spontaneous Abortion. *Electron Physician* 8, vol. 8: 2787–92. doi: 10.19082/2787.

Tas, Jeroen. Personal interview with authors, April 11, 2017.

Tas, Jeroen. 2017. Artificial Intelligence Will Save Your Life One Day: Here's Why. *LinkedIn Pulse*. https://www.linkedin.com/pulse/artificial-intelligence-save-your-life-one-day-heres-why-jeroen-tas.

Taylor, Nick Paul. 2015. 23andMe Raises $115Million as Investors Buy into Data-Driven Drug Discovery Vision. FierceBiotech (accessed April 3, 2017).

Tecco, Halle. 2017. 2016 Year End Funding Report: A Reality Check for Digital Health. Rock Health (accessed May 8, 2017).

Teng, Kathryn. Personal interview with authors, April 12, 2017.

Terhune, Chad, and Kaiser Health News. 2017. The Medical Testing Overload and How California Healthcare Organizations Are Addressing It (accessed May 24, 2017).

Terry, S. F. 2003. Learning Genetics. *Health Aff (Millwood)* 22, vol. 5: 166–71.

Terry, Sharon. Personal interview with authors, April 11, 2017.

Thompson, Dennis. 2017. "Keyhole" Surgery Not Helpful for Knee Arthritis, Experts Say.

Thomson Reuters. 2017. MetaDrug™. https://lsresearch.thomsonreuters.com/pages/solutions/18/metadrug (accessed April 6, 2017).

Topol, Eric. Personal interview with authors, April 11, 2017.

Torrieri, Marisa. 2014. What Hospitals Are Doing to Reduce Readmissions in 2015 (accessed January 30, 2017).

Toyota. 2017. Toyota Production System. Toyota Australia. http://www.toyota.com.au/toyota/company/operations/toyota-production-system.

Tozzi, John. 2015. This Medical Charity Made $3.3 Billion from a Single Pill. T15:33:58.768Z (accessed July 7, 2015).

Trachoo, O., C. Satirapod, B. Panthan, M. Sukprasert, A. Charoenyingwattana, W. Chantratita, W. Choktanasiri, and S. Hongeng. 2017. First Successful Trial of Preimplantation Genetic Diagnosis for Pantothenate Kinase-Associated Neurodegeneration. *J Assist Reprod Genet* 34, vol. 1: 109–16. doi: 10.1007/s10815-016-0833-y.

Transparency Life Sciences. 2017. How It Works. http://www.transparencyls.com/how-it-works (accessed June 1, 2017).

Transparency Market Research. 2014. Non-Invasive Prenatal Testing (NIPT) Market Expected to Reach USD $3.62 Billion Globally in 2019: Transparency Market Research (accessed March 8, 2017).

Transparency Market Research. 2015. Global Medical Tourism Market. http://www.transparencymarketresearch.com/pressrelease/medical-tourism.htm (accessed March 15, 2017).

Transplant Living. 2017. Transplant Living: Financing a Transplant: Costs. United Network for Organ Sharing. https://transplantliving.org/before-the-transplant/financing-a-transplant/the-costs/ (accessed January 27, 2017).

TransUnion. 2013. TransUnion Survey: Healthcare Cost Transparency Major Factor in Patients' Choice of Providers, Health Plans during Open Enrollment. Marketwired.

Tsotsis, Alexia. 2012. Facebook Scoops Up Face.com For $55–60M to Bolster Its Facial Recognition Tech (Updated) (accessed March 28, 2017).

Tsui, L. C., and R. Dorfman. 2013. The Cystic Fibrosis Gene: A Molecular Genetic Perspective. *Cold Spring Harb Perspect Med* 3, vol. 2. doi: 10.1101/cshperspect.a009472.

Tuller, David. 2004. Seeking a Fuller Picture of Statins. *New York Times* (July). https://www.nytimes.com/2004/07/20/health/seeking-a-fuller-picture-of-statins.html (accessed February 19, 2017).

Ťupa, O., A. Procházka, O. Vyšata, M. Schätz, J. Mareš, M. Vališ, and V. Mařík. 2015. Motion Tracking and Gait Feature Estimation for Recognising Parkinson's Disease Using MS Kinect. *Biomed Eng Online* 14. doi: 10.1186/s12938-015-0092-7.

U.S. Food & Drug Administration. 2015a. Press Announcements: FDA Approves Praluent to Treat Certain Patients with High Cholesterol.

U.S. Food & Drug Administration. 2015b. Press Announcements: FDA Approves Repatha to Treat Certain Patients with High Cholesterol.

U.S. Food & Drug Administration. 2017a. FDA Allows Marketing of First Whole Slide Imaging System for Digital Pathology. U.S. Dept. of Health & Human Services.

U.S. Food & Drug Administration. 2017b. Press Announcements: FDA Approves First Cancer Treatment for Any Solid Tumor with a Specific Genetic Feature. U.S. Dept. of Health & Human Services.

U.S. News & World Report. 2016. FAQ: How and Why We Rank and Rate Hospitals (accessed January 21, 2017).

Ubaldi, F. M., D. Cimadomo, A. Capalbo, A. Vaiarelli, L. Buffo, E. Trabucco, S. Ferrero, E. Albani, L. Rienzi, and P. E. Levi Setti. 2017. Preimplantation Genetic Diagnosis for Aneuploidy Testing in Women Older Than 44 Years: A Multicenter Experience. *Fertil Steril* 107, vol. 5: 1173–80. doi: 10.1016/j.fertnstert.2017.03.007.

Ullrich, N. J., M. W. Kieran, D. T. Miller, L. B. Gordon, Y. J. Cho, V. M. Silvera, A. Giobbie-Hurder, D. Neuberg, and M. E. Kleinman. 2013. Neurologic Features of Hutchinson-Gilford Progeria Syndrome after Lonafarnib Treatment. *Neurology* 81, vol. 5: 427–30. doi: 10.1212 /WNL.0b013e31829d85c0.

United Health Foundation. 2016. America's Health Rankings. http://www.americashealthrankings.org/ (accessed February 1, 2017).

Urban, A. E., J. O. Korbel, R. Selzer, T. Richmond, A. Hacker, G. V. Popescu, J. F. Cubells, R. Green, B. S. Emanuel, M. B. Gerstein, S. M. Weissman, and M. Snyder. 2006. High-Resolution Mapping of DNA Copy Alterations in Human Chromosome 22 Using High-Density Tiling Oligonucleotide Arrays. *Proc Natl Acad Sci USA* 103, vol. 12: 4534–9. doi: 10.1073/pnas.0511340103.

Van Arnum, Patricia. 2016. Global Oncology Market Poised for Strong Growth, IMS Says. DCAT Connect.

Van der Aa, N., M. Z. Esteki, J. R. Vermeesch, and T. Voet. 2013. Preimplantation Genetic Diagnosis Guided by Single-Cell Genomics. *Genome Med* 5, vol. 8: 71. doi: 10.1186/gm475.

Vanderbilt University Medical Center. 2017. *MyDrugGenome*. https://www.mydruggenome.org/ (accessed February 19, 2017).

Vanier, Vance. Personal interview with authors, April 12, 2017.

Vanstone, M., C. King, B. de Vrijer, and J. Nisker. 2014. Non-invasive Prenatal Testing: Ethics and Policy Considerations. *J Obstet Gynaecol Can* 36, vol. 6: 515–26.

Varret, M., J. P. Rabes, B. Saint-Jore, A. Cenarro, J. C. Marinoni, F. Civeira, M. Devillers et al. 1999. A Third Major Locus for Autosomal Dominant Hypercholesterolemia Maps to 1p34.1-p32. *Am J Hum Genet* 64, vol. 5: 1378–87. doi: 10.1086/302370.

Vemireddy, Madhavi; Juster, Iver; Mendelowitz, Paul; Sobocinski, Scott; Wiese, Kim; Benway, Bruce; Yale, Ken. 2014. ActiveHealth Management CareEngine: Advancing the Cause of Evidence-Based Care.

Ventura, Leslie. 2017. Turntable Health's Closure Leaves Downtown Patients in the Lurch. *Las Vegas Weekly* (January). https://lasvegasweekly.com/intersection/2017/jan/11/turntable-healths-closure-leaves-down town-patients/ (accessed May 4, 2017).

Verel, Dan. 2014. Can Cohealo Bring the Sharing Economy to Hospitals? (accessed October 20, 2014).

Versel, Neil. 2010. Revolution Health Kills Its PHR.

Versel, Neil. 2015. Startup Amino Has Big Plans for Medicare Claims Data (accessed April 22, 2017).

Versel, Neil. 2016. "Data Marketplace" Seeks to Apply Precision Medicine to Heart Disease (accessed February 6, 2017).

Versel, Neil. 2017. Philips Gets FDA Clearance for Inpatient Continuous Monitoring System (accessed February 20, 2017).

Vertex. 2015. Vertex Receives U.S. Food and Drug Administration Approval of KALYDECOÂ® (ivacaftor) for Children with Cystic Fibrosis Ages 2 to 5 who have Specific Mutations in the CFTR Gene. Vertex Pharmaceuticals Incorporated.

Viebeck, Elise. 2014. New Price Transparency Rules for Hospitals. TheHill (accessed January 17, 2017).

VisionGain. 2015. Checkpoint Inhibitors for Treating Cancer: Market Report with Forecasts.

Vuong, Zen. 2016. USC to Show How Wearable Technology Can Improve Cancer Treatment as Part of White House Event. *USC News* (accessed April 21, 2017).

Wah, Y. M., T. Y. Leung, Y. K. Cheng, and D. S. Sahota. 2016. Procedure-Related Fetal Loss Following Chorionic Villus Sampling After First-Trimester Aneuploidy Screening. *Fetal Diagn Ther.* doi: 10.1159/000447538.

Wakabayashi, Daisuke. 2016. Apple Watch Outpaced the iPhone in First Year. *Wall Street Journal* (April). http://www.wsj.com/articles/apple-watch-with-sizable-sales-cant-shake-its-critics-1461524901 (accessed January 26, 2017).

Wald, Christopher. Personal interview with authors, April 11, 2017.

Walker, Joseph. 2015. Gilead's $1,000 Pill Is Hard for States to Swallow. *Wall Street Journal* (April). http://www.wsj.com/articles/gileads-1-000-hep-c-pill-is-hard-for-states-to-swallow-1428525426 (accessed January 17, 2017).

Wall Street Journal. 2015. Should the U.S. Move Away From Fee-for-Service Medicine? (accessed March 20, 2017).

Wang, E., A. Batey, C. Struble, T. Musci, K. Song, and A. Oliphant. 2013. Gestational Age and Maternal Weight Effects on Fetal Cell-Free DNA in Maternal Plasma. *Prenat Diagn* 33, vol. 7: 662–6. doi: 10.1002/pd.4119.

Wang, Teresa, Tej Azad, and Ritu Rajan. 2017. The Emerging Influence of Digital Biomarkers on Healthcare. Rock Health.

Wani, M. C., H. L. Taylor, M. E. Wall, P. Coggon, and A. T. McPhail. 1971. Plant Antitumor Agents. VI. The Isolation and Structure of Taxol, a Novel Antileukemic and Antitumor Agent from Taxus Brevifolia. *J Am Chem Soc* 93, vol. 9: 2325–7.

Wapner, R. J., C. L. Martin, B. Levy, B. C. Ballif, C. M. Eng, J. M. Zachary, M. Savage et al. 2012. Chromosomal Microarray Versus Karyotyping for Prenatal Diagnosis. *N Engl J Med* 367, vol. 23: 2175–84. doi: 10.1056/NEJMoa1203382.

Ward, Andrew. 2016. Sanofi Eyes Acquisitions in Market for Rare Disease Drugs. *Financial Times* (February). https://www.ft.com/content/6025f75a-dc9b-11e5-827d-4dfbe0213e07.

Ward, Susan. Personal interview with authors, April 12, 2017.

Warsof, S. L., S. Larion, and A. Z. Abuhamad. 2015. Overview of the Impact of Noninvasive Prenatal Testing on Diagnostic Procedures. *Prenat Diagn* 35, vol. 10: 972–9. doi: 10.1002/pd.4601.

WCVB. 2015. Apple Watch Saves a Young Man's Life (accessed September 20, 2015).

Wei, James. 2007. *Product Engineering: Molecular Structure and Properties (Topics in Chemical Engineering).* Oxford University Press.

Weinberg, Zachary. Personal interview with authors, May 3, 2017.

Weintraub, Arlene. 2014. Cost Watchdogs Demand Efficacy Data on New Bayer Cancer Drugs. FiercePharma (accessed March 6, 2017).

Weise, Elizabeth. 2017. Could Your Next Prescription Come From Amazon?

Weiskopf, K. 2017. Cancer Immunotherapy Targeting the CD47/SIRPalpha Axis. *Eur J Cancer* 76: 100–109. doi: 10.1016/j.ejca.2017.02.013.

Weisman, Robert. 2015. Harvard Pilgrim Strikes "Pay-for-Performance" Deal for Cholesterol Drug. *Boston Globe* (November). https://www.bostonglobe.com/business/2015/11/08/harvard-pilgrim-strikes-pay-for-performance-deal-for-cholesterol-drug/iGIV7rBie4K20HNbKORsPJ/story.html (accessed April 3, 2017).

Welch, H. G., P. C. Prorok, A. J. O'Malley, and B. S. Kramer. 2016. Breast-Cancer Tumor Size, Overdiagnosis, and Mammography Screening Effectiveness. *N Engl J Med* 375, vol. 15: 1438–47. doi: 10.1056/NEJMoa1600249.

WellMatch. 2017. About WellMatch. https://www.wellmatchhealth.com/about_us (accessed March 14, 2017).

Westgate, Aubrey. 2015. Four Common HIPAA Misconceptions (accessed June 8, 2015).

Wharam, J. F., F. Zhang, E. M. Eggleston, C. Y. Lu, S. Soumerai, and D. Ross-Degnan. 2017. Diabetes Outpatient Care and Acute Complications Before and After High-Deductible Insurance Enrollment: A Natural Experiment for Translation in Diabetes (NEXT-D) Study. *JAMA Intern Med.* doi: 10.1001/jamainternmed.2016.8411.

Wheeler, D. L., T. Barrett, D. A. Benson, S. H. Bryant, K. Canese, V. Chetvernin, D. M. Church et al. 2006. Database Resources of the National Center for Biotechnology Information. *Nucleic Acids Res* 34: D173–80. doi: 10.1093/nar/gkj158.

Wiernik, P. H., E. L. Schwartz, J. J. Strauman, J. P. Dutcher, R. B. Lipton, and E. Paietta. 1987. Phase I Clinical and Pharmacokinetic Study of Taxol. *Cancer Res* 47, vol. 9: 2486–93.

Williams, Sean. 2017. The 19 Best-Selling Prescription Drugs of All Time. *Motley Fool* (accessed March 31, 2017).

Winnick, Ed. 2012. Verinata Sues Ariosa, LabCorp for Patent Infringement (accessed April 29, 2017).

Winslow, Ron. 2017. Mayo Clinic's Unusual Challenge: Overhaul a Business That's Working. *Wall Street Journal* (June). https://www.wsj.com/articles/mayo-clinics-unusual-challenge-overhaul-a-business-thats-working -1496415044.

Wishart, D. S., C. Knox, A. C. Guo, S. Shrivastava, M. Hassanali, P. Stothard, Z. Chang, and J. Woolsey. 2006. DrugBank: A Comprehensive Resource for In Silico Drug Discovery and Exploration. *Nucleic Acids Res* 34: D668–72. doi: 10.1093/nar/gkj067.

Wolters Kluwer. 2017. Clinician Story: A Specialist Corrects Misdiagnosis of Sarcoidosis to HLH and Lymphoma (accessed April 26, 2017).

Wong, N. S., and M. A. Morse. 2012. Lonafarnib for Cancer and Progeria. *Expert Opin Investig Drugs* 21, vol. 7: 1043–55. doi: 10.1517/13543784.2012.688950.

Wood, Laura. 2016. Global & USA Cancer Immunotherapy Market Analysis to 2020: Avastin, Nivolumab, Revlimid, Rituxan, and Xtandi Will Be the Top Five Cancer Drugs. *Business Wire* (accessed March 6, 2017).

World Bank, The 2017 Health Expenditure, Total % of GDP. http://data.worldbank.org/indicator/SH.XPD .TOTL.ZS (accessed January 24, 2017).

World Health Organization. 2016. World Health Statistics 2016: Monitoring Health for the SDGs. Geneva: World Health Organization.

World Health Organization. 2017. WHO | Cancer. World Health Organization (last modified March 23, 2017, 19:39:01, accessed April 30, 2017). http://www.who.int/mediacentre/factsheets/fs297/en/.

Xerox. 2016. Xerox Technology Solutions for Healthcare. https://www.xerox.com/en-us/services/healthcare -solutions (last modified December 13, 2016, accessed January 26, 2017).

xG Health. 2014. Geisinger Study Finds Diabetes Care "Bundle" Produces Better Health Outcomes.

xG Health. 2017. xG Healthcare Solutions. https://xghealth.com/solutions/ (accessed January 30, 2017).

Xu, Y., S. Chen, X. Yin, X. Shen, X. Pan, F. Chen, H. Jiang et al. 2015. Embryo Genome Profiling by Single-Cell Sequencing for Preimplantation Genetic Diagnosis in a Beta-Thalassemia Family. *Clin Chem* 61, vol. 4: 617–26. doi: 10.1373/clinchem.2014.228569.

Yip, K. 2016. Blockchain & Alternative Payment Models.

YouScript. 2017. YouScript Home. http://youscript.com/ (accessed February 20, 2017).

Zhang, M., and O. Lin. 2016. Molecular Testing of Thyroid Nodules: A Review of Current Available Tests for Fine-Needle Aspiration Specimens. *Arch Pathol Lab Med* 140, vol. 12: 1338–44. doi: 10.5858 /arpa.2016-0100-RA.

Zimmerman, Ron. 2014. Whole-Genome Sequencing Solving Medical Mysteries (accessed May 1, 2017).

Zitner, Aaron. 2000. An Ego in a Lab Coat Seeks Genetic "Fountain of Youth." *Los Angeles Times* (August). http://articles.latimes.com/2000/aug/23/news/mn-8952.

Zugazagoitia, J., C. Guedes, S. Ponce, I. Ferrer, S. Molina-Pinelo, and L. Paz-Ares. 2016. Current Challenges in Cancer Treatment. *Clin Ther* 38, vol. 7: 1551–66. doi: 10.1016/j.clinthera.2016.03.026.

Index